WORLD OF LANGUAGE

Nancy Nickell Ragno   Marian Davies Toth   Betty G. Gray

Contributing Author – Primary   Elfrieda Hiebert
Contributing Author – Vocabulary   Richard E. Hodges
Contributing Author – Poetry   Myra Cohn Livingston

Consulting Author – Thinking Skills   David N. Perkins

SILVER BURDETT GINN

NEEDHAM, MA   PARSIPPANY, NJ

Atlanta, GA   Irving, TX   Deerfield, IL   Santa Clara, CA

Acknowledgments

Cover: Patricia A. Courtney

Contributing Writers: Sandra Breuer, Judy Brim, Bernie Brodsky, Jack Dempsey, Anne Maley, Duncan Searl, Gerry Tomlinson

Contributing artists: Ernest Albanese, Lori Anderson, Karen Bauman, Paul Birling, Lori Bernero, Alex Block, Robert Casilla, J. Chambless, Donald Cook, Jim Cummins, Frank Daniel, Allen Davis, Cathy Diefendorf, R.R. Donnelley Cartographic Services, Don Dyen, Rae Eclund, Marlene Eckman, Michele Epstein, Fernando Fernandez, Grace Goldberg, S. Haefele, Pat Hinton, Kies deKiefte, Barbara Lanza, Robert Lee, Richard Loehle, Frank Margasak, Robert Marinelli, Claude Martinot, Fred Marvin, Richard Milholland, Kathy Munger, James Needham, Loughran O'Connor, Lisa O'Hanlon, John Holder, R.A. Parker, R.S. Pate, Tom Powers, Marcy Ramsey, Larry Raymond, David Rickman, Robert Roth, Jose Reyes, Sally Schaedler, Steve Schinler, Sandra Speidel, Susan Spellman, Cindy Spencer, Don Tate, Kyuzo Tsugami, Gary Undercuffler, Victor Valla, George Vicente, James Watling, Arieh Zeldich

Picture credits: All photographs by Silver Burdett & Ginn (SB&G) unless otherwise noted **Unit 1** 4: Leonard Lee Rue III/Shostal Associates. 8: Peter Byron for SB&G. 9: *Hudson River* by Winslow Homer, American, 1836–1910. Watercolor, 14 x 20 in. Bequest of William Sturgis Beigelow. Courtesy, The Museum of Fine Arts, Boston. 10: Bohdan Hrynewych/Stock, Boston. 15: *t.* Grant Heilman/Grant Heilman Photography; *m.* John Colwell/Grant Heilman/ Grant Heilman Photography. 20: *Twilight in the Wilderness* by Frederick Edwin Church. The Cleveland Museum of Art, Mr. and Mrs. William H. Marlatt Fund, 65.233. 35: © Ellan Young. 39: Animals Animals/Margot Conte. 44: Dan De Wilde for SB&G. 49: *t.* Jacket illustration by John Schoenherr from *Julie of the Wolves* by Jean Craighead George. Illustration copyright © 1972 by John Schoenherr. Reprinted by permission of Harper & Row, Publishers, Inc. **Unit 2** 60: Photographs by Christopher G. Knight. Reproduced by permission of Macmillan Publishing Company from *Puppeteer* by Kathryn Lasky. Photos, copyright © 1985 by Christopher Knight. 62: Robert Frerck/ Odyssey Productions. 64: Kermit the Frog © 1985 Henson Associates, Inc. 65: © 1988 Children's Television Workshop. Used by courtesy of *Sesame Street*. 76: *Vaudeville* by Jacob Lawrence. Hirshhorn Museum and Sculpture Garden, Smithsonian Institution, gift of Joseph H. Hirshhorn, 1966. 81, 82, 83, 88, 94: Photographs by Christopher G. Knight. Reproduced by permission of Macmillan Publishing Company from *Puppeteer* by Kathryn Lasky. Photos, copyright © 1985 by Christopher G. Knight. 98: Dan De Wilde for SB&G. 103: *t.* Reproduced with permission of Macmillan Publishing Company from *Puppeteer* by Kathryn Lasky and Christopher G. Knight. Copyright © 1985 by Kathryn Lasky and Christopher G. Knight. **Unit 3** 118: Lefever/Grushow/Grant Heilman Photography. 119: DPI. 122: John Lei/Stock, Boston. 125: Leo deWys, Inc./NOAA photo. 126: Michael Freeman/Bruce Coleman. 131: Alan G. Nelson/ Tom Stack & Associates. 136: Gerald L. French/Frederic Lewis, Inc. 138: *Bluebonnets* by Porfirio Salinas. Courtesy of Exxon Company, USA. 147: Rod Planck/Tom Stack & Associates. 149: E.R. Degginger/Bruce Coleman. 153: Manley Features/Shostal Associates. 158: Dan De Wilde for SB&G. 162: NASA. 163: *t.* Jacket illustration from *Dogs & Dragons, Trees & Dreams* by Karla Kuskin, copyright © 1980 by Karla Kuskin. Reprinted by permission of Harper & Row, Publishers, Inc. **Unit 4** 178: United States Information Service, India. 180: Pictorial Parade. 182: Photo No. PC8 in the John F. Kennedy Library. 184, 185: Sovfoto. 187: AP/Wide World Photos. 194: Edward Steichen, *Therese Duncan at the Parthenon* (1921). Gelatin-silver print, 13 ¾ x 10¾ in. Collection, The Museum of Modern Art, New York. Gift of the photographer. Reprinted with the permission of Joanna T. Steichen. 198: Paul Schutzer, *Life Magazine* © Time Inc. 199: Courtesy of Peter Galbraith. 200: United States Information Service, India. 204: Steve Vidler/Leo deWys, Inc. 213: *t.* Disario/The Stock Market of NY; *b.* Mel Lewis/Shostal Associates. 214: Paul Schutzer, *Life Magazine* © Time Inc. 218: Dan De Wilde for SB&G. 222: *l. Broadway Boogie Woogie* by Piet Mondrian, 1942–1943. Oil on canvas, 50 x 50 in. Collection, The Museum of Modern Art, New York. Given anonymously; *r. Circular Forms* by Robert Delaunay, 1930. Oil on canvas, 50¾ x 76¾ in. Photographed by David Heald. Collection, Solomon R. Guggenheim Museum, New York. 223: *Homesick: My Own Story* by Jean Fritz. Used by permission of Dell Books, a division of Bantam, Doubleday, Dell Publishing Group Inc. **Unit 5** 238: The Granger Collection. 239: *The Underground Railroad, detail,* by Charles T. Webber, Cincinnati Art Museum, Subscription Fund Purchase. 245: The Granger Collection. 252: Brown Brothers. 252: *New York, New Haven and Hartford* by Edward Hopper, © Indianapolis Museum of Art, The Emma Harter Sweetser Fund. 265: *r.* Ken Kerbs for SB&G; *l.* Diane K. Gentry/Black Star. 267: Ray Risley/Shostal Associates. 274: Dan De Wilde for SB&G. 279: Jacket illustration by James McMullan. From *M.C. Higgins, The Great* by Virginia Hamilton. Copyright © 1974 by Macmillan Publishing Company. Reproduced by permission of the publisher. **Unit 6** 293: The Bettmann Archive. 297: *t.* UPI/Bettmann Newsphotos; *b.* Paul J. Sutton/Duomo. 302: *Lydia at a Tapestry Loom* by Mary Cassatt (1888). Courtesy of the Flint Institute of Arts, gift of the Whiting Foundation. 306: Courtesy of the National Automotive History Collection of the Detroit Public Library. 313: The Granger Collection. 317: Paul J. Sutton/Duomo. 321: Gordon Wiltsie/Bruce Coleman. 324: Courtesy of the National Automotive History Collection of the Detroit Public Library. 328: Dan De Wilde for SB&G. 333: *t.* Illustration from *I Will Be a Doctor!* by Dorothea Clark Wilson. Copyright © 1985 by Abingdon Press. Used with permission. **Unit 7** 351: Hanging scroll, landscape in Shin style, attributed to Kenko Shokei, The Metropolitan Museum of Art, purchase, bequest of Stephen Whitney Phoenix, by exchange, 1985 (1985.7). 355: Ben Simmons/The Stock Market of NY. 357: Claude Charlier/Black Star. 359: © Earl Dibble/Photo Researchers, Inc. 362: *The East River* by Maurice Prendergast. Watercolor, 13¾ x 19¾ in. Collection, The Museum of Modern Art, New York. Gift of Abby Aldrich Rockefeller. 386: Dan De Wilde for SB&G. 391: Jacket illustration by Harru Wells from *Of Nightingales that Weep* by Katherine Paterson. (Thomas Y. Crowell) Jacket art © 1974 by Harru Wells. Reprinted by permission of Harper & Row, Publishers, Inc. **Unit 8** 402: Spencer Jones/Bruce Coleman. 409–411: The Granger Collection. 414: *t.* Animals Animals/Patti Murray; *b.* Animals Animals/Anthony Bannister. 416: *Surprise!* by Henri Rousseau. Reproduced by courtesy of the Trustees, the National Gallery, London. 428: © Pat and Tom Leeson/Photo Researchers, Inc. 432: *t.* Robert C. Simpson/Tom Stack & Associates; *b.* Animals Animals/Robert Maier. 438: Dan De Wilde for SB&G. 443: Jacket illustration by Morgan and Charles Reid Dennis. From *Misty of Chincoteague*

CONTENTS

INTRODUCTORY UNIT

UNIT 1 USING LANGUAGE TO NARRATE

Literature Model: My Side of the Mountain

UNIT THEME: The Wilderness

UNIT 2   USING LANGUAGE TO INFORM

PART 1   LANGUAGE AWARENESS ◆ NOUNS

PART 2 A REASON FOR WRITING ◆ INFORMING

UNIT THEME: Theater Arts

Literature Model: Puppeteer

UNIT 3   USING LANGUAGE TO CREATE

PART 1   LANGUAGE AWARENESS ◆ VERBS

PART 2   A REASON FOR WRITING ◆ CREATING

UNIT 4   USING LANGUAGE TO PERSUADE

PART 1   LANGUAGE AWARENESS ◆ PRONOUNS

PART 2   A REASON FOR WRITING ◆ PERSUADING

UNIT THEME: Americans Abroad

Literature Model: Letter to Peter Galbraith

UNIT 5   USING LANGUAGE TO DESCRIBE

PART 1   LANGUAGE AWARENESS ◆ ADJECTIVES

PART 2   A REASON FOR WRITING ◆ DESCRIBING

UNIT 6   USING LANGUAGE TO RESEARCH

PART 1   LANGUAGE AWARENESS ◆ ADVERBS

PART 2   A REASON FOR WRITING ◆ RESEARCHING

UNIT THEME: Pioneering Women

Literature Model: From Coast to Coast

UNIT 7   USING LANGUAGE TO IMAGINE

PART 1   LANGUAGE AWARENESS ◆ PREPOSITIONS AND CONJUNCTIONS

PART 2   A REASON FOR WRITING ◆ IMAGINING

UNIT 8   USING LANGUAGE TO CLASSIFY

PART 1   LANGUAGE AWARENESS ◆ SENTENCES

PART 2   A REASON FOR WRITING ◆ CLASSIFYING

WRITER'S REFERENCE BOOK

AWARD · LITERATURE · WINNING

My Side of the Mountain
by Jean George

Puppeteer
by Kathryn Lasky

Letter to Peter Galbraith
by John F. Kennedy

The House of Dies Drear
by Virginia Hamilton

The Crane Wife
by Sumiko Yagawa
translated by Katherine Paterson
illustrated by Suekichi Akaba

Project Panda Watch
by Miriam Schlein

...rhey
...things. In
...rooms, a
...ent. Listen
...s.

...s About It

THE HOUSE
by Virginia Hami...

Long before his fa...
Small was excited ab...
college history teach...
his son its story.
More than a...
Dies Drear had...
Underground...
and helped th...
knew that th...
not talk ab...
Now...
Thomas...
waiting...
twins...
fell...

256

LITERATURE

The Crane Wife

Retold by SUMIKO YAGAWA   **Translated by KATHERINE PATERSON**
Illustrated by SUEKICHI AKABA

This story of a poor farmer who rescues a
wounded crane from death is perhaps Japan's best-
loved folktale. Japanese children grow up hearing
this tale. As adults they continue to enjoy it, since
it has been made into plays, movies, and even an
opera.

In a faraway mountain village, where the snow falls
deep and white, there once lived all alone a poor young
peasant named Yohei. One day, at the beginning of winter,
Yohei went out into the
snow to run an errand,
and, as he hurried home,
suddenly *basabasa* he
heard a rustling sound. It
was a crane, dragging its
wing, as it swooped down
and landed on the path.
Now Yohei could see
that the bird was in great
pain, for an arrow had
pierced its wing. He went
to where the crane lay,
drew out the arrow, and
very carefully tended its
wound.

366

LITERATURE: Folktale

WORLD OF LANGUAGE

Introductory Unit

Literature in Your World

In the *World of Language* literature plays a key role. Why is it so important? What can literature mean for you in your world?

Literature unlocks your imagination. It opens your mind to the world of ideas. Through literature you can enter any time and any place. You can experience unusual adventures, meet people you would never meet, share ideas with the greatest minds. Literature is indeed a key — to expanding your world and to enriching your world of language.

Writing in Your World

Writing and reading are intertwined. They are a team, partners. Yet, like two sides of a coin, they are different. Writing begins with you the writer. Writing is a way for you to make connections with the world outside you. When you write, you write *to* someone. You write for your readers. You write to be read. Writing is also a way for you to connect with your inner world — your world of thoughts, feelings, and dreams. Sometimes you are both the writer and the reader.

Writing is creating, and you are its creator, its owner. Writing is thinking, and writing is discovering what you think. Writing is a way of finding out about your world — and writing is a way to change it. That is a powerful thought, but writing is powerful — a powerful tool in your world and in the wonderful world of language.

What Is a Writer?

A writer is anyone who writes. You probably already do a great deal of writing. For example, you might write a note to a friend or a telephone message. You do many kinds of writing, and you write for many reasons. Here are three kinds of writing you will try this year.

Writing to Inform ◆ Writing can help you get something done in the world. You might write a business letter, for example, to let someone know about a particular problem.

Writing to Create ◆ You can use your imagination to write a poem, a play, or a story.

Expressive Writing ◆ You may want to write just for yourself. Expressive writing is writing to explore your ideas, plans, and impressions. It is a kind of talking to yourself. It is writing you can do in a journal.

Journal Writing

A journal is a writer's best friend. Carry one with you and you're always prepared to

- capture an idea — jot it down before you forget it
- try things out — write a description, for instance
- think things through — draft some questions for an interview you want to do
- note your reactions to books, movies, music, poetry
- record your impressions — write about a sunset or a new friend

Keeping a journal is a way to pin thoughts in place while you work on them. It is a way to slow down your thinking so you have time to be more creative and precise. A journal is a place for your work in progress.

A journal can be a special notebook, a section of another notebook, or a folder with stapled paper. Writing ideas that you can try in your journal will appear throughout this book.

Introducing the Writing Process

Not all writing is writing you do in a journal, just for yourself. Sometimes you want to write something, make it really good, polish it, and then share it with other people. A lot of work can go into this kind of writing. It can seem scary. However, using the writing process can make writing a lot less scary — even fun.

How can a process help writing? The writing process breaks writing into small steps. For each step there are lots of *strategies* — ways of working — that you can learn. There are ways to get ideas and organize ideas. There are hints for how to get started and how to keep going. There are strategies for improving your writing and sharing it.

Think, Read, Speak, Listen, Write

At the end of each unit you will use the writing process for writing something that you will publish, or share with others. You will be well-prepared for this, because first you will have a series of lessons to get you started.

- A **Thinking Skill** lesson will give you a strategy to use in reading and writing.
- A **Literature** lesson will provide you with a model for your writing.
- A **Speaking and Listening** lesson will show you how to use oral language correctly.
- **Writing** skills lessons will show you how to do the kinds of writing you will do in the Writing Process lessons.
- Two **Connection** lessons will show you how to apply the skills you learned in the unit directly to your writing.

Using the Writing Process

As you write, it helps to know two things.

1. Purpose Why are you writing? To tell a story? To persuade someone about an opinion you have? To explain how to do something?

2. Audience Who will read what you write? Will your reader be someone your own age? Someone younger? An adult?

As you write, reminding yourself of your purpose and audience will help keep your writing on the right track.

Write a Description

Don't just read about the writing process. Try it!

On the next four pages, you will read about five stages of the writing process: *prewriting, writing, revising, proofreading,* and *publishing.* Writers often start with prewriting, and they end by publishing. However, writers sometimes go back and forth among the stages until they are satisfied with their work. You have to make those decisions with each piece of writing that you do. With each of the stages is an activity for you to do. When you have done all five, you will have written and published a description.

Read the Writer's Hint about purpose and audience. For your description your *audience* is your classmates. Your *purpose* is to describe an object so well that they can guess what it is without being told.

1 Prewriting ♦ Getting ready to write

Have you ever said, "I don't know what to write about" or "I don't have any ideas"? Welcome to the writers' club! Most writers feel that way before they start writing. How can you get the ideas to write about? There are lots of ways. For example, you can brainstorm, draw an idea cluster, keep a writer's notebook, or do an interview.

PREWRITING IDEA

Using the Five Senses

Choose an object to describe. Choose something you can observe closely right now. It might be something on or in your desk, such as an eraser, a sheet of paper, or the apple you brought for lunch. It might be something you are wearing or carrying, such as a shirt button or a ring.

Study the object for three minutes. Write everything you notice about it. Think of the five senses. What does it look like? Does it make a sound if you tap it or drop it? What does it feel like? Does it have a smell? (Don't taste it unless it is edible and clean!) Your notes can just be words. They don't have to be complete sentences.

2 Writing ◆ Putting your ideas on paper

You have decided what to write about. You have gathered some ideas. Now you are facing a blank page. It's time to start writing, but sometimes you don't know how to get started. Often, once you start, you don't know how to keep going.

The important thing is just to start writing. Don't worry if your ideas are out of order and your spelling is bad. You will be able to improve your writing when you revise and proofread.

WRITING IDEA

Starting with a Question

Put your prewriting notes in front of you before you begin writing your description. How can you begin? You might begin with a question such as *Have you ever really looked at an eraser?* After you start, think about the five senses. Tell how your object looks, sounds, feels, smells, and maybe tastes. Then add an ending sentence, such as *An eraser is a lot more interesting than you might think.*

3 Revising ◆ Making changes to improve your writing

An important revising strategy is reading to yourself. First think about your purpose. Suppose your purpose was to describe an object. Decide if you followed your plan. Or did you forget to describe and start telling a story instead? Also think about your audience. Were you writing for your classmates? Try to hear your description with their ears. Will they understand it?

Another revising strategy is sharing with a partner. Read your writing aloud. Ask your partner to make suggestions and ask questions. Listen to the answers. Then make the changes *you* feel are important.

REVISING IDEA

Read to Yourself and Read to a Partner

First read your description to yourself. Consider your purpose and audience: Did you really write a description? Did you write it so well that your classmates will be able to guess what you are describing? Make any changes you think will improve your description. You can cross out words and write in new words. You can draw arrows to show where to move words or sentences. Your writing may look very messy at this point.

Next read your description to a partner. Ask, "*What part did you like best?*" and "*Is there anything you would like to know more about?*" Listen to the answers. Then make the changes you think will improve your description.

4 Proofreading ◆ Looking for and fixing errors

After you have made sure your writing says what you want it to say, proofread for correctness. Check capital letters and punctuation, indenting, and spelling. Then make a clean copy in your best handwriting. A correct and readable copy is a courtesy to your reader.

5 Publishing ◆ Sharing your writing with others

There are all kinds of ways to share writing, including reading your writing into a tape recorder, mailing a letter to someone, reading aloud in a story circle, and posting your writing on a special bulletin board. One of the best parts of writing is hearing or seeing your audience's response.

UNIT ONE

USING LANGUAGE
TO
NARRATE

Writing
IN YOUR JOURNAL

WRITER'S WARM-UP ◆ What do you know about the wilderness? Have you camped or hiked in a wilderness area or park? Probably you have read books that are set in the wild. You have certainly seen TV specials about wild animals or unspoiled natural areas. What would you do if you found yourself in the wilderness? Write about it in your journal.

Play the "Short-and-Sweet-Yet-Complete" game with a partner. Follow the examples below to express thoughts about animals.
Birds chirp.   Lions roar.   A mosquito buzzes.

1 Writing Sentences

Read the groups of words below.

Not Sentences	**Sentences**
1. Belongs to everyone.	**3.** The wilderness belongs to everyone.
2. Our wild land.	**4.** Our wild land is disappearing fast.

The word groups on the left do not express complete thoughts. Group **1** does not name who or what *Belongs to everyone*. Group **2** does not tell what *Our wild land* is or does. The word groups on the right answer these questions. Group **3** names what *belongs to everyone*. It is *The wilderness*. Group **4** tells what *Our wild land* is or does. It *is disappearing fast*.

Groups of words that are not sentences do not make sense by themselves. The word group below does not make sense.

■ **Wilderness areas last year.**

Adding more words gives it meaning and makes it a sentence.

■ **Over sixty million hikers used wilderness areas last year.**

> **Summary** ◆ A **sentence** is a group of words that expresses a complete thought. When you write, you use sentences in many ways—to tell what you are thinking or feeling, to explain your ideas, and to ask questions.

Guided Practice

Tell which of the following groups of words is a sentence and which is not a sentence.

1. Some human activities cause damage to the wilderness.
2. Trampled by the boots of countless hikers.
3. New and better roads attract more people to the wilderness.

Practice

A. Decide whether each group of words below expresses a complete thought. Then write *sentence* or *not a sentence* for each group of words.

4. The American wilderness once stretched from sea to sea.
5. Today only one fifth of the land in the United States.
6. Each year more of our untouched land vanishes.
7. Preserving and protecting wilderness areas.
8. Many people seek quiet in the wilderness.
9. Careless tourists can spoil the experience.
10. Destroys the habitat of animals.
11. Scarred by rutted trails, campsites, and litter.
12. Campers should leave no mark on the land.
13. Really need the wilderness.
14. Finds the woods refreshing.
15. Careful planning and use will help us preserve them.

B. Be a sentence writer! Add words to make each group of words a sentence.

16. A graceful white-tailed deer _____ .
17. _____ chirped merrily from a tall hemlock.
18. _____ along the shore of the mountain lake.
19. _____ are covered with ferns and moss.
20. The gloomy forest of pines _____ .
21. _____ in a V-formation high among the clouds.
22. After the waterfall the river _____ .
23. A grove of aspens _____ .
24. The insects on the surface of the water _____ .
25. _____ glittered brightly in the clear night sky.

Apply • Think and Write

From Your Writing ◆ Look back at what you wrote for the Writer's Warm-up. Does it make sense to you now? Is it clear? Does each sentence express a complete thought? Now try to improve your sentences by changing or adding words.

> ✎ **Remember**
> to use complete sentences to express your ideas.

How do these signs differ?

| Private. No Hiking Allowed. | Private? No! Hiking Allowed. |

Can you think of other ways to use a **?** or a **!** to change messages?

2 Four Kinds of Sentences

The climbers used four types of sentences. Luis used a declarative sentence to make a statement, or tell something. Sue used an interrogative sentence to ask a question. Jon used an imperative sentence. He gave a command. Pat's sentence is also imperative, but it makes a request with the word *please*. Ana used an exclamatory sentence to show her strong feeling about the mountain. Notice how each type of sentence begins and ends.

When you write, try to use all four kinds of sentences. They will add variety and interest to your work. Also, remember to
- begin every sentence with a **capital letter**
- end a declarative or imperative sentence with a **period (.)**
- end an interrogative sentence with a **question mark (?)**
- end an exclamatory sentence with an **exclamation mark (!)**

Summary ♦ A **declarative sentence** makes a statement. An **interrogative sentence** asks a question. An **imperative sentence** gives a command or makes a request. An **exclamatory sentence** expresses strong feeling.

Guided Practice

Tell which kind of sentence each of the following is.

1. Were all mountains formed by movements of the earth's crust?
2. Some mountains are formed by volcanoes.
3. What a relief that this isn't one of them!

Practice

A. For each sentence below write *declarative, interrogative, imperative,* or *exclamatory.*

   4. Tell us more about mountains.
   5. Mountains cover one fifth of the earth's surface.
   6. What is the difference between a mountain and a hill?
   7. A mountain must be at least 2,000 feet above its surroundings.
   8. Mount Everest, the tallest mountain, is over 29,000 feet high.
   9. Why, that's over 5 miles up!
  10. Did you know that some mountains are below sea level?
  11. The West Indies are the peaks of underwater mountains.

B. Write the sentences, using capital letters and end punctuation correctly.

  12. mountainous areas usually have cool, wet climates
  13. explain the reasons for that
  14. rising air loses heat and moisture on the way up
  15. how delightful this cool breeze is
  16. why are mountains relatively unpopulated
  17. look at the thin rocky soil
  18. what crops could a farmer raise in that

C. Rewrite each sentence below. Change it to the kind of sentence asked for in parentheses ( ).

  19. The view is glorious. (exclamation)
  20. Will you sit here and enjoy it? (imperative)
  21. Imagine a road through here. (interrogative)
  22. Are logging and mining common mountain industries? (declarative)
  23. Can you name some mountains? (imperative)

Apply ◆ Think and Write

Creative Writing ◆ Pretend that you are standing on top of a majestic mountain. Using all four kinds of sentences, write about your experience.

✎ **Remember**
to use different kinds of sentences for variety.

Start with any two-word sentence. Then expand it by adding one word at a time. Follow this example.

Artists paint. Artists paint pictures. Young artists paint pictures.
Young artists paint pictures often.

3 Complete Subjects and Predicates

Every sentence has two main parts—the complete subject and the complete predicate. Both parts are necessary to write a complete sentence. In each sentence below, the complete subject is shown in blue. The complete predicate is shown in green.

> The Catskill Mountains are located in New York State.
> They lie along the western shore of the Hudson River.
> The highest peaks of the range soar to over 4,000 feet.
> Delaware Indians explored the region first.

The complete subject can be one word or many words. However, it always names someone or something. The complete predicate can also be one word or many words. It always tells what the subject is or does. When you write, use complete subjects and complete predicates to express your thoughts. This way you will make your meaning clear.

> **Summary** ◆ The **complete subject** is all the words in the subject part of a sentence. The subject part names someone or something. The **complete predicate** is all the words in the predicate part of a sentence. The predicate part tells what the subject is or does.

Guided Practice

Name the complete subject in each sentence.

1. The Catskill region belonged to the colony of New Amsterdam.
2. Dutch words for *wildcat creek* gave the Catskills their name.
3. Dutch settlers traded with Native Americans for beaver furs.

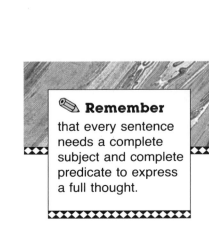

26.785 *Hudson River.* Winslow Homer, American, 1836–1910. Watercolor 14 x 20 in. Bequest of William Sturgis Beigelow. Courtesy, Museum of Fine Arts, Boston.

Practice

A. Read each sentence. Then write each complete subject.

4. The English took over New Amsterdam in 1664.
5. They renamed this former Dutch colony New York.
6. The English rulers encouraged settlement in the Catskills.
7. Large tracts of the mountainous area could not be farmed.
8. The ancient forests provided valuable timber, though.
9. Another major resource of the area is water.
10. Giant pipes carry it to New York City.

B. Write each sentence. Underline the complete subject once. Underline the complete predicate twice.

11. The writer Washington Irving lived from 1783 to 1859.
12. "Rip Van Winkle" is one of his best-known stories.
13. This humorous tale is set in the Catskills.
14. James Fenimore Cooper wrote *The Leatherstocking Tales* during the first half of the nineteenth century.
15. Some events in these tales take place in the Catskills.
16. Many artists painted the scenery of the Hudson River.
17. News of the region spread far and wide.
18. Luxury hotels were built in wilderness surroundings.

C. Each sentence below is missing one of its main parts. Add your own complete subjects or complete predicates to write full sentences.

19. _____ are found in the mountains.
20. Rivers and streams _____.
21. _____ will be tired after walking in those woods.
22. _____ carry a lunch with them.
23. A knapsack _____.

Apply ◆ Think and Write

Dictionary of Knowledge ◆ Washington Irving combines imagination, history, and folklore in his writings. What do you think you might like best about his stories? Read about him in the Dictionary of Knowledge. Write some sentences about him or his stories.

> ✎ **Remember**
> that every sentence needs a complete subject and complete predicate to express a full thought.

How many different words can you think of to complete this sentence?

A bad _____ can spoil a camping trip.

4 Simple Subjects

You have already learned that the complete subject of a sentence is all the words in the subject part. One word in the complete subject, however, is more important than the rest. This main word is called the simple subject. Like the complete subject, the simple subject names someone or something.

Read the sentences below. The simple subject of each sentence is in a blue box.

Complete Subject	Complete Predicate
1. A storm with heavy rain	can spoil a camping trip.
2. Iris Díaz	watches the weather closely.
3. She	follows a storm's progress.
4. Complete weather forecasts	may not be available.

Notice in sentence **3** that the complete subject is just one word. In such cases the simple subject is the same as the complete subject. In sentence **2** the complete subject is a name. This name is also the simple subject, although it is two words.

> **Summary** ♦ The **simple subject** is the main word in the complete subject. In your writing choose your subjects carefully to make your meaning clear.

Guided Practice

Name the simple subject in each sentence.

1. The wind is an important weather forecaster.
2. The direction of the wind can give some important information.
3. Winds from the northwest are often cooler.
4. Low pressure systems have a counterclockwise circulation.
5. You can determine the wind's direction easily.

Practice

A. Write the simple subject of each sentence.

6. You can learn the wind's direction from drifting smoke.
7. Tall trees sway in the wind, too.
8. Some people raise a wet finger in the air.
9. The cool side of the finger points to the wind's direction.
10. A simple study of the wind can tell us about the weather.

B. Write each sentence. Underline the complete subject once and the simple subject twice.

11. The best natural weather predictors are clouds.
12. The most common rainmakers are nimbostratus clouds.
13. These thick gray clouds blot out the sun completely.
14. The low-lying layers are often a sign of heavy rain.
15. Those fluffy white piles in the sky are cumulus clouds.
16. The average person considers them harmless.
17. A wise camper watches cumulus clouds carefully, though.
18. Gentle cumulus clouds can swell quickly into cumulonimbus clouds.
19. These threatening thunderheads bring rain and lightning.
20. Dangerous tornadoes can develop from some storm clouds.

C. The sentences below are each missing a simple subject. Choose a word from below to complete each sentence.

temperatures   changes   gusts   winds   weather

21. _____ bring fair weather to most places.
22. Strong _____ often bring rain, however.
23. Clear, cold _____ is associated with north winds.
24. Warmer _____ come in on southern breezes.
25. _____ in the weather occur faster with high-speed winds.

Apply ◆ Think and Write

Making Predictions ◆ What clues do you use to guess the weather? Write several sentences that tell how you sometimes predict changes in weather. Underline the simple subject of each sentence.

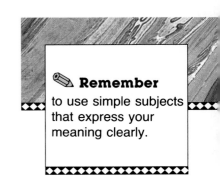

✎ **Remember**
to use simple subjects that express your meaning clearly.

GETTING
STARTED

Think of words to complete this sentence: *Arthur* ____ *the mountains.* Can you think of words beginning with each letter of the alphabet—*adores, braved, climbed, drew . . .* ?

5 Simple Predicates

You have learned that the complete predicate of a sentence is all the words in the predicate part. One or more words in the complete predicate, however, are more important than the others. This main word or words is the simple predicate. The simple predicate is always a verb. A verb expresses action or being.

Read the sentences below. The simple predicate of each sentence is in a green box.

Complete Subject	Complete Predicate
1. My friend Arthur	was in big trouble.
2. He	shivered alone on the wet mountain trail.
3. The darkness	would surround him soon.
4. This young hiker	had been wandering for over four hours.

Sometimes the simple predicate, or verb, is made up of more than one word. In sentence **3** the main verb *surround* is helped by another verb, *would*. In sentence **4** the main verb *wandering* is helped by the verbs *had* and *been*.

> **Summary** ♦ The **simple predicate**, or verb, is the main word or words in the complete predicate. In good writing the simple predicate expresses action clearly.

Guided Practice

Name the simple predicate, or verb, in each sentence.

1. The summer evening became quite cold in the mountains.
2. The weather shifted quickly from sun to rain.
3. Arthur watched the dark clouds overhead.
4. Something would happen soon.
5. Poor Arthur had carried no warm clothing with him.

Practice

A. Write the simple predicate, or verb, of each sentence.

6. Arthur made other serious mistakes, too.
7. He was carrying no compass.
8. He had forgotten his matches.
9. These items save many hikers' lives in the mountains.
10. The blisters on Arthur's feet ached.
11. Sturdy hiking boots would have prevented the blisters.
12. Arthur misjudged the distance to the mountaintop.
13. Hikers should consult maps.

B. Write each sentence. Underline the complete predicate once and the simple predicate twice.

14. Arthur told no one about his plans for the day.
15. No one knew his whereabouts.
16. The young man ignored danger signals during the day.
17. The storm clouds had formed hours ago.
18. A wiser hiker might have returned home then.
19. Sore muscles indicated Arthur's poor physical condition.
20. He should have set a more realistic goal.
21. Experienced hikers plan their trips carefully.

C. Each sentence below is missing a complete predicate. Write a complete predicate for each one. Then underline the simple predicate.

22. An experienced hiker _____ .
23. Arthur's goal _____ .
24. A forest ranger _____ .
25. Some other hikers _____ .

Apply ✦ Think and Write

Making Choices ✦ Suppose you became lost on an isolated mountain during a storm. What three pieces of equipment would you most want to have on hand? Write sentences telling what you would do with the equipment. Underline the simple predicates in your sentences.

> ✎ **Remember**
> to use simple predicates that express action clearly.

What commands do you really dislike hearing? For what questions would you like to hear Yes as an answer?

6 Locating Subjects in Sentences

You know that the subject part of a sentence names someone or something. In declarative sentences the subject part usually comes first.

Subject Part **Predicate Part**

| Some people | eat wild plants in the wilderness. |

In interrogative sentences, however, the subject part often comes after the first word of the sentence. To find the subject of an interrogative sentence, change it into a declarative sentence.

| Are | they | eating dandelions? | They | are eating dandelions. |

The subject of both sentences above is *they*. When the word *subject* is used by itself, it means simple subject.

In imperative sentences the subject is always *you*. However, the word *you* is not usually stated. It is understood. In the sentences below, the subject is understood to be *you*.

| (You) | Boil dandelion leaves. |
| (You) | Eat dandelion roots raw. |

> **Summary** ◆ In a declarative sentence the subject usually comes before the verb. In an interrogative sentence the subject often comes after the verb or between the parts of a verb. In an imperative sentence the subject is often *you* (understood).

Guided Practice

Tell the subject of each sentence.

1. Do people eat plants in the wilderness?
2. Is a guidebook to edible plants useful?
3. Fry milkweed flowers in batter.
4. Shell acorns before roasting.

Practice

A. Write the subject of each sentence.

    5. Have you had cattail cakes lately?
    6. Does flour from cattail roots taste sweet?
    7. Collect young cattail shoots in early spring.
    8. Prepare them like asparagus.
    9. Does the cattail have many uses?
    10. Do bushes with berries grow wild in this area?
    11. Eat only familiar berries.
    12. Stay away from wild mushrooms!
    13. Is milkweed as tasty as broccoli?
    14. Might weeds save your life in the woods?

B. Write the subject of each sentence. Then write whether the sentence is interrogative or imperative.

    15. Can a person find shelter from the cold in the wilderness?
    16. Wear as many layers of clothing as possible.
    17. Do spaces below rocks and cliffs form natural shelters?
    18. Keep drafts out with tree boughs, leaves, and snow.
    19. Make a lean-to with branches against a fallen tree.
    20. Is a deep trench in the snow really a warm shelter?

C. Write each sentence below as a declarative sentence.

    21. Should you stay in a snowbound car during a storm?
    22. Does an empty cabin or a barn make a good shelter?
    23. Can you cover the top of a snow hole with giant snowballs?
    24. Will a single candle keep a snow hole warm?

Apply ◆ Think and Write

Survival Solutions ◆ Follow these examples to write three questions and three commands about surviving in the wilderness.

    What is one thing you could do to prevent sunstroke?
    Always wear a hat when you are hiking under the blazing sun.

✎ Remember
to use different kinds of sentences to make your writing interesting.

What word might describe Anthony's soccer-playing ability?

As high scorer, Anthony is a _____ soccer player.

VOCABULARY ♦
Using the Thesaurus

A **thesaurus** contains lists of synonyms, or words with similar meanings. Entry words in a thesaurus and the synonyms included in each entry are arranged in alphabetical order. Often a thesaurus entry includes antonyms, or words with opposite meanings.

A thesaurus is a treasure chest of words for writers. Here is the key to unlock that treasure. Look through the Thesaurus on pages 480–497 to see how it is organized. Study this entry for *good*.

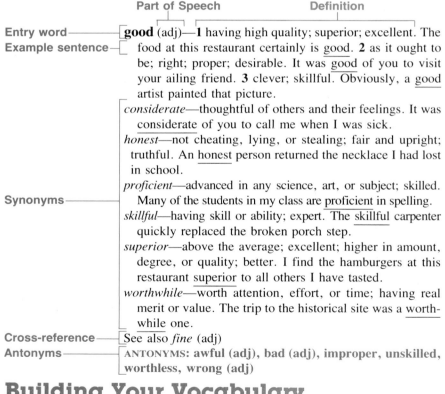

	Part of Speech **Definition**
Entry word	**good** (adj)—**1** having high quality; superior; excellent. The
Example sentence	food at this restaurant certainly is <u>good</u>. **2** as it ought to be; right; proper; desirable. It was <u>good</u> of you to visit your ailing friend. **3** clever; skillful. Obviously, a <u>good</u> artist painted that picture.
	considerate—thoughtful of others and their feelings. It was <u>considerate</u> of you to call me when I was sick.
	honest—not cheating, lying, or stealing; fair and upright; truthful. An <u>honest</u> person returned the necklace I had lost in school.
Synonyms	*proficient*—advanced in any science, art, or subject; skilled. Many of the students in my class are <u>proficient</u> in spelling.
	skillful—having skill or ability; expert. The <u>skillful</u> carpenter quickly replaced the broken porch step.
	superior—above the average; excellent; higher in amount, degree, or quality; better. I find the hamburgers at this restaurant <u>superior</u> to all others I have tasted.
	worthwhile—worth attention, effort, or time; having real merit or value. The trip to the historical site was a <u>worth-while</u> one.
Cross-reference	See also *fine* (adj)
Antonyms	ANTONYMS: **awful (adj), bad (adj), improper, unskilled, worthless, wrong (adj)**

Building Your Vocabulary

Read the **Getting Started** activity again. Which synonyms above might describe Anthony's soccer playing? Which synonym do you think *best* describes his playing? Notice how a thesaurus can help you find the best words for the meaning you want to express.

Practice

A. Find the synonyms for *good* that fit best in these sentences.
Use a different synonym in each sentence.

    1. Tomás thought the book was _____ to read.
    2. The school librarian thanked Ken for being _____ of others.
    3. This is a _____ piece of artistry.
    4. Mary Cassatt was a _____ painter.
    5. Effective writers are _____ in their use of words.

B. Use the Thesaurus to find synonyms to replace the underlined
words in the sentences below. Choose words that come as close
as possible to the original meaning of the sentence.

    6. Would you please <u>explain</u> the meaning of this note?
    7. Homer Price had many <u>funny</u> adventures.
    8. The <u>noise</u> of approaching horses echoed through the street.
    9. The village clock is always set to the <u>right</u> time.
    10. What do you <u>think</u> really happened when E.T. went home?

C. Rewrite the sentence below. Replace the underlined words with
synonyms or antonyms that you find in the Thesaurus.

Angela <u>said</u> that she <u>saw</u> a <u>small</u>, <u>sleek</u> creature <u>run</u> when it
<u>heard</u> the <u>loud</u> <u>noise</u> <u>made</u> by a passing motorcycle.

LANGUAGE CORNER • Word Meanings

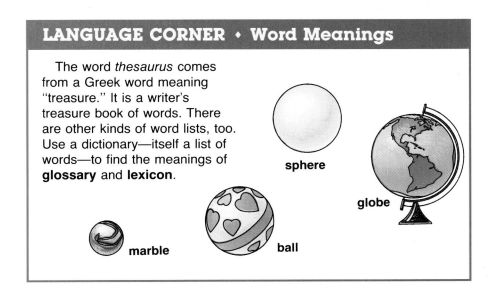

The word *thesaurus* comes
from a Greek word meaning
"treasure." It is a writer's
treasure book of words. There
are other kinds of word lists, too.
Use a dictionary—itself a list of
words—to find the meanings of
glossary and **lexicon**.

sphere

globe

marble

ball

How to Combine Sentence Parts

You can use what you have learned in this unit about sentence parts to combine sentences that contain repeated information. Read the sentences in example **1**.

> **1.** Tina went camping in Yellowstone. Her family went camping in Yellowstone.

A better, more efficient way to express this information is to combine the two sentences into one strong sentence. In example **2** the subjects of the two sentences are combined with the word *and*.

> **2.** Tina and her family went camping in Yellowstone.

The two sentences in example **3** have the same subject. In example **4**, the two predicates are combined with *and* to form a single sentence.

> **3.** They hiked. They visited lovely mountain lakes.
> **4.** They hiked and visited lovely mountain lakes.

Subjects and predicates are not the only parts of sentences that can be combined. What parts are combined below?

> **5.** They took pictures of Old Faithful. They took pictures of the hot springs.
> **6.** They took pictures of Old Faithful and the hot springs.

The Grammar Game ◆ Try it yourself! Combine each pair of sentences. Which words will you leave out? What word will you add?

◆ They arrived early Thursday afternoon. They pitched their tent in the public campgrounds.
◆ Tina went horseback riding. Her brother went horseback riding.
◆ They stopped at a small lake. They stopped at a scenic overlook.

COOPERATIVE LEARNING: Combining Sentences

Working Together

Work with your group on activities **A** and **B**. You will find that combining sentences will make your writing smoother, more efficient, and easier to read.

A. Imagine that your group organized a camping trip. Match each sentence in the first column with a sentence from the second column that repeats information. Then combine each pair of sentences, using the word *and*.

We got sleeping bags.	We looked at travel guides.
We chose a camping spot.	We packed our clothes.
We washed our clothes.	We got cooking gear.
We looked at maps.	We reserved a campsite.

B. Find pairs of sentences to combine in the paragraph below. You can combine subjects, predicates, or other parts of sentences. Then write your new paragraph.

Everyone got out of the car. Everyone rushed to the campsite. Soon we had all the tents up. Soon we had our gear unpacked. Richie went for a hike. Michael went for a hike. Meanwhile, Tina and her sister saw several deer. They saw some beavers. Afterwards, we built a fire. We cooked a wonderful dinner. Everyone enjoyed the food. Everyone enjoyed the storytelling later in the evening.

WRITERS' CORNER ◆ Choppy Sentences

Using too many short, or choppy, sentences can make your writing boring and hard to read.

CHOPPY: **Tina carried the pots and pans. She carried them to the picnic table. The table was dirty. Michael cleaned it up. He cleaned it with soap and water.**

IMPROVED: **Tina carried the pots and pans to the picnic table, but the table was dirty. Michael cleaned it up with soap and water.**

Read what you wrote for the Writer's Warm-up. Is your writing choppy? Could you improve any of your sentences?

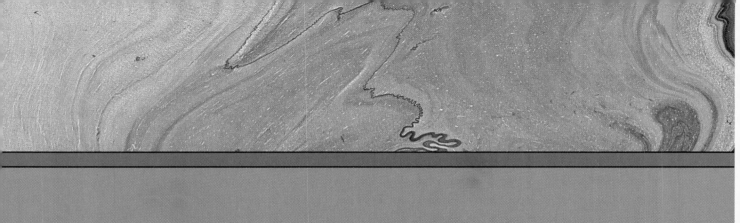

TWILIGHT IN THE WILDERNESS
painting by Frederick Edwin Church
The Cleveland Museum of Art,
Mr. & Mrs. William H. Marlatt Fund.

USING LANGUAGE
TO
NARRATE

=== **PART TWO** ===

Literature   *My Side of the Mountain* by Jean George
A Reason for Writing Narrating

CREATIVE
Writing

FINE ARTS ◆ Look at the sky in the painting at the left. Then give the sky life. What mood do you see in that sky? What would the sky want to say to the earth right now? Write a letter from the sky to the earth.

CRITICAL THINKING ◆
A Strategy for Narrating

A GOAL/PLAN/OUTCOME CHART

A story is sometimes called a narrative. The story after this lesson is *My Side of the Mountain* by Jean George. It is about a boy who struggles to survive in the wilderness. The boy uses the words *I* and *me* to narrate the story from his point of view. Later you will write a personal narrative about something that happened to you.

In a good story the main character often has a goal and makes a plan for reaching it. The writer describes the actions the character takes to reach the goal and then describes the result, or outcome. Here is an example from *My Side of the Mountain*.

After a struggle I made a fire. Then I sewed a big skunk cabbage leaf into a cup with grass strands. I had read that you can boil water in a leaf, and ever since then I had been very anxious to see if this were true. It seems impossible, but it works. I boiled the eggs in a leaf.

What was the boy's goal? What actions did he take to reach it? What was the outcome?

◆ Learning the Strategy

Suppose you want to do more chin-ups than you can do now. Could just identifying your goal help you reach it? Suppose you were reading an adventure story. Could identifying the character's goal and plan of action help you follow the story? Suppose you were writing about the time you performed your stilt-walking act in a talent contest. Could identifying your goal and your actions help you organize your ideas and tell your story clearly?

A goal/plan/outcome chart is a good strategy for thinking about goals and the actions taken to reach them. For example, think about wanting to do more chin-ups. A goal/plan/outcome chart like the one below might help you keep track of the actions you plan and the result. As you can see, two or three actions may be needed to reach your goal. Also, there are times when an action leads to more than one outcome.

Goal:

To do 30 chin-ups in a row by the end of 6 weeks

▶

Plan:

Do arm exercises daily.
Practice chin-ups Mon., Wed., and Fri.
Start with 5 chin-ups. Do 5 more each week.

▶

Outcomes:

Arms tired at first
Arms OK by third week
Did 30 chin-ups by the fifth week

Using the Strategy

A. Think of a subject in which you would like to improve your grade. It might be spelling, art, or gym. Then make a goal/plan/outcome chart. Fill in the Outcome column with the result that is most likely.

B. In *My Side of the Mountain*, a boy tries living in the wilderness. Imagine that you had to survive alone in the wilderness. What might some of your goals be? Make a goal/plan/outcome chart. Under *Goal*, write one of your goals for wilderness survival. Under *Plan*, list actions you would take to reach your goal. Under *Outcome*, list the probable result. Then read to find out how the boy in *My Side of the Mountain* met the challenges of wilderness survival.

Applying the Strategy

♦ How did you decide on the goals, plans, and outcomes for your charts?
♦ When might it be important for you to plan actions to reach goals in your own life? Why might it be important to evaluate the outcome of your actions?

from # My Side of
the Mountain

by Jean George

One spring day, Sam Gribley left his family's
crowded New York City apartment and set out for
Great-grandfather Gribley's land in the Catskill
Mountains. He had only a little money, a
penknife, an ax, a ball of cord, and a flint with
steel for building fires. With these tools and the
skills he had acquired, Sam figured that he could
survive in the mountains. He planned on living off
the land that Great-grandfather Gribley had once
tried to farm.

When Sam found the farm, though, little
remained but some stone walls, the ruins of a
house, and an old beech tree with the name
Gribley carved on it. Still, the land provided wild
plants for food, a clear stream for fishing, and
trees for firewood and shelter. At the edge of a
mountain meadow, Sam also found a hemlock
forest. Never in his life had he seen such huge, old
trees. As Sam stood before the biggest and oldest
tree of all, an idea struck him. In this entry from
his diary, Sam tells what happened then.

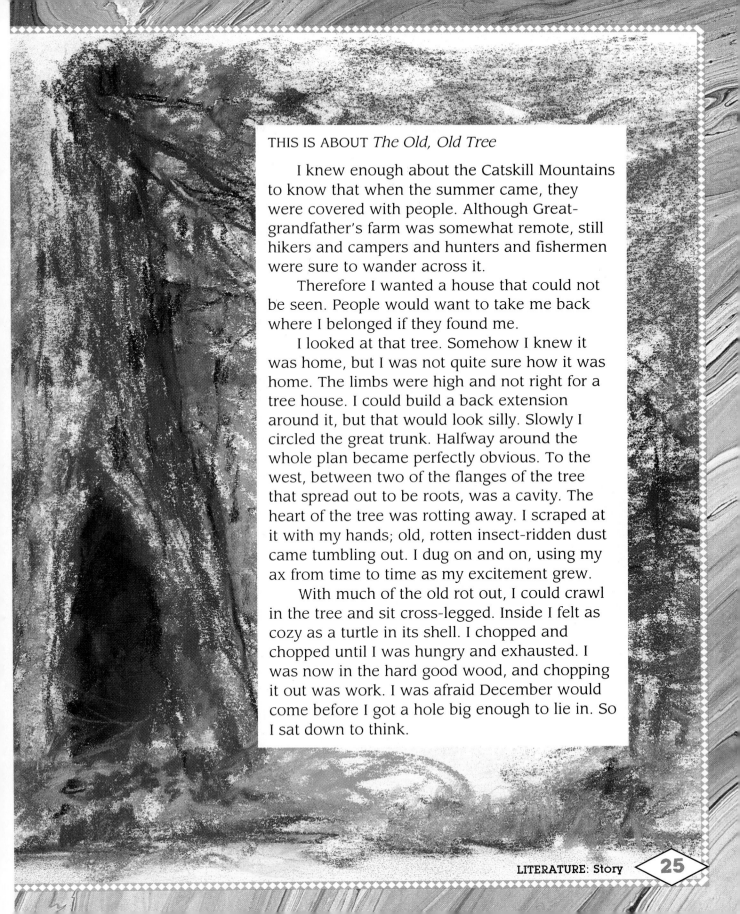

THIS IS ABOUT *The Old, Old Tree*

I knew enough about the Catskill Mountains to know that when the summer came, they were covered with people. Although Great-grandfather's farm was somewhat remote, still hikers and campers and hunters and fishermen were sure to wander across it.

Therefore I wanted a house that could not be seen. People would want to take me back where I belonged if they found me.

I looked at that tree. Somehow I knew it was home, but I was not quite sure how it was home. The limbs were high and not right for a tree house. I could build a back extension around it, but that would look silly. Slowly I circled the great trunk. Halfway around the whole plan became perfectly obvious. To the west, between two of the flanges of the tree that spread out to be roots, was a cavity. The heart of the tree was rotting away. I scraped at it with my hands; old, rotten insect-ridden dust came tumbling out. I dug on and on, using my ax from time to time as my excitement grew.

With much of the old rot out, I could crawl in the tree and sit cross-legged. Inside I felt as cozy as a turtle in its shell. I chopped and chopped until I was hungry and exhausted. I was now in the hard good wood, and chopping it out was work. I was afraid December would come before I got a hole big enough to lie in. So I sat down to think.

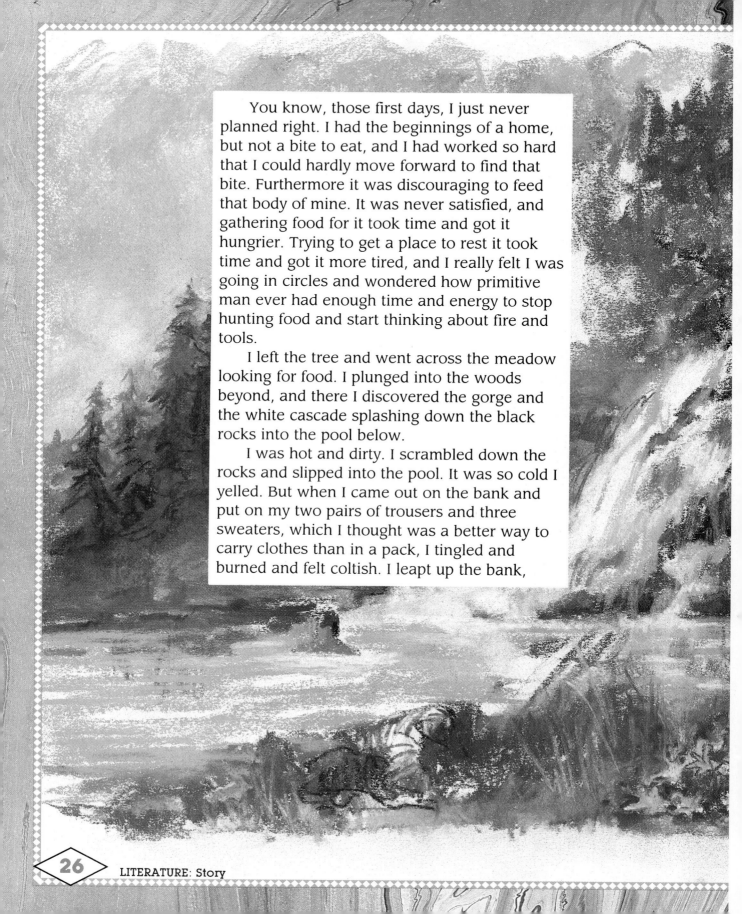

You know, those first days, I just never planned right. I had the beginnings of a home, but not a bite to eat, and I had worked so hard that I could hardly move forward to find that bite. Furthermore it was discouraging to feed that body of mine. It was never satisfied, and gathering food for it took time and got it hungrier. Trying to get a place to rest it took time and got it more tired, and I really felt I was going in circles and wondered how primitive man ever had enough time and energy to stop hunting food and start thinking about fire and tools.

I left the tree and went across the meadow looking for food. I plunged into the woods beyond, and there I discovered the gorge and the white cascade splashing down the black rocks into the pool below.

I was hot and dirty. I scrambled down the rocks and slipped into the pool. It was so cold I yelled. But when I came out on the bank and put on my two pairs of trousers and three sweaters, which I thought was a better way to carry clothes than in a pack, I tingled and burned and felt coltish. I leapt up the bank, slipped, and my face went down in a patch of dogtooth violets.

You would know them anywhere after a few looks at them at the Botanical Gardens and in colored flower books. They are little yellow lilies on long slender stems with oval leaves dappled with gray. But that's not all. They have wonderfully tasty bulbs. I was filling my pockets before I got up from my fall.

"I'll have a salad type lunch," I said as I moved up the steep sides of the ravine. I discovered that as late as it was in the season, the spring beauties were still blooming in the cool pockets of the woods. They are all right raw, that is if you are as hungry as I was. They taste a little like lima beans. I ate these as I went on hunting food, feeling better and better, until I worked my way back to the meadow where the dandelions were blooming. Funny I hadn't noticed them earlier. Their greens are good, and so are their roots—a little strong and milky, but you get used to that.

A crow flew into the aspen grove without saying a word. The little I knew of crows from following them in Central Park, they always have something to say. But this bird was sneaking, obviously trying to be quiet. Birds are good food. Crow is certainly not the best, but I did not know that then, and I launched out to see where it was going. I had a vague plan to try to noose it. This is the kind of thing I wasted time on in those days when time was so important. However, this venture turned out all right, because I did not have to noose that bird.

I stepped into the woods, looked around, could not see the crow, but noticed a big stick nest in a scrabbly pine. I started to climb the tree. Off flew the crow. What made me keep on climbing in the face of such discouragement, I don't know, but I did, and that noon I had crow eggs and wild salad for lunch.

At lunch I also solved the problem of carving out my tree. After a struggle I made a fire. Then I sewed a big skunk cabbage leaf into a cup with grass strands. I had read that you can boil water in a leaf, and ever since then I had been very anxious to see if this were true. It seems impossible, but it works. I boiled the eggs in a leaf. The water keeps the leaf wet, and although the top dries up and burns down to the water level, that's as far as the burning goes. I was pleased to see it work.

Then here's what happened. Naturally, all this took a lot of time, and I hadn't gotten very far on my tree, so I was fretting and stamping out the fire when I stopped with my foot in the air.

The fire! Indians made dugout canoes with fire. They burned them out, an easier and much faster way of getting results. I would try fire in the tree. If I was very careful, perhaps it would work. I ran into the hemlock forest with a burning stick and got a fire going inside the tree.

Thinking that I ought to have a bucket of water in case things got out of hand, I looked desperately around me. The water was far across the meadow and down the ravine. This would never do. I began to think the whole inspiration of a home in the tree was no good. I really did have to live near water for cooking and drinking and comfort. I looked sadly at the magnificent hemlock and was about to put the fire out and desert it when I said something to myself. It must have come out of some book: "Hemlocks usually grow around mountain streams and springs."

I swirled on my heel. Nothing but boulders around me. But the air was damp, somewhere—I said—and darted around the rocks, peering and looking and sniffing and going down into pockets and dales. No water. I was coming back, circling wide, when I almost fell in it. Two sentinel boulders, dripping wet, decorated with flowers, ferns, moss, weeds— everything that loved water—guarded a bathtub-sized spring.

"You pretty thing," I said, flopped on my stomach, and pushed my face into it to drink. I opened my eyes. The water was like glass, and in it were little insects with oars. They rowed away from me. Beetles skittered like bullets on the surface, or carried a silver bubble of air with them to the bottom. Ha, then I saw a crayfish.

I jumped up, overturned rocks, and found many crayfish. At first I hesitated to grab them because they can pinch. I gritted my teeth, thought about how much more it hurts to be hungry, and came down upon them. I did get pinched, but I had my dinner. And that was the first time I had planned ahead! Any planning that I did in those early days was such a surprise to me and so successful that I was delighted with even a small plan. I wrapped the crayfish in leaves, stuffed them in my pockets, and went back to the burning tree.

Bucket of water, I thought. Bucket of water? Where was I going to get a bucket? How did I think, even if I found water, I could get it back to the tree? That's how cityfied I was in those days. I had never lived without a bucket before—scrub buckets, water buckets—and so when a water problem came up, I just thought I could run to the kitchen and get a bucket.

"Well, dirt is as good as water," I said as I ran back to my tree. "I can smother the fire with dirt."

Days passed working, burning, cutting, gathering food, and each day I cut another notch on an aspen pole that I had stuck in the ground for a calendar.

Library Link ♦ *You can read the whole account of Sam Gribley's adventures in* My Side of the Mountain *by Jean George.*

Reader's Response

If you were stranded in the wilderness, would you like to have a copy of *My Side of the Mountain* with you? Why or why not?

My Side of the Mountain

 ## Responding to Literature

1. What did you learn from reading this selection from *My Side of the Mountain?* Tell one thing you know now that you did not know before you read it.

2. Solving problems often requires creative thinking and resourcefulness. Sam solved many problems. If you had been Sam, what would you have done differently? Write a page in your journal. Tell how you would have solved one problem that Sam faced.

3. Choose one classmate to play the part of Sam in *My Side of the Mountain*. Then choose another to be a television talk-show host. Plan the questions, possible responses, and follow-up questions. Remember that "Sam" must be ready with answers.

 ## Writing to Learn

Think and Solve ◆ Jean George had goals for each part of the story and knew how she might achieve them. Based on your reading, prepare a Goal/Plan/Outcome Chart that she might have prepared.

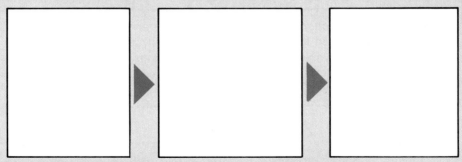

Goal-Plan-Outcome Chart

Write ◆ Focus on the outcomes to write a paragraph. Tell how the outcome made the story richer.

Tell a very brief story about an amusing incident you remember. *A skywriter trailed words across a cloudless sky. My baby sister said, "I can't read yet, but I think it says it's going to rain!"*

SPEAKING and LISTENING ♦
Telling an Anecdote

> **Miyax had to learn to "talk wolf." She grunted, whined, and "talked" with her body as she moved among the wolves.**

Everyone loves to hear a good story, especially if it is told with drama. A speaker can capture listeners' attention by telling an anecdote, or brief story, like the one above. It is about something interesting that happened in a book called *Julie of the Wolves*. Knowing how to tell an anecdote will help you add to the enjoyment of your audience.

Use the guidelines below to help you tell anecdotes and listen to them.

Telling an Anecdote	1. Think of your audience. Choose an anecdote they will enjoy. Make notes to remember all the details in order. 2. Standing up, practice speaking aloud. Repeat your story several times. Practice before a mirror to check on your posture, facial expressions, and gestures. 3. Before you speak, pause to get the audience's attention. Think of your first sentence, smile, and begin. 4. Look directly at individuals. Make eye contact. 5. Speak loud enough to be heard. Speak slowly and clearly.
Being an Active Listener	1. Be attentive. Look at the speaker and show your interest. 2. Listen for the order of events, and try to predict the story's ending. 3. As you listen, ask yourself questions. Listen for answers. 4. Watch. What do the speaker's facial expressions and body language tell you?

Summary ♦ An **anecdote** is a brief, interesting story. A well-told anecdote captures the interest of listeners and brings them enjoyment.

Guided Practice

Say each sentence two different ways to show each feeling that is named. Ask your listeners to tell what the feeling was.

1. What a surprise! (happiness, shock)
2. How did you manage to do this? (sincerity, anger)
3. Now try to do it again. (irritation, patience)

Practice

A. Practice saying the sentences aloud in ways that show how you feel. Use facial expressions and gestures, too. Ask your listeners to tell what the feeling is each time.

    4. Gently I approached the sleeping opossum. (mysterious, timid)
    5. I was hot and tired. (disgusted, sad)
    6. The water was so cold that I yelled. (surprised, amused)
    7. They will try to climb the tree. (excited, determined)
    8. You silly thing! (loving, mocking)
    9. Let's be sure to remember to watch this show every week. (enthusiastic, sarcastic)

B. Tell an anecdote to a partner. It can be real, or it can be from your imagination. Prepare by jotting down notes about the details. Build in some suspense or a surprise. Keep your listener interested in the story. Stop just before the end, and ask your partner to guess what happens next. When you are the listener, pay close attention, and think of a question to ask the speaker.

Apply ◆ Think and Write

Collecting Anecdotes ◆ Think about stories you have read recently or about films or television shows you have seen. Choose an incident you would like to use as an anecdote sometime. Jot down notes so that you will be able to remember it later. Make this the beginning of a "storehouse" of your favorite anecdotes.

> ✎ **Remember**
> to tell anecdotes in an amusing or interesting way.

◆ GETTING ◆
STARTED

"The refrigerator works fine," she announced coldly.
"A famous actor like me is always busy," he added playfully.

Can you make up more funny quotations like these?

WRITING ◆
Quotations

When you write a quotation, you show the exact words of a speaker. Quotation marks show where the speaker's words begin and end. The first word of a quotation begins with a capital letter. A comma separates the quotation from the words that tell who is speaking. The comma always comes before the quotation mark.

> **"It would scare me to live alone in the woods," said Dan.**
> **Dan confessed, "I wouldn't know what to do first."**

When a quotation is a question or an exclamation, use a question mark or an exclamation mark instead of a comma.

> **"I think it would be fantastic!" exclaimed Tanya.**
> **"How would you handle unexpected situations?" asked Dan.**

Some quotations are divided. If a divided quotation is one sentence, use commas to separate the quotation from the speaker.

> **"I would use my wits," Tanya answered, "just like Sam in *My Side of the Mountain* did."**

When a divided quotation is two sentences, use a period after the words that tell who is speaking. Capitalize the first word of the second sentence.

> **"He was amazing," said Dan. "I wish I were like him."**

When you quote a conversation, begin a new paragraph each time the speaker changes. Also, remember to vary the verb that you use. Do not use the verb *said* too often.

> **"Did the author of that book write any other stories about the wilderness?" asked Theo.**
> **"Let's ask the librarian," Susan suggested.**

> **Summary** ◆ Use **quotation marks** (" ") to show the exact words of a speaker.

Guided Practice

Tell where quotation marks and capital letters should be placed.

1. Susan asked, what was the author's name?
2. If I remember correctly, Theo replied, it was Jean George.
3. I'll check the *G* shelf, said Susan. you ask the librarian.

Practice

A. Write the sentences below, adding quotation marks and capital letters where needed.

4. here are five books by Jean George, called Susan.
5. Theo asked, do any of them sound good to you?
6. this one might be interesting, Susan replied, but you probably wouldn't read a book about a girl.
7. hey! laughed Theo. a good book is a good book!
8. do you think this Julie really lives with wolves? wondered Susan.
9. there's only one way to find out, Theo announced. hand over the book.
10. I'll borrow it next, said Susan, if you recommend it.

B. Write the following conversation about *My Side of the Mountain* correctly. Add punctuation where it is needed. Remember to start a new paragraph each time the speaker changes.

How could the boy expect to survive Jed asked. Kim replied He knew a lot before he started, and he was very resourceful. Even so Jed argued every little task was so hard at first, and a mistake could have cost him his life. Kim admitted I don't know if I could have done what he did. Me either agreed Jed.

Apply ◆ Think and Write

An Interview ◆ What questions would you like to ask Jean George? How might she answer? Write a possible conversation. Use all the rules for punctuating, capitalizing, and indenting quotations.

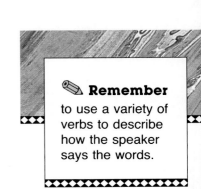

✎ **Remember**
to use a variety of verbs to describe how the speaker says the words.

At daybreak Lou was awakened by the din of rush-hour traffic. Take turns adding sentences until you finish the story. Use words and phrases such as *then, an hour later,* and *at last.*

WRITING ◆
Time Order in Narratives

When you use language to narrate, you use it to tell a story. Narratives come in all forms and lengths—oral or written, hundreds of pages long or just a paragraph. Whether long or short, narratives tell what happened and are organized in time order, telling about events in the order in which they happened. Time-order words, such as those below, help to make the order of events clear.

first	now	until	at noon	immediately	next
second	soon	at last	at once	in a minute	after
then	during	today	meanwhile	after a while	later

A narrative tells a story. When you write a narrative, you need to tell the details in the order in which they happened. Time-order words let your reader know the sequence of events. Notice the time-order words in this narrative paragraph from *Julie of the Wolves*.

Miyax stared hard at the regal black wolf, hoping to catch his eye. She must somehow tell him that she was starving and ask him for food. This could be done she knew, for her father, an Eskimo hunter, had done so. One year he had camped near a wolf den while on a hunt. When a month had passed and her father had seen no game, he told the leader of the wolves that he was hungry and needed food. The next night the wolf called him from far away, and her father went to him and found a freshly killed caribou. Unfortunately, Miyax's father never explained to her how he had told the wolf of his needs. And not long afterward he paddled his kayak into the Bering Sea to hunt for seal, and he never returned.

—Jean Craighead George

Summary ◆ A **narrative** tells what happened. It is organized by time order, the order in which events happened.

Guided Practice

The following story is based on another wilderness experience. Tell the events in order, using the time-order words as clues.

1. After tying the ends, he made sure the hammock was level.
2. Next he located two trees that would support his weight.
3. To begin with, he unrolled his mosquito-netted jungle hammock.
4. Then he tied each of the two ends securely to the tree.
5. Finally he had a peaceful night's rest, without black flies.

Practice

A. Arrange these sentences in time order, then write them.

6. Today she thought the job would be easy.
7. Ten matches later, it finally began to burn.
8. At camp last year Billie Joe had learned how to build a fire safely.
9. Then she built the log-cabin shape, with twigs in the middle.
10. Next, hoping for success with only one match, she tried to light the fire.
11. She began by collecting logs and twigs.

B. Choose one of these topics for a narrative. Write a story, using time-order words to tell what happened.

12. a favorite memory
13. a special holiday
14. a hilarious happening
15. a stroke of luck
16. a thrilling experience
17. a day best forgotten

Apply ◆ Think and Write

Dictionary of Knowledge ◆ Read the article about Robinson Crusoe. He and Friday had to survive in the wilderness. Put yourself in Crusoe's place. Write sentences that tell the first five things you would do if you were in his situation.

✎ **Remember**
that using time order will make your narrative easier to follow.

Focus on Point of View

Do you like to give your point of view? If so, that means you enjoy expressing your opinion. To a writer, however, **point of view** means something else — it means "who tells the story."

A writer can tell the story from one of two points of view: first person or third person. If a character tells his or her own story, using *I*, the point of view is **first person**. If an outsider tells the story, using *he* or *she*, the point of view is **third person**.

FIRST PERSON: *I* solved the problem of carving out *my* tree.

THIRD PERSON: *He* solved the problem of carving out *his* tree.

Choosing a point of view is an important decision for a writer. It affects what the writer can and cannot tell about the story. Here are some advantages (+) and disadvantages (−) of the two points of view.

First-Person Point of View	Third-Person Point of View
+ The reader understands and sympathizes with the narrator.	+ The writer can reveal all characters' thoughts and feelings.
+ The reader feels that he or she is on the scene.	+ The writer can tell about any event, any time, and any place.
− The writer can reveal the thoughts of only one character.	− The reader may feel more removed from the story.
− The writer must be at every event the writer tells about.	

The Writer's Voice ◆ Point of view can be either first person or third person. Finish each of these first-person sentences about yourself. Then change each of the sentences into the third person.

1. My hobbies are _____ .
2. I really dislike _____ .
3. I've always wanted to _____ .
4. I enjoy listening to _____ .

Working Together

Every piece of writing has a point of view. Factual reports are often written in the third person. First person can be a good choice for stories that you want readers to experience along with the narrator. Use both points of view as your group works on activities **A** and **B**.

A. Jean George's *My Side of the Mountain* has a first-person narrator. Reread the first four paragraphs of her story, which appear in this unit. Then go back and change the point of view from first person to third person. Have the *I* become *Sam*. When the changes have been made, name one person to read the revised version to the rest of the class. Discuss the differences between the points of view. What words had to be changed? What effect did the changes have on the story?

B. With your group, rewrite the following sentences in the *first-person plural* point of view. (Use forms of the pronoun *we*.)

1. Judy read *My Side of the Mountain* in her fourth-period class.
2. Mr. Roe, her teacher, told her that she would enjoy it.
3. The story taught Judy many things about living in the woods.
4. She agreed that it was one of her ten favorite books.
5. Judy asked, "Could I read another book by Jean George?"

THESAURUS CORNER • Word Choice

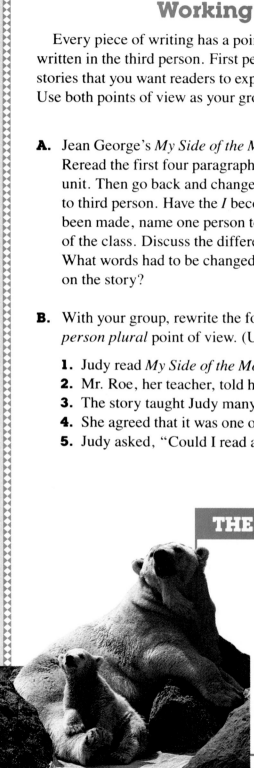

Rewrite the paragraph below. Separate it into sentences and punctuate the sentences correctly. Use the Thesaurus and Thesaurus Index to replace each word in dark type with a better word.

A wilderness animal that **expands** in captivity is the polar bear polar bears, which are found in Arctic coastal **districts**, usually live on drifting pack ice do you **fathom** why polar bears are white in fact, they aren't white their dense fur is made up of translucent hairs that reflect almost all visible light polar bears are **gigantic** fast fearless and dangerous they are **illustrious** favorites at zoos, but zookeepers must treat them with extreme caution.

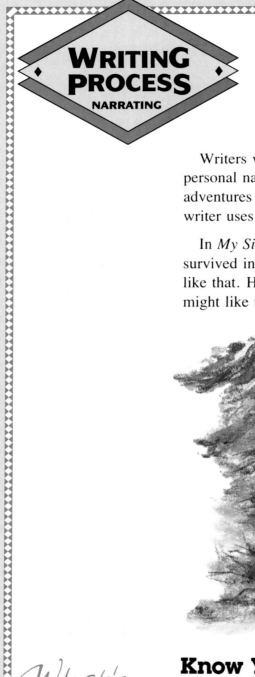
Writing a Personal Narrative

Writers write many kinds of narratives, or stories. One kind is a personal narrative. It is a story the writer tells about his or her own adventures or experiences. The point of view is first person. The writer uses the words *I* and *me*.

In *My Side of the Mountain*, for example, a boy tells how he survived in the wilderness. You may never have had an adventure like that. However, you have had many experiences that others might like to read about.

Know Your Purpose and Audience

In this lesson you will write a personal narrative about a real-life experience. Your purpose will be to tell a story about something you did that was difficult to do.

Your audience will be your classmates. Later you and your classmates can read your personal narratives aloud or make a book of them.

What's
MY PURPOSE

Who's
MY AUDIENCE

1 Prewriting

Prewriting is getting ready to write. First you need to choose a topic, then gather ideas about your topic.

Choose Your Topic ◆ Make a list of times in your life when you've had to do something difficult. Perhaps you rescued a hurt animal or learned to walk on crutches.

Think About It	Talk About It
Make a list of five difficult things you've done. Put the items in order from the least to the most difficult. Then decide which is best. Is it the one that was hardest to do? Is it the one that is the most exciting? Circle your favorite topic.	Talk to your classmates about possible topics. Your topic could be about raising prize-winning broccoli. Remember to recall events from when you were younger, too. You may remember that learning to ride a bike was hard at that time.

Topic Ideas

raising a prize-winning
steer
learning to walk on crutches
first learning to ride a bike
learning to play the tuba
singing in front of an
audience

Choose Your Strategy ◆ Here are two strategies that can help you gather ideas for your narrative. Read both strategies. Then use what you think will work best for you.

PREWRITING IDEAS

CHOICE ONE

Freewriting

One way to recall details about your experience is to freewrite about it. Quickly write ideas for about five minutes without stopping. Try to relive the experience as you write. When you have finished, underline the parts you think are the most interesting, exciting, or humorous.

Model

Fell off swing — Broke leg — Got crutches — Couldn't get up out of bed — Couldn't go up and down stairs — Then learned how to go really fast on them.

CHOICE TWO

A Goal/Plan/Outcome Chart

A goal/plan/outcome chart is another way to gather details. Fill in the details for the story you want to tell.

Model

| Goal: To learn to walk on crutches | → | Plan: Get family to help me Practice a lot on stairs | → | Outcomes: I learned to get around fast! |

2 Writing

Writing is putting your ideas on paper. First review your freewriting or your goal/plan/outcome chart. Then begin to write your personal narrative. Here are ways you might begin:

♦ Did I ever tell you about the time ____?

♦ Once when I was much younger ____.

As you write, try to do more than just list details. Remember your feelings about your experience. Sometimes it helps to think of a friend who might read your story. Think of words and phrases that would help that person understand and share your excitement, your fear, or your success.

Record each event in time order. This will help you keep your thoughts clear and organized as you write. Don't be too concerned about grammar or spelling. Just keep on writing. You can make corrections later when you revise and proofread.

Sample First Draft ♦

When I was eight years old, I broke my leg. Suddenly the rope that held the swing came loose, and for a second I flew so high I thought I would never come down. I was swinging in the backyard, admiring the sky.

My father rushed me to the hospitle. They set my leg and put it in a cast, and then came the hard part. I had to learn to walk with crutches. I had to learn to get up out of bed. Had to learn to go up and down stairs. Before long, though, I could charge around as fast on crutches as my brothers could without them. with my family to help me, I became a real expert!

3 Revising

Revising is making changes to improve your writing. Here is an idea that may help you decide what changes to make.

REVISING IDEA

FIRST Read to Yourself

As you read, review your purpose. Did you tell a story about something difficult you did? Think about your audience. Will your classmates understand why the experience was difficult? Circle any unclear or confusing words you may want to change later.

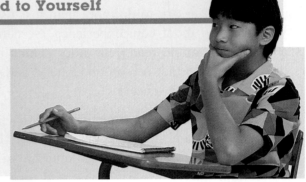

Focus: Have you used first-person point of view to make your feelings about your experience clear?

THEN Share with a Partner

Choose a partner to be your first audience. Read your narrative aloud. Ask your partner to respond honestly to your writing. Below are some guidelines.

The Writer

Guidelines: Read aloud slowly and clearly. Listen to your partner, but make only the changes you think you should make.

Sample Questions:

- Does the order of events in my story make sense?
- Focus question: Did you understand how I felt about the experience?

The Writer's Partner

Guidelines: Be honest. Say what you think, but make your comments courteously.

Sample Responses:

- It might make more sense if you first told _____.
- I wasn't sure how you felt about _____.

Revising Model ♦ Look at this sample draft that is being revised. Revising marks often look messy, but they show the changes the writer wants to make.

This sentence was not in the correct time order.

This sentence needed a subject to express a complete thought.

The writer's partner wanted to know how she felt.

Encourage is a more precise word for this sentence.

> When I was eight years old, I broke my leg. Suddenly the rope that held the swing came loose, and for a second I flew so high I thought I would never come down. I was swinging in the backyard, admiring the sky.
>
> My father rushed me to the hospitle. They set my leg and put it in a cast, and then came the hard part. I had to learn to walk with crutches. I had to learn to get up out of bed. *I felt like a baby just learning to walk.* Had to learn to go up and down stairs. Before long, though, I could charge around as fast on crutches as my brothers could without them. with my family to *encourage* help me, I became a real expert!

Read the revised draft above. Read it the way the writer has decided it *should* be. Then revise your own narrative.

Grammar Check ♦ Sentences that express complete thoughts are easier to read.

Word Choice ♦ Is there a more precise word for a word like *helped*? A thesaurus can help you improve your word choice.

Revising Checklist

☐ **Purpose:** Did I write a personal narrative about something I did that was difficult to do?

☐ **Audience:** Will my classmates understand what happened and how I felt?

☐ **Focus:** Did I use first-person point of view?

4 Proofreading

Proofreading is looking for and fixing errors. Making sure your writing is correct and easy to read is a way of being polite to your readers.

Proofreading Model ♦ Here is the sample draft of the narrative about learning to walk on crutches. Notice how red proofreading marks have now been added.

Proofreading Marks

capital letter	=
small letter	/
indent paragraph	¶
check spelling	⬭

¶ When I was eight years old, I broke my leg. Suddenly the rope that held the swing came loose, and for a second I flew so high I thought I would never come down. ⟨I was swinging in the backyard, admiring the sky.⟩

    My father rushed me to the ⟨hospitle⟩ *hospital* They set my leg and put it in a cast, and then came the hard part. I had to learn to walk with crutches, I had to learn to get up out of bed. *I felt like a baby just learning to walk.* ∧ Had to learn to go up and down stairs. Before long, though, I could charge around as fast on crutches as my brothers could without them. with my family to ~~help~~ me *encourage*, I became a real expert!

Proofreading Checklist

- ☐ Did I spell words correctly?
- ☐ Did I indent paragraphs?
- ☐ Did I use capital letters correctly?
- ☐ Did I use correct marks at the end of sentences?
- ☐ Did I type neatly or use my best handwriting?

PROOFREADING IDEA

One Thing at a Time

When you look for several kinds of errors, you may skip over mistakes. So focus on one thing at a time. Read your paper once for grammar errors. Then read it again for spelling errors.

Now proofread your personal narrative and write a title for it. Then make a neat copy.

5 Publishing

Publishing is sharing your writing with others. Try one of the ideas below for sharing your personal narrative.

Learning to Walk on Crutches

When I was eight years old, I broke my leg. I was swinging in the backyard, admiring the sky. Suddenly the rope that held the swing came loose, and for a second I flew so high I thought I would never come down.

My father rushed me to the hospital. They set my leg and put it in a cast, and then came the hard part. I had to learn to walk with crutches. I had to learn to get up out of bed. I had to learn to go up and down stairs. I felt like a baby just learning to walk. Before long, though, I could charge around as fast on crutches as my brothers could without them. With my family to encourage me, I became a real expert!

PUBLISHING IDEAS

Share Aloud	Share in Writing
Get together with three or four classmates. Take turns reading your personal narratives to each other. Allow time for the listeners to tell one outstanding feature of each.	To reach a wider audience, make a class book of personal narratives for the school library. Glue a library card case into the book with space on the book card for borrowers' comments.

CURRICULUM
◆CONNECTION◆

Writing Across the Curriculum
Social Studies

In this unit you read about a boy who planned ways to survive in the wild. You may have used a goal/plan/outcome chart to help you write about a personal experience. People who lived in the past also made plans to reach goals. Analyzing people's goals and plans and the outcomes is one way of studying history.

Writing to Learn

Think and Analyze ◆ Study the pioneers in this picture. What were their goals? How did they plan to reach them? What were some of the outcomes for them and for us? Make a goal/plan/outcome chart for the pioneers in this picture.

Goal-Plan-Outcome Chart

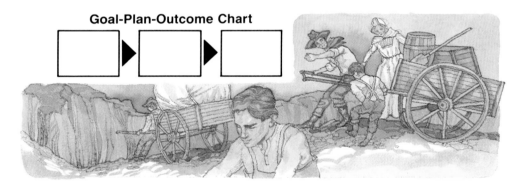

Write ◆ Imagine you live in the 1800s. You want to move from the East to the West. Write a letter to a relative. Explain why you want to make the journey. Describe how you plan to make it.

Writing in Your Journal

In the Writer's Warm-up you wrote about the wilderness. Later you read a narrative about living in the wild. Would you like living alone in the wilderness? Record your ideas in your journal.

BOOKS TO ENJOY

 ## Read More About It

Julie of the Wolves *by Jean Craighead George*
This book by the author of *My Side of the Mountain*
tells the story of Miyax, a thirteen-year-old Eskimo
girl. Lost and alone in the Arctic wilderness, she
survives by becoming part of a roving wolf pack.

Newbery Award

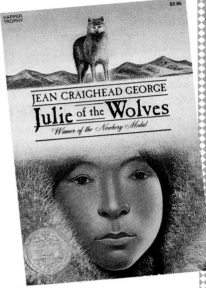

Robinson Crusoe *by Daniel Defoe*
One of the first novels in English, this book was
first published in 1719. Robinson Crusoe's wilderness
is an uninhabited desert island. Like Sam Gribley,
Crusoe must use his wits and knowledge to find shelter,
food, and tools. This exciting adventure also
explores what it is like to be truly alone.

The Boy Who Sailed Around the World Alone
by Robin Lee Graham
This is Robin Lee Graham's autobiographical
account of his successful solo sailboat voyage around
the world. With photographs, hand-drawn maps, and
logbook entries, Graham recreates his joys and
struggles in a wilderness of waves.

 ## Book Report Idea Book Jacket

The picture and information on a
book jacket can persuade
someone to read a book.

Create a Book Jacket ◆ Fold
a large piece of paper as shown.
In the middle, draw a scene from
the book. On the flaps, write a
few paragraphs about the story.
Don't give away the ending.

UNIT REVIEW

Unit 1

Sentences *pages 4–15*

A. Write the sentences using capital letters and correct end punctuation. After each sentence, write *declarative, interrogative, imperative,* or *exclamatory.*

1. how tired I am
2. shut the door
3. will you be at the dance
4. the elephant roared loudly
5. may I borrow your bicycle
6. what a difficult test this is
7. the boy on the left is my cousin
8. bring your sister to school
9. tell me the correct time
10. can you do a double somersault
11. she loves her pet dog
12. give Francisco my message

B. Write each complete subject. Then underline each simple subject.

13. Thomas Alva Edison was a great inventor.
14. Some people think him the greatest of all inventors.
15. Edison's father came from Canada to the United States.
16. The father's manufacturing business prospered.
17. A teacher in Edison's school punished the boy for asking too many questions.
18. His mother made learning a game for the boy.
19. Tom got a job on a train at age twelve.
20. His experiments with chemicals caused a fire.
21. The conductor threw him off the train.
22. Edison invented the phonograph.
23. The invention of the electric light bulb was one of his greatest achievements.
24. This man eventually became known as "the wizard of Menlo Park."

C. Write each complete predicate. Then underline each simple predicate.

25. Our band is rehearsing for the spring concert.
26. Terry plays the tuba for the middle school.
27. He has practiced for several hours every day.
28. Jeanine will do a solo at the concert.
29. She performs clever pieces on the marimba.
30. The clarinetists are learning their parts.
31. Fran's oboe sounds beautiful.
32. The school choir will sing with the band.
33. They have appeared with the band previously.
34. The concert provides wonderful opportunities for many talented people.

D. Write the subject of each sentence. Write *(You)* if the subject is understood.

35. A picnic is great fun!
36. Did Sigrid bring the pickles?
37. Dad is grilling the hamburgers.
38. Take this plate of chicken to Theresa.
39. Will Jackie pass the mustard?
40. Don't overcook the corn.
41. The baked potatoes taste delicious!
42. Has Paul tasted the cherry pie?
43. Put out the fire.
44. My brother ate too much.
45. Paul has a stomachache.
46. Give him some medicine.

Thesaurus *pages 16–17*

E. Use this thesaurus entry to answer questions **47–49**.

new (adj)–now first made, thought out, known, felt, or discovered; never having existed before; now first used; not used up or worn. Your <u>new</u> car is just beautiful.
current–of the present time.
fresh–newly made, gathered, or arrived; recent; not known, seen, or used before; new.
modern–of the present time; of times not long past; not old-fashioned; up-to-date.
recent–made or done not long ago; not long past; modern. Did you see the <u>recent</u> movie that was on television last night?
ANTONYMS: **ancient (adj), antique (adj), old (adj), outdated, outmoded, stale (adj)**

47. What part of speech is *new*?
48. Which words are synonyms of *new*?
49. Which words are antonyms of *new*?

Quotations *pages 34–35*

F. Write each sentence. Add quotation marks and capital letters where needed.

50. I think, said Jean, that summer is the best time of the year.
51. What's wrong with winter? asked Anne. then we can ice skate and go skiing.
52. I like snow and ice and cold weather generally, she added.
53. Do you really like to freeze your bones? asked Jean.
54. Anne replied huffily, the cold weather suits me very well.
55. All times of the year are great, Tim stated thoughtfully. you just have to know how to get the best out of them.
56. If we keep talking about the seasons of the year, warned Mike, we aren't going to get any of our work done.
57. Mike's right, agreed Anne. let's get back to work.

Time Order in Narratives *pages 36–37*

G. Write the following sentences in time order.

58. "Good morning," I greeted my mother. "What's for breakfast?"
59. Next I washed and dressed.
60. When the alarm clock rang, I woke.
61. After that, Mom smiled and handed me a glass of orange juice.
62. First I snuggled under the blanket for a few moments, and then I got up.
63. Then I went downstairs to the kitchen.

LANGUAGE PUZZLERS

An Animal Chain

The clue to this animal puzzle is a chain of letters. The last two letters of each simple subject are the first two letters of the simple predicate in the following sentence. The last two letters of the simple subject in the last sentence are the first two letters of the simple predicate in the first sentence. (Hint: Remember that *You* is the understood subject of an imperative sentence.)

1. A tiger _ _ _ _ _ _ _ _ its prey quickly.
2. Our Scout troop _ _ _ _ _ _ _ a glass and wood ant farm.
3. America's first zoo _ _ _ _ _ _ in New York City in 1864.
4. An octopus _ _ _ _ _ black ink for protection.
5. A snake _ _ _ _ its tongue for smelling.
6. _ _ _ _ your dog's water dish full of water.
7. An antelope _ _ _ _ _ _ the horse and rider.
8. A baby ostrich _ _ _ _ _ its way out of the egg.
9. A buffalo _ _ _ _ _ _ _ enemies in anger.
10. An alpaca _ _ _ _ _ like a small, shaggy camel.

A Story Box

How many of each kind of sentence can you find in the box? Label four columns and tally each sentence under the correct label: *declarative*, *interrogative*, *imperative*, and *exclamatory*.

look at that box what box do you mean I don't see any box look over there don't you see the box by the door do you mean that box of course I mean that box do you see any other boxes in the room it sure is a strange box what do you think is in it I don't know who do you think brought it I have no idea is it heavy I haven't the faintest idea I didn't try to pick it up go see what is in it I'll go look at it

look at those people I wonder if they are shy why don't they come over and look at us maybe they have never seen a box before don't be silly of course they have seen a box before then why don't they come over and open the box I want to get out of here get ready to jump out if they start opening it I'm scared no you're not I'm not scared why should you be scared here comes one of them I think the little girl is braver than the rest she is going to open the box when she has the top loose jump out be quiet they may be able to hear us don't tell me to be quiet all of you be quiet here she comes will she open it what a surprise she'll have

I hope our box arrived all right did you send it to the right planet I sent it to Earth what do you mean didn't you want it sent to Earth it was to be sent to Reath not Earth I'm in trouble you certainly are I only hope no one on Earth opens that box imagine all those creatures running loose on Earth help

Unit 1 Extra Practice

1 Writing Sentences

p. 4

A. Write *sentence* or *not a sentence* for each group of words.

1. Many hands make light work.
2. Lost time is never found again.
3. All work and no play.
4. Haste makes waste.
5. A bad worker.
6. Will be a new day.
7. In the bush.
8. Love will find a way.
9. Fortune helps the brave.
10. In glass houses.
11. Time flies.
12. Too many cooks.
13. Sweeps clean.
14. One good turn deserves another.
15. Are better than one.

B. Add words to make each group of words a sentence. Try to make a proverb, or wise saying. Then write the sentence.

16. Birds of a feather _____ .
17. _____ is the best policy.
18. One good turn _____ .
19. _____ spoil the broth.
20. April showers _____ .
21. _____ gathers no moss.
22. The early bird _____ .
23. _____ heals all wounds.
24. _____ is not gold.
25. All work and no play _____ .
26. _____ is worth a thousand words.
27. A stitch in time _____ .
28. The squeaky wheel _____ .
29. _____ come in small packages.
30. A barking dog _____ .

2 Four Kinds of Sentences
p. 6

A. Write each sentence. After each sentence write *declarative*, *interrogative*, *imperative*, or *exclamatory*.

1. The blue whale is the largest animal.
2. It is bigger than thirty elephants.
3. How much does it eat every day?
4. It eats from four to eight tons of food a day.
5. What a huge appetite it has!
6. Blue whales are so gigantic!
7. Does it really weigh 100 tons?
8. The Antarctic blue whale weighs up to 150 tons!
9. It spends six months a year feeding in Antarctic waters.
10. A blue whale is about twenty-five feet long at birth.
11. What a big baby that is!
12. How much does a baby blue whale weigh?
13. Please read the sign to find out.
14. It weighs about two tons at birth.
15. Note the size of that whale.
16. Whales consume hundreds of tons of plankton each year.
17. A young whale can gain as much as ninety pounds a day!
18. Its favorite food is the tiny shrimplike krill.
19. Can a blue whale stay underwater for a long time?
20. Some have stayed underwater for almost an hour.
21. What huge breaths they must take!
22. Tell me more about these amazing animals.
23. Blue whales often dive to depths of several hundred feet.

B. Write the sentence, using capital letters and correct end punctuation. Then write the kind of sentence each one is.

24. a spout of water vapor shoots into the air
25. look at the blue whale's spout
26. how high it is
27. do you know the length of this blue whale
28. this whale is almost 100 feet long
29. can you see the two flat flukes on the whale's tail
30. these strong tail fins push the whale forward
31. what an extraordinary animal the blue whale is

C. Write the sentences, using capital letters and end punctuation correctly.

32. a comet is a giant ball of frozen gas and dust
33. have you ever seen one
34. look through this telescope
35. how bright it is
36. the comet's center is called the nucleus
37. tell us more about comets
38. the fuzzy area around the center is the coma
39. what do you call the long trailing part
40. it is called the tail
41. one famous comet has a tail 200 million miles long
42. that's unbelievable
43. did you see that painting of the comet with a long silver tail
44. explain how comets are like planets
45. most comets revolve around the sun
46. however, some travel far beyond the solar system

D. Write the sentences, using capital letters and correct end punctuation. After each sentence write *declarative*, *interrogative*, *imperative*, or *exclamatory*.

47. do you have any other questions about comets
48. how often does a comet orbit the sun
49. some comets orbit the sun every few years
50. others take thousands of years to make one orbit
51. what a long time that is
52. did you see Halley's comet in 1986
53. we waited for two hours in the cold to see it
54. why are comets so bright
55. they reflect the sun's intense light
56. let me look through the telescope now
57. show me how to focus it
58. notice the comet's tail ahead of the comet
59. how can a comet's tail lead the comet
60. the sun's energy directs the tail away from the sun
61. are new comets still being discovered
62. astronomers find new comets every year

3 Complete Subjects and Predicates

p. 8

A. Write each sentence. Underline the complete subject.

1. The sun set at 5:30 P.M. on October 11, 1492.
2. Three small ships sailed west into the sunset.
3. They had been at sea since August 3.
4. Anxious sailors searched the red horizon.
5. No land was in sight.
6. The evening of October 11 passed.
7. Columbus stood alone on the deck of the *Santa María*.
8. The time was 2:00 A.M.
9. The small ship *Pinta* sailed ahead of Columbus's ship.
10. The lookout on the *Pinta* was Rodrigo de Triana.
11. He rubbed his eyes suddenly.
12. A white sand cliff was gleaming in the distance.
13. The young man yelled the Spanish word for ''land.''
14. Captain Pinzón of the *Pinta* fired a signal cannon.
15. The powerful explosion echoed over the moonlit ocean.

B. Write each sentence. Underline the complete subject once. Underline the complete predicate twice.

16. The sound thrilled Columbus.
17. His long journey into the unknown was a success.
18. Columbus shouted to Captain Pinzón.
19. A night landing would be too dangerous.
20. The hours until dawn crept by.
21. The three ships found a suitable harbor at daybreak.
22. Small boats carried the sailors ashore.
23. Tears of joy filled Columbus's eyes.
24. The thankful sailors fell on the beach.
25. Columbus named the island San Salvador.
26. Columbus discovered the island of Cuba two weeks later.
27. His fleet navigated the waters around the Bahamas.
28. Natives of Hispaniola wore golden ornaments.
29. The *Santa María* went aground near Cap Haitien.
30. Forty of Columbus's crewmen founded a small fort.
31. Storms plagued the return voyage to Europe.
32. Columbus's two ships arrived safely in Lisbon Harbor.

4 Simple Subjects

p. 10

A. Write the complete subject of the sentence. Underline the simple subject.

1. The game of table tennis was first played in 1889.
2. James Gibb invented the game.
3. He made paddles from cigar boxes.
4. Old bottle corks served as the first balls.
5. Gibb's dinner table was the playing surface.
6. Gibb called his game Gossima.
7. The English inventor developed better balls and paddles.
8. The new game was not popular at first.
9. Gibb's lawyer renamed the game Ping-Pong a few years later.
10. People in Europe played the game enthusiastically.

B. Write the simple subject of each sentence.

11. Joseph Merlin was the world's first roller skater.
12. This musician skated into an English ballroom in 1760.
13. The young Belgian skater was also playing a violin.
14. The guests stared at this strange sight.
15. Tragedy struck almost immediately.
16. The musical athlete smashed into a giant mirror.
17. Bits of glass littered the ballroom floor.
18. A valuable violin was broken.
19. Poor Joseph was badly injured.
20. The new sport was not tried again for fifty years.

C. Write each sentence. Underline the complete subject once and the simple subject twice.

21. One popular American sport is almost 100 years old.
22. A Massachusetts college teacher invented basketball in 1891.
23. His name was James Naismith.
24. The young coach needed an indoor sport for his athletes.
25. The new sport had only thirteen rules at first.
26. The first basketball was a soccer ball.
27. Two old baskets were nailed to the wall as goals.
28. A janitor with a ladder got the ball after each goal.
29. The players loved the game from the beginning.
30. Only one goal was scored in the first game.

5 Simple Predicates

p. 12

A. Write the simple predicate, or verb, in each sentence.

1. A coyote is a sly animal.
2. It runs faster than rabbits.
3. The coyote carries its bushy tail quite low.
4. The ears of a coyote are short and pointed.
5. It has slender legs.
6. The coyote inhabited the plains originally.
7. It is found in mountain areas, in valleys, and in other places now.
8. A coyote likes fresh game of any kind.
9. The doglike mammal can catch snakes with no trouble.
10. It can survive on a diet of insects.
11. Many farmers complain about coyotes.
12. The sly beasts steal poultry and baby lambs.
13. Some coyotes have raided vegetable gardens.
14. Few people mistake the howl of a coyote.
15. A coyote's wail cuts the night like a knife.
16. The howl has a lonesome sound.

B. Write each sentence. Underline the complete predicate once and the simple predicate twice.

17. Coyotes are not lonely animals.
18. They live in family units most of the time.
19. Coyotes make their homes in underground dens.
20. Some have chosen natural caves in rocky areas.
21. The female coyote guards her pups with care.
22. The babies stay near the den.
23. A mother coyote will fight all intruders savagely.
24. Coyotes hunt at night in populated areas.
25. They search for food at all hours in the wild.
26. Desert coyotes may rest during the hot midday.
27. Prairie coyotes are a brownish color.
28. The fur of some other coyotes is gray.
29. Coyotes share desert water holes with weasels and foxes.
30. Smaller animals must wait until later for their turn at the water hole.
31. The cunning coyote can catch even the swiftest rabbit.

6 Locating Subjects in Sentences *p. 14*

A. Write the subject of each sentence. If the sentence is imperative, write (*You*).

1. Please give me some tips on bird-watching.
2. Do I need a pair of binoculars?
3. Is morning the best time for bird-watching?
4. Do all birds fly south in the fall?
5. Look up *migration* in the guidebook.
6. Do you see that formation of geese?
7. Lend me your binoculars, please.
8. May I adjust these glasses?
9. Keep careful notes on the birds.
10. Compare these pictures with the real geese.
11. Look at all those birds.
12. Are they flying south?

B. Write the subject of each sentence. Then write whether the sentence is interrogative or imperative.

13. Is autumn beginning already?
14. Turn on the furnace tonight.
15. Will we harvest the corn on Saturday?
16. Do you want to help?
17. Buy a big pumpkin for Halloween.
18. Does fall begin on September 22 this year?
19. Check the calendar over there.
20. Put away your bathing suits.
21. Get out your jackets and caps.
22. Can we play football this fall?
23. Is autumn your favorite season?
24. Will you help me rake the lawn?
25. Use the leaves as mulch in the garden.
26. Should I clear the leaves off the roof?
27. Please help me with these storm windows.
28. Did your class make bird feeders?
29. Is Rosa making her Halloween costume?
30. Are they going to the football game?
31. Pick the last vegetables in the garden.

UNIT TWO

USING LANGUAGE
TO
INFORM

=== PART ONE ===

Unit Theme   *Theater Arts*

Language Awareness   Nouns

=== PART TWO ===

Literature   *Puppeteer* by Kathryn Lasky

A Reason for Writing   Informing

Writing
IN YOUR JOURNAL

WRITER'S WARM-UP ◆ What do you know about the theater? Have you ever seen a live performance or a TV production of a play? What did you like about the performance? Was it the costumes, the music, or the story? Write about the theater in your journal. Tell what kind of show you would like to see.

GETTING STARTED

Read this nonsense sentence: *The winaber gomped a burkle in the menk.* Which of the "words" seem to name a person, a place, or a thing? With what real words could you replace these "words"?

1 Writing with Nouns

Nouns are naming words. A noun may name a person, place, thing, or idea. The chart below shows examples of nouns.

Names of Persons	girl, boy, puppeteer, Shari Lewis
Names of Places	theater, city, Canada
Names of Things	puppet, stage, Bil Baird Marionettes
Names of Ideas	love, enjoyment, peace

Most nouns name things that can be seen or touched. For example, you can see a boy or a puppet. You can touch a table. Some nouns, however, name things that cannot be seen or touched. These nouns name ideas, such as happiness, anger, and success.

Each sentence below contains three underlined nouns. Which sentence is more interesting and clearer? Which gives more specific detail?

1. The <u>woman</u> moved the <u>figure</u> across the <u>floor</u>.
2. <u>Shari Lewis</u> moved the <u>puppet</u> across the <u>stage</u>.

Notice that a noun can be made up of more than one word.

When you write, use exact nouns to give details to your reader. Exact nouns help create a word picture in your reader's mind.

Summary ♦ A **noun** names a person, place, thing, or idea. Use exact nouns to give details in your writing.

Guided Practice

Name the nouns in each sentence below.

1. Puppetry is a very old branch of theater.
2. In Egypt archaeologists discovered puppets in the tombs of the pharaohs.
3. Explorers have found figures in the ruins of Greece and Rome, too.

62   GRAMMAR and WRITING: Nouns

Practice

A. The nouns in the sentences below give details about puppets. Find the nouns and write them. (Hint: There are forty-five nouns.)

   4. A puppet for the hand has a hollow head and a body of cloth.

   5. Fingers move the parts of the puppet.

   6. Two famous puppets, Punch and Judy, were stars in shows in Europe for 400 years!

   7. A marionette is a figure operated by strings or wires.

   8. A puppeteer above the stage pulls the strings that move the head, arms, hands, legs, and feet.

   9. Marionettes were once used as a tool to teach people.

 10. Puppets on long rods are popular in many lands.

 11. These figures can portray people, animals, goodness, or truth.

 12. The puppets used by a ventriloquist are called dummies.

 13. A ventriloquist moves the dummy with levers and strings.

B. Use the nouns to complete the paragraph. Write the paragraph.

emotions	armchair	justice	audience	king
sound	backyard	puppeteer	figures	city

   A puppet can portray anything—from an evil (**14.** person) to a broken (**15.** thing), from (**16.** idea) to a magic lamp. Puppets can perform anywhere—from a theater in a large (**17.** place) to a table in your (**18.** place). How do puppets come alive? A skilled (**19.** person) gives the (**20.** things) movement and (**21.** thing). Just one other thing is necessary; that's an (**22.** people). Puppets come alive by awakening (**23.** idea) in people.

C. Use the model below to write five sentences of your own. Notice how the nouns create a different word picture in each.

   24–28. The _____ saw a _____ in the _____ .

Apply ♦ Think and Write

From Your Writing ♦ Read what you wrote for page 61. Find the nouns you used. List them in these four columns:

   Persons   Places   Things   Ideas

Was it a surprise to see how many nouns you used?

✎ **Remember**
that exact nouns help to create a clear word picture in your reader's mind.

You know the meaning of each of these words: *bill*, *march*, *turkey*. What happens to their meanings when they begin with capital letters—*Bill*, *March*, *Turkey*? Can you name other words that change their meanings when they're capitalized?

2 Common and Proper Nouns

You know that a noun names a person, place, or thing. Notice the underlined nouns in the following sentences.

1. The man created the puppet.
2. Jim Henson created Kermit the Frog.

The nouns in sentence **1** do not name any particular man or puppet. *Man* is a general name for any man. *Puppet* is the name for any puppet. These nouns are called common nouns. A common noun is the general name of a person, place, or thing.

In sentence **2** the nouns give more specific information. They name a particular man, Jim Henson, and a particular puppet, Kermit the Frog. A noun that names a particular person, place, or thing is a proper noun.

A proper noun always begins with a capital letter. Some proper nouns are made up of more than one word, but only the important words begin with a capital letter.

> **Summary** ◆ A **common noun** is the general name of a person, place, or thing. A **proper noun** names a particular person, place, or thing. Using proper nouns can make writing clearer and more specific.

Guided Practice

The nouns in the sentences below are underlined. Tell whether each noun is common or proper.

1. Hasn't every child heard of Ernie, Bert, and Big Bird?
2. These characters perform on Sesame Street, a production of the Children's Television Workshop.
3. The show, made in New York City, has amused viewers for years.

Kermit the Frog

Practice

A. Write each underlined noun. Then write whether it is common or proper.

4. In <u>school</u> in <u>Maryland</u>, <u>Jim Henson</u> joined a <u>club</u> for <u>puppeteers</u>.
5. During <u>college</u> he had a daily <u>show</u> on <u>television</u> in <u>Washington, D.C.</u>
6. Later the young <u>entertainer</u> studied <u>puppetry</u> in <u>Europe</u>.
7. <u>Henson</u> made up the <u>name</u> <u>Muppet</u>.
8. These <u>creations</u> have imaginative <u>names</u> like <u>Cookie Monster</u> and <u>Oscar the Grouch</u>.

B. Write each sentence. Draw one line under each common noun and two lines under each proper noun.

9. Most figures have soft heads and are covered with fabric.
10. A person needs both hands to work with a character like Kermit.
11. The Muppets have been a big success in America.
12. The lovable puppets have made a movie in London.
13. These fuzzy creatures help young Americans to learn while having fun.

C. Use your imagination to complete the paragraph. Add a proper noun or common noun as directed. Then write the paragraph.

There is a puppet that looks a little bit like a (**14.** common) and is called (**15.** proper). This character lives in a (**16.** common), in a place called (**17.** proper). It works as a (**18.** common) in a (**19.** common). Surprisingly the character dreams of becoming a (**20.** common) someday, like its hero (**21.** proper). To reach this goal, the puppet gets a (**22.** common) and goes to (**23.** proper).

Apply ♦ Think and Write

Creative Writing ♦ Think more about the puppet you described in **Practice C.** Suppose the puppet could make its dream come true. Write what you think might happen. Have a classmate circle each common noun and underline each proper noun you use.

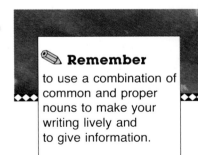

✎ **Remember**
to use a combination of common and proper nouns to make your writing lively and to give information.

GETTING STARTED

Start a game with a common noun that names a category such as puppets. Then name proper nouns that fit the category.

puppets: Big Bird, King Friday, Punch

3 Capitalizing Proper Nouns

Remember that a proper noun names a particular person, place, or thing. You also know that only the important words in a proper noun begin with a capital letter. The chart below shows when to use capital letters in proper nouns.

When to Use Capital Letters	
1. Capitalize the names of persons and pets.	Paul, Noriko Asano, Phineus T. Bluster, Patches
2. Capitalize important words in the names of particular places and things.	Carson City, Nevada, Mexico, Africa, Lake of the Woods, Mott Avenue, Port Mann Bridge, Tower of London, Rio Grande
3. Capitalize months, days, and holidays.	September, Tuesday, Fourth of July, Thanksgiving
4. Capitalize important words in names of clubs, businesses, and organizations.	Lenox Amateur Theater Club, Towne and Davis Lighting Company, Puppeteers of America

Which words are not capitalized in the proper nouns above?

Summary ◆ When you write, use capital letters for the important words in proper nouns.

Guided Practice

Name the proper nouns in these sentences. Tell which letters should be capitalized.

1. My name is sofa potato, and I'm a dummy.
2. My owner, doris dudley, made me from the arms of an old sofa from a dump on steuben avenue in downtown lakeside.
3. I have studied starches at the university of latke.

Practice

A. Write the sentences. Capitalize the proper nouns.

   4. My friend doris is no dummy; she graduated from the lakeside school of ventriloquism.

   5. We had our first performance in january at centerville park.

   6. By march we had done shows in ohio, iowa, and indiana.

   7. Our big break came around memorial day when I got a small part in a movie.

   8. Critics in hollywood complained that my acting was wooden and my delivery a bit forced.

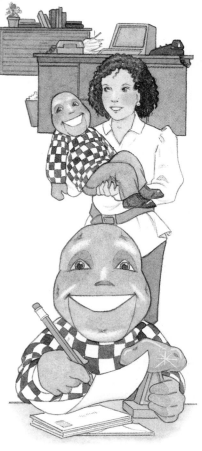

   9. Even so, from the atlantic to the pacific, americans loved my strong, silent manner and potatolike good looks.

   10. The sofa potato fan club was founded in peoria, illinois, and spread as far as shanghai, china.

   11. Doris quit her job at the spuds-in-duds department store and formed her own company—starchy productions.

   12. Perhaps my greatest thrill came last thursday when the american potato growers' union gave me their highest award.

   13. It's a good thing doris was there because, as usual, I was at a loss for words.

B. Write a proper noun for each common noun below. Then use each proper noun in a sentence.

   EXAMPLE: state
   ANSWER: Oklahoma—Many famous Americans were born in the state of Oklahoma.

   14. river   **18.** street   **22.** holiday

   15. building   **19.** school   **23.** club

   16. country   **20.** store

   17. bridge   **21.** company

Apply ♦ Think and Write

Planning a Vacation ♦ Plan a dream vacation that you would like to take someday. Write about the places you would like to visit. You might draw a map. Label the places and special sights you want to see. The places may be real or imaginary.

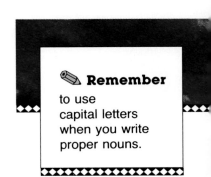

✎ Remember
to use capital letters when you write proper nouns.

To play "I Want," one person says, "I want one apple." The next says, "I want one apple and two bees." In turn, players recall all that was said, and then add a noun in alphabetical order—right down to twenty-six zebras!

4 Singular and Plural Nouns

The noun *apple* is singular. It names one thing. The noun *bees* is plural. It names more than one. Like the word *bee*, most nouns add -*s* to form the plural. Other nouns change their spelling in the plural. A few nouns have the same singular and plural.

Singular Nouns			Plural Nouns			
puppet	camel	costume	puppets	camels	costumes	
latch	dish	glass	fox	latches	dishes	glasses	foxes
berry	lady	beauty	berries	ladies	beauties	
boy	tray	monkey	boys	trays	monkeys	
thief	wife	leaf	thieves	wives	leaves	
radio	photo	hero	radios	photos	heroes	
tooth	woman	child	teeth	women	children	
moose	deer	sheep	moose	deer	sheep	

The rules for spelling plural nouns begin on page 503 of this book. Refer to the rules as you complete the exercises in this lesson.

Summary ♦ A **singular noun** names one person, place, thing, or idea. A **plural noun** names more than one person, place, thing, or idea. When you write, pay special attention to spelling plural forms.

Guided Practice

Tell how you would form the plural of each underlined noun.

1. The *Arabian Nights* have delighted <u>child</u> for <u>age</u>.
2. These <u>story</u> were collected in Arabia, India, and other <u>country</u>.
3. They tell about <u>prince</u> and <u>princess</u>, <u>hero</u> and <u>thief</u>, as well as ordinary <u>man</u> and <u>woman</u>.

Practice

A. Write each sentence. Use the plural forms of the nouns in parentheses ( ).

4. "Aladdin and His Wonderful Lamp" is one of the best-known (fantasy) of the *Arabian Nights*.
5. Puppeteer Paul Davis tells the (adventure) of Aladdin in one of his puppet (show).
6. In the far (reach) of a cave, this peasant lad finds a storehouse of (valuable), including a wonderful lamp.
7. Inside the lamp lives a spirit, or genie, who is able to fulfill all of Aladdin's (wish) and (desire).
8. The genie brings golden (dish), (ruby), and other (prize).
9. With the lamp, Aladdin leads (army) and defeats (enemy).
10. The (glory) of Aladdin's (palace) surpass all (other).
11. However, after a few (month), a magician uses (trick) and (disguise) to steal the lamp.
12. Then he uses the lamp's (power) to take away Aladdin's (rich).
13. How Aladdin recovers his (loss) is exciting indeed!

B. If a noun below is singular, write its plural form. If it is plural, write its singular form. Then use at least five of the plural forms you wrote in sentences.

14. eyelashes	**19.** tooth	**24.** bat
15. tax	**20.** branch	**25.** cherries
16. sky	**21.** guess	**26.** donkey
17. calves	**22.** business	**27.** moose
18. potatoes	**23.** woman	**28.** shelf

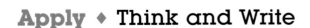

Apply ♦ Think and Write

Dictionary of Knowledge ♦ Read about Scheherazade in the Dictionary of Knowledge. Make a list of props and costumes you could use in a puppet show about this heroine. Ask a classmate to check the spelling of any plural nouns you used.

> ✎ **Remember**
> to be courteous to your reader and use correct plural spellings.

A Hink Pink is a two-word rhyme that fits a definition.

a pet's bonnets = a cat's hats

a grizzly's coat = a bear's hairs

Make up your own Hink Pinks that show ownership.

5 Possessive Nouns

You know that a noun names a person, place, thing, or idea. A noun can also show ownership, or possession. The underlined words below are possessive nouns.

The sixth grade has a stage.	It is the sixth grade's stage.
The students have puppets.	They are the students' puppets.
Many people have tickets.	They are the people's tickets.

The chart below lists rules for forming possessive nouns.

Forming Possessive Nouns	
To form the possessive of a singular noun, add an apostrophe and *s* (*'s*).	a *child's* puppet *Luisa Navarro's* house *Tomás's* good idea
To form the possessive of a plural noun that ends in *s*, add only an apostrophe (*'*).	two *puppeteers'* stage many *students'* parts the *girls'* costumes
To form the possessive of a plural noun that does not end in *s*, add an apostrophe and *s* (*'s*).	the *geese's* feathers the *children's* tools many *deer's* antlers the *oxen's* tails

Summary ◆ A **possessive noun** shows ownership. When you write, be careful to form possessive nouns correctly.

Guided Practice

Spell the possessive form of the noun in parentheses that will correctly complete each sentence.

1. The (library) collection of puppet plays is a large one.

2. However, the (students) goal was to write their own script.

3. This way the (children) ideas will come alive on the stage.

Practice

A. Complete each sentence. Write the possessive form of the noun in parentheses ( ).

4. Making the hand puppets challenged the (class) creativity.
5. The young (artists) use of wood, cloth, and paint was a success.
6. A local (women) club helped construct the plywood stage.
7. (People) attention next turned to scenery.
8. The (scenery) purpose is to provide atmosphere.
9. Beautiful and fascinating sets are a (designer) goal.
10. The (puppets) sizes and colors influence the sets.
11. Lightweight scenery is important for (economy) sake.
12. (Students) attics were a source of many imaginative props.
13. The other (classes) curiosity began to grow.

B. Rewrite each sentence so that it contains a possessive noun.

> **EXAMPLE:** The voice of each character is very important.
> **ANSWER:** Each character's voice is very important.

14. Good lighting is also a concern of a puppeteer.
15. The movements of the puppets must be clearly visible to all.
16. Open the show with music to get the attention of people.
17. The tone of the background music should fit each scene.
18. Sound effects will increase the impact of the show.
19. Careful practice usually insures the success of a production.
20. The movements and voices of the characters must be perfected.
21. The comments of your teachers should guide your practice.
22. The goal of your group should be a professional performance.
23. The delight of the audience will reward a puppeteer.

Apply ◆ Think and Write

A Dramatic Review ◆ Recall a time when you watched or took part in a play or other dramatic production. Write sentences that tell what was best about the show. Also describe how it could have been improved. Use at least five possessive nouns.

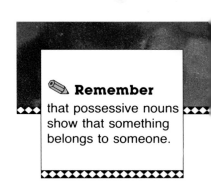

✎ **Remember**
✕✕✕ that possessive nouns ✕✕✕
show that something
belongs to someone.

✕✕✕✕✕✕✕✕✕✕✕✕✕✕✕✕

◆ GETTING ◆
STARTED

What other words can you form when you add *gate* to each of these words: *way, crasher, post, keeper, flood, toll, tail?* How many of these words can you define?

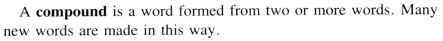

VOCABULARY ◆
Compounds

A **compound** is a word formed from two or more words. Many new words are made in this way.

■ This <u>spaceship</u> is ready for a <u>blast-off</u> from a <u>launching pad</u>.

Some compounds, such as *spaceship,* are written as one word. Other compounds, such as *launching pad,* are written as separate words. Although these compounds are written as two words, they are used together as a unit. Some compounds, such as *blast-off* and *sister-in-law,* are written with a hyphen (-) or hyphens to connect the words.

What compounds will answer these questions?

▎**What is the tip of a rocket or spaceship sometimes called?**
▎**What are the final seconds just before a space launch called?**

Building Your Vocabulary

Compounds are often used in special vocabularies, such as the vocabularies of space exploration, sports, and the theater arts.

List some compounds that begin or end with the word *space.*

Think of the sports page of a newspaper. Name some compounds used in writing about sports.

Combine words in column **A** with words in column **B** to form compounds used in the theater arts. You may use a dictionary for help.

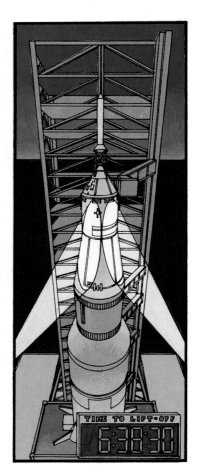

A		B	
spot	back	up	in
stand-	make	light	drop

Practice

A. Rewrite each sentence. Use the underlined words to form a compound.

> **EXAMPLE:** Darlene was always asleep by <u>the middle of the night</u>.
> **ANSWER:** Darlene was always asleep by *midnight*.

1. Darlene always awoke at <u>the light of day</u>.
2. At each <u>break of day</u> she heard a familiar sound.
3. It was a bird who chirped ''hello'' at <u>the rise of the sun</u>.
4. Darlene's feathered friend sometimes even greeted her at <u>the middle of the day</u>.
5. But at <u>the setting of the sun</u>, the bird was seldom seen.
6. Darlene decided that by <u>the fall of night</u> the bird was too tired to chirp.
7. Besides, it was <u>time for dinner</u> for both of them.

B. Write compounds by filling in the missing words. Each compound names something that might be found in a home.

8. _____ chair
9. _____ sticks
10. _____ shelves
11. _____ mat
12. table _____
13. foot _____
14. _____ place
15. door _____
16. _____ book

C. **17–21.** Use these ten words to write five compounds. The compounds will be written as separate words.

school	gloves	tape	fiction	high
boxing	science	cash	recorder	register

LANGUAGE CORNER • Anagrams

Anagrams are groups of letters that can be rearranged to form words. You can use the letters **a e l s t** to form *least, slate, stale, tales, steal,* and *teals* (river ducks).

Play a game of anagrams. Use these groups of letters to form compounds.

llabestkba   ghtoomnli   foronus   drethotsunmr

orptrai
lalbesab
orodokbn

How to Revise Sentences with Nouns

You know that nouns are used to name persons, places, things, and ideas. Now you will see that certain nouns can give important information and make your writing clearer and more interesting. For example, read the sentences below.

1. The shelves were crowded with toys.
2. The shelves were crowded with hand puppets and marionettes.

Although sentence **1** does give some information, it is not very specific. Because exact information is not given, you cannot picture the kinds of toys that are on the shelves. In sentence **2**, however, the vague noun *toys* has been replaced by the exact nouns *hand puppets* and *marionettes*. Because of these nouns, you can now picture clearly what is on the shelves.

If the vague noun *toys* were replaced with different exact nouns, new information could be given and the picture would change again.

■ 3. The shelves were crowded with model cars and trucks.

Exact nouns can really make a difference in your writing. By choosing exact nouns, you can give clarity to your writing and necessary information to your readers. You will be better able to communicate exactly what you want to say.

The Grammar Game ◆ Sharpen your noun sense! Quickly write as many exact nouns as you can for each vague noun below. Then compare lists with a classmate. Did you write any of the same nouns?

sport	boat	dwelling	jewelry
entertainment	tree	insect	bird

Working Together

While working as a group on activities **A** and **B**, you will see how exact nouns give more information. Exact nouns make your writing clearer, too.

In Your Group

- Contribute your ideas.
- Respond to the suggestions of others.
- Record the group's ideas.
- Agree or disagree in a pleasant way.

A. Rewrite each sentence below. Replace the underlined words with one or two exact nouns of the group's choice. Then write the sentences again with different exact nouns to change the information you give.

1. The <u>worker</u> walked quickly into the <u>building</u>.
2. <u>Certain qualities</u> are necessary to become an Olympic <u>athlete</u>.
3. Juan broke his <u>bone</u> at the <u>event</u> and will be out of school for a <u>while</u>.
4. In order to fix this <u>machine</u>, I need <u>tools</u> and <u>supplies</u>.
5. Tish picked up the <u>belongings</u> that she left in the <u>place</u> after she finished.

B. Replace the vague nouns in the paragraph below with more exact ones. How many replacements did your group make?

The <u>place</u> was crowded but quiet. Everyone watched the <u>people</u> on stage. The <u>show</u> was almost over. Suddenly some <u>entertainers</u> from <u>one part</u> of the stage moved forward and <u>musical instruments</u> sounded. <u>Decorations</u> fell from <u>someplace</u> and the rest of the <u>people</u> came running out from <u>another part</u> of the stage. It was quite a <u>sight</u>!

WRITERS' CORNER ◆ Exact Information

When you choose nouns, think about the kind of information you want to give. Sometimes your reader may only need general information. If more exact information is necessary, how specific do you want it to be?

GENERAL: **The storage room is filled with equipment.**
EXACT: **The storage room is filled with baseball gear.**
MORE EXACT: **The storage room is filled with gloves and bats.**

Read what you wrote for the Writer's Warm-up. Are the nouns the ones you wanted to use? Can you improve any of them?

RUBY GREEN SINGING
painting by James Chapin
Norton Gallery of Art, West Palm Beach, Florida

USING LANGUAGE
TO
INFORM

=== **PART TWO** ===

Literature *Puppeteer* by Kathryn Lasky

A Reason for Writing Informing

CREATIVE

Writing

FINE ARTS ◆ "Ruby Green Singing" is the title of this portrait at the left. Imagine that you are a singer. Write a journal entry telling what you think about before going on stage. Then tell about how it feels to appear on stage before an audience.

CREATIVE THINKING ◆
A Strategy for Informing

A CLUSTER MAP

One reason for writing is to give information. Sometimes informative writing explains how to do something. After this lesson you will read part of a book called *Puppeteer*, which is about how a puppet show is created. Later you will write an article that explains how to do something you do well.

How does a puppeteer create costumes? Here the author elaborates on, or gives many details about, the costuming for ''Aladdin and His Wonderful Lamp.''

As Paul finishes painting each head, he places it on a stand and drapes it with . . . fabrics he is considering using for the costumes. He winds the swatches into turbans, lets them fall as veils . . . or wraps them as simple peasant scarves. From the glitz box he takes a pendant and pins it to the Princess's veil so that the stars of the fake diamonds and sapphires rest in the middle of her forehead.

''Aladdin and His Wonderful Lamp'' is set long ago in the Middle East. Think of the research Paul had to do before he began to make even one costume. Think of the details he had to gather. One strategy for gathering details is a cluster map.

Learning the Strategy

There are many times when you might want to round up information or ideas about a topic. Suppose, for example, you are writing a report about the Incas of Peru. How might you organize what you already know about your topic? How might you add new information from your research? Suppose your teacher is explaining kinds of nouns. How could information about the topic be organized? Imagine that your class is brainstorming ideas for a fall festival. How can the festival committee gather and organize their ideas?

Making a cluster map is a useful strategy for generating and organizing ideas. A cluster map like the one below might help your committee round up their many ideas. The topic is in the red center circle. Subtopics are in blue circles attached to the topic circle. Details are in green circles attached to the subtopic circles. What subtopics and details might you add?

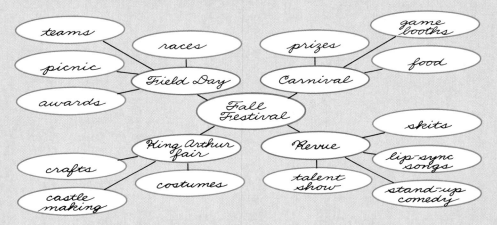

Using the Strategy

A. Make a cluster map about the contents of your desk. Write *My Desk* in the topic circle. Add subtopics such as *books* or *writing instruments*. Add detail circles about each subtopic. Use your cluster map to help reorganize your desk.

B. The passage you have read from *Puppeteer* is about making costumes. Imagine, however, how many other tasks go into making a professional puppet show. Make a cluster map to show your ideas. Write *Making a Puppet Show* in the topic circle. Elaborate on the topic by adding subtopic and detail circles. Then, when you read the rest of *Puppeteer*, compare your ideas with what Paul, the puppeteer, really does.

Applying the Strategy

- ◆ Why might two cluster maps about the same topic differ?
- ◆ Besides making a cluster map, what other ways can you think of to elaborate on a topic? When might you want to do it?

from

PUPPETEER

By Kathryn Lasky

Photographs by Christopher G. Knight

Paul Vincent Davis is a hand puppeteer. He puts his hand inside a puppet, and it comes to life. He uses his voice, and the puppet appears to speak. Like all puppeteers, Paul has the power to be any character he chooses. All by himself, he creates a world on a tiny stage.

Paul Davis produces and performs puppet shows at the Puppet Show Place in Boston. For a new show, he will perform the old tale of Aladdin and His Wonderful Lamp. He will play all nine characters, from a princess to an evil magician. First Paul must make the puppets. He begins by researching the characters and how they should look. Then he sketches their faces and sculpts each head from clay. As he works, Paul exaggerates the heads and their features. This way the faces will catch the light, and the audience will see them clearly. For a roomful of people, the puppets must come alive.

Making the Puppets

With the nine heads sculpted, Paul is ready to begin making molds. Using old cardboard cartons, he will pour liquid plaster of paris around each sculpted head until its impression is cast. The clay head of Fatima, the Princess's Servant, is the first to be immersed in the milky plaster sea. She must sit there quietly with the plaster up to her ears for one hour until it sets. Then, after rubbing the exposed part of her face with a soap solution, Paul fills the box entirely with plaster. He will let the mold set for several hours, separate the two parts, remove the clay head, and put the parts of the mold in the oven to bake at a very low temperature until they are completely dry. This process must be repeated nine times. During all this sitting and watching and baking, Paul often sketches ideas for costumes or tries out different voices in his search for each character's sound. Even as the other clay heads wait to be plunged into the plaster sea, Paul cannot resist wrapping strips of paper towel around their heads for a turban or draping the Princess with an old dishcloth secured by a circlet of plastic pearls for a crown.

These odd arrangements and improvisations of homely things might look like rags and tags, bits and pieces, but they feed Paul's imagination and will become transformed through his artistry into a special kind of magic. Months later, in a darkened theater, they will make children and grownups hold their breaths, laugh, maybe cry, gasp, look again and, for forty-five minutes, suspend disbelief as they watch *Aladdin and His Wonderful Lamp*.

Two days later Paul patches any nicks or pockmarks and bands the two parts of the plaster molds together tightly. Then he pours a liquid-rubber casting compound through the small hole at the base of each mold. It will take eight hours for the rubber to dry, becoming a hollow duplicate of the original clay head. When removed, the heads are light, weighing a few ounces at the most, so that Paul's hands will not grow tired. The neck of each of the puppets is large enough for two of Paul's fingers, so he can move the head easily. . . .

Painting a puppet's face is very similar to applying the heavy theatrical makeup of an actor. First, Paul mixes a base coat for the flesh tone and paints the entire head. Then he begins to add the color and shadowing that will reinforce the lines and contours of the face he has sculpted. It should not appear too flat under the strong stage lighting. As Paul paints the rubber head, it seems to be gathering the facial muscle and tone for its role. The head is becoming a puppet, one that will deliver its lines with expression and sometimes passion, in spite of the fact that its face is frozen forever into a single expression that is neither quite joy nor sorrow.

Paul has many makeup tricks. A touch of red on the outer part of the brow bone as well as a dot of red in the inner corner of the eye gives a youthful, lively look to the puppet's face. Its lips stand out when the lower lip is outlined with a darker color and filled in with a lighter one. The procedure is then reversed on the upper lip. "I learned that by watching a TV commercial for lipstick. But here's one they don't do on TV." Paul draws a thin black line between the upper and lower lip. "Strictly for puppets. It makes them look as if they are talking."

Paul begins to paint the head's eye spaces. When finished, the eyes will not have pupils or lashes. Instead, they will be black crescents, giving the puppet a blind look from close up.

From the audience, however, the puppets will not look blind at all. The audience will assume that the puppets have lifelike eyes, as a person, seeing another from a distance and unable to see each feature of the eyes, never doubts that the eyes are there.

The black crescent shape varies on each puppet in accordance with the eye contour that Paul has sculpted. The evil Magician's eyes are two black slashes. The Rug Merchant's eyes are like half moons, whereas the Royal Herald's eyes are slivered crescents of a new moon. Aladdin's Mother's eyes are as sleek as dolphins in their shape.

As Paul finishes painting each head, he places it on a stand and drapes it with swatches of the various fabrics he is considering using for the costumes. He winds the swatches into turbans, lets them fall as veils or burnooses, or wraps them as simple peasant scarves. From the glitz box he takes a pendant and pins it to the Princess's veil so that the stars of the fake diamonds and sapphires rest in the middle of her forehead. A child's bracelet of dark enameled beads circles the Mother's head. Close up, the puppets look overly made up and very artificial. But Paul scoots back in his rolling chair to view them. He is trying to imagine them on the small stage under theatrical lighting. Paul squints his eyes to focus better, and just as his own eyes become slits for his imagination, he sneezes. It is a huge sneeze from a very large man. The room seems to quake. Twelve puppet heads tremble on their poles. Turbans quiver. Veils flutter, "diamonds" shimmer. Light and dark shadows race across their faces, and he can almost hear the muffled voices deep in their rubber throats trying to escape. For that brief second the puppets are not facsimiles of life at all. They are actors waiting for their voices, their movement, waiting like the rest of us for that little slit between two eternities that is called life. Their lives will be played on the 3½- by 2-foot stage.

Library Link ♦ *To learn more about the production of a puppet show, read the book* Puppeteer *by Kathryn Lasky.*

Reader's Response

Paul began to work with puppets when he was eleven years old. Tell about something you enjoy doing that could become a career.

LITERATURE: Nonfiction

PUPPETEER

 ## Responding to Literature

1. Imagine that you are a puppet. Visualize how you look. Remember that you cannot move or speak until a puppeteer moves you. Write an entry in your journal. Describe yourself. Tell what your life is like and how you feel about it.

2. Make a list of the many skills a puppeteer must master to produce a successful show. Then arrange the tasks in order from least difficult to most difficult. Then decide which task would be yours if you were part of a company of puppeteers. Tell why.

3. Work in small groups. First find a story to dramatize. Then assign roles to group members. Make a simple stick puppet for each character. Perform your play for classmates. Before your performance, create a poster to advertise your play.

 ## Writing to Learn

Think and Elaborate ◆ What does it take to produce a puppet show? Make a cluster map to explore all of the possibilities. Use information from the article plus your imagination. Focus on Paul's production of *Aladdin and His Wonderful Lamp*.

Cluster Map

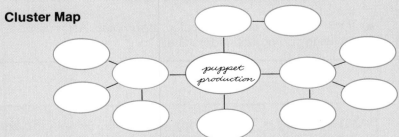

Write ◆ Use the information from the cluster map to write questions. If you could interview Paul Davis, what would you ask?

Tell how to do something simple, such as how to use a can opener. Ask your listeners to act out *exactly* what you say. You will discover just how good your directions are!

SPEAKING and LISTENING •
Directions

Have you ever been lost or confused because someone gave you poor directions or because you were not really listening? Have you ever had trouble giving someone else directions? Most of us have had these experiences. They make us realize why it is important to know how to give and follow directions.

Directions need to be complete, yet clear and easy for a listener to follow. Use the guidelines below to learn how to give and follow directions. These apply to all kinds of directions, whether they tell how to make or do something or how to get from one place to another.

Giving Directions	1. Explain the steps in order. Use words such as *first, next,* and *last* to help your listeners remember the order. 2. Give complete directions. Be sure to explain all the steps. 3. Explain any words or special terms that might be unfamiliar to your listeners. 4. Look directly at your listeners and speak clearly. 5. Use gestures and a map, diagram, or drawing to make your directions clear. 6. Make sure your listeners understand. Ask if there are any questions.
Listening to Directions	1. Look directly at the speaker and listen closely. 2. Mentally picture yourself doing each step. 3. Listen for time-order words, and repeat the directions to yourself in the correct order. 4. If the directions are complicated, take notes. Ask questions about anything you do not understand.

Summary ◆ When giving directions, be specific and arrange the steps in order. Listen to and follow directions carefully.

Guided Practice

Take turns giving clear and complete directions for each item below. As a listener, mentally picture each step that is given.

1. how to look for a seat in a dark, crowded theater
2. how to fold clean bath towels and put them away
3. how to look up a name in a telephone book and use a pay phone
4. how to roll a bowling ball down the lane to make a strike

Practice

A. With a partner, take turns giving and listening to directions, choosing from the suggestions below. You may make some notes before beginning. As the listener, mentally picture each step.

5. how to make a hand puppet appear to be frightened
6. how to make sound effects that imitate a galloping horse on a cobblestone street
7. how to find a book of plays in the library
8. how to memorize lines for a play
9. how to make a poster to advertise a puppet show

B. With a partner, take turns giving and following directions. You could explain how to draw a city's skyline, how to make a paper-bag puppet, or how to find synonyms in a thesaurus. To find out whether your directions are clear and complete, ask your partner to do *only* what you say.

Apply ◆ Think and Write

Informing with Directions ◆ What do you already know how to do? Are you a good baby-sitter, can you take a city bus, or can you operate a videocassette recorder? Write a set of step-by-step directions to fix the procedure in your mind. Then it will be easier for you to explain it to someone else.

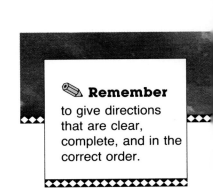

✎ Remember
to give directions that are clear, complete, and in the correct order.

Choose someone in the class, but do not reveal who it is. Give a main idea and three details about that person. See who can guess your "mystery person" first.

WRITING ◆ Topic Sentence and Supporting Sentences

A **paragraph** is a group of sentences about one main idea. Often a paragraph has one sentence that states the main idea. This sentence is called the topic sentence. The other sentences are supporting sentences that give details about the main idea. The first word of a paragraph is indented.

Not every paragraph has a topic sentence, but a topic sentence helps to make the main idea of a paragraph clear. Although the topic sentence often comes first, it may appear anywhere in the paragraph. Notice that in the second example below, the topic sentence comes last. The supporting sentences lead up to it.

Topic Sentence **Supporting Sentences**	The black crescent shape varies on each puppet in accordance with the eye contour that Paul has sculpted. The evil Magician's eyes are two black slashes. The Rug Merchant's eyes are like half moons, whereas the Royal Herald's eyes are slivered crescents of a new moon. Aladdin's Mother's eyes are as sleek as dolphins in their shape.
Supporting Sentences **Topic Sentence**	The evil Magician's eyes are two black slashes. The Rug Merchant's eyes are like half moons, whereas the Royal Herald's eyes are slivered crescents of a new moon. Aladdin's Mother's eyes are as sleek as dolphins in their shape. The black crescent shape varies on each puppet in accordance with the eye contour that Paul has sculpted.

Summary ◆ The **topic sentence** states the main idea of a paragraph. **Supporting sentences** give details about the main idea.

Guided Practice

Put the sentences in a logical order to form a paragraph. Which is the topic sentence? Which are supporting sentences?

1. Crew members are responsible for the costumes on their lists.
2. It also gives special notes, such as *a rumpled raincoat.*
3. The list tells everything worn by that character.
4. Each character in a play has a costume list.
5. The lists are given to members of the costume crew.

Practice

A. Use these sentences to write a paragraph. Begin with the topic sentence. Then write the supporting sentences in a logical order.

    6. Shape the puppet's head on your index finger with paper.
    7. You can make a hand puppet from everyday materials.
    8. Collect a square cloth, a newspaper, and three rubber bands.
    9. This will give you a puppet that has a head and hands.
    10. Now you need to give it a personality!
    11. The cloth, fastened with the rubber bands, will cover the character's head, your thumb, and your second finger.

B. Write your own topic sentence for each topic below.

    12. a movie you would (would not) like to see
    13. your favorite (least favorite) television program
    14. things you enjoy drawing

C. Choose one of the topic sentences below. Write the sentence. Then develop a paragraph by adding some supporting sentences.

    15. Costumes and makeup are important to stage productions.
    16. Music and dance play a large role in my life.
    17. It would be difficult to make (book title) into a movie.
    18. Body language sometimes communicates more than words can.

Apply ◆ Think and Write

Dictionary of Knowledge ◆ Read about Pinocchio. Then write a paragraph explaining why this character, a mere puppet, has become world-famous.

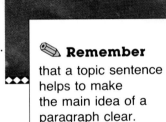

✎ **Remember** that a topic sentence helps to make the main idea of a paragraph clear.

A very puzzled Martian is standing in a living room facing a television set. Explain television to this strange life form. Take turns adding sentences. Begin with *The thing you see before you is . . .*

WRITING ♦
An Explanatory Paragraph

One of the most useful kinds of paragraphs is a paragraph that explains how to make or do something. Here is a paragraph that explains how to make a paper-bag mask. Notice that it begins with a topic sentence. Notice, too, that all the other sentences are supporting sentences that give details about the topic.

Topic Sentence

Supporting Sentences

Signal Words

It is easy to make a paper-bag mask. First, gather these materials: a paper bag large enough to fit over your head, chalk, a pencil, scissors, and crayons or poster paints. Put the paper bag over your head, and ask someone to mark the places for the eyes, nose, and mouth with chalk. Next, take the bag off your head and cut out the eye, nose, and mouth openings. Then sketch the face and ears on the bag with pencil. When you have it just the way you want it, color the mask with bright crayons or poster paints. For the final touch, cut along the outer edge of each ear, and bend the ears forward. Your mask is ready!

Here are guidelines for writing an explanatory paragraph.

How to Write an Explanatory Paragraph	1. Begin with a topic sentence that tells what the paragraph will explain. 2. List any materials that will be needed. 3. Write step-by-step instructions. Use **signal words,** such as *first, second,* and *next* to tell the order of the steps. 4. Make sure you have included all the necessary steps but have not added unnecessary information.

Summary ♦ An **explanatory paragraph** can inform someone about how to make or do something. When you write an explanatory paragraph that gives instructions, give all the necessary steps in order.

Guided Practice

State a topic sentence for each item below. Strive for variety. You may occasionally want to use a question as a topic sentence.

1. giving a child instructions on how to cross a street safely
2. explaining the designated-hitter rule in baseball
3. telling the materials needed to build a birdhouse

Practice

A. Write the following sentences as an explanatory paragraph. Begin with the topic sentence. Then write the supporting sentences in the correct order.

   4. Then the leader should go through the motions of an activity, such as brushing teeth or making pancakes.
   5. Learn how to play the game "Mirror Image" with a partner.
   6. Next stand face-to-face so that the follower can pretend to be the leader's reflection in a mirror.
   7. The follower should move with the leader as a mirror image.
   8. First decide who will lead and who will follow.

B. Study the picture of the easy-to-make puppet theater shown here. Then write a paragraph explaining how to make it. Begin with a topic sentence that tells what you will explain.

Apply ♦ Think and Write

Explanatory Paragraph ♦ Write a paragraph that gives clear instructions on how to make or do something. Illustrate it if you wish. Here are some suggestions.

how to build a . . .   how to improve . . . through practice
how to learn about . . .   how to plan a . . . for friends

✎ **Remember** that instructions for doing or making something need to be written in step-by-step order.

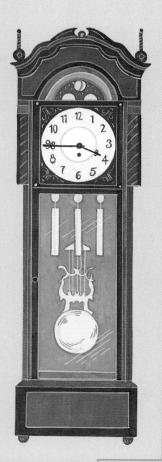

Focus on Sequence

No one knows exactly what time is, but we all know that it passes. One by one the minutes, hours, and days march by. They follow each other in a *sequence*, or dependable order. As a writer, you can use this time-order sequence to organize what you write. The author of *Puppeteer*, part of which you read earlier, uses time order to organize her information.

The clay head of Fatima, the Princess's Servant, is the *first* to be immersed in the milky plaster sea. She must sit there quietly with the plaster up to her ears *for one hour until* it sets. *Then, after* rubbing the exposed part of her face with a soap solution, Paul fills the box entirely with plaster.

The process of making a puppet is complicated. Yet we understand it because the author unfolds the process in a step-by-step order. To help us follow that order, she uses signal words, like those in italics above and listed below.

after	first	eventually	at the same time
before	second	meanwhile	following
next	during	immediately	preceding
last	now	whenever	subsequently
then	later	yesterday	while
soon	earlier	finally	often

The Writer's Voice ◆ Use this time-order framework to write a story. Copy the words below on a separate sheet of paper and fill in the blanks. Presto! You have created a "timely tale."

Just in Time

At first _____ . But soon _____ . Then _____ . During _____ .
Immediately _____ . At the same time _____ . It's now or never _____ !
Later _____ . Meanwhile _____ . At long last _____ . Finally _____ .

Working Together

Time order is often a good way to show sequence in writing. Use time-order words to help make the sequence clear as you work with your group on activities **A** and **B**.

A. Arrange these steps in their logical order. Then write a complete sentence describing each step. Use time-order words where appropriate. Your group's completed paragraph should be clearly organized and should read well.

- Makes costumes for the puppets
- Writes a script
- Puts on opening night performance
- Does research for his script
- Puts on dress rehearsal
- Makes the puppets
- Designs characters to fit the script

B. Everyone has a recipe for a favorite dish. Bring the recipe to class. Your group can decide which of the recipes to choose. Pretend that you will be putting on a television show telling the audience how to make the dish. Prepare a step-by-step script. (Begin with the ingredients.) Have one person, "The Pantomime Chef," use the script to present the recipe to the class.

THESAURUS CORNER • Word Choice

Rewrite the sentences below. Arrange them in a logical order. Replace each noun in dark type with a synonym that makes better sense. Use the Thesaurus and Thesaurus Index.

1. Few could believe that the full-time **chore** of this talented writer had once been to baby-sit for the stars' children.
2. There was no **repose** from work until after opening night.
3. When the curtain fell, a **noise** of approval rose from the audience.
4. One actor in a minor role spoke in a dreary **sound**, but most were superb.
5. The playwright had a brilliant **opinion** for a new play.
6. During the **termination** of the play, there was not a dry eye in the house.

WRITING PROCESS
INFORMING

Writing a How-to Article

In *Puppeteer*, Kathryn Lasky gives her readers a great deal of fascinating information about how a puppet show is created. A closely-related kind of informative writing is the how-to article. A how-to article tells how to do something. It tells what materials are needed and explains each step. Signal words such as *first*, *next*, or *last* show the order of the steps.

Know Your Purpose and Audience

In this lesson you will write a how-to article. Your purpose will be to explain how to do something you do well.

Your audience will be your classmates. Later you might demonstrate your activity or help create an activity box.

What's MY PURPOSE

Who's MY AUDIENCE

1 Prewriting

Before you write, you need to choose a topic to write about. Then you will need to gather supporting details.

Choose Your Topic ♦ Think about the things you do well or enjoy doing. What sports, arts, or hobbies do you enjoy? What crafts are you good at? What special skills do you have? Make a list of possible topics.

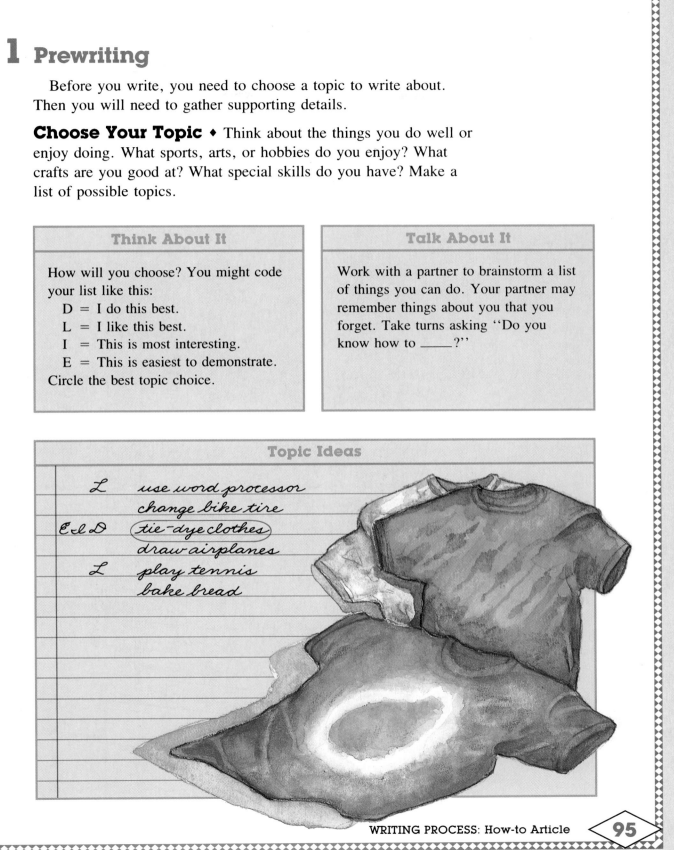

Think About It	**Talk About It**

How will you choose? You might code your list like this:
  D = I do this best.
  L = I like this best.
  I = This is most interesting.
  E = This is easiest to demonstrate.
Circle the best topic choice.
	Work with a partner to brainstorm a list of things you can do. Your partner may remember things about you that you forget. Take turns asking "Do you know how to _____?"

Topic Ideas

    L   use word processor
              change bike tire
  E L D   (tie-dye clothes)
              draw airplanes
    L   play tennis
              bake bread

Choose Your Strategy ◆ Here are two strategies for gathering supporting details. Read both. Then use the idea that seems helpful to you.

PREWRITING IDEAS

CHOICE ONE

A Cluster Map

Make a cluster map. Write your topic in the red center circle. Attach subtopics in blue circles and supporting details in green circles. Use your cluster map to gather as many ideas and details about your topic as you can.

Model

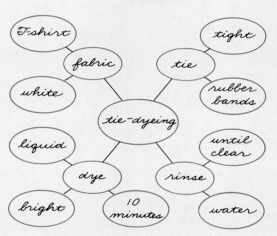

CHOICE TWO

A Step Chart

Make a step chart. Think about each step in your activity. Write the steps in order, starting on the bottom step. Use as many steps as you need. Use your step chart to help you put the steps in the correct order.

Model

4. take off bands
3. rinse
2. dip in dye
1. wrap cloth

2 Writing

Review your cluster map or step chart. Then begin to write your article. Ask yourself what readers might want to know. They might be curious about the cost, the time involved, or why the activity is fun to do. You might try to answer one question in your first sentence.

- ◆ It is a satisfying feeling to know that you can ＿＿＿.
- ◆ For the cost of only ＿＿＿ you can ＿＿＿.

As you continue to write, be sure to give the steps in time order. If you made a cluster map for prewriting, the blue subtopic circles might provide topic sentences for your paragraphs, and the green detail circles might provide the supporting details. Don't worry about errors. They can be corrected later, when you revise and proofread what you have written.

Sample First Draft ◆

For the cost of only a few cents and an hour's time, you can create works of art. The only materials you need are fabric dye, rubber bands, and a white T-shirt.
Start by wrapping a Rubber Band around a section of cloth. Put it on very tightly. Then do other sections until all the material has been tied. Now dip the stuff in dye let it sit about ten minutes or until the color is a little darker than you want it to be. Finaly take off the ties and enjoy your design. Rinse the cloth in water until the water runs clear.
Tie-dyeing is one of the best hobbys. It is fun to do. It is also fun to know that no one else will have a shirt just like yours!

3 Revising

You have written the first draft of your how-to article. Does it need to be improved? Here is one way to find out.

REVISING IDEA

FIRST   Read to Yourself

As you read, think about your purpose. Did you explain how to do something? Think of your audience. Will they understand the materials and the steps involved? Put a wavy line ~~~~ under any parts you want to clarify later.

Focus: Have you used signal words such as *first*, *then*, and *finally* to make the order of the steps clear?

THEN   Share with a Partner

Sit beside your partner and read aloud as your partner reads along silently. Ask if your partner understands how to do the activity you are telling about. Ask for suggestions on how to make the steps clearer. Below are some guidelines.

The Writer

Guidelines: Read slowly and clearly. Consider your partner's suggestions, but make only the changes you feel are important.

Sample questions:
- Did I include enough supporting details?
- **Focus question:** How can I make the order clearer?

The Writer's Partner

Guidelines: As you read along, try to visualize each step. Tell the writer when you have trouble visualizing the steps.

Sample responses:
- It would be clearer if you added some details about _____.
- At this point, I wasn't sure which step came next.

Revising Model ♦ Look at this draft of a how-to article. The marks show changes the writer wants to make.

Revising Marks

cross out	——
add	∧
move	⟲

The writer added a sentence that clearly stated the topic.

The writer replaced the vague noun *stuff* with the more precise noun *fabric*.

The writer moved this step, which was out of order.

The word *realize* is more exact than the word *know*.

For the cost of only a few cents and an hour's time, you can create works of art. *you can learn to tie-dye.* The only materials you need are fabric dye, rubber bands, and a white T-shirt.
Start by wrapping a Rubber Band around a section of cloth. Put it on very tightly. Then do other ~~sections~~ until all the material has been tied. Now dip the ~~stuff~~ *fabric* in dye let it sit about ten minutes or until the color is a little darker than you want it to be. Finaly take off the ties and enjoy your design. ⟨Rinse the cloth in water until the water runs clear.⟩
~~Tie-dyeing is one of the best hobbys. It is~~ fun to do. It is also fun to ~~know~~ *realize* that no one else will have a shirt just like yours!

Read the revised how-to article above. This shows the way the writer thinks it *should* be. Then revise your own how-to article.

Grammar Check ♦ Precise nouns can help give your reader a vivid picture of what you are writing about.

Word Choice ♦ Do you ever wish you had a more exact word for a word like *know*? A thesaurus is a source of exact words.

Revising Checklist

☐ **Purpose:** Did I write a how-to article that explains how to do something?

☐ **Audience:** Would my classmates be able to follow my directions?

☐ **Focus:** Did I use signal words to make the order of the steps clear?

4 Proofreading

Proofreading gives you another chance to improve your writing by fixing your spelling, punctuation, and handwriting.

Proofreading Model ♦ Here is the sample draft of the how-to article. Red proofreading changes have now been added.

For the cost of only a few cents and an hour's time, you can create works of art. *you can learn to tie-dye.* The only materials you need are fabric dye, rubber bands, and a white T-shirt.

¶ Start by wrapping a Rubber Band around a section of cloth. Put it on very tightly. Then do other sections until all the material has been tied. Now dip the *fabric* stuff in dye, let it sit about ten minutes or until the color is a little darker than you want it to be. *Finally* Finaly take off the ties and enjoy your design. Rinse the cloth in water until the water runs clear.

Tie-dyeing is one of the best *hobbies* hobbys. It is fun to do. It is also fun to *realize* know that no one else will have a shirt just like yours!

PROOFREADING IDEA

Using a Ruler

Hold a ruler under the line you are checking for errors. Look only at that line. After you have marked any errors, move the ruler down to the next line. Read one line at a time.

Now proofread your article, add a title, and make a neat copy.

5 Publishing

Now it's time to share your how-to article with your classmates. Here are two ways you might try.

Tie-Dyeing

For the cost of only a few cents and an hour's time, you can create works of art. You can learn to tie-dye. The only materials you need are fabric dye, rubber bands, and a white T-shirt.

Start by wrapping a rubber band around a section of cloth. Put it on very tightly. Then do other sections until all the material has been tied. Now dip the fabric in dye. Let it sit about ten minutes or until the color is a little darker than you want it to be. Rinse the cloth in water until the water runs clear. Finally take off the ties and enjoy your design.

Tie-dyeing is one of the best hobbies. It is fun to do. It is also fun to realize that no one else will have a shirt just like yours!

PUBLISHING IDEAS

Share Aloud	Share in Writing
Give a talk on how to do your activity. If possible, demonstrate the activity step by step. Ask your listeners for questions at the end.	With your classmates, make a mini-library of your articles. Put each one in a folder with the title and author's name on the tab. Keep a log with the folders for readers to record comments.

CURRICULUM ·CONNECTION·

 Writing Across the Curriculum Music

In this unit you wrote a how-to article. To gather ideas for your article, you may have made a cluster map. A cluster map can also help you gather ideas for a musical presentation.

Writing to Learn

Think and Elaborate ◆ Imagine that your class will present a musical show at a school assembly. You want to plan a show of songs, dances, and instrumental music. You have narrowed your choice of shows to either "Music of the Past" or "Music of Today." Choose one of these topics. Make a cluster map of ideas for a musical show on that topic.

Cluster Map

Write ◆ Write a program for the show you chose. List the songs, dances, and other musical offerings. Decorate the program.

 Writing in Your Journal

In the Writer's Warm-up you wrote about the theater. During the unit you learned a lot about puppetry. Before you read *Puppeteer*, did you know how much thought and work went into a puppet show? In your journal write the most interesting things that you learned about puppets.

BOOKS TO ENJOY

Read More About It

Puppeteer *by Kathryn Lasky*
For Paul Davis, mounting a puppet show is a year-long process. In *Puppeteer,* you can follow the master as he prepares for the play and enjoys the triumph of opening night.

Putting on a Play *by Susan and Stephen Judy*
This book is designed to improve your homemade play productions. Dozens of useful suggestions tell how to develop simple ideas into imaginative scripts.

Pinocchio *by Carlo Collodi*
Long before his movie fame, Pinocchio was one of the best-known puppets of our time. He appeared in this classic work over one hundred years ago.

Book Report Idea   Puppet Play

Good books often ''come alive'' for their readers. Here's how to make a book you have read come alive for your classmates.

Create a Puppet Play Report ◆ Make a few simple stick or glove puppets of the main characters in your book. Then prepare a short script that retells an interesting part of the book. Another approach is to have the characters discuss their roles in the book. Using a simple stage, have the puppets present the script to the class.

UNIT REVIEW

Unit 2

Nouns *pages 62–71*

A. Write the nouns in each sentence. Then write whether each noun names a *person, place, thing,* or *idea.*

1. My cousin grew up in Chicago.
2. Her house was on State Street.
3. Rosa met many different people.
4. People enjoyed their neighbors.
5. Rosa liked her neighborhood.
6. Mrs. Brown lived on the corner.
7. A Chinese teacher and his wife lived across the street.
8. An architect and his wife lived in the next block.
9. Rosa and her schoolmates rode the bus to school.
10. Their friends gathered at the park.

B. Write each underlined word. Then write whether it is a *common noun* or a *proper noun.*

11. Abraham Lincoln lived in troubled times.
12. This great statesman was the sixteenth President of the United States.
13. He was born on a farm in Kentucky.
14. His family moved to Indiana and then to Illinois.

15. Even as a boy, Abe showed he was a fine speaker.
16. After studying law, he became a partner in the firm of Stuart and Lincoln.
17. Later he formed a partnership with William Herndon.
18. His debate with Stephen A. Douglas made him a famous person.
19. His Gettysburg Address stands as one of the great speeches of the world.
20. When this great man was slain, Americans mourned his death.

C. Write each sentence. Capitalize the proper nouns.

21. My cousin donna manages the bon ton dress shop on shelby lane.
22. The owners, luisa campos and henry taylor, respect her abilities.
23. Many of the clothes are made by the fine art clothing company.
24. Last friday, march 18, donna held a showing of her new fashions.
25. Reporters from as far away as houston, texas, attended.
26. Next may, she will open a shop with the designer ms. rita romero.
27. They will raise funds for the twin lakes general hospital.

D. Write the plural form of each noun.

28. tomato
29. woman
30. cherry
31. shelf
32. moose
33. chimney
34. valley
35. swallow
36. millionaire
37. deer
38. mystery
39. knife

E. Write the possessive form of each noun. Write whether the noun is *singular* or *plural*.

40. teeth
41. farm
42. mice
43. Charles
44. cow
45. baboons
46. song
47. men
48. antelope
49. cheese
50. monkeys
51. elephant

Compounds   *pages 72–73*

F. Write each of the following sentences. Underline the compounds.

52. You have a letter from your pen pal in Ecuador.
53. Do you still have last evening's newspaper article about the basketball game.
54. Please put the chicken in the microwave oven.
55. The audience watched Ming Chin do a handstand.
56. There are absolutely no leftovers in the refrigerator.
57. I think that truck has the right-of-way.
58. There were four inches of rainfall last Tuesday.
59. My mother recently bought a new handbag.
60. My dog Rascal just loves ice cream on a hot day.
61. The team planned their new strategy during the time-out.
62. After the sudden snowfall, the sidewalk was slippery.

Topic Sentence and Supporting Sentences   *pages 88–89*

G. Use the sentences below to write a paragraph. Begin with the topic sentence. Then write the supporting sentences in logical order.

63. That training usually begins when a dancer is very young.
64. After barre work, dancers practice center work without the supporting rod.
65. Ballet dancing requires many years of training.
66. Classes end with practice in leaping for males and practice in dancing for female dancers.
67. Dance class starts with work at the barre, a rod used for support.

Explanatory Paragraph   *pages 90–91*

H. Read the following paragraph. Then answer the questions.

You can make a fine omelet with a little practice. First, crack two or three eggs into a bowl. Then blend the eggs with a fork. Add some seasonings. Next, melt some butter in a small frying pan. Add the eggs and stir them as they cook. Then with a fork or spatula, fold one half of the omelet over the other. Finally, slide the cooked omelet onto a plate.

68. Which sentence is the topic sentence?
69. What actions must be performed? List the actions in order.
70. What signal words help to show the order of steps?

Unit 1: Sentences *pages 4–15*

A. Write the sentences, using capital letters and correct end punctuation. After each sentence write *declarative*, *interrogative*, *imperative*, or *exclamatory*.

1. this week the circus came to our town
2. look at the funny clowns
3. do you see the baby elephant
4. how clever the juggler is
5. get us some popcorn
6. the tightrope walker does dangerous stunts
7. a family of acrobats performs together
8. is the lion tamer in control of her animals
9. what a dangerous profession that is
10. the ringmaster introduces all the acts
11. may Angela and I go to the sideshow
12. don't throw peanuts at the dancing bears
13. what a wonderful time we have had
14. the circus will come again next year

B. Write each complete subject. Then underline each simple subject.

15. My older brother is a photographer.
16. This profession takes him to many interesting places.
17. His camera goes everywhere with him.
18. His photograph of a polar bear and her cubs won an award.
19. The mother was very protective of her young.
20. Her growl alerted my brother to the danger.
21. This kind of situation was not new to him.
22. Photography of wild animals is one of his specialties.
23. His years of experience have made him cautious.
24. Many different people have also been snapped by his camera.
25. A famous actress called him her favorite photographer.
26. Her producer has often employed my brother.
27. The results of his photography please almost everyone.
28. A career in photography can be very rewarding.

C. Write each complete predicate. Then underline each simple predicate.

29. Giraffes are the tallest animals in the world.
30. An adult giraffe can grow to nearly eighteen feet.
31. A large male giraffe weighs about two thousand pounds.
32. A giraffe's hoof is split into two parts.
33. Each part consists of one toe.
34. An average giraffe can gallop up to thirty miles an hour.
35. Lions and hunters have reduced the giraffe population.
36. People use the giraffe's tail hairs for bracelets.

D. Write the subject of each sentence.

37. Have you read this book?

38. Is it very exciting?

39. Tell me about it.

40. Emmy reads two books every week.

41. The librarian suggests interesting books.

42. Did Carl return that mystery story to the library?

43. Don't reveal the surprise ending.

44. Has this author written other mystery stories?

45. Her books are popular with young people.

46. Lend me her latest novel.

Unit 2: Nouns *pages 62–71*

E. Write the nouns in each sentence. Then write whether each noun names a person, place, thing, or idea.

47. My uncle traveled to India.

48. His purpose was to write a book about that land.

49. Many people roam the streets.

50. Even so, the man was struck by the beauty of the country.

51. The people make beautiful jewelry and vases.

52. His conclusion is that the nation has many problems but also much beauty.

F. Write each noun. Then write whether it is a common noun or a proper noun.

53. Ohio River
54. tiger
55. Switzerland
56. snowstorm
57. bicycle
58. sandal
59. Albert Payson
60. Ms. Fermi

G. Write each sentence. Capitalize the proper nouns.

61. I spent thanksgiving with aunt martha and uncle ed in phoenix.

62. They met me on wednesday and took me to their house on hayden road.

63. On thursday evening we went to a concert at symphony hall.

64. The next day I was taken to a photography show at phoenix civic plaza.

65. That afternoon we went to the phoenix art museum.

66. I admired a painting by jackson pollock.

67. On saturday we had a picnic at south mountain park.

68. On sunday, at the phoenix international airport, I thanked my relatives for a wonderful time.

H. Write the plural form of each noun.

69. wish
70. knife
71. moose
72. baby
73. leash
74. woman
75. city
76. berry
77. goose
78. mouse
79. tomato
80. deer
81. ostrich
82. sheep

I. Write the possessive form of each noun. Then write whether the noun is singular or plural.

83. Ms. Nevins
84. mice
85. people
86. bottles
87. poems
88. violin
89. glass
90. ladies
91. ox
92. students
93. berry
94. patches
95. children

LANGUAGE PUZZLERS

Word Clues

Write the word that can be used before or after each of the three words in the group to make a two-word proper noun. (Hint: Each missing word begins with a capital letter.)

1. Mother's   Memorial   Thanksgiving   _ _ _
2. Hudson   Red   Colorado   _ _ _ _ _
3. Superior   Tahoe   Swan   _ _ _ _
4. Grant   Fifth   Pennsylvania   _ _ _ _ _ _
5. England   Jersey   Mexico   _ _ _
6. Middle   Germany   Virginia   _ _ _ _
7. Divide   Britain   Dane   _ _ _ _ _
8. Ben   Dipper   Sur   _ _ _
9. Nations   States   Kingdom   _ _ _ _ _ _
10. Everest   McKinley   Vernon   _ _ _ _ _

Shape a Noun

Use the clues below to figure out eight capitalized names.

1. a state: *d*, *h*, and three vowel letters
2. a continent: *s* and three vowel letters
3. a month: *p*, *r*, *l*, and two vowel letters
4. a country: *r*, *l*, *n*, *d*, and three vowel letters
5. a president: *b*, *r*, *h*, *m*, *l*, *n*, *c*, *l*, *n*, and five vowel letters
6. a city: *d*, *t*, *r*, *t*, and three vowel letters
7. a tree-planting day: *r*, *b*, *r*, *d*, *y*, and three vowel letters
8. a language: *t*, *l*, *n*, and four vowel letters

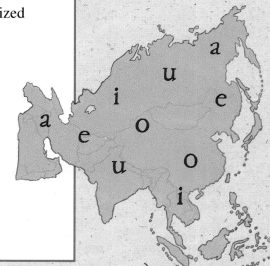

Unit 2 Extra Practice

1 Writing with Nouns

p. 62

A. Write the nouns in these sentences.

1. Paul Bunyan is the hero of many tales.
2. Lumberjacks made up stories about his strength.
3. This powerful man could easily cut down a whole forest.
4. Paul was a fast runner, too.
5. The friendly giant could beat his own shadow!
6. A great blue ox named Babe lived with Paul.
7. The very heavy pet left his footprints in solid rock!
8. The ox could haul a forest of logs.
9. The logger and his crew lived in a huge bunkhouse.
10. The chimney almost touched the sun.
11. Paul Bunyan cut down trees in Minnesota.
12. His sawmill was in Louisiana.
13. The giant needed logs for his mill.
14. No rivers or roads had been built.
15. So Paul and Babe dug the Mississippi River!

B. Write the nouns in these sentences. Then write whether each noun names a person, place, thing, or idea.

EXAMPLE: Paul made his own ax.

ANSWER: Paul (person), ax (thing)

16. Paul Bunyan had tremendous power.
17. His voice shook every tree in the forest.
18. Paul dug Lake Michigan for a bathtub.
19. His handkerchief was a sheet.
20. The giant used a tree as a comb.
21. For breakfast the great lumberjack ate 140 eggs.
22. Paul drank thirty buckets of milk.
23. The logger met Pecos Bill in Arizona.
24. Bill was a legendary cowboy.
25. The two men became friends.
26. Pecos Bill once rode a wild cyclone.
27. Heavy rains from the cyclone created the Grand Canyon.

2 Common and Proper Nouns p. 64

A. Write each underlined word. Then write whether it is a common noun or a proper noun.

1. A class from Ridgevale School went to Virginia.
2. Pupils saw Mount Vernon, the home of George Washington.
3. The beautiful Potomac River flows near the house.
4. The students also visited the Tomb of the Unknown Soldier.
5. This monument is located in Arlington.
6. Virginia has a rich past.
7. Thomas Jefferson was a famous president from that state.
8. He was the author of the Declaration of Independence.
9. The class saw Monticello, his home near Charlottesville.
10. They visited Jamestown, too.
11. Settlers from England arrived there in 1607.
12. Nearby Williamsburg is a historic city.
13. Craft House and other buildings have interesting exhibits.
14. The battlefield at Yorktown was the scene of a big event.
15. The last major battle of the American Revolution took place there in 1781.
16. Two years later the Treaty of Paris established the independence of the colonies.
17. Virginia was also a major battlefield during the Civil War.

B. Write each sentence. Draw one line under each common noun and two lines under each proper noun.

18. Norfolk is the largest city.
19. Ships from Norfolk sail across Chesapeake Bay to the Atlantic Ocean.
20. Nearby Virginia Beach is a great place for a vacation.
21. Ships are built in Newport News.
22. The Pentagon is in Arlington.
23. The students also visited the capitol at Richmond.
24. Richmond was the capital of the Confederacy.
25. On Monument Avenue are statues of great heroes.
26. The trip ended on Skyline Drive.
27. The Blue Ridge Mountains can be seen from this road.
28. These mountains extend into North Carolina.

3 Capitalizing Proper Nouns   p. 66

A. Write the sentences. Capitalize the proper nouns.

1. A reporter from a newspaper spoke to the class in may.
2. Students visited the newspaper's office on main street.
3. On thursday, luis cruz of micrex company told the class about careers in computers.
4. His company has offices in mexico, israel, and france.
5. Members of the lamonte computer club enjoyed the talk.
6. beth lang of the professional engineering society also spoke.
7. She showed her plans for the honey river bridge.
8. Finally, celia garcia and her owl, charlie, visited the class.
9. She told about working in yellowstone national park.
10. After memorial day, students reported on other careers.

B. Write a proper noun for each common noun below.

EXAMPLE: state
ANSWER: Oklahoma

11. river
12. building
13. country
14. bridge
15. street
16. school
17. store
18. company
19. holiday
20. club

C. Write the paragraph, capitalizing each proper noun.

A man named pierre l'enfant designed the city of washington, d. c. george washington himself chose the site on the potomac river. The construction of the white house began in 1792. The first one to live there was thomas jefferson. Earlier capitals had been in new york and philadelphia. During the war of 1812, the british burned most of the public buildings. dolley madison saved a famous painting from the flames. Visitors today often spend hours at the smithsonian institution. The declaration of independence and the bill of rights are on view at the national archives building. The lincoln memorial is another favorite tourist spot.

4 Singular and Plural Nouns   *p. 68*

A. Write the plural form of each noun.

1. fox	**6.** cry	**11.** self	**16.** deer
2. body	**7.** lunch	**12.** radio	**17.** sky
3. stone	**8.** rodeo	**13.** hero	**18.** church
4. valley	**9.** eyelash	**14.** day	**19.** lock
5. thief	**10.** loss	**15.** tooth	**20.** play

B. Write each sentence, using the plural forms of the nouns in parentheses ( ).

21. The (child) saw many (exhibit) at the county fair.
22. (Business) and farm (society) sponsored the event.
23. The (pen) of (calf) and (sheep) interested Hana.
24. Taro liked the (pony), (donkey), and (lamb).
25. One girl was brushing the (mane) of her (horse).
26. (Man) and (woman) were showing (duck) and (turkey).
27. The biggest and best (tomato), (cabbage), and (beet) were also on view.
28. These (vegetable) were stored in (box) on (shelf).
29. Taro sampled some excellent (jam) and (jelly) made from (blackberry) and (peach).
30. Then Hana and Taro each drank two (glass) of milk and ate two (sandwich).

C. Write the sentence. Then write the plural form of each word in the list next to the correct clue.

potato	half	turkey	peach
sheep	reindeer	mouse	thief

31. Cats chase these animals.
32. They have eyes, but they do not see.
33. One of these animals is named Rudolph.
34. This type of fruit grows on trees.
35. They are lambs when they are young.
36. Two of these make a whole.
37. Many of these are eaten on Thanksgiving.
38. Another word for them is *robbers*.

5 Possessive Nouns

p. 70

A. Write the possessive noun in each sentence. Then write whether it is singular or plural.

1. Our country's first nationwide day of thanksgiving was celebrated in 1789.
2. Each state's date for Thanksgiving was soon different.
3. It was Sarah Hale's idea to make Thanksgiving a national holiday, like the Fourth of July.
4. Mrs. Hale was editor of a popular women's magazine.
5. Many of her magazine's articles were about Thanksgiving.
6. Sarah Hale sought important people's help.
7. Her plan for a national holiday had many governors' support.
8. Finally it attracted President Lincoln's attention.
9. He met Mrs. Hale and discussed the woman's plan.
10. In 1863 the President's proclamation made the last Thursday of November our national Thanksgiving Day.

B. Write the possessive form of each noun. Then write whether the noun is singular or plural.

11. house	16. turkey
12. mice	17. dish
13. glass	18. cranberries
14. men	19. Mr. Jones
15. plates	20. guests

C. Write the possessive form of the noun in parentheses ( ).

21. What are your (family) special customs for Thanksgiving?
22. The turkey is the center of most (families) Thanksgiving dinners.
23. Beyond that, different (areas) customs may vary.
24. Near Chesapeake Bay, the (turkey) stuffing may be made with oysters.
25. A southern (cook) choice might be cornbread stuffing.
26. (New Englanders) side dishes may be creamed onions and acorn squash.
27. The (Pilgrims) feast included meat pies and squash pies.

UNIT THREE

USING LANGUAGE TO
CREATE

Writing
IN YOUR JOURNAL

WRITER'S WARM-UP ◆ Is there a special spot in nature that you like to visit? It might be a wooded park, a seashore, or an open field. You might enjoy watching the moon and stars from your window at night. Write in your journal about your favorite part of nature. Tell why it is your favorite.

Think of several words that name common actions, such as *climb* and *jog*. Pantomime these actions. See how quickly others can guess the actions you act out.

1 Writing with Verbs

The simple predicate, or verb, is the main word in the complete predicate. In the following sentences the verbs are underlined.

> The first daffodil <u>struggles</u> into the thin spring light.
> A soft wind <u>shuffles</u> through the dry summer grass.
> Autumn's leaves briefly <u>flare</u> a brilliant red.

The verbs *struggles*, *shuffles*, and *flare* are action verbs. These verbs express, or tell about, action that can be seen.

Some action verbs express action that cannot be seen.

> Most poets <u>appreciate</u> nature.
> The natural world <u>affects</u> poets deeply.

Other verbs do not express action at all. Instead, they state what is. These verbs are called state-of-being verbs.

> Each drop of dew <u>is</u> a diamond.
> The thunderclouds <u>are</u> angry.

The following forms of the verb *be* are the most common state-of-being verbs.

| am | is | are | was | were | be | being | been |

> **Summary ♦** A **verb** expresses action or being. Using strong verbs can make your writing more interesting.

Guided Practice

Name the verb in each sentence.

1. The mysteries of nature are all around us.
2. Nature's splendor impresses people everywhere.
3. Many poets write about the natural world.
4. Their poems often contain powerful natural images.

Practice

A. Write the verb in each sentence.

    5. The ocean pounds rhythmically against a rocky coast.

    6. A brilliant star blazes across the purple sky.

    7. A herd of deer bound nimbly through an open field.

    8. Scenes of incredible natural beauty amaze everyone.

    9. Sometimes these scenes also cause strong feelings within us.

  10. Poets think about these scenes and feelings.

  11. Their poems express their experiences and emotions.

  12. These experiences and feelings are often familiar to us.

B. Write the verb in each sentence. Then write *action verb* or *state-of-being verb* after the verb.

  13. A poet spots a cocoon on a tree bough.

  14. Inside, a wormlike caterpillar slowly forms wings.

  15. For a while the poet herself is the caterpillar.

  16. She describes her need for peace and quiet for her change.

  17. The poet's message is clear to the reader.

  18. Change and self-improvement are possible.

  19. These changes require purposeful and intense activity.

C. Complete each sentence with a verb that expresses action in a colorful or exact way.

  20. Snowflakes _____ gently downward in a forest.

  21. A poet _____ one of the unique crystals.

  22. The flake's beautiful pattern _____ the poet.

  23. In the poet's hand the snowflake instantly _____ .

  24. How quickly natural beauty _____ !

Apply ◆ Think and Write

From Your Writing ◆ Read what you wrote for the Writer's Warm-up. List the verbs that you used. Can you think of stronger, more colorful verbs to better express the actions you described?

> ✏ **Remember**
> to use colorful, precise verbs when you speak and write.

Think of something and tell others whether it is animal, vegetable, or mineral. To find out what it is, the others take turns asking no more than twenty questions. Each question must contain a form of the verb *be*: *Is it alive? Is it a four-footed animal?*

2 Linking Verbs

State-of-being verbs can be linking verbs. A linking verb connects, or links, the subject of a sentence with a word or words in the predicate. In the following sentences the underlined words are linking verbs.

1. May is a poet.   **2. Her poems seem beautiful to us.**

In sentence **1** the linking verb *is* connects the subject *May* with the noun *poet*. A noun that follows a linking verb and renames the subject is a **predicate nominative**. In sentence **2** the linking verb *seem* connects the subject *poems* with the adjective *beautiful*.

Forms of *Be*	Other Linking Verbs
be, am, is, are, was, were	appear, become, feel, look, seem, smell, taste

Read the sentences below. Notice that a singular noun is used as a subject with *is* and *was*. A plural noun is used as subject with *are* and *were*.

May's favorite place is a forest.	That tree was an oak.
These foxgloves are lovely.	The beavers were busy.

> **Summary** ◆ A **linking verb** connects the subject with a word or words in the predicate.

Guided Practice

Name the linking verb in each sentence.

1. The whippoorwill's call is an invitation to the forest.
2. These wildflowers are Dutchman's-breeches.
3. The delicate blossoms smell so sweet.
4. Here the moss becomes a thick, green carpet.

Practice

A. Write the sentences. Underline each linking verb.

    5. The forest is a peaceful place.
    6. The spruces, pines, and firs are evergreens.
    7. Because of them, the entire forest smells fragrant.
    8. In winter the green boughs seem especially warm.
    9. The cool water of this rocky spring tastes tangy.
   10. The overflow becomes a brook farther down.
   11. The brook's babbling song sounds mysterious to me.

B. Write each linking verb. Then write the noun or adjective that the linking verb connects to the subject.

   12. Once again the deer are plentiful.
   13. Their wide, dark eyes appear almost shimmery.
   14. To the squirrels the shadow of a hawk is a threat.
   15. This strangely colored butterfly looks scarlet.
   16. Those wild asparagus stalks were delicious.
   17. For a gray fox this hollow ash tree was a convenient house.
   18. The bear on the hillside seems young.
   19. That shallow cave in the rocks recently became its den.
   20. The air in the cave feels damp.

C. Complete each sentence with a linking verb (LV) and a predicate nominative (PN).

   21. The noise of the insects (LV) a low (PN).
   22. Woodland mushrooms (LV) a springy (PN).
   23. Warm rocks (LV) comfortable (PN) for snakes.
   24. Dense underbrush (LV) a (PN) for wild grouse and turkeys.
   25. At night the forest (LV) an enchanted (PN).

Apply ◆ Think and Write

Caring for Nature ◆ Write a paragraph telling how you think people should behave when they hike or camp in forests. Try using some of the following words after linking verbs: *majestic*, *responsible*, *wise*, *natural resource*, *heritage*, *preservation*.

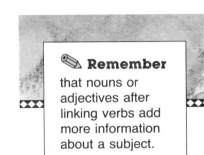

> ✎ **Remember**
> that nouns or adjectives after linking verbs add more information about a subject.

How many different ways can you think of to complete this sentence? *I _____ finish my homework.* How does each word change the meaning of the sentence?

3 Main Verbs and Helping Verbs

A verb can consist of more than one word.

> The world <u>can be seen</u> as one huge ocean.
> Here and there the ocean <u>is broken</u> by continents.
> Few people <u>are</u> not <u>inspired</u> by the ocean.

When a verb is more than one word, the most important word is called the **main verb**. The other words are called **helping verbs**. The main verbs in the sentences above are *seen*, *broken*, and *inspired*. Notice that the word *not* can separate a helping verb and the main verb. It is not part of the verb. Common helping verbs are listed below.

am	be	had	did	may
is	being	can	shall	might
are	been	could	should	must
was	has	do	will	
were	have	does	would	

Some verbs in the box, such as *is* and *has*, can stand alone in a sentence. When they stand alone, they are the main verbs.

■ Waves <u>are</u> rough.   Seas <u>have</u> power.

> **Summary** ◆ A **helping verb** works with the main verb to express action or being.

Guided Practice

Name the helping verbs and the main verbs in each sentence.

1. At all times the ocean is moving.
2. Small waves might lap gently across the sand.
3. A stormy sea can batter the earth with fearsome power.
4. The sea's movements have been shaping our coastlines.

Practice

A. Write the sentences below. Underline the helping verbs once and the main verbs twice.

5. What a tremendous variety of life can be found in the sea!
6. A microscope will reveal countless one-celled organisms.
7. Yet the largest animals, blue whales, are living here, too.
8. Jellyfish and sharks, giant turtles and skates have joined this sea world.
9. The extraordinary range of life forms would amaze anyone.
10. More and more is being learned about life in the sea.
11. We have not discovered all the sea's mysteries yet.

B. Write the verbs in each sentence. Then write *MV* if the sentence has only a main verb. Write *HV + MV* if the sentence has both a helping verb and a main verb.

12. The sea has fascinated people throughout history.
13. The restless sea has tremendous power.
14. It can carve rocks, cliffs, and caves.
15. Currents are great rivers of water within the ocean.
16. Currents of warm or cold water have an effect on climate.
17. The moon's gentle pull is the cause of tides.
18. A tidal wave might create an image of the sea's power.

C. Complete each sentence by adding a helping verb (HV), a main verb (MV), or both.

19. The sea (HV) not yield its riches easily.
20. In fragile boats, early traders (HV) (HV) feared the sea.
21. For centuries fishers have (MV) the sea for food.
22. The sea (HV) (MV) a major source of mineral wealth.
23. Someday it (HV) (MV) abundant energy and fresh water.

Apply ◆ Think and Write

A Watery Planet ◆ It has been suggested that *Sea* would be a better name for our planet than *Earth*. Write a paragraph that tells why someone might make such a suggestion. Also tell whether you agree with the idea. Try to use some helping verbs.

> ✎ **Remember**
> to use helping verbs to express actions and shades of meaning.

Think of some three-word sentences that follow this pattern: subject, action verb, noun. For fun, have each word begin with the same letter. For example: *Automobiles amuse Americans. Bears bite berries. Crow criticizes crocodiles.*

4 Verbs with Direct Objects

When Lonato checked his homework assignment, part of it was torn off and missing.

Each student must write a about a season.

The part of the sentence that is missing is the direct object. Without the direct object, the meaning of the sentence is not complete. A direct object receives the action of the verb. It is often a noun. In the sentence below, the noun *poem* is the direct object. It answers the question *what* after the verb.

■ Each student must write a <u>poem</u> about a season. (must write what?)

A direct object can also answer the question *whom* after the verb. In the following sentence, *friend* is the direct object.

■ Lonato will call a <u>friend</u> for the assignment. (will call whom?)

When you include a direct object in a sentence, you tell who or what receives the action of the verb. This often makes your sentences clearer. To find the direct object in a sentence, ask who or what receives the action of the verb.

> **Summary** ◆ The **direct object** receives the action of the verb.

Guided Practice

Name the direct object in each sentence. Tell whether it answers the question *whom* or *what*.

1. Spring breezes awaken the earth.
2. Warm sunlight thaws the stubborn snow.
3. In the pasture, lambs and foals nuzzle their mothers.
4. Bright flowers and budding trees delight the children.

Practice

A. Write the direct object in each sentence. Then write *whom* or *what* to show which question the direct object answers.

5. For spring the cherry trees wear pink dresses.
6. Young rabbits nibble the sweet new grass.
7. How busily the songbird weaves its nest.
8. Rich, brown earth thrills a farmer.
9. Soon summer will surround us.
10. Slowly the sun ripens the fruit in fields and orchards.
11. Cool waters support the joyful swimmers.
12. A dusty farmer cuts his fragrant hay.

B. Write the action verb and the direct object in each sentence.

13. A sudden thundershower shakes the earth.
14. Cider and apples satisfy the guests.
15. Red, yellow, and brown leaves cover the forest floor.
16. In a hazy field a grateful farmer harvests corn.
17. High above, the honk of southbound geese interrupts the still night.
18. A squirrel gathers acorns for the days ahead.
19. A chilly wind warns the neighborhood of winter.

C. Complete each sentence by adding a direct object.

20. A layer of snow covers the ____ .
21. A sorrowful sparrow cannot find any ____ .
22. In his hidden den a fat-bellied bear enjoys a ____ .
23. A pale and distant sun provides the ____ with little warmth.
24. People patiently await the ____ of another spring.
25. Soon birds will sing their ____ again.

Apply ♦ Think and Write

A Seasonal List ♦ Which of the four seasons is your favorite? Make a list of things you do during your favorite season. Follow these examples: *eat berries*, *sweep sidewalks*, *watch thunderstorms*, *enjoy the sun*.

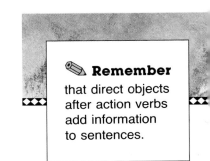

✎ **Remember**
that direct objects after action verbs add information to sentences.

Make up three sentences. Begin the first sentence with the word *Yesterday*, the second with *Now*, and the third with *Tomorrow*.

5 Tenses of Verbs

Calendars, clocks, and watches all tell time. Verbs tell time, too. You use verbs in all of your sentences, and tenses of the verbs you use show time.

A verb in the present tense shows action that happens now.

> Storm clouds <u>linger</u> above the mountains.
> A river of rain <u>sweeps</u> the sky.

A verb in the past tense shows action that already happened. The past tense of a verb usually ends in *-ed*.

> Yesterday a gentle fog <u>settled</u> down in the village.
> It <u>touched</u> us all with its powdery mist.

A verb in the future tense shows action that will happen. The future tense is usually formed with the helping verb *will* or *shall*.

> Tomorrow the radiant sun <u>will blaze</u> above.
> How we <u>shall welcome</u> its warmth and light.

When you write about something that happened in the past, make sure all your verbs are in the past tense. Similarly, when you write about something that will happen, use future-tense verbs.

Summary ♦ The **tense** of a verb shows time.

Guided Practice

Tell whether the underlined verb in each sentence is in the present, past, or future tense.

1. Lightning <u>flashed</u> a familiar warning.
2. Angry clouds <u>thundered</u> from on high.
3. With watery darts the storm <u>attacks</u> us.
4. The dusty earth <u>absorbs</u> the flow.
5. The air <u>will turn</u> cool and clear soon.

Practice

A. Write the verb in each sentence. Then write *present tense*, *past tense*, or *future tense* to show the time of the action.

    6. Slow-motion snow floats steadily toward the earth.
    7. The silent flakes will dust the earth with a powdery white layer.
    8. Cold air etched a secret message on the windows.
    9. Frosty breath punctuates our conversation.
    10. Dull gray clouds loitered aimlessly all day.
    11. At last a luminous sun breaks through the milky clouds.
    12. It chased away the snow by noon.
    13. The warmth will awaken the still earth.
    14. Stiff breezes wildly whip the weather vane.
    15. The whole world squints in the thin, bright light.

B. Think of an appropriate verb to complete each sentence. Write it in the tense shown in parentheses.

    16. Out at sea a swirling hurricane _____ . (present)
    17. Tomorrow it _____ the coast with fearful force. (future)
    18. The wary villagers _____ for the worst. (present)
    19. A fast-moving funnel of wind _____ across the plains. (past)
    20. The violent twister _____ through fields and towns. (past)
    21. For decades residents _____ a cyclone's fury. (future)
    22. A blinding blizzard _____ a northern city. (past)
    23. High-speed, howling winds _____ the streets of people. (future)
    24. Storm-torn wires _____ in a tangle. (present)
    25. Repair crews _____ quickly. (present)

Apply ◆ Think and Write

Then, Now, Later ◆ Write three sentences about yourself as a young child. Then write three sentences about yourself right now. Finally write three sentences about yourself as an adult. Underline all the verbs. Did you use verbs in past, present, and future tenses?

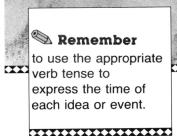

✎ **Remember**
to use the appropriate verb tense to express the time of each idea or event.

Read this nonsense sentence: *An alpy kerred the draf because the moigs had diffled a pirkop.* Which of the words seem to be verbs? How do you know? With what real verbs could you replace them?

6 Principal Parts of Verbs

All verbs have basic forms called principal parts. The first principal part of a verb is the present. The second principal part is the past. It is usually formed by adding *-ed*. The third principal part is called the past participle. Most past participles are also formed by adding *-ed*. The helping verb *has*, *have*, or *had* is used with the past participle.

> **Present:** Each night people <u>watch</u> the moon and stars.
>
> **Past:** Last month we <u>watched</u> an eclipse of the sun.
>
> **Past Participle:** For centuries people have <u>watched</u> for comets.

When the past and the past participle of a verb are formed by adding *-ed*, the verb is called a **regular verb**. Read the principal parts of these verbs.

Present	Past	Past Participle
call	called	(has, have, had) called
splash	splashed	(has, have, had) splashed
worry	worried	(has, have, had) worried
trap	trapped	(has, have, had) trapped

Notice that verbs that end in a consonant and *y*, such as *worry*, change the *y* to *i* and add *-ed* to form the past. One-syllable verbs that end in a vowel and a consonant, such as *trap*, double the final consonant and add *-ed* to form the past.

> **Summary** ◆ The **principal parts** are the basic forms of a verb. They include the present, past, and past participle.

Guided Practice

Tell the present, past, and past participle of each verb. Use the helping verb *has* with each past participle.

1. drop   **2.** hurry   **3.** ask   **4.** move   **5.** search

Practice

A. Write the three principal parts of each verb. Use the helping verb *has* with each past participle.

6. flap   **9.** rely
7. serve   **10.** close
8. knock   **11.** contract

B. Write the verb in each sentence. Then write *present*, *past*, or *past participle* to show which principal part is used.

12. Over 200 billion stars fill the known universe.
13. Throughout time this vast expanse has thrilled people.
14. The sun, moon, and stars inspired people in many ways.
15. These bright orbs enchant us still.
16. Travelers have used stars as direction finders since the days of the ancient Phoenicians.
17. These distant lights now symbolize the future.
18. Another heavenly body, the moon, has influenced the earth.
19. The moon's gravity creates our ocean tides.
20. At night moonlight has illuminated many dark paths.
21. The moon's loveliness inspired poets and composers.

C. Complete each sentence with an appropriate verb from the list below. Use the principal part indicated in parentheses ( ).

inspire   caused   depends   worshiped   have explained

22. All life on the earth _____ on the sun. (present)
23. Many ancient people _____ the sun. (past)
24. A solar eclipse _____ great terror. (past)
25. Many myths _____ the sun's movement. (past participle)
26. Even today sunrises and sunsets _____ people. (present)

Apply ◆ Think and Write

Dictionary of Knowledge ◆ Scientists and observers throughout the ages have been puzzled and fascinated by the movements of the sun, moon, and stars. Read about Stonehenge in the Dictionary of Knowledge. Write some sentences about that ancient astronomical observatory.

✎ **Remember**
to double-check the spelling of the verbs you use.

What verbs do you think people use most often in everyday speech? What are their principal parts? Do all of them add *-ed* to form the past and past participle?

7 Using Irregular Verbs

Regular verbs have past and past participle forms that end in *-ed*. Some verbs, however, are irregular. They do not add *-ed* to form the past and past participle. Here are the principal parts of some common irregular verbs.

Present	Past	Past Participle
begin	began	(has, have, had) begun
blow	blew	(has, have, had) blown
do	did	(has, have, had) done
drink	drank	(has, have, had) drunk
eat	ate	(has, have, had) eaten
fly	flew	(has, have, had) flown
give	gave	(has, have, had) given
go	went	(has, have, had) gone
grow	grew	(has, have, had) grown
know	knew	(has, have, had) known
ring	rang	(has, have, had) rung
sing	sang	(has, have, had) sung
swim	swam	(has, have, had) swum
take	took	(has, have, had) taken
throw	threw	(has, have, had) thrown
write	wrote	(has, have, had) written

Summary ◆ **Irregular verbs** do not form the past and past participle by adding *-ed*.

Guided Practice

Name the three principal parts of these verbs.

1. know   **2.** give   **3.** take   **4.** write   **5.** begin

Practice

A. Write the three principal parts of each verb below.

6. fly   **8.** drink   **10.** write   **12.** do   **14.** blow

7. ring   **9.** throw   **11.** sing   **13.** eat   **15.** go

B. Write each sentence, using the past or past participle of the verb in parentheses ( ).

16. The hike to our campsite (take) a long time.
17. The sun had (go) down, and the mosquitoes were out.
18. In the darkness we (begin) to make camp.
19. We (know) we should have double-checked the packs.
20. Everyone thought someone else had (take) the tent.
21. Gradually we (grow) accustomed to sleeping on the ground.
22. Jo said a bat had (fly) past her nose.
23. Then suddenly the wind (blow) harder.
24. By midnight a steady drizzle had (begin).
25. Mom (give) a sigh and muttered, ''Nature.''

C. Use the past or past participle of irregular verbs from the list in this lesson to complete the story.

At about 4:00 A.M. the birds (**26.** _____) us a loud wake-up song. ''If I had (**27.** _____) so much poison ivy (**28.** _____) here,'' Dad remarked, ''I would have (**29.** _____) elsewhere.''

''Look!'' shouted Jo. ''Some raccoons have (**30.** _____) our food.''

I had just (**31.** _____) a gulp of fresh spring water when Dad shouted, ''You shouldn't have (**32.** _____) that! Polluted water has (**33.** _____) many campers serious diseases!''

It was time for some fun. I had (**34.** _____) only three strokes in the pond when a snapping turtle (**35.** _____) past my arm. ''Maybe I should go fishing,'' I thought.

Apply ✦ Think and Write

A Nature Paragraph ✦ Think of a time when you felt Mother Nature double-crossed you. For example: *The wind blew your homework into a puddle.* Write a paragraph about your experience. Try to use some of the verbs from this lesson.

✎ **Remember**
to check the past forms of any irregular verbs you use.

Talk, *pick*, *arrive*, and *instruct* are regular verbs. Think of irregular verbs that are synonyms for those four verbs. Use the past-tense forms of the synonyms in sentences.

8 Using Irregular Verbs

As you know, irregular verbs do not form their past or past participle by adding *-ed*. Many irregular verbs, however, do follow other patterns when forming their principal parts.

Some form the past participle by adding *-n* to the past.

Present	Past	Past Participle
break	broke	(has, have, had) broken
choose	chose	(has, have, had) chosen
freeze	froze	(has, have, had) frozen
speak	spoke	(has, have, had) spoken

Some have the same present and past participle.

Present	Past	Past Participle
become	became	(has, have, had) become
come	came	(has, have, had) come
run	ran	(has, have. had) run

Some have the same past and past participle.

Present	Past	Past Participle
bring	brought	(has, have, had) brought
catch	caught	(has, have, had) caught
say	said	(has, have, had) said
teach	taught	(has, have, had) taught
think	thought	(has, have, had) thought

Summary ◆ Some irregular verbs follow a pattern in the way they are formed.

Guided Practice

Name the form of the verb that completes each sentence. Tell which principal part is needed, the past or the past participle.

1. Nature (bring) us a backyard full of wonders.
2. This delicate creature has (break) its cocoon.
3. A wormlike caterpillar has (become) a silvery butterfly!

Practice

A. Write the three principal parts of each verb below.

    4. become   **5.** catch   **6.** bring   **7.** think   **8.** speak

B. Write each sentence, using the past or past participle of the verb in parentheses ( ).

  9. Who has (teach) this spider such clever weaving skills?

 10. Its glistening wheel-like web has (catch) a careless fly.

 11. Warm temperatures have (bring) the fireflies, or lightning bugs, of summer.

 12. Their cool lights have (break) up the shadows.

 13. With a sudden, soft murmur, a hummingbird (come) by.

 14. Pausing in midflight, it (choose) to sip a rose.

 15. A woodpecker (speak) in a rat-a-tat roar.

 16. Its drill-bit beak (break) through bark and into wood.

 17. A hard-shelled turtle (freeze) at the sound of our voices.

 18. The sightless mole's tunnel (run) beneath the grass.

 19. Whatever (become) of the snake that left this patterned skin behind?

 20. It must have (choose) some other spot to slither in.

 21. The buzzing of bees has (break) the garden's silence.

 22. The bees (teach) each other where to find pollen and nectar in a special ''dance.''

 23. A flying squirrel has (run) up to a roughly-made nest.

 24. Gracefully gliding, it has (come) down the easy way.

C. Use the past or past participle of each verb in a sentence of your own.

    25. say **26.** teach **27.** freeze **28.** choose **29.** come

Apply ✦ Think and Write

A True-False Test ✦ Create ten items for a true-false principal parts test. For example:

1. *Teach* has the same past and past participle.   **T** ____ **F** ____

2. *Burst* is the past participle of *break*.   **T** ____ **F** ____

3. *Catched* is the past of *catch*.   **T** ____ **F** ____

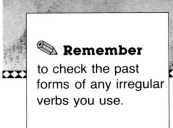

✐ **Remember** to check the past forms of any irregular verbs you use.

USAGE: Irregular Verbs   **131**

9 Using Troublesome Verb Pairs

Certain pairs of verbs are sometimes confused. For example, the verbs *can* and *may* are often used incorrectly. When you ask or tell if someone is able to do something, use *can*. When you ask or give permission, use *may*.

> **Can** you come with me to the Wild Animal Center today?
> **May** visitors help feed the animals at the center?

The verbs *lie* and *lay* have different meanings. *Lie* means "to rest" or "to recline." *Lay* means "to put or place something."

> **Three baby rabbits <u>lie</u> in a box. We <u>lay</u> grass inside it.**

Sit and *set* have different meanings, too. *Sit* means "to rest" or "to stay." *Set* means "to put or place something."

> A hawk with a broken wing <u>sits</u> on a perch.
> I will <u>set</u> this bowl of water in its cage.

Some people also confuse the verbs *teach* and *learn*. *Teach* means "to instruct" or "to show how." *Learn* means "to gain understanding" or "to find out how to do something."

> Workers at the center <u>teach</u> us about wild animals.
> We <u>learn</u> a great deal on our visits to the center.

> **Summary** ◆ Some pairs of verbs are often confused. Use these verbs carefully when you speak and write.

Guided Practice

Tell which verb correctly completes each sentence.

1. (Can, May) the hawk fly well?
2. No, Mrs. Hart has to (sit, set) its wing in a splint.
3. (Can, May) we please watch her? Yes, but (sit, set) down here.
4. (Lie, Lay) the dressing carefully on the wound.
5. Experience (teaches, learns) us how to help wild animals.

Practice

A. Write each sentence. Use the correct verb in parentheses ( ).

   6. (Can, May) I please leave this orphan fawn here?
   7. It's so weak that it just (lies, lays) there.
   8. (Lie, Lay) it down here in this pen.
   9. We did (sit, set) out food for the fawn, but it was too weak to eat.
   10. (Can, May) you help it?
   11. (Sit, Set) here by the fawn.
   12. I'll (teach, learn) you how to feed it with a bottle.
   13. In no time the fawn (teaches, learns) to use the bottle to take its food.
   14. It (can, may) stand on its own legs now.
   15. Soon it will want to (lie, lay) down and sleep.

B. Write each sentence. Use the word *can*, *may*, *sit*, *set*, *lie*, *lay*, *teach*, or *learn* in place of the blank.

   16. After being hit by a car, this raccoon had to ____ how to walk again.
   17. Now it ____ walk well enough to be returned to the wild, where it must exist on its own.
   18. ____ we help you free it?
   19. The helpers ____ the cage down in the woods and open it.
   20. They ____ on a stone and watch the surprised raccoon.
   21. The ring-tailed mammal ____ even climb now!
   22. The frightened opossums ____ on the floor of their cage.
   23. Did their mother ____ them how to play dead?
   24. They're alive and healthy and ____ live on their own in the wild now.
   25. We will ____ them down and watch them scurry off.

Apply ◆ Think and Write

A Friendly Letter ◆ If you had a pet that learned very quickly, what would you teach it? Write a letter to tell a friend about your pet and its training. Use the verbs *lie*, *lay*, *teach*, *learn*, *sit*, and *set* in your letter.

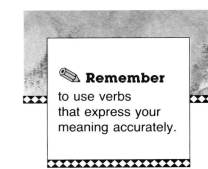

✎ **Remember**
to use verbs that express your meaning accurately.

Prepare for this presentation on prefixes with this preview. In two minutes, think of as many words as you can that begin with *pre-*.

VOCABULARY ♦
Prefixes

A **prefix** is a word part added to the beginning of a word. A prefix changes the meaning of the word to which it is added. Look at the web of words connected to the prefix *un-*. Add *un-* to each word. What happens to the meaning of each?

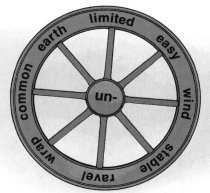

Some common prefixes and their meanings are listed below.

Prefix	Meaning	Examples
dis-	opposite of, away from	dislike, disapprove
mis-	wrong, wrongly	mislead, mistrust
un-	not, opposite of	unhappy, unfold
re-	again, back	reuse, rewind
pre-	before	prehistoric, prepay
im-	not, opposite of	imperfect, impatient
in-	not, opposite of	incapable, invisible

Building Your Vocabulary

Choose prefixes from the chart above to make the words below *opposite* in meaning. You might wish to check the new words you form in a dictionary.

correct	possible	sure	connect
safe	understand	agree	active
honest	patient	complete	reliable

Practice

A. Using words with prefixes can help you write more clearly. Add a prefix from the lesson to one of the underlined words in each sentence. Then rewrite the sentence using the new word.

> **EXAMPLE:** The umpire <u>wrongly called</u> the play.
> **ANSWER:** The umpire *miscalled* the play.

1. Don't drink the water; it is <u>not pure</u>.
2. The measures taken against the raging fire were <u>not effective</u>.
3. We <u>filled again</u> the car's leaking radiator.
4. Ron <u>told again</u> the story of his rescue from the river.
5. Mary <u>wrongly judged</u> her score on the exam.
6. They decided to <u>not regard</u> the warning.
7. Before baking Mom always <u>first heats</u> the oven.
8. The frightened kitten might have been <u>wrongly treated</u>.
9. His letter to me seemed <u>not personal</u>.
10. Did the beagle puppy <u>not obey</u> Lucía's commands?
11. The baggage handlers <u>wrongly placed</u> our suitcases.
12. I was <u>not attentive</u> during the talk, so I remember little.

B. The prefix *pre-* is used with many words. Add *pre-* to the words below. Then use the words you form in sentences of your own.

13. shrunk	**15.** school	**17.** view	**19.** paid
14. teen	**16.** measure	**18.** arrange	**20.** soak

LANGUAGE CORNER • Clipped Words

A *prefab* is a building made of parts that are ready to assemble, or put together. *Prefab* is a short, or clipped, way of saying *prefabricated*.

Be a word detective. Find the longer word for each word below.

math gym van vet bike

lube flu bus gas taxi

How to Revise Sentences with Verbs

In this unit you have learned that verbs are words that express actions or states of being. Your choice of verbs can make a difference in your writing. Choosing exact verbs can make your writing lively and interesting. Read the examples below.

1. The clear brook water moved across the stones.
2. The clear brook water scurried across the stones.

Sentence **1** is a perfectly fine sentence, but the verb *moved* is not very detailed or interesting. The verb *scurried* in sentence **2** gives us more information. It tells us exactly how the water moved. It helps us see the action of the water more clearly.

Replacing the verb *moved* again can completely change the image of the water in the brook.

■ 3. The clear brook water drifted across the stones.

Look for opportunities to use exact verbs in your writing. A carefully chosen verb can make the difference between a dull sentence and an interesting one.

The Grammar Game ◆ Energize with verbs!
◆ Write as many exact verbs as you can for each verb below.
◆ Try to choose new verbs that differ in meaning.
◆ Give yourself one point for each new verb up to a score of 18 points.
◆ Give yourself two points for each one after that.

said	rain	call
look	put	went
got	cook	write
walk	laugh	do

Working Together

Use exact verbs to make your writing lively and interesting while doing activities **A** and **B** with your group.

In Your Group

♦ Remember to listen to each other.
♦ Address people by name.
♦ Encourage others to talk.
♦ Help the group reach agreement.

A. Complete the news headlines below with exact verbs of the group's choice. Then rewrite the headlines, using different verbs to change their meaning.

1. CIRCUS _____ TODAY
2. JANITOR _____ THOUSANDS
3. ACTOR _____ RARE PAINTINGS
4. STUDENTS _____
5. JUDGE _____ TESTIMONY
6. LION CUB _____ IN ZOO
7. COACH _____ DECISION
8. WEATHER _____ PARADE
9. SPACE SHUTTLE _____
10. CRITICS _____ FILM

B. Write the paragraph below, using an exact verb of the group's choice to replace the verb in each sentence.

At noon the tired hikers <u>walked</u> up the last hill. The clouds <u>were</u> heavy and dark in the sky. A soft rain <u>fell</u> briefly down on them. Small animals <u>ran</u> about looking for cover. At the top of the hill, the hungry hikers <u>got</u> their lunch and <u>ate</u> under the trees. Some hikers <u>talked</u> and others <u>slept</u> until the sky cleared.

WRITERS' CORNER ♦ Overused Verbs

Avoid using the same verbs too many times in a piece of writing. Overused verbs can make your writing less effective.

EXAMPLE: **The children ran noisily around the park. The rabbits ran away, and the raccoons ran up a tree. Even the pigeons ran for safety.**

IMPROVED: **The children ran noisily around the park. The rabbits hopped away, and the raccoons scampered up a tree. Even the pigeons rushed for safety.**

Read what you wrote for the Writer's Warm-up. Did you overuse any verbs? If you did, change some of them.

BLUEBONNETS
painting by Porfirio Salinas
Courtesy, Exxon Company, USA.

UNIT
THREE

USING LANGUAGE
TO
CREATE

PART TWO

Literature *Poetry*

A Reason for Writing Creating

CREATIVE
Writing

FINE ARTS ◆ Step into the painting at the left. Walk through the bluebonnets and stand beside the tree. Someone will come down the road to meet you very soon. Who will it be? What adventures will you have together? Write a story about those adventures.

CREATIVE THINKING ◆
A Strategy for Creating

A THOUGHT BALLOON

Creative writing expresses fresh and imaginative ideas. Poets, for example, sometimes imagine that they are something else, such as a mushroom or a seed. In their poems, the poets speak as if they were that other thing. After this lesson you will read poems in which poets speak as something else. Later you will write this kind of poem yourself.

Here is an example, some lines from Lilian Moore's poem "How Frog Feels About It."

This warm wet stone	I uncoil my
is just my	tongue surprise
size.	some flies.

How do you suppose Lilian Moore imagined what a frog would think? How does a poet see things from another point of view?

 ## Learning the Strategy

You may not have to put yourself in a frog's place very often. However, you do often need to imagine the points of view of other people. One way to put yourself in someone else's place is to think about experiences you have had. For example, suppose your best friend lost a swimming race. Have you ever lost a contest you wanted to win? How might your experience help you know what to say to your friend?

Understanding other viewpoints is also an important reading skill. Suppose you are reading a book about a girl who went west in a covered wagon. What experiences of your own can help you understand this girl who lived over a hundred years ago?

Making a thought balloon is a strategy that can help you think from another person's point of view. That same strategy can help you imagine the point of view of an object or an animal. For example, what about an eagle soaring overhead? What is it thinking? This thought balloon shows one possibility. What others can you imagine?

> *My, it's crowded up here these days. I wish the air-traffic controllers would keep those big, shiny birds out of my lane!*

an eagle

Using the Strategy

A. Think of an article of clothing in your closet. What if it could think? Imagine its point of view about the other clothes in the closet. Imagine its point of view about the places you go when you wear it. Imagine its point of view about *you*! Make a balloon to show its thoughts.

B. In each of the poems that follow in this unit, the poet writes from the point of view of a thing. There are poems about mushrooms, seeds, a frog, the prairie, and a little swamp fish. Choose one of these and make a thought balloon for it. Then read the poem to find out what ideas the poet had about it.

Applying the Strategy

♦ How is making a thought balloon for an animal or thing different from making a thought balloon for a person?

♦ Describe one time when you needed to understand someone else's point of view.

Poets may talk to us in many voices. They sometimes put on masks to speak as other things. In these poems, the poets pretend to be mushrooms, a prairie, and other things that are usually silent. Listen to what they say in their strange, new voices.

How Frog Feels About It

I'm green and
gold
in this bright sun.

This warm wet stone
is just my
size.

I uncoil my
tongue   surprise
some flies.

Green and gold
and still as stone
I sit

listening.

Grass whispers   a
warning and I
leap

into the glistening
muck of the
pond.

Sunned
Sated
Safe

Why should I want to be kissed?
Why should I want to be a prince?

— Lilian Moore

Trees: THE SEEDS

We are
given light wings,
parachutes, downy legs
that we may be carried aloft
by wind

and drop
where some kind mouse
will bury us in earth;
some squirrel will forget we are food,
leave us

to sprout
green shoots, to weave
rootlets, that we may eat
and drink and grow in time our own
small seeds

— *Myra Cohn Livingston*

from MUSHROOMS

So many of us!
So many of us!

We are shelves, we are
Tables, we are meek,
We are edible.

Nudgers and shovers
In spite of ourselves
Our kind multiplies.

We shall by morning
Inherit the earth.
Our foot's in the door.

— *Sylvia Plath*

from Cornhuskers

I am the prairie, mother of men, waiting.
They are mine, the threshing crews, eating beefsteak, the farmboys driv-
    ing steers to the railroad cattle pens.
They are mine, the crowds of people at a Fourth of July basket picnic,
    listening to a lawyer read the Declaration of Independence, watch-
    ing the pinwheels and Roman candles at night, the young men and
    women two by two hunting the bypaths and kissing-bridges.
They are mine, the horses looking over a fence in the frost of late Octo-
    ber saying good morning to the horses hauling wagons of rutabaga
    to market.
They are mine, the old zigzag rail fences, the new barbwire.

— *Carl Sandburg*

from My Song Is a Piece of Jade

I am the little fish
of the swamp grass
I sigh
How I long to sing

O Most High and Great Prince of the Turtles
I beg you
I want to be like my brothers
    the locust
    the hornet
    the bee

How precious their songs are
and the song
of the green frog
sitting in the sun
Listen!
How he is singing in his house
on the lentil leaf

I am gold
I am a little golden fish
but I have no song

The turtledove has
bells of gold
in his throat

I cry out!

O God of all creatures
I want to speak
I want to sing
too

    — adapted by Toni de Gerez

Soy el pescadito
de la ciénaga
Suspiro
quisiera cantar

¡Oh!
Gran Señor y Alto Príncipe de las Tortugas
yo te suplico
quisiera ser como mis hermanas
    la cigarra
    la avispa
    la abeja

qué preciosas son sus canciones
y también
el canto de la rana verde
que está tomando el sol
¡Escucha!
Cómo canta en su casa
sobre la hoja de lenteja

Soy el pescadito
soy de oro
pero no puedo cantar

La tórtola tiene
campanillas de oro
en su garganta

¡Lloro!

¡Oh!
dios de las criaturas
quisiera hablar
quisiera cantar

Reader's Response

Which poem was the most interesting to you? Explain why.

Poetry

 ## Responding to Literature

1. Choose one of the poems to read aloud. Think about what the subject of the poem is saying to us. When you read aloud, use your voice to help convey the message. Allow your poem's subject to "speak" to the class.

2. Work with a partner to "talk back" to the speaker in one of the poems. Select a poem. Then compose a short dialogue. Begin by directing a question to the poem's speaker. One of you may ask questions, and the other may answer as the speaker in the poem. Share your dialogue with the class.

3. Find a mask poem from this collection or from another book. As a class, decide on one poem to prepare as a choral reading. Select which lines could be read together and which could be read as separate voices. After practicing, invite another class to hear your poem.

 ## Writing to Learn

Think and Create ◆ Sketch the frog from "How Frog Feels About It" by Lilian Moore. Draw a thought balloon above the frog.

Thought Balloon

Write ◆ Fill the thought balloon with the frog's words. Tell what the frog might have said if a princess had picked him up and carried him to a castle.

What clue in the way the following words are written tells you how a robot talks? "Hold   your   hand   out.   Close   your   hand   now.   Ro   bot   hand   shake."

SPEAKING AND LISTENING ♦
Reading Poetry Aloud

Every poem waits patiently on a page for a voice to speak it. Every poem is waiting to be heard. If *you* are that voice, you will want to look closely at the poem for clues to its sounds, its rhythms, and its phrasing. If you do look closely and carefully, you will find that the poet has left many clues to how the poem should be said.

These guidelines will help you find the poet's clues and use them in your reading and listening. Your own imagination and feelings for the poem will do the rest.

Reading a Poem Aloud	1. Select a poem you like for oral reading. 2. Practice reading it silently and then aloud until you know it well. 3. Follow the poet's clues to the poem's sounds, rhythms, complete thoughts, and phrasing. The poem's shape on the page and the length of its lines are visual clues you will want to note. Other clues are the pauses at commas, semicolons, and between verses. Sometimes, large spaces between words indicate pauses as well. 4. Consider how your own imagination and feeling for the poem can help you read it with expression. Think about which words you would like to emphasize or where you might raise or lower your voice to reflect a change of feeling. 5. Keep your own images for the poem in mind as you are speaking. 6. Speak clearly in an expressive, but natural, voice.
Being an Active Listener	1. Create your own images for the poem as you listen. 2. Listen for the poet's clues to imagery and sound.

Summary ♦ Choose a poem you like and practice reading it aloud. Use the poet's clues to complete thoughts, sounds, and phrasing, as well as your own ideas and imagination. Use your voice expressively as you speak.

Guided Practice

Speak the words below, using your voice to fit the thing you've become. The clues will help you speak with expression. Commas and large spaces indicate pauses; stress the words in *italics*.

1. "Here in my home it's warm and wet, dark and dreary, slimy and still—good earthworm weather!" (earthworm)
2. "I'm tired and old, but remember *this*: If you steal my gold, you'll feel the *hissssss* of hot dragon breath   behind you." (dragon)

Practice

A. Work with a partner to present an oral reading of the poem "Mushrooms" on page 143. Make your own copy of the poem to mark with notes for reading. Read the poem aloud, picturing the images and looking for clues to sound, rhythm, and phrasing. Discuss these questions as you mark your copy.

3. What images and mood does this poem convey to you?
4. What are the poem's complete thoughts? Which words would you like to stress in each one? Where will you pause?
5. How will you say the lines that end with exclamation marks?
6. Compare the meek mushrooms at the beginning of the poem with the strong, teeming mushrooms at the end. How can you use your voice to show the mushrooms' growing strength?

Use your notes to practice reading the poem. Then take turns reading it aloud and listening. How are your readings different?

B. One way to know a poem is to put it into your own words. Choose a poem on pages 142–144 to tell to a small group. You may want to write your story of the poem before telling it. Be sure to tell your story in the voice of the thing that is speaking.

Apply • Think and Write

Dictionary of Knowledge ◆ Read about Carl Sandburg. Copy the poem in the entry and practice reading it aloud. When you are ready, read the poem to a friend or relative.

✎ **Remember**
to use the poet's clues and your own voice and imagination to read poetry aloud.

◆ GETTING ◆
STARTED

Do you remember the tongue twisters "Peter Piper picked a peck of pickled peppers" and "She sells seashells by the seashore"? Say them as fast as you can.

WRITING ◆
Poets Use Sound

In poetry, as in music, sounds blend together to produce many different moods and effects. Some sounds relax us and are pleasant, like the rhymes poets often use. Other sound wake us up and may even be jarring. Listen for the sounds in this poem.

Living Tenderly

My body a rounded stone
with a pattern of smooth seams.
My head a short snake,
retractive, projective.
My legs come out of their sleeves
or shrink within,
and so does my chin.
My eyelids are quick clamps.

My back is my roof.
I am always at home.
I travel where my house walks.
It is a smooth stone.
It floats within the lake,
or rests in the dust.
My flesh lives tenderly
inside its bone.

—May Swenson

Read the first two lines aloud. Listen to how calm and quiet they seem, yet strong as a turtle's shell. Next read the third and fourth lines. Notice how the words imitate the way a turtle pops its head in and out in jerky movements. A few lines later, notice how the words *quick clamps* mimic the movements of a turtle's eyelids.

Using words to imitate sounds is known as onomatopoeia, from a Greek word meaning "name-making." Some examples of onomatopoeia are *hiss, zoom*, and *scratch*. These words imitate natural sounds.

Working Together

In a poem the poet's voice may not be a person's voice. It may be the voice of something else — the wind or a river, for example. Keep this in mind as your group does activities **A** and **B**.

A. A choral reading is an oral reading with many voices. Plan a choral reading of "River's Song." Ask a volunteer to copy the poem on a large sheet of chart paper or on the chalkboard. Then decide how to divide the poem into parts for speaking. The following example shows how the first verse can be spoken by two groups of voices.

> **GROUP 1:** Here I am where you see me
> Strong and brown.
> **GROUP 2:** Still, I am far away
> Where yesterday I was.

What other lines can these two groups speak? Will you assign any parts for a solo, or single, voice? What lines can the whole group say together? Make sure all lines are assigned.

B. When the parts of the poem have been assigned (activity **A**), practice reading the poem. Try to imagine yourself as actually being the river. After reading, discuss ways in which the reading might be improved. You may wish to try several different ways to arrange your choral reading.

In Your Group

- Make sure everyone understands the directions.
- Use people's names during a group discussion.
- Remind group members to listen carefully.
- Show appreciation for everyone's contribution.

THESAURUS CORNER • Word Choice

Look up the verb **go** in the Thesaurus. Use four of its synonyms in four sentences in which a glacier is speaking about itself. Before beginning to write, you may want to find out more about glaciers in your science book or an encyclopedia. By doing so, your information will be accurate and your use of the synonyms will be appropriate.

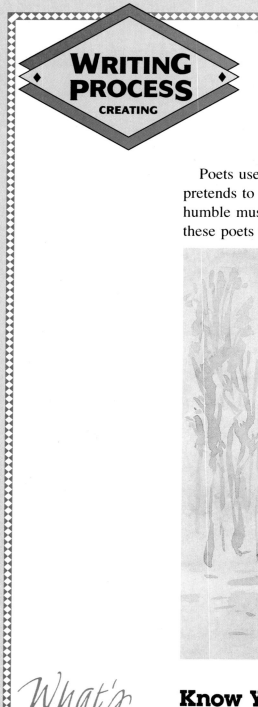

Writing a Poem

Poets use the mask to speak as animals and things. Lilian Moore pretends to be a frog, green and gold. Sylvia Plath speaks as the humble mushroom. Carl Sandburg speaks as the prairie. All of these poets use the mask to give voice to things that cannot speak.

Know Your Purpose and Audience

In this lesson you will write a poem. Your purpose will be to express an original or imaginative viewpoint. You will use the mask to write as if you were an object.

Your audience will be your classmates. Later you and your classmates can have a poetry party or make poetry posters.

What's
MY PURPOSE

Who's
MY AUDIENCE

1 Prewriting

First decide on a topic, an object you will write about. Then gather ideas that will help you write your poem.

Choose Your Topic ♦ When poets look for topics, they often reflect on their own experiences. You can do this, too. Choose a topic that you like best of all.

Think About It	Talk About It
Choose one event you remember best. Then list objects you associate with that event. From a football game, you might remember the goal posts, the football, or band instruments. List as many as you can. Then decide which object it would be most fun to be.	Brainstorm with classmates about special school days you remember. Make a big list on the chalkboard. Perhaps you remember a football game, a school picnic, or a class play. Then pick an event. What objects do you associate with that event?

Topic Ideas

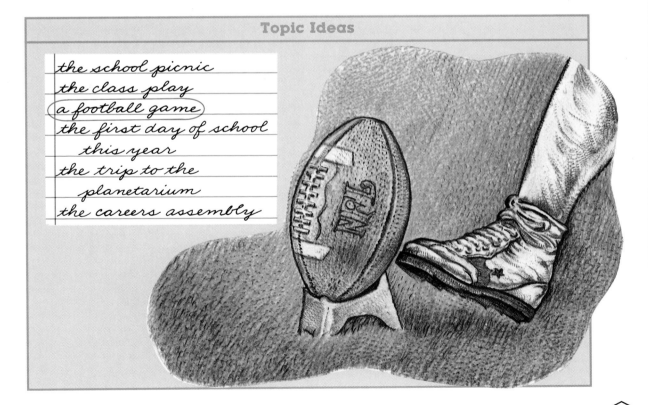

the school picnic
the class play
a football game
the first day of school
    this year
the trip to the
    planetarium
the careers assembly

Choose Your Strategy ◆ Here are two idea-gathering strategies. Read both of those strategies. Then decide which strategy you prefer to use.

PREWRITING IDEAS

CHOICE ONE

Presto Change-o   Model

"Presto change-o" are the words a magician says to turn one thing into another. Pretend you are a magician. Turn yourself into the object you have chosen to be, such as a football. Then use the words *I* and *me* to tell a partner about the event you were a part of, such as a football game. Make notes about what you say.

CHOICE TWO

A Thought Balloon   Model

Close your eyes and pretend you are the object you chose, such as a pom-pom or the tug-of-war rope. Imagine the event, such as the football game or the picnic, from the object's point of view. Sketch the object and make a thought balloon for it. Write the object's thoughts in the balloon. If you like, make a lot of thought balloons.

> *Listen to how loudly the fans are cheering.*

> *Sometimes I feel like a bird soaring through the air.*

> *Look out! You're going to fumble me!*

> *I get kicked around a lot.*

2 Writing

Review your prewriting notes. Then read the poems in this unit to see how poets begin. Look at these two opening lines, the first by Lilian Moore and the second by Sylvia Plath.

- ◆ Statement: I'm green and gold in this bright sun.
- ◆ Exclamation: So many of us!

Remember that sound is an essential part of poetry. As you write, consider trying to use onomatopoeia or alliteration. The main thing is to have fun as you write. Play with your words. Shift lines around. Decide what sounds please *you*.

Sample First Draft ◆

I am kicked hard,

Thrown far.

Like a wingless bird, I soar

through the air.

thump, I'm caught.

all brown and leathery.

I am fumbled

into the dust and dirt,

I am captered by the other side,

held tightly in strong arms.

Someone runs with me

into the end zone.

Cheers! Cheers! Cheers!

3 Revising

After you have done a first draft of your poem, you may want to polish it. Here is an idea to help you revise.

REVISING IDEA

FIRST   Read to Yourself

As you read, review your purpose. Have you written a poem that expresses an original or imaginative viewpoint? Consider your audience. Will your classmates enjoy your poem? Which part do *you* like best? Try to explain to yourself why you like it.

Focus: Have you used the mask? Have you spoken as if you were the object your poem is about?

THEN   Share with a Partner

Choose a partner to be your first audience. First read your poem aloud to your partner. Then sit side by side and let your partner read along silently as you work together. These guidelines may help you and your partner.

The Writer

Guidelines: Read your poem with expression. Then ask for your partner's ideas.

Sample questions:
- I'm trying to use alliteration. Can you help me?
- **Focus question:** Is the mask clear? Can you tell I'm speaking as a _____?

The Writer's Partner

Guidelines: Listen carefully. If you see a way to improve the poem, offer it politely as a suggestion.

Sample responses:
- For alliteration you could use the word _____ here.
- You've really captured the point of view of a _____. Maybe you could tell how it felt when _____.

Revising Model ♦ Here is a poem the writer is revising. Notice the revising marks and changes in blue.

Revising Marks

cross out ——
add ∧
move ⟳

The writer's partner asked who or what is speaking here.

Fumbled, feeble, and *fingers* are examples of alliteration.

Cradled is a more exact and poetic verb than *held*.

Sprints is more vivid and adds alliteration with *someone*.

The long *o* sounds in *goalposts* echo the sound in *zone*.

I am a football,
I am kicked hard,
        Thrown far.
Like a wingless bird, I soar
        through the air.
thump, I'm caught.
All brown and leathery.
I am fumbled by feeble fingers
        into the dust and dirt,
I am captered by the other side,
        cradled
        held tightly in strong arms.
        sprints
Someone runs with me
        through the goalposts
        into the end zone.
Cheers! Cheers! Cheers!

Read the poem above with all the writer's changes. Then revise your own poem.

Grammar Check ♦ Exact verbs can add spice to your writing.

Word Choice ♦ Are you searching for a special word, one with a precise meaning or a certain beginning sound? A thesaurus is a good place to look.

Revising Checklist

☐ **Purpose:** Have I written a poem that expresses an original or imaginative viewpoint?

☐ **Audience:** Will my classmates enjoy my poem?

☐ **Focus:** Did I use the mask? Did I speak as if I were an object?

4 Proofreading

Poets do not always follow strict writing rules. They often use punctuation and capitalization and indenting for different effects. Look at the poems in this book as models. Is your spelling correct? Have you used punctuation and capitalization correctly?

Proofreading Model ◆ Here is the draft poem about the football. The writer has added proofreading changes in red.

Proofreading Marks

capital letter	=
small letter	/
check spelling	⬭

I am a football,
I am kicked hard,
    Thrown far.
Like a wingless bird, I soar
    through the air.
thump! I'm caught.
All brown and leathery.
I am fumbled by feeble fingers
    into the dust and dirt,
    captured
I am captered by the other side,
    cradled
    held tightly in strong arms.
    sprints
Someone runs with me
    through the goalposts
    into the end zone.
Cheers! Cheers! Cheers!

Proofreading Checklist

- ☐ Did I spell words correctly?
- ☐ Did I use capital letters correctly?
- ☐ Did I use correct marks at the end of sentences?
- ☐ Did I use my best handwriting?

PROOFREADING IDEA

Handwriting Check

Make sure that your handwriting is neat and legible. Have you dotted your *i*'s and crossed your *t*'s? Have you left space between words? Are the ends of words written as clearly as the beginnings?

Now proofread your poem and make a neat copy. Do not forget to give your poem a title.

5 Publishing

To share your poem with others, try one of these ideas.

Wingless Flight

I am a football, all brown and leathery.
I am kicked hard,
    thrown far.
Like a wingless bird, I soar
    through the air.
Thump! I'm caught.
Fumbled by feeble fingers
    into the dust and dirt,
I am captured by the other side,
    cradled tightly in strong arms.
Someone sprints with me
    through the goalposts
    into the end zone.
Cheers! Cheers! Cheers!

PUBLISHING IDEAS

Share Aloud	Share in Writing
Have a poetry party with classmates. First practice, using all you have learned about reading poetry aloud. Then take turns reading your poems to each other. If possible, dress like the objects in your poems. After you read, ask your listeners to suggest other things your object might say.	Make a poetry poster. Copy your poem in large letters and attach it to a colorful piece of posterboard. Illustrate your poster with magazine pictures, photographs, or your own drawings. Then you and your classmates can choose five of the posters to display in your school. Write your choices on voting ballots.

Writing Across the Curriculum   Science

It can be interesting and useful to take a different point of view. In this unit you wrote a poem from the point of view of an object. Scientists also like to adopt different viewpoints.

Writing to Learn

Think and Imagine ◆ Astronauts were the first to see the earth from space. Before spaceflights, no one knew that the earth looked like a blue marble from above. With their special viewpoints, astronauts have had ideas about everything from agriculture to world peace. Imagine that you are an astronaut. Write a thought balloon telling your ideas as you look down on the earth.

Thought Balloon

Write ◆ Consider your thought balloon. Then explain how you think seeing the earth from space could help a scientist.

Writing in Your Journal

In the Writer's Warm-up you wrote about nature. Then you read nature poems. Look over the poems you read. Which gave you the clearest picture? Find the words that helped you see that picture. Then, in your journal, write about a special day you spent outdoors.

BOOKS TO ENJOY

Read More About It

Wind Song *by Carl Sandburg*
The poems in *Wind Song* express Sandburg's search
for meaning in history and his enthusiasm for the
American land and people.

What a Wonderful Bird the Frog Are
edited by Myra Cohn Livingston
Many poems are meant to make us laugh. As proof,
a well-known American poet offers us this
anthology.

Dogs & Dragons, Trees & Dreams
by Karla Kuskin
Karla Kuskin wrote all these poems and drew the
pictures. All through the book she talks to her
readers in side notes about writing poetry.

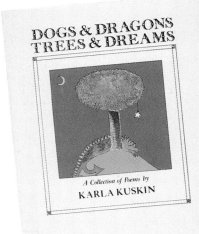

Book Report Idea Tape Recording

The best way to share poetry is
by reading aloud. A book report
on tape is an ideal way to tell
about a collection of poetry.

Record Your Poems
Practice the poems until you can
read them clearly and
comfortably. You will want to
accent some words and to pause
after others. Begin your recording
with one poem. Then give the
title and author and tell what you
liked about the poetry. End your
recording by reading more poems.

UNIT REVIEW

Unit 3

Verbs *pages 116–133*

A. Write each of the following sentences. Draw one line under the linking verb. Draw two lines under the words that the verb connects.

1. The weather is chilly.
2. Gerry looks uncomfortable.
3. The snow feels cold.
4. I am warm in my overcoat.
5. This green apple tastes sour.
6. It also smells strange.
7. The day becomes even colder.
8. Jamie is fond of winter.
9. She appears pleased.
10. However, Gerry is unhappy.
11. He feels chilly.
12. Gerry is happiest in the summertime.
13. Summer smells wonderful.
14. It becomes a holiday for him.
15. He looks relaxed.
16. We are happy.

B. Write the following sentences. Underline the helping verbs once. Underline the main verbs twice.

17. We are rehearsing for the class play.
18. Six students have written the script.
19. The play will be shown to all the students in the school.
20. Tim has learned all his lines.
21. He will make a fine hero.
22. Mary should work harder during rehearsals.
23. She might act her role with greater emotion.
24. The stagehands have attended our last two rehearsals.
25. They are building the set for the play.
26. Ms. Torres has trained all of the actors well.
27. The play will open next week.
28. My parents and my sister are coming.

C. Write the direct object in each sentence.

29. The dog wagged its tail.
30. The batter hit the ball into left field.
31. The mother cat held the kitten by its neck.
32. Snow covered the rusty, old car.
33. Lucy loves games.
34. The little girl lost her mittens.
35. Bobbie fed his pet skunk.
36. The carpenter sawed the board in half.
37. Mother cooked the meatballs.
38. The nurse cradled the baby in her arms.

D. Write the past tense and the future tense of each verb.

39. push
40. provide
41. watch
42. laugh
43. join
44. melt
45. measure
46. smile
47. roll
48. jump
49. move
50. count

E. Write the three principal parts of each verb. Use the helping verb *has* with each past participle.

51.	ask	**62.**	hurry
52.	grow	**63.**	stop
53.	begin	**64.**	bring
54.	choose	**65.**	carry
55.	drag	**66.**	swim
56.	laugh	**67.**	write
57.	know	**68.**	look
58.	think	**69.**	sing
59.	act	**70.**	fly
60.	give	**71.**	take
61.	finish	**72.**	run

F. Write each sentence. Use the correct verb in parentheses ( ).

73. Will you (learn, teach) me to do a swan dive?

74. (Lie, Lay) that heavy package on the shelf.

75. I will (set, sit) it down here for you.

76. (Can, May) you solve this math problem?

77. Please do not (lie, lay) in the sun too long.

78. (Can, May) I go with you to the rock concert?

79. (Sit, Set) down next to Frank.

80. I will (learn, teach) my dog a new trick.

81. My dog (teaches, learns) new tricks quickly.

82. Will you (sit, set) the forks to the right of the plates?

83. Did you (lie, lay) these books here?

84. (May, Can) I give you my frank opinion?

Prefixes   *pages 134–135*

G. Write a word with a prefix for each group of words.

85. opposite of honorable

86. discover again

87. not exact

88. recorded before

89. understand wrongly

90. opposite of polite

91. opposite of like

92. not correct

93. not visible

94. opposite of fold

95. opposite of appear

96. not opened

97. opposite of wrap

98. sharpen again

99. opposite of patience

100. opposite of lock

101. check again

Proofreading

H. Proofread each sentence for an error in capitalization or punctuation. Write the correct form for each error.

102. Sallys plan included shopping and then seeing a movie.

103. "I really would like to see that movie!" exclaimed pat.

104. "May I please come with you," asked her sister.

105. "The movie is playing at the newton theater," said Sally.

106. "Good — that theaters seats are the most comfortable," said Pat.

107. "saturday night is fun!" Sally exclaimed.

LANGUAGE PUZZLERS

A Verb Square

A verb square is a set of verbs that read the same from left to right and from top to bottom. Here is a five-letter verb square.

```
d a r e d
a t o n e
r o a s t
e n s u e
d e t e r
```

Unscramble each underlined set of letters to make a verb. Then use the clues to make a four-letter verb square. (Hint: The first verb begins with a vowel.)

1. past tense of <u>esu</u>   **3.** present tense of <u>edesa</u>
2. present tense of <u>tyadse</u>   **4.** past tense of <u>yde</u>

Secret Messages

Here is a system that can be used to send secret messages. First, a sentence is broken into five-letter groups.

The letter was delivered to the wrong girl.
Thele / tterw / asdel / ivere / dtoth / ewron / ggirl.

Then each group is written backward, without punctuation or capitalization.

eleht wrett ledsa erevi htotd norwe lrigg

Write the message hidden in the four sentences below.

sumew ttegt teleh rfret rehmo
ltaht rette revsi opmiy tnatr
adnil tlliw motyr worro
evahi gsida fesiu rehro

Unit 3 Extra Practice

1 Writing with Verbs

p. 116

A. Write the sentences. Underline each verb.

1. An architect draws the plans for a house.
2. She wants a beautiful house.
3. Workers pour a concrete foundation.
4. Trucks bring lumber to the house site.
5. Carpenters lay long, thick beams across the foundation.
6. A power saw is a useful tool at this time.
7. The builders follow the architect's plans.
8. They enjoy their work very much.
9. Carpenters build the frame of a house.
10. They construct each wall separately.
11. Then the workers raise the walls into place.
12. A steel beam supports the second floor of the house.
13. This beam is very strong.
14. Next the carpenters install windows and doors.
15. They also cover the inside walls with plasterboard.
16. Roofers nail shingles on the roof.
17. The shingles protect the wooden part of the roof.
18. The outer walls of this house are brick.

B. Write the verb in each sentence. Then write *action verb* or *state-of-being verb* after the verb.

19. That worker was a bricklayer.
20. She built the fireplace, chimney, and front steps.
21. The plumbers were here last week.
22. They connected the pipes for the kitchen and bathrooms.
23. The plumbers are also responsible for the heating system.
24. An electrician is in the house now.
25. He brought a truckload of electrical cable and light fixtures with him.
26. The painters, paperhangers, and carpet installers arrive next week.
27. Then the lucky owners move into the house.
28. They love their new home already!

2 Linking Verbs

p. 118

A. Write the sentences. Underline each linking verb.

1. Jody is a gardener.
2. Her plants look healthy.
3. That flower is a rose.
4. The garden was large.
5. The eggplants were purple.
6. Jody's garden is a sunny spot.
7. The land seems quite flat.
8. The soil appears rich and dark.
9. Those tomatoes are so red!
10. The tomato plants smell strong.
11. That tool is a hoe.
12. It was very useful.
13. Those vegetables are squashes.
14. They taste delicious with onions.
15. The pumpkins finally appear ripe.
16. The watering cans look heavy.
17. They were very full.
18. These peppers become red in October.
19. The herbs smell pleasant.
20. The garden feels especially peaceful in the evening.

B. Write each sentence. Draw one line under the linking verb. Draw two lines under the words that the verb connects.

EXAMPLE: The large orange flower is a zinnia.
ANSWER: The large orange <u>flower</u> <u>is</u> a <u>zinnia</u>.

21. These yellow roses smell so sweet.
22. Their petals feel very soft.
23. The marigolds appear dry now.
24. Yellow and white daisies are my favorite flowers.
25. That bench in the garden looks comfortable.
26. This garden becomes beautiful in the spring.
27. Those white insects are mealybugs.
28. Flowers taste great to them.
29. The bees were busy earlier.
30. I am always happy in the garden.

3 Main Verbs and Helping Verbs *p. 120*

A. Write the sentences below. Underline the helping verbs once and the main verbs twice.

1. The batter is not hitting the ball.
2. The crowd has left the stadium.
3. I must have lost my ticket.
4. Reggie did play yesterday.
5. The runner will steal second base.
6. The pitcher is being replaced.
7. Our team did not score in the first inning.
8. The ball was hit over the fence.
9. Dominic had walked the first batter.
10. The fans are walking on the field.
11. The ball has bounced into the stands.
12. The batter should have swung.
13. A pinch hitter may bat for the catcher.
14. The game was not shown on television.
15. The Little League game is being postponed.
16. The rain had started in the second inning.

B. Write the verbs in the sentences. Then write *MV* if the sentence has a main verb but no helping verb. Write *HV +
MV* if the sentence has both a helping verb and a main verb.

EXAMPLE: The umpire has the ball.
 ANSWER: has, MV

17. The umpire has called the pitch a strike.
18. I am playing third base.
19. The game is in extra innings.
20. The manager would not agree with the umpire.
21. The scoring cards are in the stands.
22. The umpire always has the final word.
23. Our local newspaper does not cover sports.
24. Our team could play in a championship game.
25. We must win two more games.
26. Jo Ann has the new uniforms.
27. You must watch the World Series.
28. We can learn much from professional ballplayers.

4 Verbs with Direct Objects   *p. 122*

A. Write the direct object in each sentence. Tell whether it answers the question *whom* or *what*.

1. Luisa was watching a television news program.
2. Much of Center City has lost its electricity.
3. Luisa called her older brother into the room.
4. They watched the news report.
5. Thick ice covered the trees.
6. A strong wind broke a large branch.
7. The falling branch tore an electrical wire.
8. The house suddenly lost its power.
9. The blackout worried Mother.
10. Mother made a call to the power company.
11. The power company received many calls.
12. The company sent some workers.
13. The workers repaired many wires.
14. By now the house had lost its heat.
15. Luisa built a big fire.
16. She lit candles, too.
17. Mother telephoned the neighbors.
18. They had also lost their electricity.
19. The family cooked dinner over the fire.
20. Father watched the street from time to time.

B. Write the sentences. Underline each action verb once and each direct object twice.

21. He did not see any lights yet.
22. Mother piled more wood on the fire.
23. Luisa found a radio with batteries.
24. She heard her favorite program.
25. The family invited some friends to the house.
26. Everyone sang songs by the firelight.
27. Mother and Father told long funny stories.
28. Luisa suddenly noticed the television.
29. She saw a reporter on the screen.
30. The reporter at the TV station announced the end of the blackout.

5 Tenses of Verbs

p. 124

A. Write the verb in each sentence. Then write *present tense*, *past tense*, or *future tense* after the verb.

1. A huge sheet of ice covers the Antarctic continent.
2. The scientists study this icy glacier.
3. During the Ice Age, glaciers moved over North America.
4. These glaciers melted long ago.
5. The scientists will measure a glacier.
6. I shall join the scientists next week.
7. The scientists drilled a deep hole in the glacier.
8. They measured the ice.
9. The edges of the glacier touch the ocean.
10. Giant chunks of ice form icebergs.
11. These icebergs will float in the ocean.
12. A large iceberg weighs more than one million metric tons.
13. The biggest ones tower four hundred feet above the ocean's surface.
14. Winds and ocean currents move the mountains of ice away from Antarctica.
15. In time the icebergs will reach warmer waters.
16. Then they will melt.
17. In northern waters, icebergs cause problems for sailors.
18. The famous ship *Titanic* rammed an iceberg in 1912.
19. Water poured into the ship.
20. Many people died in the tragedy.
21. Later the United States and England formed the International Ice Patrol.
22. Today the Coast Guard watches large icebergs.
23. Their work will prevent many tragedies in the future.

B. Write the past tense and future tense of each verb below. Use *will* with the future tense.

24. laugh
25. believe
26. show
27. invite
28. push
29. pour
30. count
31. watch
32. smile
33. crash

C. Write the verb in each sentence. Write *present tense*, *past tense*, or *future tense* to describe the verb.

34. Years ago many ships sailed into South Street Seaport.
35. This section of lower Manhattan bustled with activity.
36. Now the area looks quite different.
37. Soon it will thrive again.
38. The Fulton Fish Market still stands in the same place.
39. Workers restored many of the old buildings.
40. Merchants opened new shops and restaurants.
41. Other businesses will open there, too.
42. Many of the Tall Ships docked there for the Bicentennial celebration.
43. Sightseers flock to the area.

6 Principal Parts of Verbs   *p. 126*

A. Write the three principal parts of each verb. Use the helping verb *has* with each past participle.

1. smile   **6.** pass
2. drag   **7.** snap
3. try   **8.** plant
4. serve   **9.** supply
5. walk   **10.** subtract

B. Write the verb in each sentence. Then write *present*, *past*, or *past participle* to show which principal part of the verb was used.

11. My brothers and I raise pigeons.
12. People originally raised pigeons for food.
13. We have raised pigeons for three years.
14. Pigeons race great distances.
15. The swift birds cover about 500 miles a day.
16. Owners have timed pigeons at speeds of eighty miles per hour.
17. The racers travel around storms and bad weather.
18. Homing pigeons always hurry back to their homes.
19. Many amazing stories have resulted.
20. One homing pigeon returned to China from France!

C. Write the verb in each sentence. Then write *present*, *past*, or *past participle* to show which principal part of the verb was used.

    21. Pigeons have served as messengers throughout history.
    22. In Greek mythology a pigeon acted as a guide for Jason and the Argonauts.
    23. Ancient Egyptians carried the birds aboard their ships.
    24. They communicated with their homeland by pigeon.
    25. Soldiers have used pigeons during times of war.
    26. Some Army pigeons have received medals for bravery!
    27. Pigeon owners describe their pets as loyal.
    28. Pigeons provide much pleasure for their owners.

D. Write the past and past participle of each verb. Use the helping verb *has* with each past participle.

    29. fix   **33.** cry
    30. arrive   **34.** drop
    31. drip   **35.** trot
    32. bury   **36.** hurry

7 Using Irregular Verbs   *p. 128*

A. Write each sentence, using the past or the past participle of the verb in parentheses ( ).

    1. At last our vacation had (begin).
    2. The ride to our campsite (take) a long time.
    3. It (grow) darker and darker.
    4. We finally (begin) to unpack.
    5. Mother had (give) everyone a job to do.
    6. Father and I (take) the tent to the campsite.
    7. We (sing) our favorite songs.
    8. No one (know) the tent poles were still at home.
    9. By now it had (grow) even darker.
    10. Finally we (throw) the tent over a rope between two trees.
    11. A big bat (fly) overhead.
    12. Had it (fly) into our tent?
    13. We all (go) into the tent.
    14. Meanwhile our dog had (eat) all our sandwiches!

B. Write each sentence, using the past or the past participle of the verb in parentheses ( ).

15. Then the rain (begin).
16. The wind (blow) harder and harder.
17. Soon rainwater had (begin) to leak into the tent.
18. We (do) the only possible thing.
19. We (go) to a motel for the night.

C. Write the three principal parts of the verbs below.

20. do   **22.** fly   **24.** throw   **26.** blow   **28.** go
21. eat   **23.** ring   **25.** drink   **27.** know   **29.** write

D. Complete each sentence by writing the past or past participle of the verb in parentheses ( ).

30. My pen pal had (write) me an invitation from camp.
31. I (take) the invitation to my parents.
32. They (know) how much I wanted to go.
33. Dana and I have (do) so many things together.
34. He had (fly) here to see me many times.
35. My trip (begin) well.
36. After takeoff I (drink) some orange juice.
37. After I had (eat) lunch, I fell asleep.
38. From the airport we (go) to Dana's farm.

8 Using Irregular Verbs
p. 130

A. Write the three principal parts of the underlined verbs.

1. We brought a personal computer home.
2. I thought it would be difficult to use.
3. My parents run their business with it.
4. The computer taught French to my sister.
5. We chose programs that were easy to use.
6. I caught my brother playing action games on it.
7. Some computers speak with a funny voice.
8. They come with many exciting games.
9. Father says that computers will make writing easier.
10. They have become an important part of our lives.

B. Write the past and past participle of each verb.

11. freeze   **13.** break   **15.** say   **17.** catch   **19.** become
12. speak   **14.** think   **16.** run   **18.** teach   **20.** choose

C. Write the past or past participle of the verb in parentheses ( ) to complete each sentence. Then label the principal part you used.

21. Many English words have (come) from foreign languages.
22. The word *typhoon* (come) from the Chinese word for "a great wind."
23. Immigrants from Hamburg (teach) Americans about one food.
24. This food (become) the American hamburger.
25. Germans from Frankfurt (bring) frankfurters to America.
26. Some experts have (say) that the word *mouse* comes from an early word for "steal."
27. Long ago a Frenchman (think) a certain flower looked like a lion's tooth.
28. He (speak) the French words *dent de lion.*
29. Those words (become) *dandelion* in English.
30. In England someone (choose) to call a flower "the day's eye."
31. That flower has (become) the American daisy.
32. The ancient Greeks (run) in a contest called an *agōn.*
33. If you have (run) a long way, you may know what agony is.
34. Long ago a Greek runner (bring) news of a victory in battle from Marathon to Athens.
35. Many runners have (break) records in today's marathons.
36. Many English words have (come) from French.
37. In fact, French once (become) the official language of England.
38. In 1066 a French king (come) to power in England.
39. He and his followers (bring) their language with them.
40. Many English people (choose) their new king's language.
41. Soon most people of wealth and power (speak) French.
42. Some people have (say) that only the peasants still spoke English.
43. The English finally (break) free from French rule.
44. The English (think) they should have an English ruler.
45. By that time many French words had (become) part of the English vocabulary.

9 Using Troublesome Verb Pairs *p. 132*

A. Write each sentence. Use the correct verb in parentheses ( ).

1. You (can, may) make life more pleasant for everyone by showing cooperation.
2. Don't (lie, lay) your things everywhere.
3. (Can, May) you find a way to help?
4. Did you (lie, lay) your books on the chair?
5. You (can, may) not borrow something without permission.
6. (Can, May) I borrow your pen?
7. Do you (lie, lay) things in the proper place?
8. (Lie, Lay) your things neatly on shelves or in drawers.
9. You (can, may) not open someone else's mail.
10. You (can, may) help others in many ways.
11. You (can, may) practice good telephone manners.
12. Ask if you (can, may) take a message.
13. (Lie, Lay) out messages clearly for others.
14. Keep activities quiet while others (lie, lay) down to rest.

B. Write each sentence. Use the word *can*, *may*, *lie*, or *lay* in place of the blank.

15. You ____ serve dinner now. 16. ____ you think of an interesting story to tell? 17. Please ____ your napkin next to your plate when you have finished eating. 18. ____ I be excused now? 19. I wish to ____ down for a while.

C. Write the verb in parentheses ( ) that is correct in each sentence.

20. (Can, May) you help me unpack the car?
21. (Can, May) you lift that cooler?
22. (Lie, Lay) the plates over there.
23. (Can, May) we use this picnic table?
24. (Lie, Lay) out the tablecloth first.
25. It will not (lie, lay) flat in this breeze.
26. (Can, May) we eat now?
27. Yes, you (can, may) begin.
28. (Can, May) I take your picture now?
29. (Can, May) you give me a big smile?
30. Will you (lie, lay) down for a nap now?

176 Extra Practice

D. Write each sentence. Use the correct verb in parentheses ( ).

31. You can (teach, learn) an old dog new tricks.
32. Younger dogs (teach, learn) more quickly.
33. A dog should (sit, set) when its owner says so.
34. Many people (teach, learn) their dogs to heel and to stay.
35. You should try to (sit, set) aside thirty minutes a day for training your dog.
36. Any dog can (teach, learn) to walk beside its owner.
37. It is important to (teach, learn) a dog to heel.
38. A dog should (sit, set) when its trainer stops.
39. (Teach, Learn) the dog the correct sitting position.
40. Dogs (teach, learn) quickly when they are praised often.
41. (Sit, Set) a time limit for lessons.
42. Dogs (teach, learn) best with two short lessons a day.
43. Many fine books (teach, learn) people how to train dogs.

E. Write each sentence. Use the word *teach*, *learn*, *sit*, or *set* in place of the blank.

44. The dog-show judges ____ the trophies on the table.
45. A trainer will ____ a hurdle at its lowest level.
46. Another will ____ the planks for the long jump in place.
47. The people ____ quietly in the stands.
48. Trainers ____ dogs to ignore other dogs at shows.
49. Dogs must ____ this in order to perform well.
50. Trainers also ____ their dogs to walk in figure eights.
51. Dogs must ____ still for minutes at a time.
52. A new dog owner can ____ many things at a dog show.

F. Write the verb in parentheses ( ) that correctly completes each sentence.

53. First the coach will (sit, set) the rule books on the table.
54. We players (sit, set) and listen.
55. We want to (teach, learn) all we can from the coach.
56. The coach may (sit, set) a chart on the easel.
57. He will use it to (teach, learn) us new plays.
58. Some players practice and others (sit, set) on the bench.
59. He will (teach, learn) them the play first.
60. The rest of us will (teach, learn) the moves by watching.

UNIT FOUR

USING LANGUAGE TO
PERSUADE

Writing
IN YOUR JOURNAL

WRITER'S WARM-UP ◆ If you could choose one foreign country to live in for a year, where would you go? You will probably name a country that you know something about and that interests you. Imagine for a moment that you have been transported to this place. What might you expect to see and do there? Write in your journal about one typical day there.

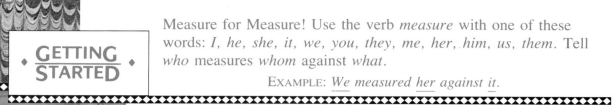

◆ GETTING ◆
STARTED

Measure for Measure! Use the verb *measure* with one of these words: *I, he, she, it, we, you, they, me, her, him, us, them.* Tell *who* measures *whom* against *what.*

EXAMPLE: *We measured her against it.*

1 Writing with Pronouns

Words that take the place of nouns are called pronouns. In the sentences below, the pronouns are shown in blue. The words they take the place of are shown in red.

> John F. Kennedy was the 35th President. He was elected in 1960. Kennedy gave good speeches. People still remember them. Kennedy's ideas inspired many. His ideas were exciting.

Singular	Plural
I, me, my, mine	we, us, our, ours
you, your, yours	you, your, yours
he, she, it, him	they, them, their, theirs
her, his, hers, its	

When you write, use pronouns to avoid awkward repetition.

Kennedy was proud that Kennedy's family produced many leaders.
Kennedy was proud that his family produced many leaders.

> **Summary** ◆ A **pronoun** takes the place of a noun or nouns. Using pronouns in your writing can help you avoid repeating the same nouns over and over.

Guided Practice

Name the pronoun in each sentence below.

1. John F. Kennedy was named after his grandfather John Fitzgerald.
2. John Fitzgerald had been mayor of Boston, and he served in Congress.
3. Kennedy's father was our ambassador to Great Britain.
4. Several Kennedys worked to solve problems we still face today.
5. They were part of a strong family.

Practice

A. These sentences tell about the Kennedy family in London.
Write the pronouns in each sentence.

    6. John F. Kennedy stayed with his parents in London in 1939.

    7. As part of the ambassador's family, he was an unofficial
representative of our country.

    8. ''I want you to travel in Europe,'' John's father told him.

    9. ''Find out the thoughts of the leaders of Europe for me.''

   10. Young Kennedy interviewed European leaders about their
views.

   11. They told him about a growing crisis in Europe.

   12. ''I was interested in the things they told me,'' he said.

   13. ''I had to express my views on the problems we faced.''

   14. So, back in college, he wrote a book about his findings.

   15. It was called *Why England Slept*, and it was popular.

B. Rewrite each sentence using pronouns in place of the
underlined words.

   16. After <u>Kennedy's</u> graduation, Kennedy traveled abroad
again.

   17. The Navy made <u>Kennedy</u> commander of a patrol boat in
the South Pacific.

   18. On August 2, 1943, a Japanese destroyer hit Kennedy's
boat and cut <u>the boat</u> in two.

   19. Ten men clung to the wreckage in <u>the men's</u> life jackets.

   20. Kennedy ordered <u>the men</u> to swim to a nearby island.

   21. Kennedy said that <u>Kennedy</u> would go for help.

   22. <u>Kennedy's</u> men were starving; <u>the men</u> ate only coconuts.

   23. At last two islanders found <u>Kennedy and his men</u>.

   24. <u>Kennedy</u> persuaded them to help <u>Kennedy</u> and the crew.

   25. <u>Kennedy and the other men</u> were rescued by the
Australians.

Apply ◆ Think and Write

From Your Writing ◆ Read what you wrote for the
Writer's Warm-up. List the pronouns you used. Can
you list the noun or nouns each pronoun stands for?

✎ **Remember**
that you can
use pronouns to
avoid repeating the
same nouns too
often.

Imagine that there were no pronouns in English. How would that change the way we speak? To find out, tell the class what you did yesterday. Remember, don't use any pronouns!

2 Pronouns and Antecedents

Remember that pronouns are words that take the place of nouns. For a pronoun to make sense, a reader or listener must know what noun it replaces. The word or words that a pronoun refers to is called the antecedent. Every pronoun needs a clear antecedent.

antecedent   pronoun
<u>John Kennedy</u> wanted a political career, so <u>he</u> ran for Congress.

          antecedents   pronoun
He had seven <u>brothers and sisters</u>, and <u>they</u> helped Jack win.

In the examples above, the pronouns come after their antecedents. A pronoun can also come before its antecedent. Sometimes the antecedent is not in the same sentence.

"<u>I</u> want to run for President in 1960," <u>Kennedy</u> announced.
<u>The supporters</u> cheered. <u>They</u> had been waiting for years.

> **Summary** ◆ An **antecedent** is the word or words to which a pronoun refers. Every pronoun needs a clear antecedent.

Guided Practice

Name the antecedent of each underlined pronoun.

1. The election was close, but Kennedy won <u>it</u>.
2. The country had problems, and Kennedy wanted to solve <u>them</u>.
3. Kennedy's name for <u>his</u> program was the New Frontier.

Practice

A. Write the pronouns in these sentences. Then write the antecedent of each pronoun. The pronoun and its antecedent might not be in the same sentence.

4. Space and its exploration was part of the New Frontier.
5. Kennedy wanted a moon landing, so he pushed for success.
6. The government also said it would ban nuclear bomb tests.
7. Kennedy founded the Alliance for Progress. It was a program to aid Latin American nations.
8. The alliance helped the nations develop their economies.
9. The President identified with people and their need for freedom.
10. "I am a Berliner," Kennedy told the people of West Berlin.
11. They felt threatened by the Soviets.
12. Kennedy worked for civil rights; he helped to integrate schools.
13. He wanted Americans to get involved and told them so.

B. Complete the paragraph with the pronouns below.

they	its	she	their	he	them	his	it

The Peace Corps was created by Kennedy in 1961. (**14.** ____) is still a popular program. Peace Corps volunteers are chosen because (**15.** ____) are skilled. Teachers and farmers bring special skills with (**16.** ____). Peace Corps workers teach (**17.** ____) skills to people in poor and underdeveloped nations. The new skills help the people to improve (**18.** ____) standard of living. For example, an American carpenter helped an African village build (**19.** ____) first school. (**20.** ____) wife became the first teacher. (**21.** ____) taught her students to read and write. In their own way, both (**22.** ____) and (**23.** ____) had become ambassadors for peace.

Apply ◆ Think and Write

Persuasive Sentences ◆ Tell what you think you can do to make the world a better, safer place. Underline each pronoun that you use in your sentences.

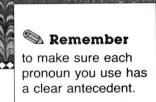

✎ **Remember**
to make sure each pronoun you use has a clear antecedent.

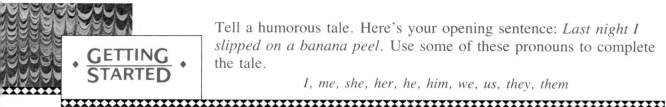

Tell a humorous tale. Here's your opening sentence: *Last night I slipped on a banana peel.* Use some of these pronouns to complete the tale.

I, me, she, her, he, him, we, us, they, them

3 Subject and Object Pronouns

The chart below lists two types of pronouns—subject pronouns and object pronouns. Notice that *you* and *it* can be either type.

Subject Pronouns		Object Pronouns	
Singular	Plural	Singular	Plural
I	we	me	us
you	you	you	you
she, he, it	they	her, him, it	them

How do you know when to use each type of pronoun? A subject pronoun may be used as the subject of a sentence. Any subject pronoun, for example, can be the subject of the following sentence:

■ _____ **can travel to another country.**

An object pronoun may be used as direct object of a sentence. In the first sentence in each pair below, the direct object is a noun. In the second sentence, an object pronoun replaces the noun.

> The Russians welcomed <u>Samantha</u>. The Russians welcomed <u>her</u>.
> Samantha enjoyed <u>the trip</u>. Samantha enjoyed <u>it</u>.

> **Summary** ◆ The **subject pronouns** are *I, you, she, he, it, we,* and *they*. The **object pronouns** are *me, you, her, him, it, us,* and *them*.

Guided Practice

Tell if the underlined words are subject or object pronouns.

1. "The idea of war worries <u>me</u>," thought Samantha Smith.
2. "But what can <u>I</u> do?" the ten-year-old student wondered.
3. <u>She</u> decided to write a letter to the Soviet leader.

Practice

A. Write *subject pronoun* or *object pronoun* for each underlined word.

    4. <u>She</u> sent <u>it</u> to Mr. Yuri Andropov, The Kremlin, Moscow, USSR.

    5. ''Why do <u>you</u> want to conquer the world?'' Samantha wrote.

    6. The return letter from the Soviet Union surprised <u>her</u>.

    7. <u>It</u> was from Yuri Andropov, the most powerful Soviet.

    8. <u>He</u> was the General Secretary of the Central Committee of the Communist Party of the Soviet Union.

B. Write the pronouns in these sentences. Then write whether each is a subject pronoun or an object pronoun.

    9. The letter said, ''I invite you to come to the Soviet Union.''

   10. ''We want peace for all peoples of the planet,'' the leader said.

   11. He compared her to Becky in Mark Twain's *Tom Sawyer*.

   12. Mr. and Mrs. Smith read the letter. They would go, too.

   13. The chance to build friendship between nations thrilled them.

C. Rewrite each sentence. Replace the underlined subject or direct object with the correct pronoun.

   14. <u>Samantha and her parents</u> toured the Soviet Union in style.

   15. The family met the Soviet leader and thanked <u>the leader</u>.

   16. The Soviets praised <u>Samantha</u> for being a peacemaker.

   17. <u>Samantha</u> made <u>the Soviets</u> her friends.

   18. ''I hope you can visit <u>Samantha</u> someday,'' she said.

   19. ''<u>My friends and I</u> have learned from each other,'' she said.

   20. Many people praised <u>Samantha's adventure</u>.

   21. Television reporters interviewed <u>the Smith family</u>.

   22. <u>The reporters</u> called Samantha ''the littlest ambassador.''

   23. Samantha published a book about the trip; <u>the book</u> is called *Journey to the Soviet Union*.

Apply ◆ Think and Write

A Travel Paragraph ◆ If you could visit any place in the world, where would you go? Write a paragraph telling what you would hope to do and see there. Use some pronouns in it.

✎ **Remember**
to use subject
and object pronouns
to express ideas
simply and clearly.

Some words—*ewe* and *you*, for instance—sound alike but have different meanings. Use the words below in sentences. Then use their "sound-alike twins" in sentences.

hour   aisle   heel   hours   weave

4 Possessive Pronouns and Contractions

Remember that possessive nouns show ownership. Pronouns can also show ownership. The following possessive pronouns are used before nouns: *my, your, her, his, its, our, their*. Pronouns that are used alone are: *mine, yours, hers, his, ours, theirs*. Notice that *his* can be used both ways.

> The ambassador's duty is to serve <u>her</u> country. The duty is <u>hers</u>.
> The President chose <u>his</u> ambassador. The choice is <u>his</u>.

The possessive pronouns *its*, *your*, and *their* are often confused with the contractions *it's*, *you're*, and *they're*. A contraction is a shortened form of two words. An **apostrophe** (') shows where a letter or letters have been left out. A possessive pronoun never has an apostrophe. Study how these contractions are formed.

> ■ **it's** (it is)   **you're** (you are)   **they're** (they are)

For more about contractions formed with pronouns such as *he'll* and *we've*, see page 504.

> **Summary** ◆ A **possessive pronoun** shows ownership. A **contraction** is a shortened form of two words. When you are proofreading, pay special attention to possessive pronouns and contractions.

Guided Practice

Tell whether each underlined word is a possessive pronoun or a contraction. Tell how you know.

1. <u>It's</u> important for America to keep <u>its</u> ties with other nations.
2. <u>Our</u> President sends ambassadors to <u>their</u> capitals.
3. <u>They're</u> also sent to look after American interests abroad.

Practice

A. Write the one possessive pronoun in each sentence.

   4. Our President has just appointed you as an ambassador.
   5. "You're best qualified," he says, "so the job is yours."
   6. Your family thinks it's a great chance to live abroad.
   7. However, they're sad about leaving their friends and home.
   8. They feel a duty toward the President and his program.
   9. You meet the country's top leader and her assistants.
  10. It's important to understand their language and culture.
  11. "Do you think I prepared well for my new assignment?"
  12. The work, with its many social events, seems like fun.
  13. "Is this mine?" you exclaim upon seeing the new office.

B. Complete the paragraph with words from the list below. Read each sentence completely before choosing a possessive pronoun or contraction.

| its | your | their | it's | you're | they're |

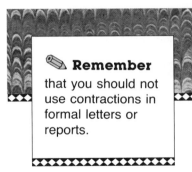

   As ambassador you must explain and support (**14.** ____) country's position on various issues. Your hosts may have different views on a subject. (**15.** ____) going to present these forcefully to you. As a diplomat (**16.** ____) expected to listen politely to (**17.** ____) views, just as they will listen to (**18.** ____) views. Knowing about the host country and (**19.** ____) history, culture, and economy can help overcome some differences. (**20.** ____) all right for two nations to disagree, if (**21.** ____) able to communicate with each other. As ambassador (**22.** ____) responsible for good communication. An ambassador's work affects the world and (**23.** ____) people in many ways.

Apply ◆ Think and Write

Dictionary of Knowledge ◆ Clare Boothe Luce was an effective American ambassador. Read about her in the Dictionary of Knowledge. Then write some sentences about how her special skills and her background helped her in working abroad. Use some possessive pronouns in your sentences.

> ✏️ **Remember**
> that you should not use contractions in formal letters or reports.

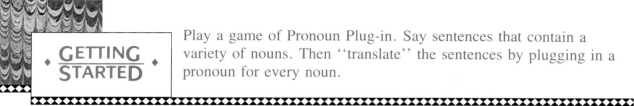

GETTING STARTED

Play a game of Pronoun Plug-in. Say sentences that contain a variety of nouns. Then "translate" the sentences by plugging in a pronoun for every noun.

5 Using Pronouns

Now that you have learned about the different kinds of pronouns, you will want to use them correctly. To decide which pronoun is correct, ask yourself how the pronoun is used in the sentence.

Always use a subject pronoun as the subject of a sentence. When you use pronouns, it is polite to name yourself last.

Wrong: My friend and me have pen pals.
Right: My friend and I have pen pals.

Use an object pronoun as a direct object after an action verb.

Wrong: Mr. Rios told Denise and I about pen pals.
Right: Mr. Rios told Denise and me about pen pals.

Use a subject pronoun after a linking verb. Pronouns that follow linking verbs are predicate nominatives.

Wrong: The writer of the letter was her.
Right: The writer of the letter was she.

> **Summary** ◆ Use a subject pronoun as the subject of a sentence and after a linking verb. Use an object pronoun after an action verb.

Guided Practice

Tell which pronoun correctly completes each sentence. Then tell whether the pronoun is a subject pronoun or an object pronoun.

1. My classmates and (I, me) have pen pals.
2. My teacher helped Denise and (I, me) with the letters.
3. The writer of the best letter was (she, her).
4. (She, her) and Diego decided to work together.
5. Denise asked (him, he) and Carl some helpful questions.

Practice

A. Write each sentence using the correct pronoun in parentheses ( ). Then write whether it is a subject or an object pronoun.

6. Allison and (I, me) both wrote letters to our pen pal Jan.
7. Jan's sister and (she, her) wrote back to us.
8. The girls in this photo are (they, them).
9. (They, Them) and their aunt live on a ranch in Australia.
10. Jan's letters delight our friends and (we, us).
11. (We, Us) and our teachers have studied that country.
12. We tell Jan's sister and (she, her) about life here.
13. Our descriptions of freeways, beaches, and suburbs interest (they, them) and their friends.
14. What amazing travelers are (we, us)!
15. Both (we, us) and (they, them) can travel around the world without leaving home.

B. Complete the body of the letter. Use subject and object pronouns. The first is done for you.

Mother and (**16.** _**I**_) just heard some wonderful news. Dad is going on a two-week business trip. Normally his trips do not make Mom and (**17.** ___) happy. This one is different. Dad's boss and (**18.** ___) are going to Australia! Their Australian partners and (**19.** ___) have to discuss plans for a new factory. What an excited pair Mom and (**20.** ___) are. Why? Dad can take Mother and (**21.** ___) with him on the trip! We will accompany his boss and (**22.** ___) on the thirty-hour flight. On July 24 (**23.** ___) will be the most exhausted-looking travelers in the Sydney Airport.

Can Mom and (**24.** ___) visit you on your ranch? Please write and let my parents and (**25.** ___) know. Then we can be pals as well as pen pals!

Apply ◆ Think and Write

Planning a Letter ◆ From what country would you like to have a pen pal? What would you want to learn about life there? What would you tell your pen pal about life here? Plan your letter. Make a list of things you would like to talk about.

✎ **Remember**
to choose carefully the subject and object pronouns you use.

Is a *notorious* person different from a *famous* person? If you were advertising a product, would you call it *inexpensive* or *cheap*? Why?

VOCABULARY ♦
Connotations

Words can convey many meanings. All words have a main meaning, called the **literal** meaning of the word. Words with similar main meanings can suggest different feelings and reactions. **Connotation** is the positive or negative meaning associated with a word.

Eric and Aaron, twin brothers, went camping in Yellowstone National Park. They kept journals of their experiences. Here are some excerpts from their journals.

ERIC: Our guide was very <u>youthful</u> and <u>brave</u>.
AARON: Our guide was very <u>childish</u> and <u>reckless</u>.
ERIC: We came upon some <u>plump</u> and <u>curious</u> bears.
AARON: We came upon some <u>fat</u> and <u>nosy</u> bears.
ERIC: Setting up camp was a <u>challenge</u>.
AARON: Setting up camp was a <u>chore</u>.

Look at the underlined words above. Eric and Aaron used words with similar meanings. However, the words Eric chose show that he enjoyed his experiences. The words Aaron chose show that he did not. Even though the words have similar main meanings, the connotations of the words are very different.

It is important to be aware of the connotations of words you use in order to write exactly what you mean. A thesaurus and a dictionary can help you.

Building Your Vocabulary

Think of words to replace *talked* in the sentence below. Notice how the meaning of the sentence changes when you replace *talked* with other verbs. (Hint: You may have to change the sentence slightly to use some synonyms for *talk*.)

Wilma <u>talked</u> about her trip to Alaska.

Practice

A. Write each sentence. Use the word in parentheses ( ) that has the more positive connotation.

    1. Jason has (asked, pestered) his parents for a new bike.
    2. Ana thought the book was (amusing, silly).
    3. Dave saw a (group, mob) of people standing on the corner.
    4. Carlos enjoys (unusual, bizarre) science fiction films.
    5. Karen is being (firm, stubborn) about her opinions.

B. Write the word in each pair that has a negative connotation.

    6. flimsy, delicate   **8.** odor, aroma   **10.** gaze, glare
    7. confident, arrogant   **9.** gossip, news   **11.** smile, smirk

C. Find words that are similar to the underlined word in each sentence, but that are different in connotation. Then figure out the word in parentheses ( ). Replace the underlined word with that word, and write the new sentence.

    12. They lived in a small <u>house</u> on the hill. (sh _ _ _)
    13. Maria is very <u>thrifty</u> with her money. (sti _ _ _)
    14. Luis's parrot has been known to <u>speak</u> all day. (bab _ _ _)
    15. The kitten was very <u>thin</u>. (scr _ _ _ _)
    16. Aaron and Eric were engaged in a noisy <u>argument</u>. (deb _ _ _)

LANGUAGE CORNER • Word Histories

The meanings of some words have changed over time. *Boy* once meant "servant" or "knave". *Girl* once meant "child," whether male or female.

Use the clues below to complete the puzzle and find out what the words at the right meant long ago.

hobby
handsome
snob
nice
gossip

Down
1. easy to handle
2. a pony, a small horse
3. foolish, ignorant

Across
4. a godparent
5. a shoemaker

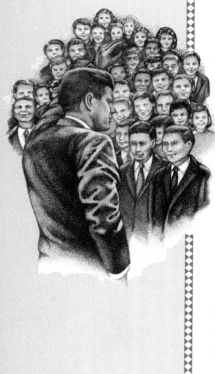

How to Revise Sentences with Pronouns

You know that pronouns are mainly used to replace nouns. Pronouns do important work in sentences. By using pronouns, you can often avoid needlessly repeating words. Without pronouns, you would frequently come across sentences like the first one below.

1. **John Kennedy was the youngest President ever elected, and John Kennedy's ability as a public speaker made John Kennedy very popular.**
2. **John Kennedy was the youngest President ever elected, and his ability as a public speaker made him very popular.**

Sentence **1** repeats the name *John Kennedy* so often that the sentence becomes awkward and difficult to read. Sentence **2**, however, uses the name only once and replaces the repeated name with pronouns. As a result the sentence becomes more sensible and easier to read.

You have also learned that there are different kinds of pronouns, depending on their use in a sentence. In sentence **2** above, there are no subject pronouns. There are, however, an object pronoun and a possessive pronoun. Can you identify each one?

The Grammar Game ♦ Exercise your pronoun power! Replace the underlined words with subject, object, or possessive pronouns. Then identify the kinds of pronouns you used.

<u>the speech</u> begins	<u>the student's</u> grades
<u>grandmother's</u> visits	for <u>the people</u>
to <u>the reporter</u>	because of <u>Rosa</u>
<u>Richard and I</u> joined	around <u>the world</u>
all of <u>the books</u>	<u>the elephant's</u> trunk
<u>the children's</u> stories	<u>my brother's and my</u> recorder
if <u>Don</u> wins the election	<u>the members</u> meet

Working Together

As your group works on activities **A** and **B**, you will find that using pronouns can result in smoother, less repetitive writing.

In Your Group

- Encourage everyone to share ideas.
- Ask questions to encourage discussion.
- Keep the group on the topic.
- Take turns recording information.

A. Find the pronouns in each line of letters and write them. Then tell what kinds of pronouns you found in each line.

1. Inbyouchebxshejuitwrbwedftheyco
2. lumeghyoucahimsshercxitlusrtthem
3. mineyourshishersitsourstheirsmyheryourhisourtheir
4. hebbyourlowuminertbtheyjuhistxlsherwemnourlmy
5. themnoxtheircbmertminepphimwuhislcittuxitsly

B. Decide which nouns your group wishes to replace with pronouns in the paragraph below. Then write your new paragraph.

John Kennedy was not the only public servant in John Kennedy's family. John had two brothers, Robert and Ted. Robert and Ted were also active in politics. Robert was appointed attorney general of the United States by Robert's brother, John, the President. Robert served as attorney general from 1961 to 1964. In 1965, the state of New York elected Robert as the state of New York's congressional senator. After John died, the members of John's family grieved deeply, but the members handled the members' grief with dignity. Then Robert decided to launch Robert's own campaign for the presidency. The campaign was well under way when the campaign was tragically ended by Robert's assassination in 1968.

WRITERS' CORNER ◆ Fuzzy Sentences

Be careful not to overuse pronouns. Sometimes replacing too many pronouns can make your sentences fuzzy, or unclear. It should always be clear to your reader what noun is replaced by a pronoun.

FUZZY: **Robert worked hard for John. He always respected him.**

IMPROVED: **Robert worked hard for John. Robert always respected him.**

Read what you wrote for the Writer's Warm-up. Did you use pronouns clearly?

THERESE DUNCAN: REACHING ARMS. The Parthenon (1921)
gelatin-silver print by Edward Steichen
Collection, The Museum of Modern Art, New York.

UNIT FOUR

USING LANGUAGE TO
PERSUADE

=== **PART TWO** ===

Literature *Letter to Peter Galbraith* by John F. Kennedy

A Reason for Writing Persuading

CREATIVE
Writing

FINE ARTS ◆ The title of the photograph at the left is "Reaching Arms." When you first glimpsed the photograph, what was your first thought? Rename the photograph. Give it a title that explains to others how you first felt about the image.

CRITICAL THINKING ◆
A Strategy for Persuading

A VENN DIAGRAM

Persuading means getting someone to agree with you. After this lesson you will read an example of persuasive writing. It is a letter from President John F. Kennedy to his friend's son, Peter. Peter didn't want to move to India. President Kennedy tried to persuade him to change his mind. Here is how the president began his letter.

> Dear Peter:
>
> I learn from your father that you are not very anxious to give up your school and friends for India. I think I know a little about how you feel. More than twenty years ago our family was similarly uprooted when we went to London where my father was ambassador . . . .

One powerful persuasive technique is to emphasize that you and the other person have something in common. That is, you emphasize your likenesses rather than your differences. Did President Kennedy do that? How? What do you think he might have said next?

Learning the Strategy

It is often useful to notice likenesses and differences. For example, suppose you are going to have a substitute teacher for a week. Would it help to know how the new teacher is like or different from your regular teacher? Have you ever read a book, then seen a movie made from the book? Would it be interesting to discuss with your friends how the two versions differ? In Europe, soccer is known as football. Would you be able to describe the likenesses and differences between American football and European football to a pen pal in Germany?

A Venn diagram is one strategy for noting likenesses and differences. It is two circles that overlap. The one below is about two teachers. The words in the middle show how they are alike. The words on the outside show how they are different.

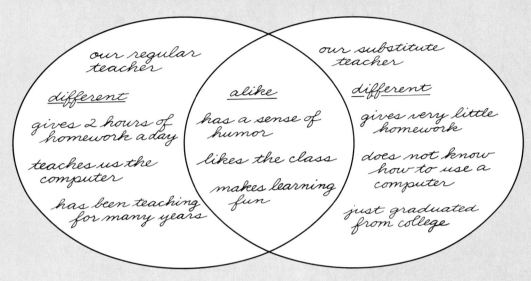

our regular teacher

different

gives 2 hours of homework a day

teaches us the computer

has been teaching for many years

alike

has a sense of humor

likes the class

makes learning fun

our substitute teacher

different

gives very little homework

does not know how to use a computer

just graduated from college

How are the two teachers alike? In what ways are they different? How does this type of diagram help you decide?

Using the Strategy

A. People often have friends who are both like and different from themselves. Think of one of your friends. Make a Venn diagram to show how the two of you are alike and different.

B. Put yourself in Peter's place and imagine suddenly having to move to India and go to school there. Make a Venn diagram about America and India. Fill in as many likenesses and differences between the two countries as you know about or can imagine. Then read President Kennedy's letter in the next lesson to see if he used any of these points to persuade Peter.

Applying the Strategy

- ◆ How did your Venn diagram for **A** above help you appreciate that other person and yourself?
- ◆ When might you need to notice likenesses and differences?

LITERATURE

A letter from President Kennedy

Early in his presidency John F. Kennedy appointed John Kenneth Galbraith, a Harvard professor, to the post of ambassador to India. Soon after the appointment Kennedy learned that Galbraith's son Peter was unhappy about going to India. He did not want to leave his friends and familiar surroundings to go with his family to this faraway land. Having been in a similar situation himself as a young man, the President took time from his busy schedule to write this letter of encouragement to Peter Galbraith.

On page 200 you can read about what happened to Peter in India. Going to India really did change his life. When he found out that we were printing the Kennedy letter, Peter Galbraith wrote an essay about his experience for you.

THE WHITE HOUSE

WASHINGTON

March 28, 1961

Dear Peter:

I learn from your father that you are not very anxious to
give up your school and friends for India. I think I know
a little about how you feel. More than twenty years ago
our family was similarly uprooted when we went to London
where my father was ambassador. My younger brothers
and sisters were about your age. They had, like you, to
exchange old friends for new ones.

But I think you will like your new friends and your new
school in India. For anyone interested, as your father
says you are, in animals, India must have the most
fascinating possibilities. The range is from elephants
to cobras, although I gather the cobras have to be handled
professionally. Indians ride and play polo so you will come
back an experienced horseman.

But more important still, I think of the children of the people
I am sending to other countries as my junior peace corps.
You and your brothers will be helping your parents do a good
job for our country and you will be helping out yourself by
making many friends. I think perhaps this is what you will
enjoy most of all.

My best wishes,

Sincerely yours,

[signature: John Kennedy]

I a little wish I were going also.

Mr. Peter Woodard Galbraith
30 Francis Avenue
Cambridge, Massachusetts

The handwritten note reads, "I a little wish I were going also."

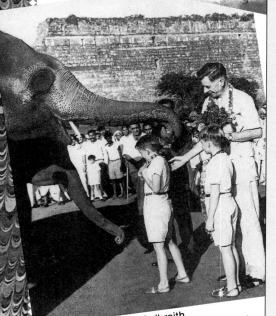

Left to right: Catherine Galbraith, Prime Minister Nehru, Peter Galbraith, Indira Gandhi.

MY EXPERIENCE IN INDIA
by Peter W. Galbraith

I was, of course, very excited to get a letter from the President of the United States, and I began to look forward to India. In terms of animals, India did not disappoint me. My pets included two peacocks, two deer (named Veni and Son), a mare and her filly (I ended up training the filly), a Siamese cat, a puppy, parrots, an ever increasing population of white mice, and a leopard cub. Some of the animals were more suited as pets than others. The leopard, for example, grew out of being a cuddly cub and had to be returned to the zoo.

India was the experience of a lifetime. With my parents, I traveled throughout the country. At different times, I slept in maharajahs' palaces, vacationed in a houseboat on a Kashmir lake, climbed over high passes in the Himalayas, and even went tiger hunting on elephant back. (Fortunately, we shot no tigers on this trip, and such hunting is now banned.)

I also got to learn about India. I studied its many religions (Hinduism, Islam, Buddhism), its millennia-old history, and its peoples. I got to know India's leaders, including its first prime minister, Jawaharlal Nehru, his daughter Indira Gandhi, who also became prime minister, and his grandson Rajiv Gandhi, who is now prime minister. When we visited, Nehru would take my brother and me to pet the tigers that he kept in his garden. I also saw, and was much affected by, the poverty in which so many of India's people live.

My time in India changed the course of my life. It gave me a taste for the exotic and a strong sense of adventure. I have devoted my professional life to international issues. Now, as an advisor to the Senate Foreign Relations Committee, I work hard for better understanding between the United States and India.

Left to right: Peter Galbraith, James Galbraith, John Kenneth Galbraith.

Library Link ♦ *You may wish to read about the boyhood of another President.* Before the Trumpet: Young Franklin Roosevelt 1882–1905 *is a book about Roosevelt's early years.*

Reader's Response

If the President of the United States were to send a personal letter to you, how might you respond?

A letter from **President Kennedy**

Responding to Literature

1. Write a page in your journal to explore the problems that moving to another country might create. Read your journal entry aloud. Then listen to the entries your classmates wrote. How are they like or different from your response?

2. Reread President Kennedy's letter. As you read, think about what kind of person he was. Make a character cluster about him. In the center circle, write *President Kennedy*, then add other circles with words and phrases that describe him.

3. In his essay Peter tells how his experiences in India changed his life. How do you think your life might change if you moved to another country?

Writing to Learn

Think and Compare ♦ Make a Venn diagram like the one below. Record the likenesses and differences between Peter Galbraith and President Kennedy.

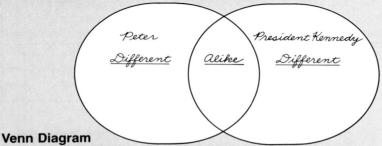

Venn Diagram

Write ♦ Write a paragraph. Explain why President Kennedy's letter to Peter may have been successful. How might their likenesses or differences have helped Peter adjust to the idea of living in a distant country?

Recite a jingle or sing a song used to advertise a popular product. Then put the jingle or song into your own words. See if it really gives any information.

SPEAKING and LISTENING ♦
Recognizing Propaganda Techniques

When President Kennedy wrote to Peter Galbraith, he used persuasion on a person-to-person basis. You use persuasion that way, too. You need to be aware, though, of another kind of persuasion—propaganda. **Propaganda** is an organized effort to spread ideas. It is used to sell products, to sway voters, and to otherwise influence public opinion. Sometimes it gives accurate information. Sometimes it does not. That is why you need to be able to recognize propaganda when you hear it. Here are four commonly used propaganda techniques.

Technique	Definition	The Speaker Says	A Critical Listener Asks
Bandwagon	Suggests you should do something because everyone is doing it	Millions of people have switched to Stay-Well vitamins. Shouldn't you?	Is there evidence to support this claim? Is this a convincing reason to switch?
Testimonial	Uses a famous person to endorse a product or opinion	Screen star Cindy Lee: "Bright tooth-paste gives me a winning smile."	Can the product do what it says, or am I being influenced by the star's beauty or personality?
Loaded Words	Appeal to the emotions; play on people's hopes and fears	Is your hair drab and lifeless? Give your hair new vitality with Glow.	Am I being swayed by my feelings? Will this product make me feel different about myself?
Faulty Cause	Gives the wrong cause for a good (or bad) effect	I ate CornO's for breakfast and hit a home run.	Is there a logical connection between the cause and the effect?

Summary ♦ **Propaganda techniques** are used to sway public opinion. Listen critically and learn to recognize when those techniques are being used to influence you.

Guided Practice

Name the propaganda technique used in each example.

1. If you believe in honesty, justice, and the American way of life, vote for Ernest.
2. Join the hundreds of Americans who have taken Manilla Tours to Puerto Rico. Don't be left out. Take Manilla today!
3. Baseball great Tony Lopez says, "Protect your eyes the way I do. Get yourself a pair of Shazam sunglasses."
4. Now that I'm using Glisten toothpaste, I'm popular!

Practice

A. Write the propaganda technique used in each statement.

   5. Buy the car most Americans prefer—the Pluto.
   6. Singer Ted Bear says, "I'd be lost without my Ace Atlas."
   7. When in Italy, drink cool, refreshing Aetna bottled water.
   8. People notice me now that I'm carrying Atlas luggage!
   9. Everyone must see Paris at least once!

B. 10–20. Listen as a classmate reads the following campaign speech aloud. Then list the loaded words in the speech.

   A vote for our candidate is a vote for justice, honor, freedom, and all that is beautiful in our state. It is time for unfair, unwanted taxes and outdated ideas to be replaced by intelligent changes. We need courageous, reliable leaders to give our state government new vitality.

C. Write a one-line ad for each item. Use the propaganda technique in parentheses ( ).

   21. radio station (bandwagon)   **23.** sneakers (testimonial)
   22. wristwatch (faulty cause)   **24.** cereal (loaded words)

Apply ◆ Think and Write

Listening for Propaganda ◆ Listen for examples of the four propaganda techniques on television and radio. Write an example of each. You might wish to read them aloud to your class to see if others agree with you about the kind of techniques used.

✎ **Remember**
to evaluate messages critically and to recognize the use of propaganda.

Complete this sentence: *The best place for a vacation is ____ .*
Then tell why.

WRITING ◆
Supporting an Opinion

An opinion is what a person *thinks* about something. People
become fond of their opinions. They are not eager to change them.
Therefore, when you want someone to agree with your opinion,
you must be convincing. You need to show that your opinion is
reasonable and that it is well supported. Basically, there are three
kinds of support you can give: (1) facts, (2) reasons, and (3)
examples.

Ways to Support an Opinion

1. A **fact** is information that can be proved to be true.

   Venice has a network of 177 narrow canals that act as its streets.

2. A **reason** tells why your reader should agree with you.

   **If you visit Venice, you will be dazzled by its beauty and awed by its
   history and art.**

3. An **example** is a case or instance that proves the point.

   **In Venice you can climb to the roof of the famed clock tower to
   watch the bronze figures strike the bell on the hour.**

Facts are easy to obtain from dictionaries, encyclopedias, and
almanacs. They will impress your readers and lead them to believe
that you are careful and accurate. The best *reasons* are those that
personally affect the reader—that show how he or she will benefit
by agreeing with you. *Examples* illustrate your argument. They
create word pictures that show what you mean.

Summary ◆ Writers use facts, examples, and reasons to
support their opinions. Choose those that will appeal to your
readers.

Guided Practice

Support each of these opinions by giving a fact, a reason, or an example as indicated in parentheses ( ).

1. Everyone should learn a foreign language as a child. (reason)
2. Nothing is more thrilling than a safari in Africa. (example)
3. There is no place like home! (reason)
4. Our state has many attractions for tourists. (fact)
5. Traveling overseas is an education in itself. (example)

Practice

A. Write a fact or an example to support each of these opinions.

6. Fall is the best time of year to travel.
7. Summer is the best time of year to travel.
8. Tourists can help a country's economy.
9. Tourists can be very annoying.
10. Traveling by car has many advantages.

B. Write a reason to support each of these opinions.

11. Before traveling abroad, you should see America.
12. It is a good idea to read about a country before planning a trip to visit it.
13. No sight in the world compares with the American Grand Canyon!
14. Cruises to the Caribbean area are becoming popular because they are so restful.
15. It is best to travel with as little baggage as possible.

Apply ◆ Think and Write

Discovering Opinions ◆ Even if you are only an "armchair traveler," you probably have opinions about foreign lands. Use writing to discover what those opinions are. Choose a country, such as France, Italy, Brazil, or Egypt. Think of its food, styles, customs, and people. Write an opinion you have about the country. Then list facts, reasons, or examples to support your opinion.

✎ **Remember**
to support your opinions with convincing facts, reasons, or examples.

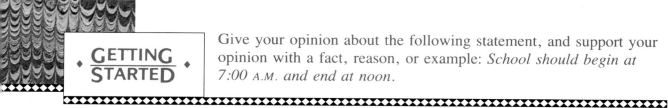

GETTING STARTED

Give your opinion about the following statement, and support your opinion with a fact, reason, or example: *School should begin at 7:00 A.M. and end at noon.*

WRITING ◆
A Persuasive Paragraph

When you write, you write for a reason. Sometimes that reason is to persuade others. You want to share your opinion about something and convince the reader to agree with you. That is the purpose of a persuasive paragraph. Here are some suggestions to help you prepare to write a persuasive paragraph.

How to Plan a Persuasive Paragraph
1. Decide exactly what your opinion is.
2. Think about your audience. Whom are you trying to convince? Why would it be to their advantage to agree with you?
3. Think of facts and reasons that support your opinion. Think of examples from your own experience, too.

When you are clear about what you want to say, you are ready to write your paragraph. People tend to remember what you say first and last, so aim for a strong beginning and ending. Begin, for example, by stating your opinion. Come right out with it. End by asking your readers to agree with you or to take action. Use the body of the paragraph to support your opinion.

The best way to travel is by train. Trains can take you almost anywhere you want to go. They travel into all major cities and also to many out-of-the-way places. Traveling by train lets you relax and enjoy the scenery. You don't have to plan routes, read maps, or deal with traffic jams. Modern trains are fast and comfortable, too. They even have dining cars where you can get meals or snacks. On your next trip, travel the fast, easy way—travel by train.

Summary ◆ A **persuasive paragraph** tries to convince the reader to agree with the writer's opinion. An effective persuasive paragraph has a strong beginning and ending.

Guided Practice

Think of a good first sentence for a persuasive paragraph about each topic. The sentence should state an opinion.

1. eating a healthful diet
2. pollution of our water
3. violence on television programs
4. registering to vote

Practice

A. Write the first sentence of a persuasive paragraph about each of these topics. In your sentence, state an opinion.

5. how to behave when visiting a foreign country
6. how much sleep a student needs
7. the length of the school year
8. the best time to exercise
9. the most interesting place to visit in your town

B. Write the following sentences as a persuasive paragraph. Write the sentence that states an opinion first. Then write the sentences that support the opinion in an order that makes sense. End with the sentence that gives a strong conclusion.

10. You may need inoculations to protect you against diseases in certain areas.
11. When you traveling abroad, you should take health precautions.
12. The water in some places is not safe to drink; make sure you know where to avoid it.
13. Take precautions to stay healthy and enjoy your trip.
14. Remember, too, that ice is usually made from drinking water.

C. Choose your favorite opinion from the ones you wrote for **Practice A.** Then list at least three facts, reasons, or examples to support the opinion.

Apply • Think and Write

A Persuasive Paragraph • Use the opinion and supporting facts, reasons, or examples from **Practice C** to write a persuasive paragraph.

> ✎ **Remember**
> to begin and end persuasive paragraphs with strong sentences.

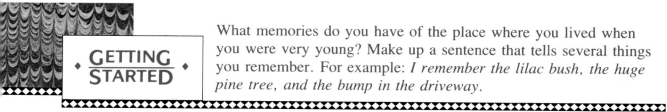

What memories do you have of the place where you lived when you were very young? Make up a sentence that tells several things you remember. For example: *I remember the lilac bush, the huge pine tree, and the bump in the driveway.*

WRITING ♦
Using Commas

The comma (,) helps to make written language clearer. This chart explains some rules for using commas.

Explanation	Example
Commas separate words or groups of words in a series (three or more items). No comma is needed after the last item.	Sid, Paolo, and Hans were in Katy's class. The class read books, saw films, and heard stories about China.
A comma is used after a word such as *yes, no,* or *well* at the beginning of a sentence.	Yes, Katy was born in China. No, she isn't Chinese. Well, her parents are Americans.
The names of people directly spoken to are set off by commas.	Katy, what is China like? Do you like it there, Katy? Please, Katy, tell us more.
When a last name appears first, a comma separates it from the first name.	Waxman, Katy Romanelli, Sofia Mbeli, Mr. S.R.

Summary ♦ When you write, use commas
- ♦ to separate words or groups of words in a series;
- ♦ after *yes, no,* or *well* at the beginning of a sentence;
- ♦ to set off the names of people spoken to;
- ♦ to separate a last name from a first name when the last name is written first.

Guided Practice

Tell where commas belong in these sentences.

1. Were you born in the Chinese capital of Beijing Katy?
2. Yes but I'm an American because my parents are Americans.
3. My father has been learning to speak read and write Chinese.
4. Well his Chinese now is almost as good as his English.
5. I think Hans that we will return to America next summer.

Practice

A. Write the sentences, adding commas where needed.

6. Katy has classmates from England Germany Italy and Africa.
7. They study the history art and music of China at school.
8. Well Katy's father studied Chinese art in Beijing.
9. Yes her mother also taught mathematics there.
10. Katy are you anxious to see America again?
11. Yes Lien but I will miss China.
12. Let's take a walk along the river Katy.
13. People are catching fish washing clothes and selling food there.
14. Look Lien. There is a beautiful wooden junk.
15. The sail is painted with a dragon for good luck Katy.
16. Just imagine it Lien beside a modern ocean liner!
17. Did you know Katy that some people live on junks?
18. No I thought they were only used to transport goods.
19. Well here is a junk carrying a large family.
20. Lien I brought a snack along for us to share.
21. Would you like plums litchis or a pork bun?

B. Some of Katy's friends were Sebastian Graham, Kei Tama, Angelo DeMeo, Vera Hill, Jossi Ngema, and Hilda Breuer. They signed up for a school trip to the opera. Copy the form below. Enter the names, last name first, on the form.

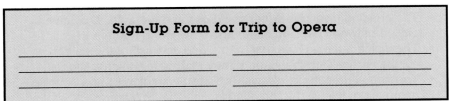

Sign-Up Form for Trip to Opera

Apply ◆ Think and Write

Questions and Answers ◆ Author Jean Fritz wrote a book about her childhood in China in the 1920s. The book is called *Homesick: My Own Story*. Write some *yes* or *no* questions you might want to ask Jean Fritz. Then make up possible answers. If you read *Homesick*, you may learn some of the real answers.

✎ **Remember**
to use commas to show readers when to pause.

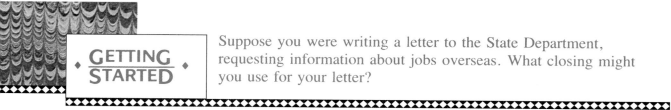

GETTING STARTED

Suppose you were writing a letter to the State Department, requesting information about jobs overseas. What closing might you use for your letter?

WRITING ♦
A Business Letter

Study the placement of the six parts of a business letter.

Heading	54 Ashley Road Columbus, OH 43216 December 16, 1990
Inside Address	Dr. Thomas Mott, Director American Schools Abroad P.O. Box 14523 Washington, DC 20008
Greeting	Dear Dr. Mott:
Body	My family and I will be spending the next several years in India. I have been teaching sixth grade in Columbus for the past five years. I also run the computer club. I would appreciate information about teaching opportunities at American schools in India.
Closing **Signature**	Sincerely yours, *Mimi Winter* Mimi Winter

- The heading gives the writer's address and the date. A comma is placed between city and state, and between the date and year.
- The inside address gives the name and address of the person or company receiving the letter. It may include a person's title.
- The formal greeting is always followed by a colon (:). If a specific name is not known, the greeting is *Dear Sir or Madam*.
- The body states the purpose of the letter. Facts are given in a brief, logical way. Each new paragraph is indented.
- The formal closing is followed by a comma. Only the first word is capitalized, for example *Yours truly* and *Sincerely yours*.
- The writer's name is typed four lines below the closing.

Summary ♦ When you write a business letter, make your message clear and brief.

Guided Practice

Tell the word or words that best complete each sentence.

1. The name of the person or company receiving a business letter appears in the ———— .

2. A business letter uses a ———— after the formal greeting.

3. *Yours truly* is a suitable ———— for a business letter.

Practice

A. Write each item as if it were part of a business letter. Use proper capitalization and punctuation.

4. dear sir or madam

5. respectfully yours

6. Ms. Joan Wangler, principal

7. dear ms. wangler

8. february 20 1990

9. dear job service

10. sincerely yours

11. Dr. Jacob Soong
edin foreign job service
5530 new york avenue
washington DC 20002

12. 2813 woodley road
peekskill ny 10566
april 4 1990

B. Write the following business letter in the correct form. Then label each of the six parts of the letter.

297 Pell Road Gary, IN 46402 May 3, 1990 Director Youth Hostels, Inc. 2700 Wilson Street New York, NY 10012 Dear Sir or Madam I plan to be traveling in Europe during the next two months and would like to stay at youth hostels while I am there. Please send me a copy of the pamphlet "European Youth Hostels" as soon as possible. Thank you. Sincerely

Paul Buenita

Apply ◆ Think and Write

Dictionary of Knowledge ◆ Many Americans have served as Peace Corps volunteers, working with people in developing countries. Read about the Peace Corps in the Dictionary of Knowledge. Then, using correct business letter form, write to this agency to request more information about its program.

✎ **Remember**
to state the facts briefly and clearly in the body of a business letter.

Focus on Reasons

President John F. Kennedy wrote a very persuasive letter to young Peter Galbraith, as you saw earlier. He gave Peter convincing reasons to feel better about moving to India. Notice the order in which President Kennedy put those reasons.

Peter will like his new friends and new school in India.
4. He will help himself out by making new friends.
3. He will help his parents do a good job for their country.
2. He will come back an experienced rider.
1. India has fascinating animals.

Kennedy begins by giving reasons **1** and **2**. Those are not major reasons for someone to move to India, but they will certainly interest Peter. Reasons **3** and **4**, on the other hand, are important reasons for Peter to want to move to India.

Kennedy's reasons are organized in the order of their importance. He uses an **ascending**, or rising order. That is, he begins with less important reasons and builds up to more important ones.

Reasons can also be given in **descending** order. Then the more important reasons are first and the less important ones last. Writers use this arrangement to persuade readers quickly.

Both methods work well because the beginning and the end are the two most powerful parts of a composition.

The Writer's Voice ◆ Suppose there is a new girl in class who has just moved from a distant state. She needs to be persuaded that she will like living in your part of the country. What would you say to convince her? List at least four reasons. Arrange them as President Kennedy did, from least important to most important.

Working Together

When you write to persuade the reader, you might use reasons to support your opinion. With your group, work on activities **A** and **B**.

A. Discuss the topics below, filling in the blanks. Whether you fully accept every answer or not, discuss reasons that could be used to support each statement. Suggest at least three reasons for each statement below.

1. Today's most enjoyable movie is _____ .
2. An interesting place to visit in our state is _____ .
3. A great way to earn spending money is _____ .
4. The most intelligent animal is _____ .
5. Television will never replace _____ .
6. The most enjoyable reading is _____ .
7. The best vacation is _____ .

B. Arrange each set of reasons in activity **A** from most important (number 1) to least important (number 3).

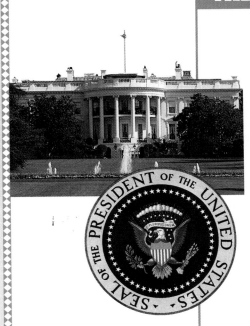

THESAURUS CORNER • Word Choice

The reasons below support the statement "The President of the United States must play many roles." Rewrite the sentences. Arrange the reasons from least important (number 1) to most important (number 5). In each sentence, replace the word *President* or *President's* with a pronoun. Replace each word in dark type with a better word. Use the Thesaurus and Thesaurus Index.

1. Perhaps more important than the President's dealings with Congress is the President's power to nominate Supreme Court justices.
2. Above all, the President must be a leader of all the people.
3. Of course, the President has to **labor competently** with Congress—and Congress with the President; he must **reap** their respect.
4. The President's ceremonial **jobs,** such as **saying** his thanks to astronauts, are highly visible but perhaps less vital than the President's other duties.
5. Even higher on the list is the President's role as commander-in-chief of America's armed forces.

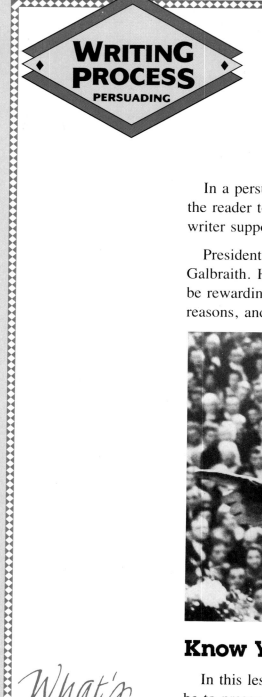

WRITING PROCESS
PERSUADING

Writing a Persuasive Letter

In a persuasive letter, a writer states an opinion and tries to get the reader to agree with that opinion. To persuade the reader, the writer supports his or her opinion with facts, reasons, or examples.

President John F. Kennedy wrote a persuasive letter to Peter Galbraith. He wanted to convince Peter that moving to India would be rewarding. The President supported his opinion with facts, reasons, and specific examples.

Know Your Purpose and Audience

In this lesson you will write a persuasive letter. Your purpose will be to present an opinion about something that is important to you. You will try to convince your audience that your opinion is right.

Once you select a topic, you will choose your audience, the person to whom you address your letter. Later you can mail or deliver your letter. You and your classmates can also share your opinions by giving speeches.

What's MY PURPOSE

Who's MY AUDIENCE

1 Prewriting

First choose a topic. Then gather ideas for your letter.

Choose Your Topic ♦ Write a phrase similar to one of the following: "I firmly believe that ____" or "I feel strongly that ____." Complete the sentence as many times as you can. Choose your favorite as your topic.

Think About It

Read your list of opinions. Which do you care most strongly about? Which can you support with facts, reasons, and specific examples? Underline your choice. Then decide whom you want to persuade. Who can act on your suggestion? Write to that person.

Talk About It

Work with a partner. Take turns saying the phrase and completing it with an opinion. Help each other think of opinions by suggesting topics. For example, the topic of whether or not school should be held all year should spark some opinion.

Topic Ideas

the playground needs new equipment
the park needs to be cleaned up
our library needs new reference books
people should not litter
our town needs a youth center

Choose Your Strategy ◆ Here are two strategies for gathering details. Read both. Then try the one you think will help you the most.

PREWRITING IDEAS

CHOICE ONE

An Opinion Notebook

Collect information that supports your opinion. Visit the library. Find books and articles related to your topic. Talk with an expert. Discuss your topic with classmates, family, and friends.

Record the supporting information you find in a notebook. You can use this example as a model.

Model

Our school library needs new encyclopedias.

Facts	Reasons	Examples
thirty yrs. old two volumes gone	better papers better grades	space program old data

CHOICE TWO

A Venn Diagram

Begin with a statement that tells your reader what ideas you both share. Either talk to the person you will write to or predict his or her opinion. Then complete the diagram.

Model

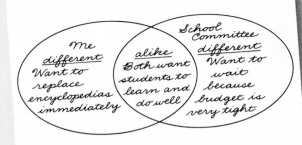

Me
different
Want to replace encyclopedias immediately

alike
Both want students to learn and do well

School Committee
different
Want to wait because budget is very tight

2 Writing

Before you write, review your notebook or your Venn diagram. Begin your letter with a statement of belief that you share with your reader. Then explain why your opinion results from this belief. Here are some ways to begin.

- ♦ I feel exactly as you do about _____ and that is why _____.
- ♦ You and I share the belief that _____.

As you write, support your opinion with facts, reasons, and examples. Try to conclude with a strong summary of your opinion. When you have finished the body, add the other parts of a business letter. Add a heading, an inside address, a greeting, a closing, and your signature.

Sample First Draft ♦

Dear Mr. Hogan

I believe that we all want littleton students to do well. However, our goal is not helped by the bad condition of our school library reference books. Our school desparately needs a new set of encyclopedias to help students write better papers. Our encyclopedias are hopelessly out of date. Our encyclopedias are almost thirty years old.

I know the school budget is very tight. Isn't it outrageous, however, when students get incorrect facts in their own school library? Im sure that you and the school committee will agree.

Sincerely Yours,

Howin Ping

3 Revising

Now that you have written your persuasive letter, would you like to improve it? Here is an idea to help you revise your work.

REVISING IDEA

FIRST Read to Yourself

As you read, review your purpose. Did you write a persuasive letter about something important to you? Think about your audience. Will that person be convinced that you are right? Mark any unclear sentences with a wavy line ～～～ so you can go back and improve them after you finish reading.

Focus: Did you support your opinion with facts, reasons, and examples?

THEN Share with a Partner

Ask a partner to take the role of the person receiving your letter. Ask your partner to read the letter silently. Then ask for suggestions. Here are some guidelines.

The Writer

Guidelines: Listen to your partner, but make only the changes you think you should make. This is *your* letter.

Sample questions:
- Could I use better persuasive techniques?
- **Focus question:** Do I need to add facts, reasons, or examples?

The Writer's Partner

Guidelines: Be honest but courteous. Use a helpful tone.

Sample responses:
- It might be more persuasive if you said _____.
- You might want to explain why _____.

Revising Model ♦ In the revised letter below, the blue marks show changes the writer wants to make.

Poor is a more precise word for this sentence.

This sentence gives the letter a strong conclusion.

The pronoun *they* replaces the repeated noun *encyclopedias*

The writer's partner thought an example was needed.

Dear Mr. Hogan

I believe that we all want littleton students to do well. However, our goal is not helped by the ~~bad~~ *poor* condition of our school library reference books. Our school desparately needs a new set of encyclopedias to help students write better papers. Our encyclopedias are ~~hopelessly~~ out of date. ~~Our encyclopedias~~ *They* are almost thirty years old. *according to our encyclopedias, we haven't even landed on the moon yet.*∧
I know the school budget is very tight. Isn't it outrageous, however, when students get incorrect facts in their own school library? Im sure that you and the school committee will agree.

           Sincerely Yours,

           Howin Ping

           Howin Ping

Read the revised letter above the way the writer has decided it *should* be. Then revise your own persuasive letter.

Grammar Check ♦ Replacing some nouns with pronouns can make your writing less repetitive.

Word Choice ♦ Do you ever want a more precise word for a word like *bad*? A thesaurus can help you find the word you want.

Revising Checklist

☐ **Purpose:** Did I write a persuasive letter?

☐ **Audience:** Will my reader be convinced?

☐ **Focus:** Did I give facts, reasons, and examples to support my opinion?

4 Proofreading

Now is the time to proofread your letter for mistakes. A correct letter is more persuasive.

Proofreading Model ♦ Here is the persuasive letter about research books. Red proofreading marks have been added.

<table>
<tr><td colspan="2">

Proofreading Marks

capital letter	=
small letter	/
indent paragraph	¶
check spelling	⬭

</td></tr>
</table>

Dear Mr. Hogan:

    I believe that we all want littleton students to do well. However, our goal is not helped by the ~~bad~~ *poor* condition of our school library reference books. Our school ~~desparately~~ *desperately* needs a new set of encyclopedias to help students write better papers. Our encyclopedias are hopelessly out of date. ~~Our encyclopedias~~ *They* are almost thirty years old. *according to our encyclopedias, we haven't even landed on the moon yet!*
    I know the school budget is very tight. Isn't it outrageous, however, when students get incorrect facts in their own school library? ~~Im~~ *I'm* sure that you and the school committee will agree.

                    Sincerely Yours,

                    Howin Ping

                    Howin Ping

Proofreading Checklist

- [ ] Did I spell words correctly?
- [ ] Did I indent paragraphs?
- [ ] Did I use capital letters correctly?
- [ ] Did I use correct marks at the end of sentences?
- [ ] Did I type neatly or use my best handwriting?

PROOFREADING IDEA

Trading with a Partner

    To be sure you find all errors, ask a classmate to proofread your work. Ask her or him to make a check next to any line that contains a mistake. Then find and correct your errors.

After you have proofread your letter, make a neat copy.

5 Publishing

Would you like to share your persuasive letter with others? Here are two ways you might try.

168 Schoolhouse Road
Littleton, MA 01460
February 9, 1991

Mr. Arthur Hogan, Chairperson
Littleton School Committee
1238 Summer Lane
Littleton, MA 01460

Dear Mr. Hogan:

I believe that we all want Littleton students to do well. However, our goal is not helped by the poor condition of our school library reference books.

Our encyclopedias are hopelessly out of date. They are almost thirty years old. According to our encyclopedias, we haven't even landed on the moon yet!

I know the school budget is very tight. Isn't it outrageous, however, when students get incorrect facts in their own school library? I'm sure that you and the school committee will agree. Our school desperately needs a new set of encyclopedias to help students write better papers.

Sincerely yours,

Howin Ping

Howin Ping

PUBLISHING IDEAS

Share Aloud

Give a short speech about your topic. Include facts, reasons, and examples from your persuasive letter. Then ask your classmates whether they agree or disagree.

Share in Writing

Mail or deliver your persuasive letter to the person you wrote it to. If you mail it, be sure the envelope is correctly addressed. You might receive a reply!

CURRICULUM
·CONNECTION·

Writing Across the Curriculum Art

In this unit you wrote a persuasive letter. First you may have made a Venn diagram to note how your ideas and your reader's ideas were alike and different. Art lovers also enjoy noting likenesses and differences when they compare works of art.

Writing to Learn

Think and Compare ◆ Look carefully at the two paintings below. On a Venn diagram list likenesses and differences you observe.

Venn Diagram

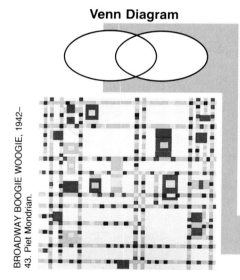

BROADWAY BOOGIE WOOGIE, 1942–43. Piet Mondrian.

CIRCULAR FORMS, 1930. Robert Delaunay.

Write ◆ Compare the paintings and then select the one you like better. Tell why you prefer this painting to the other.

Writing in Your Journal

In the Writer's Warm-up you wrote about visiting another country. Later you read about President Kennedy and Samantha Smith. Both believed that travel abroad was a valuable experience for Americans. In your journal write about the country you would most like to visit and why.

BOOKS TO ENJOY

Read More About It

Samantha Smith: Journey to the Soviet Union
by Samantha Smith

Samantha Smith's first-person account of her journey to the Soviet Union gives us an important look at a young American abroad. The lively prose and photos give us a portrait of our youngest "ambassador."

Homesick: My Own Story *by Jean Fritz*

Jean Fritz's entertaining works of historical fiction are found in most libraries. *Homesick,* however, is an autobiography. In it she recounts her experiences as a young American girl in an English school in China. Finding her place in this new world takes adjustment. With honesty and humor, young Jean overcomes obstacles and benefits from living abroad.

Newbery Honor

Book Report Idea Newspaper Ad

Advertising is one way to persuade others to read a book that you have enjoyed. The next book report you write could be a full-page newspaper ad.

Advertise Your Book ◆ Your ad doesn't have to tell a lot. The ad should make people curious to read the book. An exciting passage, a word portrait of a main character, or a description of the story conflict are all possibilities for the ad. Of course, you will have to include the title and author.

> Can you read this message?
>
> PEEK RIGHT
>
> If not, you know how Sam Mott feels.
>
> Sam is smart, funny, good-looking, and... learning disabled. His brain just won't make sense out of letters of words.
>
> Sam can't hide his problem much longer. School is torture, and things aren't working out so well at home or in the neighborhood either.
>
> Is help on the way?
>
> *Do Bananas Chew Gum?* by Jamie Gilson

UNIT REVIEW

Unit 4

Pronouns *pages 180–189*

A. Write the pronoun in each sentence. Then write *subject* or *object* to show what kind of pronoun it is.

1. Liz Ortega and I skate twice a week.
2. She is an excellent skater.
3. Liz's father taught her some marvelous stunts.
4. He used to ice skate professionally.
5. People admire them greatly.
6. Mr. Ortega is teaching me to do a figure eight.
7. I have practiced for a month now.
8. We now do figure eights together.
9. People watch us and applaud.
10. Then they ask for Mr. Ortega's autograph.

B. Write each of the following sentences. Use the correct pronoun in parentheses ( ).

11. That painting of my grandfather's old barn is (my, mine).
12. Jennie brought (her, hers) pet guinea pig to school.
13. (Her, Hers) is the report on birds.
14. Which stamp album is (your, yours)?
15. (Our, Ours) was the song that received the most applause.

16. (Her, Hers) mother is president of our parent-teacher association.
17. Where are (their, theirs) gloves?
18. (My, Mine) cousin is a lieutenant in the Air Force Reserve.
19. (Our, Ours) poodle is more affectionate than (their, theirs).
20. Will you show me (your, yours) photographs of Mexico City?

C. Write the pronoun or the contraction that correctly completes each sentence.

21. Ann and (he, him) wash the dishes.
22. Emilio and Sheila gave me (their, they're) address.
23. The best athlete on our team is (she, her).
24. The directions confused Cara and (I, me).
25. (They, Them) asked for the tape recording of our band.
26. (Your, You're) going too fast!
27. Noriko and (I, me) wrote a song.
28. Mrs. Wong and (she, her) looked at some snapshots of my trip to Hong Kong.
29. The ones who got the highest grades are (they, them).
30. Richard, tell me (your, you're) opinion of the movie.
31. Peter's cocker spaniel followed (we, us) home.
32. The enthusiastic reaction to his poem delighted (he, him).
33. The Matsuos and (they, them) are going to Yellowstone National Park.
34. (Their, They're) the ones who will paint the scenery for the play.

Connotations *pages 190–191*

D. Write each of the following sentences. Use the word in parentheses ( ) that has the more positive connotation.

35. Andrea is a very (proud, conceited) person.
36. Going over the waterfall in a canoe was a (reckless, brave) feat.
37. Ms. Moss is an extremely (careful, finicky) supervisor.
38. After she won the contest, Bena (smiled, smirked) at us.
39. Lani Akana is wearing (striking, outlandish) clothes.

E. Write the word in each pair that has the more negative connotation.

40. nonchalant, careless
41. curious, snoopy
42. fat, plump
43. group, mob
44. tedious, painstaking

Commas *pages 208–209*

F. Write each of the following sentences. Add commas where they are needed.

45. Yesterday Betty Susie and I paid a visit to the Chinese section of our city.
46. Chinese markets selling meat fish and vegetables were everywhere.
47. Yes we did have lunch at a Chinese restaurant.
48. We had fried rice steamed vegetables a meat dish and fortune cookies.
49. No my fortune cookie did not promise bad luck.

50. Susie's aunt was listed in the telephone directory as *Kwan Marie*.
51. Mrs. Kwan her husband and her six-month-old child were at home.
52. Well you should have seen that pretty baby!
53. Mrs. Kwan Susie and I took turns holding him in our laps.
54. He was smiling gurgling and clapping his tiny hands.
55. Can you Susie show us a picture of him?

Business Letter *pages 210–211*

G. Write each of the following items as if it were in a business letter. Use proper capitalization and punctuation.

56. alicia lopez chairperson
57. may 9 1990
58. dear ms.eng
59. yours truly
60. dr. wesley cohen
    somerset hospital
    231 elm avenue
    east palo alto california 94303
61. respectfully
62. 2142 acorn ridge dr
    corvallis oregon 97330
63. dear congresswoman
64. dr. elena montero
    chief of pediatrics
    university medical center
    101 tunxis avenue
    albuquerque new mexico 81170
65. mr. taro wada
    national accounting company
    1000 third avenue
    spokane washington 99206

Unit 1: Sentences *pages 4–15*

A. Write the sentences, using capital letters and correct end punctuation. After each sentence write *declarative, interrogative, imperative* or *exclamatory*.

1. our class is reading books about kites
2. how high that kite soars
3. did Pedro build that kite
4. several kinds of kites are common
5. help me make a box kite
6. what a pretty kite you have
7. don't fly that flat kite near the wires
8. most kites have frames made of sticks
9. will you enter your kite in the contest
10. Ted Osato's kite is the best of all

B. Write each complete subject. Then underline the simple subject.

11. Jennie Leigh is teaching her dog a new trick.
12. The poodle can sit up and beg.
13. An instructor at the obedience school taught it.
14. This friendly dog must learn patience.
15. The command of a pointed finger will prevent it from moving.
16. My spaniel is very frisky.
17. Moving vehicles excite it.
18. The sound of a car makes it sit up.
19. Patience is not one of my dog's virtues.
20. This lively animal will never be as obedient as Jennie's poodle.

C. Write each complete predicate. Then underline each simple predicate.

21. Goats have provided humans with milk, meat, and wool.
22. The mountain goat is descended from the wild goat of Asia.
23. Goats can vary greatly in size.
24. Some goats stand only one and a half feet tall.
25. Some Indian goats have grown as high as four feet.
26. The milk of the goat tastes tangy.
27. The Greeks use goat cheese in their cooking.
28. Wild goats prefer mountainous areas.
29. Some domestic goats stay in stables for protection.
30. Other domestic goats can range freely.
31. Mohair wool comes from the Angora goat's outer coat.
32. Cashmere is produced from the cashmere goat's fleece.

D. Write the subject of each sentence.

33. Put those plates on the buffet table.
34. Did Thelma make the party decorations?
35. Tom is bringing the cake.
36. Did Theresa bake the cherry pie?
37. Give Peter the paper cups filled with lemonade.
38. Is the lemonade too sour?
39. Serve the pot of chili.
40. Has Cynthia Gooding arrived yet?
41. Did Katja invite her parents?
42. Take the unused paper plates to the car.

Unit 2: Nouns *pages 62–71*

E. Write the nouns in each sentence. Then write whether each noun names a person, place, thing, or idea.

43. Jack Persoff is my favorite uncle.
44. His family lives in Crystal Spring.
45. My mother and Jack have a close relationship.
46. Jack repairs automobiles.
47. His garage is packed with tools, testing instruments, and old cars.
48. My sister works at his shop.
49. Tanya is learning a valuable skill.
50. By the end of the day, her gloves and overalls are covered with grease.
51. My uncle says, "Happiness is a smooth-running vehicle."
52. My mother says, "Contentment is the right person in the right job."

F. Write each underlined word. Then write whether it is a common noun or a proper noun.

53. My <u>cousin</u> went to <u>Oregon</u>.
54. He spent two <u>days</u> in <u>Portland</u>.
55. His <u>family</u> took a <u>trip</u> on the <u>Scenic Drive</u> to <u>Mount Table</u>.
56. Then they drove to <u>Ashland</u> and saw four <u>plays</u> at the <u>Globe Theater</u>.
57. Two were <u>comedies</u> by <u>William Shakespeare</u>.
58. The <u>Shakespearean Festival</u> was started in 1935 by <u>Angus Bowmer</u>, a <u>teacher</u> at a local <u>college</u>.
59. They took a <u>road</u> to <u>Crater Lake</u>.
60. This <u>attraction</u> was formed when <u>Mount Mazama</u>, a <u>volcano</u>, erupted.

G. Write each sentence. Capitalize the proper nouns.

61. One of my best friends is carly nichols.
62. I often visit her home on bellevue drive.
63. Last saturday carly and I went to fiske concert hall.
64. My friend's mother performed with the danville symphony orchestra.
65. Her mother is better known by her professional name, ornella frasscati.
66. She sang songs by mozart, schubert, and gian carlo menotti.
67. Afterward a reception was held at the terrace hotel.
68. When mrs. nichols saw me, she smiled.
69. She and arthur friedman, the orchestra's conductor, signed my autograph book.
70. Next monday I will show the autographs to my friends at the elementary school.

H. Write the possessive form of each noun. Then write whether the noun is singular or plural.

71. workshop	81. rodeos
72. elephants	82. automobiles
73. bush	83. monkey
74. children	84. farmers
75. thinker	85. toys
76. thorns	86. thrush
77. men	87. uniforms
78. geese	88. goose
79. laboratory	89. balloon
80. mice	90. women

Unit 3: Verbs   *pages 116–133*

I. Write each sentence. Draw one line under the linking verb. Draw two lines under the words that the verb connects.

91. Sandy is my cousin.
92. You appear tired.
93. That cave seems dangerous.
94. These grapes taste sweet.
95. The Kwans are both doctors.
96. That warm stew certainly smells delicious!
97. After the third television commercial, we became bored.
98. Timmie was first in line.
99. Danielle looks very sad.
100. The water in the lake feels chilly in the evening.

J. Write each sentence. Underline the helping verbs once and the main verbs twice.

101. We are watching the baseball game on television.
102. Mike Pérez has batted a home run.
103. The fans in the stadium are cheering.
104. The program will show an instant replay of the great moment.
105. The pitcher has placed his feet squarely on the mound.
106. You can see the expression on his face.
107. He is frowning at the batter.
108. A run by Pérez could win the game.
109. The pitcher is winding up.
110. Crack! Pérez has hit the ball over the fence.

K. Write the direct object in each sentence.

111. Alicia put the letter in the mailbox.
112. Hank plays the accordion.
113. The dog sniffed the bone.
114. Ms. Ferrell drives a bus.
115. The animal tamer faced the angry tiger.
116. Mr. Johnson mended the wooden fence.
117. Bobbie Jo Sterling recited a poem.
118. In winter we enjoy a hot breakfast.

L. Write the past tense and future tense of each verb. Use *will* with the future tense.

119. cry   **121.** push   **123.** spy
120. stop   **122.** measure   **124.** arrive

M. Write the three principal parts of each verb. Use the helping verb *has* with each past participle.

125. ask   **128.** go   **131.** know
126. ring   **129.** carry   **132.** sing
127. swim   **130.** blow

N. Write each sentence. Use the correct verb in parentheses ( ).

133. (Can, May) Laura study with me?
134. We (learn, teach) to move gracefully in dance class.
135. Please (sit, set) down to eat.
136. (Lie, Lay) the keys on the table.
137. (Sit, Set) the vase of roses here.
138. Ms. Flores (can, may) run the mile in four minutes fifty seconds.
139. We will (lie, lay) in the sun.
140. (Learn, Teach) me to play the piano.

Unit 4: Pronouns   *pages 180–189, 208–209*

O. Write the pronoun in each sentence. Then write *subject* or *object* to show what kind of pronoun it is.

141. Jim and Sara met, and they walked up the hill.
142. She was walking faster than Jim in the beginning.
143. People began to pass them on the hill.
144. Jim told her about swimming.
145. Then she told him about sailing.
146. She was born near the Atlantic Ocean.
147. I asked her to speak further.
148. We will listen carefully.
149. Then you can ask questions.
150. Sara will answer you.

P. Write each sentence. Use the correct word in parentheses ( ).

151. We all brought (our, ours) pets to class.
152. The Jones twins brought (their, they're) guinea pig home from the pet show.
153. The French poodle with the pink collar is (my, mine).
154. (Your, You're) Siamese cat is very friendly.
155. The rabbit with the twitching nose is (their, theirs).
156. (My, Mine) cousin left his guppies at home.
157. (They're, Their) happy swimming in (they're, their) fishbowl.
158. Which animal is (your, yours)?

Q. Write each sentence. Use the correct pronoun in parentheses.

159. My favorite actress is (she, her).
160. The stars of the play are (they, them).
161. The play's author is (he, him).
162. The stage crew are (we, us).

R. Write the pronoun that correctly completes each sentence.

163. Garry and (I, me) gave oral reports about gorillas.
164. Ms. Levin told (we, us) about these animals.
165. The one who knows most about them is (she, her).
166. (They, Them) are the largest of apes.
167. You can find (they, them) in central Africa.
168. (We, Us) showed color slides of gorilla bands to Marcia.
169. (She, Her) returned (they, them) at the end of the day.

S. Write each sentence. Add commas where they are needed.

170. Yes Marjorie we enjoyed the dinner.
171. I like broccoli asparagus and cauliflower.
172. No the vegetables are not overcooked.
173. Will you have some more of the asparagus Betty?
174. Tell me Steve did you enjoy the food?
175. Potatoes onions and grated cheese make a hearty dish.
176. You can find that cookbook in the library's card catalog under the name Simonson Mary.

LANGUAGE PUZZLERS

Unit 4 Challenge

Pronoun Homophones

Homophones are words that sound alike. Write each pair of homophones. The first word fits the definition. The second is a pronoun. (Hint: Apostrophes may be needed for some blanks.)

1. there is: _ _ _ _ _ _ _ and _ _ _ _ _ _
2. what you see with: _ _ _ and _
3. a female sheep: _ _ _ and _ _ _
4. a religious song: _ _ _ _ and _ _ _
5. it is: _ _ _ _ and _ _ _
6. very small: _ _ _ and _ _
7. sixty minutes: _ _ _ _ and _ _ _
8. they are: _ _ _ _ _ _ _ and _ _ _ _ _ _
9. note of the scale: _ _ and _ _
10. twenty-four make a day: _ _ _ _ _ and _ _ _ _

A Pronoun Mystery

Detective Cannata has all the suspects together at Bailey Mansion. Now he must figure out who the culprit is.

To solve the mystery, use the clues below. Substitute pronouns for all the suspects and groups of suspects. Then write the last letter of each pronoun. Arrange the letters to form the culprit's name.

1. Detective Cannata spotted Professor Flores and Nurse Peterson in the hall.
2. Mr. Chang saw Mr. Akana in the parlor.
3. Mrs. Wright found Ms. Meyere in the library.
4. The people in the kitchen were Professor Flores and I.
5. Detective Cannata noticed Colonel Bly and me in the game room.

Unit 4 Extra Practice

1 Writing with Pronouns

p. 180

A. Write each sentence. Underline the pronouns.

1. Robots are helpful, but they are expensive to build.
2. Robot builders call their science *robotics*.
3. It is a rapidly growing field.
4. Some robots already work in our factories and offices.
5. People find them fascinating.
6. You may have seen the robot Silent Sam.
7. He directs traffic in many states.
8. The tall robot never tires of his work.
9. People cheerfully obey him.
10. Robots in factories do their jobs quickly and well.
11. They are connected to computers.
12. The computers direct them.
13. Robots will do many of our routine jobs in the future.
14. Mother thinks a robot could make her work easier.
15. Maybe it could help with my chores, too!

B. The second sentence in each pair contains a pronoun. Write the pronoun. Then write the noun that the pronoun takes the place of.

16. **a.** Hero of Alexandria described a robot long ago.
    b. He called the invention an automaton.
17. **a.** A Czech writer's play told about robots.
    b. His play was called *R.U.R.*
18. **a.** Robots became very popular during the 1920s.
    b. People saw them in movies and magazines.
19. **a.** A robot's appearance may be humanlike.
    b. Its size may be large or small.
20. **a.** Two Viking Landers were built for a spaceflight to Mars.
    b. They were very expensive robots.
21. **a.** Another space probe will travel to Io, a moon of Jupiter.
    b. It is named *Galileo*.
22. **a.** This robot will work where humans could not.
    b. It is not hurt by harmful radiation.

2 Pronouns and Antecedents   *p. 182*

A. Write the pronouns in these sentences. Then write the antecedent of each pronoun. The pronoun and its antecedent might not be in the same sentence.

  1. The Wright brothers are famous for their work.
  2. They operated a bicycle shop in Dayton, Ohio.
  3. The brothers built different aircraft in it.
  4. They attached an engine to a glider.
  5. The men had planned their work carefully.
  6. They took the airplane with them to Kitty Hawk.
  7. It is a village on the coast of North Carolina.
  8. Orville was the first of them to take off.
  9. His new engine worked fine.
 10. The brothers continued their experiments.
 11. They built several more planes.
 12. Their flights made them world famous.
 13. Their original bicycle shop has been restored.
 14. Visitors can see the shop just as it was in 1903.

B. Complete the paragraph with pronouns from the list below.

it   their   she   her   he   his

   Charles Lindbergh made (**15.** ____) famous flight in 1927.
(**16.** ____) was the first man to fly across the Atlantic alone.
(**17.** ____) took off from Roosevelt field in New York and
landed at Le Bourget near Paris thirty-three and a half hours
later. (**18.** ____) plane was called the *Spirit of St. Louis*.
(**19.** ____) now hangs on display in the Air and Space Museum in
Washington, D. C. Amelia Earhart is also known for (**20.** ____)
aviation skill. (**21.** ____) was the first woman to fly across the
Atlantic. During a flight around the world, (**22.** ____) plane was
lost. The mystery surrounding (**23.** ____) disappearance
continues to puzzle historians. Lindbergh and Earhart have
established (**24.** ____) places in aviation history. Another
important pilot is Chuck Yeager. (**25.** ____) piloted the Bell
X-1 faster than the speed of sound. (**26.** ____) success on
October 14, 1947, made space flight a possibility.

3 Subject and Object Pronouns   *p. 184*

A. Write each sentence. Underline the subject pronouns.

1. "Would you like to make a clay bowl?" asked Aunt Anna.
2. "I would love to," said Lucas.
3. "We can work together," said the boy's aunt.
4. They rolled the clay into long coils.
5. "I make the bowls from these coils," said Aunt Anna.
6. "First we must join the ends of the coils."
7. She showed Lucas how to do that.
8. Then he stacked the coils on top of each other.
9. They pressed the coils tightly together.
10. "Now it looks like a bowl!" said Lucas.

B. Write the second sentence in each pair. Underline the object pronouns.

11. The Bird Watchers is a club. Jason will join it.
12. Club members look for birds. Members spot them all over.
13. Rita is the president. Jason asks her about the club.
14. The Bird Watchers go to the woods. Mrs. Lee takes them.
15. A song sparrow sings happily. The children hear it.
16. "Look at the sparrow," Rita says. "It doesn't see us."
17. The Bird Watchers see a cardinal. The bird startles them.
18. Mrs. Lee walks toward a wren's nest. Rita follows her.
19. The wren flies off. "The wren just saw you," Rita says.
20. A woodpecker hammers on a tree. Jason watches it.

C. The second sentence in each pair contains two pronouns. Write the pronouns. Then underline the subject pronouns once and the object pronouns twice.

21. A hummingbird flitted away. "I didn't see it!" Ann cried.
22. "Don't worry," said Mrs. Lee. "We will spot it again."
23. A goldfinch landed near the children. They all admired it.
24. A lark flew overhead. "It is watching us," said Rita.
25. "What bird is that?" asked Don. "Can you tell me?"
26. "That is an owl," said Rita. "We have seen it before."
27. "Do eagles live nearby?" asked Don. "I want to see them."
28. "An eagle lives on that cliff," said Rita. "I have seen it."

4 Possessive Pronouns and Contractions

p. 186

A. Write the possessive pronoun in each sentence. Then write *before* if it comes before a noun or *alone* if it stands alone.

1. Our neighborhood is having a cat show.
2. Sal says the white Persian cat with long hair is his.
3. Your cat has a tortoise-shell pattern.
4. Patches of brown, yellow, and black make up her coat.
5. Is the male calico cat yours?
6. Did you notice its curly hair?
7. Mrs. Stein says the Manx cat is hers.
8. Our show was a great success.

B. Write each sentence. Use the correct pronoun in parentheses ( ).

9. The Egyptians used (their, theirs) cats for hunting.
10. The first tame cats were probably (their, theirs).
11. This Russian Blue cat is (my, mine).
12. Russian Blues are known for (their, theirs) blue coats.
13. Which cat is (your, yours)?
14. My dad and I think (our, ours) cats are graceful.
15. The cat that just won a prize is (our, ours).

C. Choose the correct word in parentheses ( ) to complete the paragraph. Read each sentence completely before choosing the possessive pronoun or the contraction.

16. Do you take (your, you're) calendar for granted?
17. (Its, It's) surprising to learn that calendars didn't always begin on January 1. 18. The Egyptians based (their, they're) calendar on the annual flooding of the Nile. 19. (Their, They're) known to have used a lunar calendar. 20. (Its, It's) connection to the moon's cycles eventually put it out of phase with the seasons. 21. The Romans began (their, they're) calendar in March. 22. December was the tenth and final month of (their, they're) year. 23. If (your, you're) wondering where our modern calendar came from, Julius Caesar adjusted the calendar year to 365 ¼ days.

5 Using Pronouns

p. 188

A. Write each sentence, using the correct pronoun in parentheses ( ). Then write whether the pronoun you used is a subject or an object pronoun.

1. My brother and (I, me) visited Mexico's capital.
2. Benito told Frank and (I, me) about Mexico City.
3. Frank and (he, him) toured the National Palace.
4. A friend led Frank and (he, him) to Constitution Plaza.
5. The only people there were (we, us).
6. Rosa and (I, me) went to the Aztec ruins.
7. (We, Us) returned to the main square of the city.
8. I asked (she, her) about Montezuma.
9. That statue is (he, him)!
10. Frank and Benito found Rosa and (I, me) there.
11. I told Benito and (he, him) about the ruins.
12. Then our friends and (we, us) boarded a bus.
13. The bus took (we, us) to Chapultepec Park.
14. Frank and (I, me) wanted to see the forest.
15. Benito and (she, her) wanted to visit the famous museum.
16. They met Frank and (I, me) by the bus.
17. Later we took Benito and (she, her) to dinner.
18. Then a charter plane flew other tourists and (we, us) to Acapulco.

B. Write the pronoun in parentheses ( ) that correctly completes each sentence. Then write whether the pronoun is a predicate nominative or a direct object.

19. The girl on the beach at Acapulco is (I, me).
20. The boy on water skis is (he, him).
21. Mother met Frank and (I, me) in Mérida.
22. I led Frank and (she, her) to the ancient city.
23. I photographed (they, them) in several places.
24. The tourists next to the pyramid are (they, them).
25. The next day, Mother drove some friends and (we, us) to Veracruz.
26. The riders in the back seat were Frank and (I, me).
27. Mexico's sights impressed my family and (I, me).
28. The friendly people delighted (we, us), too!

UNIT FIVE

USING LANGUAGE TO
DESCRIBE

=== PART ONE ===

Unit Theme   *Your Place in Space and Time*

Language Awareness   Adjectives

=== PART TWO ===

Literature   *The House of Dies Drear* by Virginia Hamilton

A Reason for Writing   Describing

Writing
IN YOUR JOURNAL

WRITER'S WARM-UP ◆ Countless factors help to establish your place in the world. They include geography, history, community, family, customs, and individual talents. Moreover, as time passes and the world changes, your place in it changes, too. In a way, your place in space and time is like a photograph album. The album contains many snapshots. Each shows a different place in which you belong. Choose one place from your special album and write about it in your journal.

For each letter of your name, write a word that begins with the letter and describes you. Carlos, for example, wrote these words:
Courageous, Artistic, Reliable, Lucky, Optimistic, Serious.
You can write words for both your first and last names.

1 Writing with Adjectives

An adjective is a word that describes a noun or a pronoun. Adjectives often answer the question *What kind?* or *How many?* The underlined adjectives in this sentence describe the noun *house*.

How many? What kind?

■ One huge gray house provides the setting for the story.

Adjectives often come before the nouns they describe. Sometimes, however, they follow the nouns they describe.

▌The house, <u>old</u> and <u>mysterious</u>, was a stop on the Underground Railroad.

The words *a*, *an*, and *the* are special adjectives called **articles.** Use *a* before a word that begins with a consonant sound. Use *an* before a word that begins with a vowel sound.

■ a house   a small cottage   an apartment   an old mansion

Adjectives can change the meaning of a sentence. The adjectives in both sentences below describe the same two nouns, *house* and *town*. Find the words that create a bright picture or a sad picture.

▌The gloomy old <u>house</u> overlooked a lifeless, shabby <u>town</u>.
▌The cheerful new <u>house</u> overlooked a lively, clean <u>town</u>.

> **Summary** ♦ An **adjective** describes a noun or a pronoun. Use adjectives to add details to your writing.

Guided Practice

Name the adjectives in each sentence. Don't forget the articles!

1. The famous secret road to freedom helped many slaves.
2. Free blacks and some whites led the slaves to the North.
3. Each risked a large fine or a long term in prison.

Practice

A. Write the adjectives in these sentences. Include articles.

4. Along the various routes were some safe places to hide.
5. They might include a grand mansion or an empty hut.
6. Sympathetic people provided free food and helpful advice.
7. The final destination of the determined blacks was Canada.
8. Harriet Tubman, a former slave, led hundreds to freedom.

B. Write each sentence. Use the correct article.

9. Find (a, an) empty barn.
10. Cross (a, an) icy river.
11. Travel (a, an) dark roadway.
12. Follow (a, an) bright star.

detail, THE UNDERGROUND RAILROAD, Charles T. Webber, Cincinnati Art Museum, Subscription Fund Purchase

C. Use the words below to complete the paragraph.

industrial	close	many	runaway	public
famous	twenty	strong	one	dangerous

Harriet Beecher Stowe lived in Cincinnati, an (**13.** *What kind?*) city on the Ohio River, for almost (**14.** *How many?*) years. While there, she was a (**15.** *What kind?*) friend of John Rankin, a (**16.** *What kind?*) foe of slavery. Rankin sheltered (**17.** *How many?*) (**18.** *What kind?*) slaves and told Stowe about his (**19.** *What kind?*) activities. Stowe later published a (**20.** *What kind?*) book based on his stories. This (**21.** *How many?*) book, *Uncle Tom's Cabin*, did much to bring the problem of slavery to (**22.** *What kind?*) attention.

D. Complete these sentences by writing descriptive adjectives.

23. The ____ runaways traveled on ____ nights.
24. They had no ____ protection against their pursuers.
25. ____ sounds echoed in the shadows.
26. The ____ goal was to reach freedom.
27. The voyage across Lake Erie was ____ .

Apply ◆ Think and Write

From Your Writing ◆ Try to improve what you wrote for the Writer's Warm-up. Change some of the adjectives you used. Replace them with fresh words that give details.

✎ **Remember**
that adjectives create word pictures for your readers.

Imagine you are on a trip around the world. At each stop, you pick up a souvenir. List the souvenirs you find and the places they come from. For example: *Australian sheepskins, Swedish crystal, Bolivian rugs, Chinese figures.*

2 Proper Adjectives

Marta was writing a report about the history of Ohio. Her notes included these phrases.

| explorers from Europe   soldiers from England
| settlers from Virginia

The words *Europe*, *England*, and *Virginia* are proper nouns naming particular persons, places, or things. Proper nouns are always capitalized. Marta could have written her notes like this:

| European explorers   English soldiers
| Virginian settlers

The words *European*, *English*, and *Virginian* are proper adjectives. A proper adjective is formed from a proper noun. Like a proper noun, a proper adjective always begins with a capital letter.

The ending of a proper noun is usually changed to make a proper adjective. The endings *-ish*, *-an*, and *-ese* are often used to form proper adjectives. Sometimes a proper adjective has the same form as a proper noun. If you are not sure of the spelling, check it in a dictionary.

■ traders from New England   New England traders

> **Summary** ◆ A **proper adjective** is formed from a proper noun. Use proper adjectives to make your writing more specific.

Guided Practice

Name the proper adjective. Tell how it should be written.

1. La Salle, an explorer, claimed a large area of north american land for France.
2. This claim was ignored by the british authorities, however.
3. These european nations fought over the region for nine years.

Practice

A. Write each proper adjective correctly.

4. Early french explorers found major waterways.
5. In 1783 the former english colonies won Ohio.
6. The new american land was the Northwest Territory.
7. Many ohio settlements were begun after 1800.
8. In the War of 1812, Ohio played a major role in the attack on british naval forces in canadian waters.
9. Settlers were often virginian and connecticut farmers.
10. Then irish and german newcomers established farms.
11. The swiss settlers came in great numbers, too.
12. Later, Ohio's coalfields, steel mills, and factories attracted italian and other european immigrants.

B. Copy each sentence. Rewrite the underlined words to form a proper adjective followed by a noun.

EXAMPLE: Ohio's plateau of Appalachia is rich in coal and gas.
ANSWER: Ohio's Appalachian plateau is rich in coal and gas.

13. The 981-mile Ohio River is a major river of North America.
14. This waterway of the Midwest links Ohio to the world.
15. Ships from Japan go up the Mississippi to the Ohio River.
16. Tankers from Saudi Arabia navigate the St. Lawrence Seaway to ports of Ohio on Lake Erie.
17. Metal, glass, and rubber products manufactured in Ohio are shipped to nations in Europe, Latin America, and Africa.

C. Write each sentence. Complete it with a proper adjective.

18. _____ restaurants serve my favorite kind of food.
19. I would enjoy attending an exhibit of _____ art.
20. Someday I hope to study the _____ language.

Apply ♦ Think and Write

Dictionary of Knowledge ♦ Read about the explorer La Salle in the Dictionary of Knowledge. Write a paragraph about his expeditions in North America. Use some proper adjectives.

✏️ **Remember**
to make sure you capitalize each proper adjective that you use.

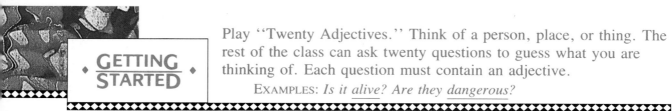

Play "Twenty Adjectives." Think of a person, place, or thing. The rest of the class can ask twenty questions to guess what you are thinking of. Each question must contain an adjective.
EXAMPLES: *Is it alive? Are they dangerous?*

3 Predicate Adjectives

Remember that a predicate nominative is a noun or pronoun that follows a linking verb and renames the subject of the sentence.

That house is a castle!   **The house in this picture is it.**

Sometimes linking verbs are followed by adjectives.

Many styles of architecture are unusual.

Victorian homes appear very mysterious.

In the sentences above, the adjectives *unusual* and *mysterious* are predicate adjectives. A predicate adjective follows a linking verb and describes the subject of the sentence.

In the first sentence the adjective *unusual* follows the linking verb *are* and describes the noun *styles*. In the second sentence the adjective *mysterious* follows the linking verb *appear* and describes the noun *homes*.

A list of common linking verbs appears on page 118. You may want to review them now.

> **Summary** ◆ A **predicate adjective** follows a linking verb and describes the subject of the sentence.

Guided Practice

Name the predicate adjective in each sentence.

1. In the nineteenth century, Great Britain was powerful.
2. The British monarch, Queen Victoria, became very influential.
3. Styles of architecture from this period are "Victorian."
4. Some Victorian homes seem elaborate.
5. Other homes look cozy.

Practice

A. The following sentences tell about Victorian architecture. Write the sentences. Underline the predicate adjectives.

6. The Gothic Revival style was popular.
7. The roofs of these homes are steep.
8. Often houses with fancy decorations are Gothic, too.
9. The mansard style is French in origin.
10. Its sloping, boxlike roof is unusual.
11. Some houses of this period are huge and ornate.
12. Others look extremely scary.
13. A veranda, or porch, looks pleasant and comfortable.
14. Pillars, or columns, seem important for support.
15. Gables are valuable for letting light into dark rooms.

B. Use the words below to complete the sentences. Underline each predicate adjective once and each predicate nominative twice.

features   royalty   dark   castlelike   mansion   ideal

16. Certain Victorian styles look _____ .
17. This imposing structure is a Victorian _____ .
18. A setting on a hill seems _____ for it.
19. Stone turrets, or little towers, were common _____ .
20. Inside these homes the rooms were sometimes _____ .
21. The Victorian family could be _____ in one of these!

C. Copy the paragraph. Complete the sentences with predicate adjectives that tell about the Victorian house shown here.

This Victorian home appears quite (**22.** _____). The windows are (**23.** _____), and the door appears (**24.** _____). Inside, the rooms are probably bright and (**25.** _____).

Apply ◆ Think and Write

A Description ◆ Think about an unusual house that you have seen or visited. Write a paragraph that tells what makes this dwelling special. Use predicate adjectives to describe the features of the house.

GABLE
MANSARD ROOF
DORMER WINDOW
VERANDA
PILLAR
EAVES

✎ **Remember**
that predicate adjectives help to create exact word pictures.

Play ''This and That.'' Say *this and that, these and those, these and that*, or *this and those*. Another person must say two words (commonly used together) that can be substituted for those words.

this and that = ham and cheese   *these and that* = peaches and cream

4 Demonstrative Adjectives

Most adjectives answer the questions *What kind?* and *How many?* The underlined adjectives in the following sentences, however, answer the question *Which one?*

> **This** town has a unique history.
> **That** history is the subject of a display.
> **These** students found historical clues in their town.
> **Those** clues helped students understand their town's history.

The words *this*, *that*, *these*, and *those* can be used as adjectives. They are called demonstrative adjectives, and they point out a specific person or thing.

This and *these* point out people or things nearby. *That* and *those* point out people or things farther away. Use *this* and *that* with singular nouns. Use *these* and *those* with plural nouns.

Sometimes *this*, *that*, *these*, and *those* are used alone in sentences. Then they are pronouns.

> **This** is dated 1874.   **These** were built before 1900.
> **That** is an old canal lock.   What were **those** used for?

Summary ◆ A **demonstrative adjective** points out the noun it describes.

Guided Practice

Name the demonstrative adjective in each sentence.

1. A local historical society shared these old town photographs.
2. Back issues of that newspaper are on microfilm in the library.
3. This oral history is a recording of the town's senior citizens.
4. Those students recorded interviews with experts.

Practice

A. Write each sentence. Underline each demonstrative adjective.

   5. From the architecture, we know this part of town is oldest.
   6. Why are many of these sturdy old buildings empty today?
   7. Those old railroad tracks haven't been used for decades.
   8. What was the name of that railroad?
   9. Those houses across the river were built in the 1920s.
  10. What happened to make this town grow so fast?
  11. This six-lane highway skirts the eastern edge of town.
  12. Why was that route chosen for the new highway?
  13. The name on this old brick factory is National Machines.
  14. What were those machines called?

B. Write each sentence. Use the correct demonstrative adjective in parentheses ( ).

  15. (This, Those) creek is called Oscoda Creek. Who named it?
  16. (These, That) signs say swimming in the river is unsafe.
  17. Did (those, this) factories upriver pollute the water?
  18. Did (this, those) trolley track run across town?
  19. Let's ask (this, those) senior citizens about it.

C. Write *adjective* or *pronoun* to tell how the underlined word is used.

  20. This is the corner of Quarry and Penn Streets.
  21. Does that mean stone was once quarried here?
  22. Is this street named after the Penn family?
  23. That family had a great impact on the town.
  24. Do you see this bridge?

Apply ◆ Think and Write

Forming Questions ◆ Ask six specific questions about the history of your own town or community. Think of things that you have actually wondered about. Use *this*, *that*, *these*, or *those* as adjectives in your questions. Then suggest how you might find the answers.

✎ **Remember**
to use *this*, *that*, *these*, and *those* to make your descriptions more specific.

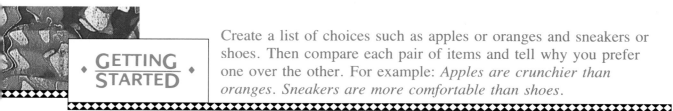

◆ GETTING ◆
STARTED

Create a list of choices such as apples or oranges and sneakers or shoes. Then compare each pair of items and tell why you prefer one over the other. For example: *Apples are crunchier than oranges. Sneakers are more comfortable than shoes.*

5 Adjectives That Compare

Adjectives have different forms to show comparisons. Many adjectives add *-er* or *-est*.

> **1.** Our new house is <u>warm</u>.
> **2.** It is <u>warmer</u> than our last home.
> **3.** It is the <u>warmest</u> house on our block.

In sentence **2**, *warmer* is the comparative form of *warm*. The comparative form of an adjective compares two persons, places, or things. It is formed by adding *-er* to the adjective. In sentence **3**, *warmest* is the superlative form of *warm*. The superlative form compares three or more persons, places, or things. It is formed by adding *-est*. Turn to page 503 for help in spelling adjectives.

Most adjectives with two or more syllables use *more* and *most* to form their comparative and superlative forms. Never use *more* or *most* and the *-er* or *-est* ending with the same adjective.

> Leaving my baseball team was <u>difficult</u>.
> Leaving my house was <u>more</u> <u>difficult</u> than leaving my team.
> Leaving my friends was the <u>most</u> <u>difficult</u> thing about moving.

Some adjectives have special comparative and superlative forms.

Adjective	Comparative	Superlative
good	better	best
bad	worse	worst

> **Summary** ◆ Use the **comparative** form of an adjective to compare two items. Use the **superlative** form to compare three or more items.

Guided Practice

Tell the comparative and superlative form of each adjective.

1. short **2.** unusual **3.** good **4.** sad **5.** comfortable

Practice

A. These sentences tell about the experience of moving to a new place. Write each sentence. Use the *-er* or *-est* form of the adjective.

   6. Moving to a new town was (easy) than I expected.

   7. Having a garage sale was (smart) than packing all my things.

   8. Bike riding was the best and (fast) way to explore my new neighborhood.

   9. Facing a school full of strangers was the (hard) part of all.

 10. I was (brave) than usual and started up some conversations.

 11. Writing to old friends was (nice) than forgetting them.

 12. I was much (happy) joining groups than just staying home.

B. Write each sentence. Use *more* or *most* with the adjective.

 13. Thinking about what a new town offers is a (positive) way to overcome sadness about moving.

 14. The (emotional) time of all was just before we moved.

 15. Time helps, too; I'll feel (comfortable) next month than today.

 16. Adjusting to a move is (difficult) for some than for others.

 17. My new town's history is (interesting) than I thought.

 18. The street I moved to was the (convenient) street in town.

C. Write each sentence. Use the correct form of the adjective.

 19. The (good) idea I had after moving in was to give a party.

 20. After all, it's (good) to make friends now than to wait.

 21. The soccer team in my old town was the (bad) in the league.

 22. Here my team has the (fine) record in the county.

 23. One player is (skillful) than the others.

 24. She finds scoring goals the (satisfactory) experience of all!

 25. I guess I'm (certain) than ever that we made the right move.

Apply ◆ Think and Write

A Paragraph ◆ If your family were to move, what would you be looking forward to? What would you hope would be different in your new community? Write a paragraph. Use comparative and superlative adjectives.

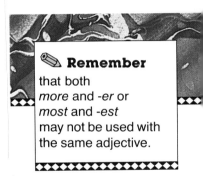

> ✏ **Remember**
> that both
> *more* and *-er* or
> *most* and *-est*
> may not be used with
> the same adjective.

The furry, chubby puppy had a noisy bark. What other adjectives ending in *-y* might describe a puppy's appearance?

VOCABULARY ◆
Adjective Suffixes

On pages 256–260 you will read about fourteen-year-old Thomas Small and the house he moves into. Look at the house pictured on this page. Which of the adjectives below might describe it?

luxurious
attractive   glorious
mysterious   sizable
affordable   scary

cheerful
harmless   famous
massive   funny
restful   livable

Each adjective above was formed by adding a suffix to a common word. A **suffix** is a letter or letters added to the end of a word to form a new word.

rest + -ful = restful   fun + -y = funny   fame + -ous = famous

What spelling changes occur when the suffixes *-ous* and *-y* are added to *fame* and *fun*?

Building Your Vocabulary

What other common words were used above to form adjectives? The suffixes that were used and their meanings are listed below.

Suffix	Meaning	Example
-able	worthy of, able to	livable
-ful	full of, having the qualities of	cheerful
-ive	tending to	massive
-less	without, not having	harmless
-ous	full of, having	glorious
-y	having, being like	funny

Practice

A. Write the adjective in each sentence formed with a suffix. Then circle the suffix.

1. Thomas thought that the house was impressive.
2. It also seemed somewhat gloomy.
3. Many thought that the house was mysterious.
4. People were so fearful that the house was uninhabited for almost ten years.
5. Thomas had read about its notable history.
6. He knew about the dangerous events that had occurred here.
7. At first Thomas felt strange and shaky.
8. But he also felt hopeful and adventuresome.
9. Thomas's interest in the house was endless.
10. Would the house ever reveal its momentous secrets, he wondered?

B. Complete the paragraph. Paint a word picture of a pleasant scene. Use adjectives formed with the suffixes in this lesson.

It was a (**11.** _____) day to be out on the river. Our (**12.** _____) canoe glided silently past the (**13.** _____) autumn woods. (**14.** _____) farmers waved from their (**15.** _____) tractors. (**16.** _____) white clouds rolled gently over our heads. A (**17.** _____) breeze blew from the west. All was calm and (**18.** _____). I remember leaning over the boat to pick a (**19.** _____) flower. Because of that flower, our day was not only (**20.** _____), it was wet!

LANGUAGE CORNER ◆ Nationalities

The suffix *-ish* means "related to" or "characteristic of." It is used to form adjectives such as *childish* and *foolish*. It is also used to form names that indicate the country of a person's origin, such as *English*.

What countries do the words below refer to?

**Danish   Finnish   Turkish
Spanish   Swedish**

How to Expand Sentences with Adjectives

In this unit you have been working with adjectives and using them to describe nouns and pronouns. Adjectives can make a big difference in your writing. They can add colorful details and information to your sentences. For example, which sentence below gives you more information?

1. The house was built on a hill.
2. The old Victorian house was built on a remote hill.

Sentence **1** does tell something about the house, but it would be difficult to picture the scene. Sentence **2**, however, gives much more information about the house. Adding the adjectives *old* and *Victorian* creates a detailed picture of the house, and adding *remote* allows us to clearly see its location. Does the scene seem mysterious to you?

The scene could be completely changed if different adjectives were used to describe the house. Read the sentence below. What kind of an image do you get of the house now?

3. The modern white house was built on a plush green hill.

If the nouns you use do not add enough detail to your writing, use adjectives to describe them.

The Grammar Game ◆ Create instant word pictures! Write adjectives or pairs of adjectives for each word below. Then do it again, choosing different adjectives to change the picture.

field	park	mountain	castle
story	cave	boat	tiger
dog	hat	jungle	doll

Working Together

Notice how adjectives add detail and information to your writing as you work on activities **A** and **B** with your group.

In Your Group
♦ Help everyone follow directions.
♦ Encourage others' ideas.
♦ Don't interrupt each other.
♦ Get the group back to work, if necessary.

A. Expand each sentence below with adjectives. Choose adjectives that begin with the same sound as the underlined noun they describe. Then make up more sentences to add to the list.

EXAMPLE: Chris arrived with a cap.

ANSWER: Clever Chris arrived with a colorful cap.

1. The <u>ship</u> sailed the <u>sea</u>.
2. <u>Tailors</u> worked on <u>ties</u> and <u>trousers</u>.
3. <u>Fans</u> cheered the <u>fighter</u>.
4. <u>Creatures</u> moved into the <u>cave</u>.
5. The <u>detective</u> inspected the <u>den</u> and the <u>desk</u>.

B. Complete the paragraph below with adjectives of the group's choice. Can you write it again with different adjectives?

The _____ building stood in the middle of the _____ block. _____ dogs found _____ places to sleep in the _____ shade. _____ children played around the _____ steps. _____ people sat on _____ chairs talking about the _____ weather. It was a _____ day. The _____ streets were crowded with _____ cars. A _____ summer in the _____ city had begun.

WRITERS' CORNER ♦ Overusing Adjectives

Choose adjectives for nouns that need more description, but be careful not to use too many adjectives to describe a noun. Sentences with too many adjectives can make your writing boring and hard to read.

EXAMPLE: **The littlest, brown, cute, furry puppy chewed on Father's soft, new, red slipper.**

IMPROVED: **The littlest puppy chewed on Father's new slipper.**

Read what you wrote for the Writer's Warm-up. Did you use too many adjectives in any of your sentences? Can you improve them?

NEW YORK, NEW HAVEN AND HARTFORD
painting by Edward Hopper
© Indianapolis Museum of Art,
The Emma Sweetser Fund.

Thomas did not wake in time to see the Ohio River. Mr. Small was glad he didn't, for through the gloom of mist and heavy rain, most of its expanse was hidden. What was visible looked much like a thick mud path, as the sedan crossed over it at Huntington.

Thomas lurched awake a long time after. The car went slowly; there was hardly any rain now. His mother spoke excitedly, and Thomas had to shake his head rapidly in order to understand what she was saying.

"Oh dear! My heavens!" Mrs. Small said. "Why it's huge!"

Mr. Small broke in eagerly, turning around to face Thomas. "You've waited a long time," he said. "Take a good look, son. There's our new house!"

Thomas looked carefully out of his window. He opened the car door for a few seconds to see better, but found the moist air too warm and soft. The feel of it was not nice at all, and he quickly closed the door. He could see well enough out of the window, and what he saw made everything inside him grow quiet for the first time in weeks. It was more than he could have dreamed.

The house of Dies Drear loomed out of mist and murky sky, not only gray and formless, but huge and unnatural. It seemed to crouch on the side of a hill high above the highway. And it had a dark, isolated look about it that set it at odds with all that was living.

A chill passed over Thomas. He sighed with satisfaction. The house of Dies Drear was a haunted place, of that he was certain.

"Well," Mr. Small said, "what do you think of it, Thomas?"

"It must be the biggest house anyone ever built," Thomas said at last. "And to think—it's our new house! Papa, let's get closer, let's go inside!"

Smiling, Mr. Small kept the car on the highway that now curved up closer toward the house. In a short time they were quite near.

At the base of the hill on which the house sat, a stream ran parallel to the highway. It was muddy and swollen by rain; between it and the hill lay a reach of fertile land, lushly tangled with mullein weed and gold wildflower. The hill itself was rocky and mostly bare, although a thaw had come to the rest of the land and countryside. At the very top of the hill Thomas noticed a grove of trees, which looked like either pine or spruce.

The house of Dies Drear sat on an outcropping, much like a ledge, on the side of the hill. The face of the ledge was rock, from which gushed mineral springs. And these came together at the fertile land, making a narrow groove through it before emptying into the stream. Running down the face of the ledge, the springs coated the rock in their path with red and yellow rust.

Thomas stared so long at the ledge and springs, his eyes began to play tricks on him. It seemed as if the rust moved along with the spring waters.

"It's bleeding," he said softly. "It looks just like somebody cut the house open underneath and let its blood run out! That's a nice hill though," he added. He looked at the clumps of skinny trees at each side of the house. Their branches were bare and twisted by wind.

Thomas cleared his throat. "I bet you can see a lot from the top of that hill." He felt he ought to say this. The hill was hardly anything compared to the mountains at home. Otherwise the land in every direction was mostly flat.

"You can see the college from the top of the hill," Mr. Small said. "And you can see the town. It's quite a view. On a clear day those springs and colored rock make the hill and house look like a fairyland."

"All those springs!" Thomas said. He shook his head. "Where do they come from? I've never seen anything like them."

LITERATURE: Story

"You'll get used to the look of the land," Mr. Small said. "This is limestone country, and always with limestone in this formation you'll find the water table percolating through rock into springs. There are caves, lakes and marshes all around us, all because of the rock formations and the way they fault."

Mrs. Small kept her eye on the house. It was her nature to concentrate on that which there was a chance of her changing.

"No, it's not," she said softly. "Oh, dear, no, it will never be pretty!"

"Everything is seeping with rain," Mr. Small said to her. "Just try to imagine those rocks, that stream and the springs on a bright, sunny day. Then it's really something to see."

Thomas could imagine how everything looked on a day such as his father described. His eyes shone as he said, "It must look just about perfect!"

They drove nearer. Thomas could see that the house lay far back from the highway. There was a gravel road branching from the highway and leading to the house. A weathered covered bridge crossed the stream at the base of the hill. Mr. Small turned off the highway and stopped the car.

"There's been quite a rain," he said. "I'd better check the bridge."

Now Thomas sat with his hands folded tightly beneath his chin, with his elbows on his knees. He had a moment to look at the house of Dies Drear, the hill and the stream all at once. He stared long and hard. By the time his father returned, he had everything figured out.

They continued up the winding road, the house with its opaque, watching windows drawing ever nearer.

The stream is the moat. The covered planks over it are the drawbridge, Thomas thought. And the house of Dies Drear is the castle.

But who is the king of all this? Who will win the war?

There was a war and there was a king. Thomas was as sure of this as he was certain the house was haunted, for the hill and house were bitten and frozen. They were separated from the rest of the land by something unkind.

"Oh dear," Mrs. Small was saying. "Oh dear. Dear!"

Suddenly the twins were scrambling over Thomas, wide awake and watching the house get closer. By some unspoken agreement, they set up a loud, pathetic wail at the same time.

"Look!" Thomas whispered to them. "See, over there is clear sky. All this mist will rise and get blown away soon. Then you'll feel better."

Sure enough, above the dark trees at the top of the hill was deep, clear sky. Thomas gently cradled the boys. "There are new kinds of trees here," he told them. "There will be nights with stars above trees like you've never known!" The twins hushed, as Thomas knew they would.

Up close the house seemed to Thomas even more huge, if that were possible. There were three floors. Above the top floor was a mansard roof with dormer windows jutting from its steep lower slopes. Eaves overhanging the second story dripped moisture to the ground in splattering beats. There was a veranda surrounding the ground floor, with pillars that rose to the eaves.

Thomas liked the house. But the chill he had felt on see-ing it from the highway was still with him. Now he knew why.

It's not the gray day, he thought. It's not mist and damp that sets it off. There are things beyond weather. The house has secrets!

Thomas admired the house for keeping them so long.

But I'm here now, he thought happily. It won't keep anything from me.

Library Link ♦ *Virginia Hamilton has written two books that tell Thomas's story:* The House of Dies Drear *and* The Mystery of Drear House.

Reader's Response

Would you like to read the rest of the book *The House of Dies Drear?* Why or why not?

THE HOUSE OF DIES DREAR

Responding to Literature

1. Choose your favorite descriptive passage from this selection. Read it aloud to classmates. Use your voice to add to the description. Then tell classmates why you selected the passage.

2. One way to learn about story characters is by paying attention to what they say. For example, when Mr. Small says "There's been quite a rain, . . . I'd better check the bridge," we can assume he is cautious and careful. Find a quotation that tells you something about one of the other characters. Read aloud the quotation and explain what it tells you about the character.

3. Make a map and show the setting of *The House of Dies Drear*. Identify the roads, the spring, and other important places. Include the details from the story in your map.

Writing to Learn

Think and Discover ◆ The name *Dies Drear* is an unusual one. What does the name mean to you? Make cluster maps to explore the meanings the words might have. Allow each word in the name to suggest another word. The second word may remind you of a third word. Let your map grow as large as possible.

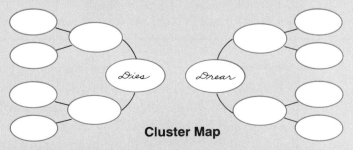

Cluster Map

Write ◆ Use the information in your cluster maps to write a paragraph about the meaning of the name *Dies Drear*.

Make description chains. The person who starts might say, "This is a book." Each person adds a detail: *This is a red book."* . . . *"This is a red book with 523 pages."*

SPEAKING and LISTENING ◆
Descriptive Details

Do you know someone everyone likes to talk to, someone whose conversation is never dull? Chances are, that person knows the secret of sparkling speech—how to use vivid descriptive details. Here are some guidelines to help you be that kind of speaker and be an active listener, as well.

Giving a Description	1. Before you describe something, ask yourself, "What makes this special? Why is it unique?" Focus your description on these details to hold your listeners' attention. 2. Be specific. Choose exact, precise words for your purpose: *amble* instead of *walk*, *cottage* instead of *house*. Precise words create clearer pictures for listeners. 3. Use vivid descriptive words: *scarlet* instead of *red*, *kindly* instead of *nice*. 4. Use words that appeal to the senses—words that help your listener see, hear, feel, smell, or taste what you describe.
Being an Active Listener	1. While you listen, try to picture what the speaker describes. 2. Listen for vivid descriptive words. 3. Listen for words that help you see what you hear.

Summary ◆ When you describe something, use vivid descriptive words, precise words, and words that appeal to the senses. These help your listeners picture what you are describing. Listen for these words and try to picture what the speaker is describing.

Guided Practice

Replace the words below with words that are more vivid or precise.

1. house **3.** body of water **5.** clothes

2. run **4.** pretty **6.** happy

Practice

A. Write each word below. Then write a more vivid or more precise word to replace it.

7. nice **9.** fish **11.** hat

8. bad **10.** ground **12.** building

B. Pick any illustration up to this page in this book. Describe it to a partner. Give your partner five minutes to identify the picture you describe. Let your partner ask one question. Remember to use strong descriptive words that appeal to the senses.

C. Work with a partner. Take turns describing a place you really like. When you are the listener, ask questions to learn what makes this place special. Here are some places you might want to describe: a barn, a park, the bank of a river, a mountain, a favorite reading or thinking corner.

Apply ◆ Think and Write

A Descriptive Word Bank ◆ Begin a list of vivid and precise words to use in your writing. As you read and listen, be on the lookout for such words to add to your list.

✎ **Remember**
to use words that paint vivid word pictures when you describe something.

Find a photograph in this book that shows some things at a distance and other things up close. This effect of distance on the way things look is called <u>perspective</u>. Tell where you think the photographer was standing when taking the picture.

WRITING ♦
Space Order in Descriptions

When you observe, you mentally collect all kinds of details. When you are ready to use those details in a description, you need to sort them out and put them in an order that makes sense. One way to organize details is to list them in space order. Space order works especially well when you are describing a place.

What is meant by *space order?* It is simply the way things are arranged in space. When you use space order to describe something, you tell what it looks like from where you are. You might describe something from left to right, from inside to outside, from top to bottom, or from near to far.

In this passage, Virginia Hamilton uses space order to describe the marvelous underground treasure-house of Dies Drear.

The barrel-shaped cavern ceiling rolled up and up over them. It was half a football field long. High up, on all sides, hung Persian carpets and rich tapestries. Their colors glowed in the flame light of Mr. Pluto's torches, grouped in the center. On the cavern floor between the hangings were whole painted canoes and finely crafted totem poles. Tens upon tens of bureaus and breakfronts, inlaid with delicate woods, had drawers packed with small treasures. There were scores of barrels bursting with silken and embroidered materials set in rows between canoes and poles. Riches spilled from kegs and crates—gold coins and gold watches, pearls and other jewelry that sparkled and nearly blinded their eyes. The astonishing hoard went on and on, practically as far as the eye could see.

> **Summary** ♦ **Space order** is one way to organize details in a paragraph. It is especially useful when you describe a place.

Guided Practice

In the example paragraph you read, the observers are standing at the entrance to a huge hall inside a cavern and are looking in. Explain how the author uses space order to describe this cavern. Which of these describes the organization most accurately: *near to far, top to bottom, bottom to top, or left to right?*

Practice

A. Name the kind of space order you would use to describe the room you are in now: *top to bottom, left to right, near to far,* or *front to back*. Then write your reason for making that choice.

B. Write the topic sentence below. Then write the five detail sentences in left-to-right space order.

> **TOPIC SENTENCE:** This mural shows events in Texas history.

1. To the right of the Alamo, cowhands drive cattle, and workers drill for oil.
2. On the far left an Indian village appears.
3. The battle at the Alamo is shown in the center.
4. Spanish missionaries are beside the Indian village.
5. Modern-day Dallas appears on the far right.

Apply ◆ Think and Write

Dictionary of Knowledge ◆ Read the entry on the Alamo. Then write a descriptive paragraph about that historic landmark. Use space order to organize your details.

> ✎ **Remember**
> that using space order can help you organize details.

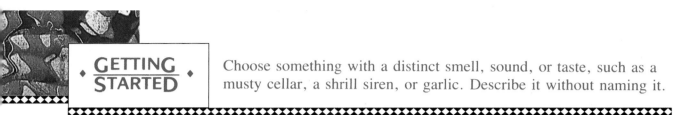

Choose something with a distinct smell, sound, or taste, such as a musty cellar, a shrill siren, or garlic. Describe it without naming it.

WRITING ♦
A Descriptive Paragraph

The ability to describe things clearly, accurately, and vividly is important, not only in school but also in everyday life. To give good descriptions, you need to be a careful observer. Train yourself to look for details. Think of yourself as a detective who notices all sorts of little things—mud on a pair of shoes, the hour being struck by a clock, the smell of a log fire burning in the next room. Being a good observer can help you write a descriptive paragraph.

A descriptive paragraph creates a word picture. It often has a topic sentence that states the main idea of the paragraph. The other sentences give details that help to create a vivid picture for the reader. Details that appeal to the senses are especially effective. Those are details that describe how something looks, sounds, feels, smells, or tastes.

Read the following descriptive paragraph from *The Mystery of Drear House*. Notice how the details create a mood of tension. They help you see, hear, and feel the blizzard raging outside.

Topic Sentence

Supporting Details

> Outside, the wind rose, building a blizzard from out of the darkness. It soon raged against the house. Drear house shuddered but stood its ground. The night was blinded snow-white. Animals dug deep for safety.
>
> —*Virginia Hamilton*

Summary ♦ A **descriptive paragraph** creates a word picture. It often includes details that appeal to the five senses and that suggest a mood.

Guided Practice

Give a detail that supports each of these topic sentences.

1. The brown hills looked lonely. **3.** A forest walk is relaxing.
2. A busy street is joyful. **4.** Sun baked the parched earth.

Practice

A. Write a detail sentence for each topic sentence below.

5. The office was a shambles.
6. A tower loomed above us.
7. Sunshine brightened every imaginable corner.
8. Driving rain dampened our spirits as well as our clothes.
9. As he entered the courtroom, he felt a sense of dread.
10. Thinking about the little cabin in the woods cheered us.

B. Read the topic sentence below. Then read sentences **11–15.** Write *yes* if the sentence gives a detail that supports the topic sentence. Write *no* if it does not.

TOPIC SENTENCE: The old house had an eery feeling about it.

11. Somewhere from deep in the house, a floorboard creaked.
12. The sky suddenly darkened, and the wind howled a warning.
13. A bright light made the room feel warm and inviting.
14. Loaves of bread were cooling on the kitchen table.
15. Only the buzzing of a fly broke the strange stillness.

C. Write a paragraph, describing a place you know well. First write a topic sentence. Then write four detail sentences to support it. Be sure to include details that appeal to the senses or that create a mood.

Apply ◆ Think and Write

A Descriptive Paragraph ◆ Study the picture of the house. What is your main impression? What details do you notice? Write a paragraph that describes the house. Remember to include details that appeal to the senses or that create a mood.

🖉 **Remember** to use details that create vivid word pictures.

Focus on Setting

How does a writer create the atmosphere, or mood, of a story? One important way is through the story's **setting** — the place, time, and even the weather in which the story occurs.

The setting of a story is the background against which the story's action takes place. A vivid setting creates emotion. It helps you feel joy, amusement, fear, dread, or suspicion as you read the story.

Look back at *The House of Dies Drear*, which you read earlier. Notice how Virginia Hamilton uses setting to create a mood of fear and suspicion.

BLEAK MOOD: The house looms "out of the mist and murky sky." It is "gray and formless, huge and unnatural." It appears to "crouch" on the hill. It looks "dark, isolated." It seems to be at odds with everything living.

Suppose you want to describe a very different kind of house, one that is cheerful and pleasant. You will choose descriptive details that create the mood you want to achieve.

HAPPY MOOD: The house stood out jauntily against the blue summer sky. Its white shingles, accented by bright red shutters, had the snappy, happy look that gleaming new paint gives a comfortable old dwelling. Three young children frolicked in the front yard, chattering gaily about jump ropes and hopscotch.

The Writer's Voice ♦ Suppose you are going to write a mystery story. Its setting is a room in your school. What details would you include to create a mood of suspense?

Working Together

The setting of a story affects the story's mood. Choose words carefully to create a setting as your group does activities **A** and **B**.

A. Suggest words and phrases for the blanks in this description. The goal of your group is to change the happy mood conveyed in the paragraph on page 268 to a bleak, dismal mood. (Add all the words you want for each blank. The part-of-speech labels are provided merely to guide you.)

 The house stood out __(adv.)__ against the __(adj.)__ sky. Its __(adj.)__ shingles, accented by __(n.)__, had the __(adj.)__ look that __(n.)__ gives __(n.)__. Three __(n.)__ __(v.)__ in the __(n.)__, __(v.)__ ing about __(n.)__.

B. Decide on the setting for an original story. Also decide the mood you want to create. List some words and phrases that would be appropriate for the setting and mood. Discuss these choices with the rest of your classmates.

THESAURUS CORNER • Word Choice

Rewrite the paragraph below. Use the Thesaurus and Thesaurus Index to fill in each blank with an appropriate adjective. Then write a second paragraph about the imaginary story. Use at least three *antonyms* for words that appear in the first paragraph.

 The author's _____ mystery story is set in a _____ town in the Midwest. The townspeople are _____ in the August heat. A hideous scream breaks the _____ silence of the _____ streets. The heroine is _____ to leave her house. Even before the _____ wail, she knew there was something dreadfully _____ in Hayes Center.

 Now add a second paragraph. Use your imagination to create the details. Review the instructions before you begin.

Writing a Description

When you read *The House of Dies Drear*, you saw Thomas Small's new home through his eyes and with his feelings. Good writers of description do more than just list a lot of details. They choose details to convey a special viewpoint or mood.

Know Your Purpose and Audience

What's MY PURPOSE

Who's MY AUDIENCE

In this lesson you will write a description. Your purpose will be to describe a special place.

Your audience will be a friend who has never seen it. Later you can read or send the description to your friend. You can also give a travel lecture to classmates or help make an illustrated travel guide.

1 Prewriting

First choose a topic—a place to write about. Then choose a strategy for gathering details for your description of it.

Choose Your Topic ◆ Consider places that a visitor to your area might want to see. You might mention an old one-room schoolhouse, a historic cemetery, a monument, or a natural wonder. Choose the place that is most interesting to you.

Think About It	**Talk About It**
Make a list of possible places. List as many as you can. Then consider your list. If you cannot think of at least three details about a place, cross it off your list. Choose from those that are left. Which would be most interesting?	Talk with your classmates about places that you think you know well. Are you able to name three specific details about any of them? Which place mentioned seems to interest others the most? Which do they stop to hear about?

Topic Ideas

the old one-room schoolhouse
the old cemetery
the Daniel Boone monument
Stone Mountain
the Alamo
the Giant Oak
Turner's Inn

Choose Your Strategy ♦ Here are two strategies that can help you gather details for your description. Read both. Then use the idea you think will work best for you.

PREWRITING IDEAS

CHOICE ONE

A Writer's Work Sketch

One way to recall details for your description is to make a writer's work sketch. Close your eyes and imagine your special place. Try to picture it from a distance, from close up, from a different angle, or from inside. Then sketch as many details as you can. Try drawing different views of your special place.

Model

CHOICE TWO

A Cluster Map

A cluster map is another way to gather and organize details for your description. Write your topic in the center circle. Choose subtopics that work for your topic. Then add as many details as you can around each subtopic.

Model

2 Writing

Before you begin, look over your writer's work sketch or your cluster map. Then begin to write. Try to set a mood with the first sentence. Here are some ways to begin.

- ◆ Laughter and happy music fill the air at _____.
- ◆ The first time I saw _____ , I felt _____.

As you write, organize your details in space order. For example, you might describe the place first from a distance, then from close up, and last from inside. Choose words and details that will convey the mood the place conveys to you.

Sample First Draft ◆

From the road the famous tourist attraction was mostly hidden by a high wooden fence. But even from far away, I could see its enormous limns. They stretched over the fence and crept out over the street. Inside the fence, Giant Oak was awesome. It stood in the middle of a yard like a terrible monster. The Tree was so big that the big grassy yard looked tiny.

I felt nervous. Would one of the tree's huge limns capture me? Up close to the tree, I reached out and touched the trunk. Slowly I climbed up and sat on a wide branch. A breeze rustled the leaves. I held my breath, but nothing happened. Giant oak wasn't an unfriendly monster after all.

3 Revising

You will probably find that your first draft has some rough spots. Here is an idea that can help you improve it.

REVISING IDEA

FIRST Read to Yourself

As you read, review your purpose. Have you written a description of a special place? Consider your audience. Have you described it so well that a friend who has never seen it will know what it is like? Decide which part of your description you yourself like best and why.

Focus: Have you chosen words and details that convey the mood of your special place?

THEN Share with a Partner

Ask a partner to read your description aloud to you. Here are some guidelines for you and your partner.

The Writer

Guidelines: Listen as if you were hearing your description for the first time. As you listen, try to decide if your meaning is clear.

Sample questions:
• Will my description help my friend "see" this place?
• **Focus question:** How can I better convey the mood?

The Writer's Partner

Guidelines: Read the description slowly so the writer can listen carefully.

Sample responses:
• Can you explain to me the mood you feel in this place ___?
• Maybe you could add a detail about ___.

WRITING PROCESS: Description

Revising Model ♦ This description is being revised.

The first time I visited Giant Oak, I felt small, unimportant, and a little frightened.

From the road the famous tourist attraction was mostly hidden by a high wooden fence. But even from far away, I could see its enormous limns. They stretched over the fence and crept out over the street. Inside the fence, Giant Oak was awesome. It stood in the middle of a yard like a terrible monster. The Tree was *~~so~~ gigantic ~~big~~* that the big grassy yard looked tiny.

~I felt nervous. Would one of the tree's huge limns capture me? ⟨Up close to the tree,⟩ I reached out ~~and touched~~ the *spongy, moss-covered* trunk. Slowly I ~~climbed~~ up and sat on a wide branch. A breeze rustled the leaves. I held my breath, but nothing happened. Giant oak wasn't an unfriendly monster after all.

The writer's partner suggested setting the mood at the beginning.

Gigantic is a more precise word than *big*.

This phrase was moved to make the space order clearer.

The writer wanted to add descriptive details.

Read the draft description the way the writer has decided it *should* be. Then revise your own description.

Grammar Check ♦ Adjectives provide descriptive details.

Word Choice ♦ Some words, like *big*, are vague and often overused. A thesaurus is a source of synonyms you can use.

Revising Checklist

☐ **Purpose:** Did I write a description of a special place?

☐ **Audience:** Will my friend who has never seen it know what my special place is like?

☐ **Focus:** Have I used words and details that convey the mood of my special place?

4 Proofreading

Proofreading Marks

capital letter =

small letter /

indent paragraph ¶

check spelling ⬭

Now that you have revised your description for clarity and meaning, it is time to correct surface errors. Proofreading helps you provide your readers with a neat, readable copy.

Proofreading Model ♦ Here is the description of Giant Oak. Notice that proofreading changes have been added in red.

The first time I visited Giant Oak, I felt small, unimportant, and a little frightened.
From the road ^ the famous tourist attraction was mostly hidden by a high wooden fence. But even from far away, I could see its enormous *limbs* (limns). They stretched over the fence and crept out over the street.
¶ Inside the fence, Giant Oak was awesome. It stood in the middle of a yard like a terrible monster. The Tree was so *gigantic* big that the big grassy yard looked tiny.
I felt nervous. Would one of the tree's huge *limbs* (limns) capture me? (Up close to the tree,) I reached out and touched the *spongy, moss-covered* ^ trunk. Slowly I climbed up and sat on a wide branch. A breeze rustled the leaves. I held my breath, but nothing happened. Giant oak wasn't an unfriendly monster after all.

Proofreading Checklist

☐ Did I spell words correctly?

☐ Did I indent paragraphs?

☐ Did I use capital letters correctly?

☐ Did I use correct marks at the end of sentences?

☐ Did I type neatly or use my best handwriting?

PROOFREADING IDEA

Reading Backward

When you think about meaning, you might miss small mistakes. To block out meaning and to find errors, try reading backward from the end to the beginning.

Now proofread your description and write a title for it. Then make a neat copy.

5 Publishing

Now it is time to share your description with an audience. Here are some ideas you might try.

A Giant Oak

The first time I visited Giant Oak, I felt small, unimportant, and a little frightened. From the road the famous tourist attraction was mostly hidden by a high wooden fence. But even from far away, I could see its enormous limbs. They stretched over the fence and crept out over the street.

Inside the fence, Giant Oak was awesome. It stood in the middle of a yard like a terrible monster. The tree was so gigantic that the big grassy yard looked tiny.

Up close to the tree, I felt nervous. Would one of the tree's huge limbs capture me? I reached out and touched the spongy, moss-covered trunk. Slowly I climbed up and sat on a wide branch. A breeze rustled the leaves. I held my breath, but nothing happened. Giant Oak wasn't an unfriendly monster after all.

PUBLISHING IDEAS

Share Aloud	Share in Writing
You have written your description for a friend who has never seen your special place. If that friend is nearby, you might read your description aloud to him or her. Or you might read it aloud to your classmates. Draw a travel poster to go with your description.	If the friend you wrote your description for is far away, you might mail him or her a copy. Include an invitation to visit and see your special place. Or assemble your descriptions into an illustrated travel guide. Take turns taking the guide home for your families to read.

CURRICULUM
•CONNECTION•

 ## Writing Across the Curriculum Health

In this unit you elaborated on the name *Dies Drear* by making cluster maps. Later you may have used ideas from another cluster map as you wrote a description. Cluster maps can help you find and organize ideas on many subjects, including health.

Writing to Learn

Think and Elaborate ◆ Make two cluster maps, one for *tired* and the other for *full of energy*. Write as many subjects and details as possible for each of these two topics.

Cluster Map

Write ◆ Use your cluster maps to write a paragraph on the topic "How to Feel Energetic."

 ## Writing in Your Journal

In the Writer's Warm-up you wrote about your place in space and time. During the unit you read about events that occurred in a variety of places and times. Of all that you read about in the unit, what did you find most interesting and why? Record your ideas in your journal.

BOOKS TO ENJOY

Read More About It

M. C. Higgins, the Great *by Virginia Hamilton*
Pollution and dangerous wastes from a nearby coal mine make M. C. Higgins want to leave his home in the Cumberland Mountains. His father's attachment to the family's ancestral home, however, seems to block M. C.'s goal.   **Newbery Award**
National Book Award

A Wrinkle in Time *by Madeleine L'Engle*
Along with some extraordinary friends, Meg Murray must travel through time and space to find her father and free him from the power of IT.   **Newbery Award**

Underground Man *by Milton Meltzer*
This fictionalized account of Joshua Bowen's life concentrates on his efforts to lead runaway slaves to freedom on the Underground Railroad.

Book Report Idea Book Tour

Reading a book is a little like taking a trip. The next time you give a book report, pretend you are a tour guide.

Create a Slide Show ◆ The "slides" in your show will be sketches of characters and settings in your book. On the back of each slide, write a few descriptive sentences about the setting or character. As you display your slides, read the descriptions. Tell your listeners why they should go on the trip.

UNIT REVIEW

Unit 5

Adjectives *pages 238–249*

A. Write the adjectives in each of the following sentences. Include articles.

1. The loud blare of a trumpet disturbed Al's thoughtful mood.
2. Then came the soft sounds of flutes.
3. A huge drum made a loud noise.
4. Cymbals, abrupt and harsh, clashed again and again.
5. A noisy horn made Al's ears ache.
6. Colorful wagons rolled in a long line.
7. An old man led the merry parade.
8. He twirled a silvery baton with intense concentration.
9. Clowns — short and tall, fat and skinny — marched behind them.
10. The greatest circus in the world had come to the small town.

B. Write each proper adjective in the following sentences correctly.

11. Joseph Turner is a famous english painter.
12. Paul Klee, a modern swiss artist, is much admired.
13. My aunt collects chinese vases.
14. I prefer american antiques.
15. Ms. Smith has just purchased a german car.

16. Origami is the art of japanese paper folding.
17. Manuela is looking for a book about ancient egyptian art.
18. Kim learned the mexican folk dance.
19. This marble statue was carved by an ancient greek sculptor.
20. Your shawl is made of scottish wool.

C. Write each sentence. Underline each predicate adjective.

21. Jeanette O'Toole is very comical.
22. Her comedy routines are famous.
23. On stage she seems silly.
24. In fact she is extremely bright.
25. Her costumes look shabby.
26. She appears awkward in front of us.
27. Her hands and feet seem restless.
28. Actually, her words and gestures are deliberate.
29. Her remarks about current events are witty.
30. O'Toole's physical comedy seems hilarious.

D. Write each sentence. Underline each demonstrative adjective.

31. These small pears are not yet ripe.
32. That banana has a few brown spots.
33. I have never tasted those vegetables.
34. What is the name of this fruit?
35. Can you hand me those onions?
36. I will use this leek in a baked chicken dish.
37. These tomatoes will go into a spaghetti sauce.
38. That bag of cherries will make a fine pie.

E. Write the comparative and superlative forms of each of the following adjectives.

39.	strong	**49.**	beautiful
40.	famous	**50.**	fair
41.	sad	**51.**	merry
42.	high	**52.**	grand
43.	unusual	**53.**	expensive
44.	serious	**54.**	nice
45.	cold	**55.**	big
46.	powerful	**56.**	large
47.	sunny	**57.**	brave
48.	enormous	**58.**	tiny

F. For each of the following sentences, write the adjective that is formed with a suffix.

59. Kathy likes a considerable change in her routine.
60. That tennis player has a mighty backhand.
61. The chairperson's speech seemed endless.
62. The playful otter swam just out of reach.
63. That small garden snake is in fact harmless.
64. A wonderful time was had by all the picnickers.
65. The courageous little dog barked at the lion.
66. Your cousin seems to be a friendly person.
67. Don't put your dirty feet on my clean rug.
68. That huge bow must have been made for a powerful person.

Space Order   *pages 264–265*

G. Write the topic sentence. Then write the four detail sentences in left-to-right space order.

TOPIC SENTENCE: This is a photograph taken inside our library.

69. Beyond the card catalog, the farthest to the right, is the stairwell.
70. In the center of the library stands the computer terminal.
71. A microfiche reader is on the far left.
72. Beside the reference desk stands the card catalog.

Descriptive Paragraph   *pages 266–267*

H. Write a sentence to describe each of the following.

73. how an ice cube feels
74. the sounds of a spring morning
75. the size, shape, and color of a pear
76. what a kitchen smells like while dinner is cooking
77. the sights or sounds of a playground during recess

I. Read the topic sentence below. Then read sentences **78–81**. For each sentence, write *yes* if it gives a detail that supports the topic sentence. Write *no* if it does not.

TOPIC SENTENCE: An indoor ice-skating rink is a fascinating place.

78. A husband and wife skate arm in arm.
79. Sounds of traffic can be heard.
80. A small girl twirls on the ice.
81. A boy practices figure eights.

Adjective Add-Ups

Try to find twenty-four adjectives in this puzzle. Make the words by using letters that touch each other horizontally, vertically, or diagonally. No letter box may be used twice for the same word. To start you off, the adjective *sweet* has been circled. (Hint: Get extra adjectives by including *est* and *er*.)

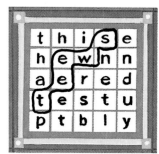

What words other than adjectives can you find in the puzzle?

Make an adjective puzzle like the one above. Ask a classmate to solve it.

Scrambled Adjectives

Unscramble each set of letters to make six adjectives. Then arrange the first letters of the adjectives to make a noun to complete this sentence: *We drank from the cool mountain _____.*

ygslsa	auantrl	nlrpsakig
tpnlaesa	rtandai	rdsetnceii

Unit 5 Extra Practice

1 Writing with Adjectives

p. 238

A. Write the adjectives in these sentences. Include articles.

1. Several unusual plants catch their food!
2. The flytrap, small and delicate, traps insects.
3. The interesting flytrap grows only in a few bogs.
4. The soil, damp and rich, lacks nitrogen.
5. Nitrogen is an important chemical for all plants.
6. A flytrap gets the necessary nitrogen from insects.
7. The curious plant traps and digests many insects.
8. The flowers, small and white, attract insects.
9. The plant lures hungry insects with a sweet liquid.
10. Each green leaf has two lobes.
11. The lobes have fine hairs on the inner surface.
12. Sharp bristles line the edges.
13. An unfortunate insect may land on a sensitive hair.
14. Then the two lobes close quickly.
15. The helpless insect cannot escape.
16. The plant uses a special liquid to digest the insect.

B. Write each sentence. Use the correct article in parentheses ( ).

17. The pitcher plant is also (a, an) extraordinary plant.
18. Each leaf forms (a, an) pitcher, or tube.
19. The leaves produce (a, an) sweet substance.
20. (A, An) insect may fly down a leaf after the juice.

C. Write each sentence. Underline the adjectives that tell *what kind* once and the adjectives that tell *how many* twice. Do not include articles.

21. Some bristly hairs at the top of the tube trap the insect.
22. Most insects cannot hang on to the slippery inner walls.
23. The tiny insect falls into a deep pit.
24. Here a special liquid digests the unlucky victim.
25. The peculiar plant is found in many states.
26. Like the flytrap, the pitcher grows in damp places.

2 Proper Adjectives

p. 240

A. Write each proper adjective in the sentences correctly.

1. Tablecloths of irish linen are lovely.
2. This jacket is made of heavy scottish wool.
3. Our neighbors have just bought a swedish car.
4. They plan to visit some german castles on their vacation.
5. Many european countries have a favorite instrument.
6. Everyone knows the sound of scottish bagpipes.
7. The same instruments are also played for irish folk dances.
8. Some hungarian dances call for violin music.
9. A viennese waltz usually features violins, too.
10. The strumming of guitars suggests spanish dances.
11. Several portuguese musicians developed their own guitar.
12. Horns of different sizes produce the german band sound.
13. Many european countries are known for particular foods.
14. Have you ever eaten polish sausage?
15. Some people like norwegian sardines for a snack.
16. Delicious austrian pastries are famous around the world.
17. A popular item on the menu is alaskan crab.
18. A favorite dessert is hawaiian pineapple.
19. In supermarkets you can often find australian lamb.
20. Sushi is a japanese dish made with raw fish.

B. Write each proper adjective correctly. Then write the proper noun from which it was formed.

EXAMPLE: This museum has a large collection of asian art.
ANSWER: Asian, Asia

21. These bronze figures were made by an indian artist.
22. A special exhibit of persian rugs is now on display.
23. Have you seen the collection of russian coins?
24. The pottery in this case dates from roman times.
25. This ancient egyptian statue was carved from wood.
26. These african masks were worn in religious ceremonies.
27. Gold and silver were used to make this mexican jewelry.
28. A brazilian artist painted these scenes of common people.
29. These woolen blankets were made by bolivian weavers.

3 Predicate Adjectives

p. 242

A. Write each sentence. Underline each predicate adjective.

1. The seas around Scandinavia are very rough.
2. Viking ships were seaworthy.
3. The Vikings felt comfortable in their strong ships on long voyages.
4. Viking sailors seemed very adventurous at first.
5. Later they became quite warlike.
6. The Vikings did not seem fierce at home.
7. Their agricultural society was fair to men and women.
8. The Vikings became skillful in carpentry and crafts.
9. However, fertile land was scarce.
10. Life in Scandinavia became difficult for many Vikings.
11. Their voyages were successful for many reasons.
12. All Viking sailors were equal in rank and training.
13. They seemed proud of their fine ships.
14. The sturdy sailors became familiar with Europe's coasts.
15. Their ability to sail without maps and compasses seems unbelievable today.

B. Write each sentence. Underline each predicate adjective once and each predicate nominative twice.

16. The Vikings were fearless in battle.
17. Many countries looked weak to the Vikings.
18. Viking traders soon became raiders.
19. England and Ireland were the sites of the first raids.
20. Towns in France, Italy, and Spain were victims, too.
21. Fear of the Vikings was common throughout Europe.
22. The Vikings eventually became peaceful again.
23. Many Vikings were important explorers.
24. Leif Eriksson was a famous Viking leader.
25. Eric the Red was the founder of a colony in Greenland.
26. The Russian state was an eastern colony of the Vikings.
27. The Vikings were proud of their seafaring skills.
28. Their long, slim boats looked very graceful.
29. Another name for Vikings was Norsemen.
30. The history of the Vikings is full of adventure.
31. Their influence on European history was great.

4 Demonstrative Adjectives

p. 244

A. Write each sentence. Underline each demonstrative adjective.

1. This month is Black History Month.
2. That display shows famous black Americans.
3. These books are by outstanding black authors.
4. Those filmstrips are about black scientists.
5. This book was written by Alex Haley.
6. In these chapters he traces his family's history.
7. The woman in that picture is Harriet Tubman.
8. She led those people to freedom from slavery.
9. This article tells how she helped 300 slaves to escape.
10. These drawings are by the astronomer Benjamin Banneker.
11. Pages from his 1792 almanac appear in those books.
12. In this filmstrip we will see how Banneker taught himself astronomy and math.
13. He used those skills to help design our nation's capital.
14. Mary McLeod Bethune is the subject of this book.
15. With these students she began a college for black women.
16. That photo shows her with President Franklin D. Roosevelt.
17. Two of the greatest jazz musicians of this century were Louis Armstrong and Duke Ellington.
18. Some of their best recordings are on that tape.
19. The origins of jazz in America are traced in this book.

B. Write whether the underlined word is used as an adjective or a pronoun.

20. That is the great black leader Martin Luther King, Jr.
21. Some of his speeches are collected in this book.
22. The baseball player in this film is Jackie Robinson.
23. Those are his teammates on the Brooklyn Dodgers in 1947.
24. That was the first time a black played major league ball.
25. Marian Anderson is one of the greatest singers this country has produced.
26. These are some very special recordings of hers.
27. That voice has thrilled millions all over the world.
28. This is a book about the scientist Dr. Charles Drew.
29. These pages tell how he set up the first blood bank.

5 Adjectives That Compare   *p. 246*

A. Write each sentence. Use the correct form of the adjective in parentheses ( ).

EXAMPLE: The continent of Asia is (big) than Africa.
ANSWER: The continent of Asia is bigger than Africa.

1. Asia is the (big) continent of all.
2. The (cold) continent is Antarctica.
3. The Atlantic Ocean is (deep) than the Indian Ocean.
4. The Pacific Ocean is the (deep) ocean on the earth.
5. It is also the (large) ocean.
6. The (high) mountain in North America is Mount McKinley, in Alaska.
7. Asia's Mount Everest is (high) than Mount McKinley.
8. The (long) river in South America is the Amazon River.
9. It is (long) than North America's Mississippi River.
10. Lake Ontario is the (small) of the five Great Lakes.
11. Europe has a (large) population than Africa.
12. The (low) point on the earth is the Dead Sea, in Asia.
13. The Dead Sea is (low) than Death Valley, in North America.
14. The Sahara is one of the (dry) spots on the earth.

B. Write each sentence. Use the correct form of the adjective in parentheses ( ).

15. Florida is the (southern) of the mainland states.
16. Only Alaska has a (extensive) coastline than Florida.
17. Florida's (popular) beach is Miami Beach.
18. Winters in Florida are (moderate) than elsewhere.
19. Florida is one of America's (famous) resort states.
20. Disney World, near Orlando, Florida, is one of the world's (extraordinary) amusement parks.
21. Everglades National Park is the (large) tropical wilderness in the United States.
22. Farming is a (important) industry than fishing.
23. Oranges are the state's (valuable) crop.
24. Florida is (populous) than forty-two other states.
25. Tourism is Florida's (important) industry.
26. Many think Florida has the (good) climate of any state.

UNIT SIX

USING LANGUAGE TO
RESEARCH

PART ONE

Unit Theme *Pioneering Women*
Language Awareness Adverbs

PART TWO

Literature "From Coast to Coast" by Louise Boyd James
A Reason for Writing Researching

Writing
IN YOUR JOURNAL

WRITER'S WARM-UP ◆ For centuries, society had definite ideas of what activities were proper for women. These ideas slowly changed, as women began to enter many fields that were once closed to them. These women were pioneers, overcoming obstacles to achieve success and pave the way for others. Many women today are still pioneers in many ways. Write in your journal about a woman whom you consider to be a pioneer.

• GETTING •
STARTED

Play the game "How Did You Do It?" The first player says a simple sentence that tells how something was done: *I spoke loudly.* Each player repeats the sentence, adding another word to describe the verb: *I spoke loudly, clearly, intelligently, humorously . . . .*

1 Writing with Adverbs

The underlined words in the following sentences are adverbs. They describe the verbs in the sentences. Adverbs answer the question *How? When? Where?* or *To what extent?*

How: Amelia Earhart walked <u>bravely</u> across the airstrip.
Where: Her small, single-engine plane stood <u>nearby</u>.
When: <u>Soon</u> she would be flying above the ocean by herself.
To what extent: Amelia could <u>hardly</u> wait to take off.

Notice that an adverb can come before or after the verb it describes. It can also come between a helping verb and a main verb.

Not all adverbs describe verbs. An adverb can also describe an adjective or another adverb. Then it usually comes directly before the word it describes.

In 1932 <u>very</u> few women were pilots. (describes adjective)
Amelia Earhart could fly <u>extremely</u> well. (describes adverb)

Adverbs often end in *-ly*. Some common adverbs that do not end in *-ly* are shown below.

almost	ever	never	rather	soon
already	here	not	seldom	there
also	just	often	so	too
always	later	quite	somewhat	very

> **Summary** ◆ An **adverb** describes a verb, an adjective, or another adverb.

Guided Practice

Name the adverbs in the sentences.

1. In 1932 no woman had successfully flown across the Atlantic.
2. This famous pilot planned her flights very carefully.
3. She was extremely precise about her navigation.

Practice

A. Write each sentence. Underline each adverb.

4. The trip from North America to Europe was quite dangerous.
5. Earhart's plane became completely ice-covered.
6. It lost altitude and spun wildly toward the dark Atlantic.
7. Earhart fortunately regained control in time.
8. The plane's altimeter broke, too.
9. Without it, Earhart could not know her altitude.
10. Later a crack developed in the engine.
11. Streaks of flame shot menacingly into the darkness.

B. Write the word that each underlined adverb describes. Then write whether the word is a verb, an adjective, or an adverb.

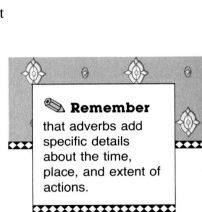

12. Earhart's plane was battered <u>rather</u> seriously in a storm.
13. The fuel tanks were <u>nearly</u> empty.
14. However, she landed <u>safely</u> in an Irish pasture.
15. Amelia Earhart returned home an <u>extremely</u> popular hero.
16. That same year she flew <u>nonstop</u> across the United States.
17. She was the <u>very</u> first person to do that alone.
18. <u>Somewhat</u> later, Earhart became the first person to fly from Hawaii to the mainland of the United States.

C. Write the paragraph using adverbs that answer the questions.

In 1937 Amelia Earhart (**19.** *How?*) announced her next extraordinary flight. She told a (**20.** *To what extent?*) impressed nation that (**21.** *When?*) she would fly around the world. The trip began well, but radio contact with Earhart's plane was lost as she was flying over the South Seas. Rescue ships and planes searched (**22.** *Where?*). No trace of brave Amelia Earhart was (**23.** *When?*) found.

Apply ◆ Think and Write

From Your Writing ◆ Read what you wrote for the Writer's Warm-up. Write the labels below on your paper. Then list the adverbs you used in these columns.

How?   **When?**   **Where?**   **To What Extent?**

> ✎ **Remember**
> that adverbs add specific details about the time, place, and extent of actions.

Describe a "mystery" person in your class by comparing his or her actions with other people's actions. For example: *My mystery person draws faster than Kurt and more creatively than Don.* See if classmates can guess the person from the clues.

2 Adverbs That Compare

Like adjectives, adverbs have a comparative and a superlative form. The comparative form is used to compare two things. The superlative is used to compare three or more things.

One-syllable adverbs usually add *-er* to form the comparative and *-est* to form the superlative.

> People work <u>hard</u> to reach a goal. (Adverb)
> They work <u>harder</u> than we do. (Comparative)
> She works <u>hardest</u> of all. (Superlative)

Most adverbs that end in *-ly* and adverbs with two or more syllables use *more* to form the comparative and *most* to form the superlative.

> Anne Bradstreet, America's first poet, was read <u>widely</u>. (Adverb)
> She was read <u>more widely</u> in England than here. (Comparative)
> She was the <u>most widely</u> read of all colonial poets. (Superlative)

Some adverbs have special comparative and superlative forms.

Adverb	Comparative	Superlative
well	better	best
badly	worse	worst

Summary ◆ Use comparative forms of adverbs to compare two things. Use superlative forms to compare three or more.

Guided Practice

Tell the correct form of the adverb in parentheses.

1. Men became published poets (frequently) than women long ago.
2. Of all American poets, Anne Bradstreet was published (early).
3. Some told her that, as a woman, she was (well) suited to using a sewing needle than a poet's pen, but they were wrong.

Practice

A. Write the comparative and superlative form of each adverb.

4.	gently	**9.**	badly
5.	harshly	**10.**	loud
6.	high	**11.**	hopefully
7.	fast	**12.**	well
8.	strongly	**13.**	seriously

B. Write each sentence. Use the correct form of the adverb in parentheses ( ). Each woman was a pioneer in her field.

14. Phillis Wheatley lived (late) than Anne Bradstreet.

15. She was (well) educated than other slaves of the time.

16. In all she wrote, she spoke (movingly) about freedom.

17. In 1852 no book affected Americans (directly) than *Uncle Tom's Cabin* by Harriet Beecher Stowe.

18. Of all evils, Stowe (angrily) rejected slavery.

19. We see women news reporters (often) now than in the past.

20. The first newswoman, Nellie Bly, may have worked (effectively) than other reporters.

21. Bly used disguises and gathered news (fast) than others.

22. Of all her feats a rapid trip around the world is known (well).

23. Helen Keller was America's (severely) disabled writer.

24. Blind and deaf, she wrote (sensitively) than many authors who could see and hear.

25. Her work was (widely) translated than other writers' books.

26. Gwendolyn Brooks describes the struggle for equality (effectively) than many poets.

27. Some feel she writes (well) when she tells of the life of blacks in the cities.

28. Her book of poetry *Annie Allen* was (highly) praised than any other when she won the Pulitzer Prize in 1950.

Apply ◆ Think and Write

Dictionary of Knowledge ◆ Read the article about Gwendolyn Brooks. Write a few sentences that tell about her and the ideas and feelings she shared in her poetry. Use some comparative and superlative adverbs.

🖉 **Remember**
to use appropriate forms of adverbs to describe actions specifically.

Describe an object by saying what it *isn't*. For example: *It isn't blue or red. It has no wooden parts. We never use it during science.* Keep giving negative clues until others guess the object.

3 Avoiding Double Negatives

A negative is a word that means "no" or "not." Some common negatives are *no*, *no one*, *not*, *none*, *never*, *nothing*, *nowhere*, and *nobody*. Contractions formed with *not* are also negatives.

Two negatives used in the same sentence are called a **double negative**. Double negatives should be avoided because they make the meaning of a sentence unclear.

Wrong: Motorcars won't never work well!
Right: Motorcars will never work well!
Right: Motorcars won't ever work well!

Notice that a double negative can be corrected in different ways. In the second and third sentences above, an affirmative, or "yes" word, has been substituted for one of the negatives. This chart shows the affirmatives for other words.

Negative	Affirmative	Negative	Affirmative
no	any, a, one, some	nothing	anything, something
no one	anyone, someone	nowhere	anywhere, somewhere
none	all, some	nobody	anybody, somebody

> **Summary** ◆ Some negative words, such as *not*, are adverbs. Avoid using two negative words in the same sentence.

Guided Practice

Tell which word makes each sentence negative.

1. Some people had (nothing, anything) good to say about the early automobile.
2. Those newfangled motorcars will (ever, never) replace horses.
3. A car (can't, can) go as fast or as far as a train.

Practice

A. Write each sentence. Use the word in parentheses ( ) that makes the sentence negative.

   4. In 1903 nine out of ten roads in the United States (weren't, were) paved.
   5. (No, A) motorist could escape dust and deep mud.
   6. (None, Some) of the first cars were comfortable.
   7. (Anybody, Nobody) could drive for long in comfort.
   8. Gas stations were (nowhere, anywhere) to be found.
   9. There were (no, some) driving tests for motorists either.
   10. Horses (could, couldn't) stand the noisy automobiles.
   11. (No one, Anyone) could control a horse terrified by a car.
   12. There seemed (an, no) end to the accidents caused by cars.
   13. Saying ''Get a horse!'' was (no, a) joke back then.

B. Rewrite each sentence to correct the double negative.

   14. In 1900 carmakers couldn't persuade nobody that cars would replace horses and trains someday.
   15. Cars couldn't go nowhere without gasoline and service.
   16. Nobody had never printed any decent road maps.
   17. There wasn't no safe way to drive on unpaved roads.
   18. Alice Ramsey didn't have no easy time as the first woman to drive across the United States.

C. Add words to make each word group into a negative sentence. Write the sentence. Be careful to avoid double negatives.

   19. A long, hot ride was not _____ .
   20. No one expected that _____ .
   21. The car never failed to _____ .
   22. The early cars had endurance, but _____ .
   23. Sometimes when the car's motor stopped, _____ .

Apply ◆ Think and Write

A Pioneer Motorist ◆ Imagine that you were one of the first motorists. Describe some car problems you might have had. Use some ''no'' words in your sentences.

✎ **Remember**
to proofread your sentences to be sure you have not used any double negatives.

Play "Switcheroo." Use an adverb that ends in *-ly* in a sentence: *She paints creatively.* Then find the adjective that it came from. Use that adjective in a similar sentence: *She is a creative painter.*

4 Using Adjectives and Adverbs

Which word would you use to complete each sentence?

> **1.** In the 1850s Dr. Blackwell treated patients (skillful, skillfully).
> **2.** Elizabeth Blackwell was (skillful, skillfully) in medicine.

In sentence **1**, the adverb *skillfully* is correct. It describes the verb *treated*. In sentence **2**, the correct word is *skillful*. *Skillful* is a predicate adjective that describes *Elizabeth Blackwell*. When you are not sure whether to use an adjective or an adverb, find the word being described.

The words *good* and *well* are often confused. *Good* is always an adjective. Use it to describe a noun or a pronoun.

> **Blackwell, the first woman in the United States to practice medicine, was a good doctor.**

Well is an adjective when it describes a noun or pronoun and means "healthy." It usually comes after a linking verb.

> ■ **Many patients became well again under her care.**

Well is an adverb when it tells how something is done.

> ■ **She used her skills well in training other women doctors.**

Summary ♦ Use adjectives to describe nouns and pronouns. Use adverbs to describe verbs, adjectives, and other adverbs.

Guided Practice

Tell which word correctly completes each sentence.

1. Maria Mitchell studied the skies (careful, carefully).
2. In 1847 the self-taught amateur astronomer felt very (proud, proudly).
3. (Surprising, Surprisingly) she had discovered a new comet!

Practice

A. Read about these women and their accomplishments. Then write the word that correctly completes each sentence.

4. Louise Bethune studied architecture (intense, intensely).

5. In the 1880s she designed buildings (regular, regularly).

6. Marie Curie became (famous, famously) for her discoveries.

7. In 1900 she studied radioactivity (thorough, thoroughly).

8. It was (unusual, unusually) to win two Nobel prizes, one for physics and one for chemistry, but Marie Curie did.

9. Rosa Parks acted (brave, bravely) as one of the first heroes of the civil rights movement.

10. She was treated (unfair, unfairly) on a bus, and she resisted.

11. Civil rights laws came about (quick, quickly) after her arrest in 1955 for defending her rights.

12. Jackie Joyner-Kersee runs (beautiful, beautifully).

13. In a heptathlon she is (outstanding, outstandingly).

B. Write each sentence. Use the word *good* or *well* in the blank. Then write whether the word is an adjective or an adverb.

14. Ella Grasso served the state of Connecticut _____ .

15. The changes made by this first elected woman governor were _____ for all the state's people.

16. Junko Tabei's mountaineering skills were very _____ .

17. Scaling Mount Everest showed how _____ she could climb.

18. On the world's highest peak, she felt healthy and _____ .

19. Ramona Bañuelos did very _____ in business in California.

20. Her work as Treasurer of the United States was also _____ .

21. As America's first woman astronaut, Sally Ride performed _____ during her six days in space.

22. Her skills as a physicist served her purpose _____ .

23. Ride also felt _____ about her accomplishments.

Apply • Think and Write

An Encyclopedia Entry ◆ What would you like to be the first person to do? Write a brief entry for an encyclopedia of the future to describe your "famous first." Remember to use adjectives and adverbs to make your writing colorful.

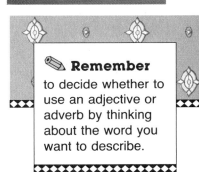

✎ **Remember**
to decide whether to use an adjective or adverb by thinking about the word you want to describe.

After the storm we were <u>soaked</u>, quite <u>drenched</u>, and thoroughly <u>sopping</u>. How many sentences can you think of that use three words that mean just about the same thing?

VOCABULARY ◆
Synonyms and Antonyms

Synonym comes from an ancient Greek word meaning "like name." **Synonyms** are words that have similar meanings. *Antonym* comes from Greek, too. It means "opposite name." **Antonyms** are words that have opposite meanings.

In the following sentences the words *beautiful* and *beauty* have been overused.

> It was a <u>beautiful</u> afternoon. We had a <u>beautiful</u> meal and later watched as the sun set in all its <u>beauty</u>.

Rewritten with synonyms, the sentences take on a much more precise meaning.

> It was a <u>delightful</u> afternoon. We had a <u>terrific</u> meal and later watched as the sun set in all its <u>splendor</u>.

Rewritten with antonyms, the sentences take on a very different meaning.

> It was an <u>awful</u> afternoon. We had a <u>disgusting</u> meal and later watched as the sun set in all its <u>dullness</u>.

Building Your Vocabulary

On pages 306–308 you will read about the first woman to drive an automobile across the United States. Do you think a trip by auto in 1909 would have been exciting, or unexciting?

The words below are synonyms for the antonyms *exciting* and *unexciting.* Try the different synonyms in the sentence. Notice how the meaning is changed by the adjectives you choose.

exciting:	thrilling	stimulating	stirring	spectacular
unexciting:	dull	monotonous	boring	lackluster

Alice Ramsey had a ＿＿＿ trip across the country.

What other synonyms for *exciting* and *unexciting* could you use?

Practice

A. The adverbs below are synonyms that mean "speedily." Use a different synonym to complete each sentence. Write the sentence.

quickly   abruptly   rapidly   suddenly   swiftly   briskly

1. Mia watched the dog _____ run into the path of a car.
2. She marveled at how _____ the driver tried to stop.
3. It all happened so _____ , yet Mia felt time had stopped, too.
4. She felt her heart beating _____ .
5. With a sigh of relief, she watched the dog scamper _____ across the street.

Use the remaining adverb to write a sentence of your own that adds to Mia's story.

B. Write each "Reasoning Rhyme" below. Use a synonym or an antonym of the underlined word to complete the rhyme.

6. Day is to night as <u>black</u> is to _____ .
7. Squirm is to wiggle as <u>laugh</u> is to _____ .
8. In is to out as <u>whisper</u> is to _____ .
9. Bottom is to top as <u>start</u> is to _____ .
10. Equal is to same as <u>domestic</u> is to _____ .

C. Make a "Reasoning Rhyme" of your own and share it with your classmates.

LANGUAGE CORNER • Given Names

Alice is a name that came from a word long ago that meant "of noble kind." It was a very popular name in England after *Alice's Adventures in Wonderland* was published there in 1865. *Alison*, *Alicia*, and *Alissa* are forms of *Alice*.

Can you find out the meaning of your first, or given, name?

How to Expand Sentences with Adverbs

You have been using adverbs to describe verbs, adjectives, and other adverbs in sentences. Because adverbs tell *how, when, where* or *to what extent,* they add important details and information to your writing. For example, read the two sentences below.

> 1. **Jeremy skated across the ice.**
> 2. **Jeremy skated gracefully across the ice.**

Both of these sentences tell us what Jeremy did. Sentence **2,** however, gives us more information. It tells *how* Jeremy skated. The adverb *gracefully* makes the sentence more detailed and interesting. The addition of the adverb allows us to see more clearly the image of Jeremy on the ice.

As you know, different adverbs give different information. Changing the adverb again can turn the picture of a masterful skater into a less accomplished one.

> ■ 3. **Jeremy skated clumsily across the ice.**

If the verbs in your sentences do not give enough detail, use adverbs to describe the verbs. Adverbs can make a difference in your writing.

The Grammar Game ◆ Concentrate on adverbs! The list of verbs below are ones that you might use in your writing. Write as many adverbs that could describe each verb as quickly as you can.

feel	read	sleep	laugh
wait	start	think	watch

Compare your list of adverbs with a classmate's. How many of your adverbs were the same?

COOPERATIVE LEARNING: Expanding Sentences

Working Together

While working as a group on activities **A** and **B**, notice how adverbs add interest and information to your writing.

In Your Group

- Pay attention to each person's ideas.
- Build on other ideas.
- Show appreciation for different opinions.
- Record the group's suggestions.

A. Add adverbs to describe each underlined verb in the sentences below. Choose one adverb that tells *how* and one that tells *when* for each sentence.

1. Fred and Ginger <u>dance</u> together.
2. The writer <u>worked</u> at her desk.
3. Carlos <u>rehearsed</u> and <u>recited</u> his lines for the play.
4. Jean <u>walked</u> into the room and <u>sat</u> in the back row.
5. Picking up the paddle, I <u>aimed</u> and <u>hit</u> the ball.

B. Find the verbs in the paragraph below. Then write the paragraph, adding adverbs of the group's choice to describe each verb. Can you write the paragraph again, choosing different adverbs to change the story of the flight?

   The pilot climbed into the airplane. She buckled her seatbelt and checked the controls. A crowd formed and waited by the hangar. The pilot signaled her departure. The single engine started, and the plane rose off the ground. Its wings dipped to the left. The pilot performed some tricks. She did a double loop, and she did a large figure eight. The plane landed, and the crowd cheered.

WRITERS' CORNER • Word Position

You know that adverbs can often appear anywhere in a sentence. Changing the position of an adverb, however, *can* sometimes change the meaning of a sentence.

EXAMPLE: **Sometimes I take swimming lessons and play basketball.**

CHANGE: **I take swimming lessons and sometimes play basketball.**

Read what you wrote for the Writer's Warm-up. Did you use any adverbs in your writing? Are they positioned to express exactly what you mean to say?

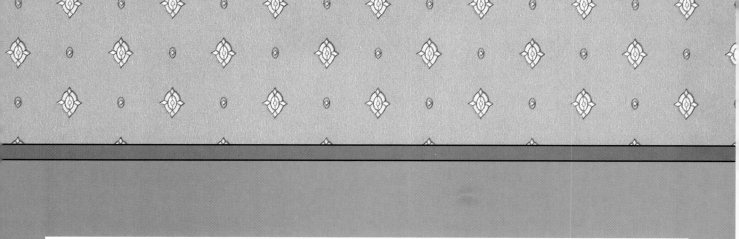

LYDIA AT A TAPESTRY LOOM (1881)
painting by Mary Cassatt
Courtesy, Flint Institute of Arts,
Gift of The Whiting Foundation.

USING LANGUAGE
TO
RESEARCH

=== PART TWO ===

Literature   "From Coast to Coast" by Louise Boyd James
A Reason for Writing Researching

CREATIVE
Writing

FINE ARTS ◆ What do you suppose the woman in the painting at the left is thinking? Is she worrying about her tapestry, planning a political speech, or wondering what to feed her family for the evening meal? Write down her thoughts in a notebook for her. Let others know what is going on in the woman's mind.

CRITICAL THINKING ◆
A Strategy for Researching

A GOAL/PLAN/OUTCOME CHART

Writers often do research about people who have reached special goals. One such person was Alice Ramsey. Over eighty years ago she set out on a very challenging journey. After this lesson you will read an article about her. Later you will write a research report about a special person.

Here is a passage from "From Coast to Coast," the article about Alice Ramsey.

> On June 9, 1909, twenty-one-year-old Alice Ramsey . . . cranked the four-cylinder, thirty-horsepower touring car to life and . . . began a historic journey of four thousand miles from New York City to San Francisco, making her the first woman to drive an automobile across the United States.

People often have a plan of action to reach a goal. What was Alice Ramsey's goal? What actions do you think she had to take to reach it? Was the outcome successful?

◆ Learning the Strategy

Often you have to plan actions to reach a goal. Suppose you want to run in a marathon. What actions would you have to take? What if you are writing a report about the first person to reach the South Pole. How could identifying the explorer's goals and actions help you organize your report?

A goal/plan/outcome chart is a good strategy for tracing the actions needed or already taken to reach a goal. For example, suppose it is your job to get a disc jockey for the end-of-year party. In three weeks you will have to make a report to the planning committee. A chart like the one below could help you keep track of your actions and the results.

Goal:	Plan:	Outcome:
Get a DJ for the party.	Get DJ phone numbers. Talk to 5 DJs. Find out about prices, tape collections, equipment. Go to hear 2 DJs.	Hired a terrific DJ for the party!

Using the Strategy

A. Think of something you would like to accomplish over the next few months. It might be learning to play a musical instrument. It might be fixing up your room. Make a goal/plan/outcome chart. Write your goal and the action or actions you might take to reach it. Then write the most likely outcome. Save your chart and write the real outcome later.

B. "From Coast to Coast" describes Alice Ramsey's drive to California in 1909. Think about what the trip may have been like. Then make a goal/plan/outcome chart. List her goal (to be the first woman to drive cross-country). Then list several actions you think she must have planned to achieve her goal. Read the article in the next lesson to learn the outcome.

Applying the Strategy

♦ How did you figure out your plan of actions for **A** above?
♦ How can identifying goals, plans, and outcomes help you in school subjects?

←From Coast to Coast→

by Louise Boyd James

The early 1900s were a time of change in the United States. A new contraption called the automobile was attracting the adventurous. In 1900 there were only 8,000 automobiles in the whole country, but by 1910 there were 450,000 on the road. Unfortunately, the nation's roads were not quite ready for the automobile. Yet major obstacles did not stop a brave pioneer motorist named Alice Ramsey.

On June 9, 1909, twenty-one-year-old Alice Ramsey impatiently answered questions and posed for pictures in a torrential rainstorm at the New York City Maxwell automobile headquarters. Suddenly she announced, "If we're going to go, let's go." She cranked the four-cylinder, thirty-horsepower touring car to life and climbed behind the right-hand-drive steering wheel.

With a last kiss for her husband, John, Ramsey and her three women passengers (two sisters-in-law and one family friend) began a historic journey of four thousand miles from New York City to San Francisco, making her the first woman to drive an automobile across the United States.

In 1909, there were few paved or marked highways, only a scattering of service stations, and no road maps as we know them. A coast-to-coast trip was an adventure, one that only about two dozen automobiles—all driven by men—had completed.

Few women drove cars, and some doctors had suggested it was dangerous for women even to ride in them. They said that women became too excited at speeds of fifteen to twenty miles an hour and would be unable to sleep at night. There was also the danger of "automobile face"—a perpetually open mouth that resulted in sinus trouble! Thus, many people believed that Alice Huyler Ramsey would be unable to complete her transcontinental trip. But this young woman was determined, saying, "I'll drive every inch of the way—if it kills me!"

The easiest part of the journey was from New York City to Chicago. Roads were best in this part of the country, even though many were designed for horses and wagons, not cars. Travel went so smoothly on the Cleveland Parkway, between Cleveland and Toledo, Ohio, that Ramsey reached her top speed of forty-two miles per hour.

Travel east of the Mississippi River was guided by the Blue Book, which gave directions and mileage from one town to another. But even the Blue Book could be wrong, as Ramsey discovered. Outside of Cleveland, it had directed: "At 11.6 miles, yellow house and barn on rt [right]. Turn left." There was no yellow house and barn; both were painted green. The man who owned them disapproved of automobiles and had hoped the changed colors would confuse drivers. Alice reached Chicago, one-third of her journey, in two weeks. From there west, there was no Blue Book, and the roads were much worse.

The trip was a promotion for the Maxwell Briscoe Motor Company. Officials had realized that a woman driving a Maxwell cross-country, over practically uncharted wilderness, was a great advertising opportunity. The auto company had furnished the forest-green car and hired J.D. Murphy as the advance man.

Murphy traveled ahead of Ramsey, usually by train. He arranged publicity, located gasoline and service stations, plotted the route, and found food and lodging for the women. One morning their breakfast consisted of corn flakes, canned tomatoes, and coffee. Another day was started with lamb chops and chocolate cake.

Travel across Iowa was the worst. It rained for thirteen days, and Ramsey drove through mud, mud, mud. "Roads were horrible!" she said later. "The accumulated rains of the past several days had already soaked deep enough below the surface of the roads to render them bottomless. We plowed our way along, forced to keep the transmission in low gear most of the time."

When the roads began to dry, potholes remained. In many places, it was impossible to avoid these; Ramsey had to weave the Maxwell around them, hitting as few as possible. "The Maxwell careened back and forth, diving in one direction, then another. Dodge a hole! Catch a breath! Now another! and another!" Ramsey wrote in her diary.

Once the right front and rear tires both got stuck in deep holes. Ramsey and Murphy jacked up the front wheel and used a fence post to force the rear wheel out. On one especially muddy section in Nebraska, the Maxwell was towed by a team of horses for thirteen miles. A dozen flat tires, a broken spring and two broken axles, and a sheared tie-rod bolt failed to stop Ramsey.

On August 7, sixty days after she had begun, Ramsey pulled into San Francisco amid a parade of honking Maxwells. She made the coast-to-coast trip at least thirty more times before her death, at age ninety-five. Alice Ramsey never had a traffic accident, and she received only one traffic ticket—for making a U-turn. In 1960, the Automobile Manufacturers Association named her Woman Motorist of the Century in honor of her adventurous spirit and contributions to the industry.

Library Link ♦ *This article is from* Cobblestone, *a historical magazine for young people. The July 1987 issue is about automobiles.*

Reader's Response

Would you like to have traveled with Alice Ramsey on her journey? Explain why or why not.

From Coast to Coast

Responding to Literature

1. "From Coast to Coast" revealed interesting information. Tell one fact or idea that surprised you.

2. Work in small groups to make a large "Then and Now" poster. Under two headings, show appropriate pictures for 1909 and now. Draw sketches and use magazine pictures. Choose one group member to explain your poster to the class.

3. Alice Ramsey was the first woman to drive across the United States. Research the facts and make a parade of other "famous firsts." Pretend to be the person who accomplished a "first." Wear a hat or the suggestion of a costume, if you like. Take turns telling who you are and what you did to be first.

4. If you could show Alice's trip on television, what three scenes would you include? Draw three television screens on paper. In each one, write a sentence that briefly describes a scene. Share your work with classmates.

Writing to Learn

Think and Plan ◆ Be like Alice Ramsey, and set a goal for yourself. What do you want to accomplish? Make a goal/plan/outcome chart to show how you will reach your goal.

Goal-Plan-Outcome Chart

Write ◆ Focusing on the outcome, write a journal entry to tell how you feel about reaching the goal you set.

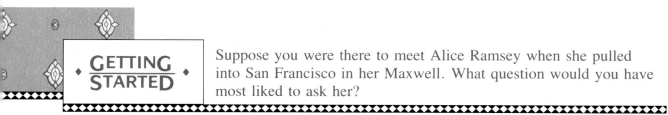

GETTING STARTED

Suppose you were there to meet Alice Ramsey when she pulled into San Francisco in her Maxwell. What question would you have most liked to ask her?

SPEAKING and LISTENING ◆ Interviews

When you are doing research on a topic, there are two ways to get the facts you need. One way is to read books and articles about your topic. From the printed material you can learn additional information, and you may also gain new insights.

Another way to get the information you need is to interview an expert—someone who knows a great deal about your topic. Asking questions in an interview is an excellent way to gather firsthand information. Through carefully planned questions you may learn information that is not available in printed form.

Here are some guidelines for interviewing.

Conducting an Interview	1. Write or call to request an interview. Explain the purpose of the interview at this time. 2. Prepare questions in advance. Make sure all the questions deal with your topic. 3. Begin your questions with the interviewing words *who, what, when, where, why,* and *how.* Avoid questions that can be answered with *yes* or *no.* 4. Thank the person for the interview.
Being an Active Listener	1. Listen carefully during the interview. Do not be thinking ahead to what you are going to say next. 2. Ask follow-up questions to clarify an answer or to explore a point. 3. Allow the person to talk freely, but do not let the discussion stray too far from the topic. 4. If possible, tape-record the interview. Otherwise, take notes.

Summary ◆ An **interview** is a useful means of getting firsthand information. Interview questions should be carefully planned in advance.

Guided Practice

Imagine you were one of the reporters interviewing Alice Ramsey in New York City as she began her cross-country drive. Tell one question you would have asked her about each of the following.

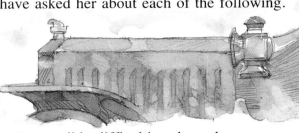

1. her preparation
2. road conditions
3. traveling time
4. possible difficulties along the way
5. people's attitudes about her attempt
6. overnight accommodations

Practice

A. Choose a topic for an interview with each person below. Write the topic. Then write three questions you would ask the person about the topic.

7. your favorite musician
8. your state's governor
9. your school's principal
10. a race-car driver

B. Write the name of one well-known person you would like to interview. Then write at least four questions you would ask that person.

C. With a partner, role-play an interview with Alice Ramsey, or with someone else who set a record. Each person should take a turn being the interviewer. If you wish, you may make up both the record and the record setter.

Apply ♦ Think and Write

Research Questions ♦ Are you familiar with the *Guinness Book of World Records?* The world records described in the book have been said to be "amazing," "astounding," and even "downright silly!" Make up a world record suitable to be included in this book. Name the record. Then write three questions you would ask the person who set that world record.

✎ **Remember**
to stick to the topic when you interview someone.

Tim decided to title his report "Space." What's wrong with this title? Think of better titles for a report on this topic.

STUDY SKILLS ◆
Choosing a Topic

Writing a good research report takes thought and planning. The first step is to choose a suitable topic. Here are some guidelines that will help you do this.

◆ Choose a topic that interests you. Your interest will help make the report more interesting, and writing the report will be easier.
◆ Think about the knowledge and interests of your audience, your readers. Well-chosen topics encourage reader attention.
◆ Narrow the topic enough to fit the size of your report.

Jerry chose the topic *cars* for his report. He knew it was a high-interest topic for himself and his classmates. However, he also knew that *cars* was too broad a topic for a short report. Jerry worked to narrow his topic by using this diagram.

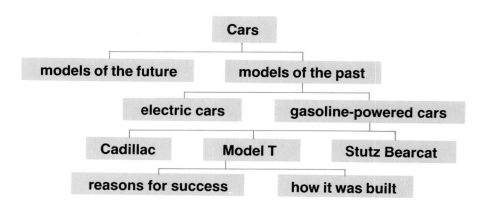

Jerry picked *reasons for the success of the Model T* as his final topic. It was narrow enough to cover in a three-paragraph report. It was also suitable to the knowledge and interests of his audience.

> **Summary** ◆ Choose a report topic that interests you. Then narrow the topic to fit the size of your report.

Guided Practice

Name the narrowest topic in each group.

1. roads, superhighways, New Jersey Turnpike
2. assembly lines, factories, automobile plants
3. types of fuel, gasoline, energy sources
4. adventurers, famous women, Alice Ramsey
5. cameras, black-and-white photographs, photography

Practice

A. Write each group of topics in order from broadest to narrowest.

    6. early vehicles, transportation, horse-drawn wagons
    7. sports, Indianapolis 500, automobile racing
    8. midwestern states, Iowa, United States of America
    9. reference materials, travel guides, Nebraska Blue Book
   10. changing flat tires, auto care, simple auto repairs

B. For each broad topic below, write a narrow topic suitable for a short report.

    EXAMPLE: American cities
    ANSWER: important products of Detroit, Michigan

11. inventions	**18.** weather
12. mountains	**19.** automobile parts
13. farming	**20.** Olympic Games
14. music	**21.** adventurers
15. hobbies	**22.** office workers
16. sports	**23.** entertainment
17. rivers	**24.** planets

C. Choose one of the broad topics given in **Practice B**. Narrow it step by step, using a diagram similar to the one on page 312.

Apply ◆ Think and Write

Narrow Topics ◆ Alice Ramsey kept a diary during her cross-country automobile trip. List some narrow topics that she might have written about.

> ✏️ **Remember**
> to narrow a topic to fit the size of your report.

Imagine that someday you are the first to accomplish something important. What would your "famous first" be? What topic might someone look under to read about you in an encyclopedia?

STUDY SKILLS ◆
Using an Encyclopedia

An encyclopedia is a useful reference tool. It contains information on a wide range of topics. Most encyclopedias contain many books, or volumes. The spine of each volume lists the beginning letter or letters of the topics in that volume. Topics are arranged alphabetically.

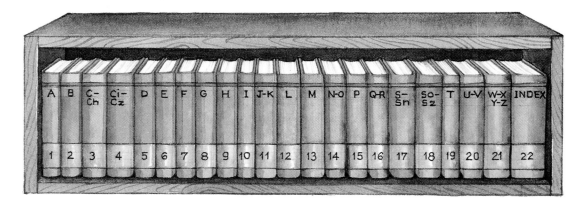

To use an encyclopedia, determine the key word or words in the topic or question you are researching. For example, Megan wanted to know when the first automobile was invented. She decided *automobile* was the key word. Megan knew that Volume 1 had articles on topics beginning with the letter *A*. Guide words at the top of each page helped her locate the article. Some encyclopedia articles include cross-references at the end. These are titles of other articles related to the topic.

You can also look up a topic in an encyclopedia's index. The index alphabetically lists all topics included in the encyclopedia and tells the volumes and page numbers where information on each topic can be found.

Summary ◆ Topics in an encyclopedia are arranged in alphabetical order.

Guided Practice

State the key word or words in each question.

1. When was the Lincoln Highway built?
2. How many bridges cross the Mississippi River today?
3. What was the first mass-produced automobile?

Practice

A. Write the key word or words in each question.

  4. What did Garrett Augustus Morgan invent?
  5. Does a diesel engine burn gasoline?
  6. What are some interesting sights in San Francisco?
  7. What river forms the eastern border of Iowa?
  8. How does advertising get people interested in a product?

B. For each question, write the key word and the volume number in which you would look it up. Use the illustration on page 314.

  9. Who was Ransom Eli Olds?
  10. Why are there so many auto factories near Detroit?
  11. How did Henry Ford change the way cars were made?
  12. What process was invented by Charles Goodyear?
  13. How does a patent protect an invention?

C. Each question below has two separate key words. Write both key words and both volume numbers in which articles would appear.

  14. How did discoveries in Texas affect automobile use?
  15. Is a tire the same as a wheel?
  16. Which is longer, a kilometer or a mile?
  17. What do Gottlieb Daimler and Karl Benz have in common?
  18. Is Chrysler Corporation larger than General Motors?

Apply ◆ Think and Write

Topic Research ◆ Choose a topic that you want to know more about. Determine the key word in the topic and look it up in an encyclopedia index. List the volumes and page numbers where information on the topic can be found.

✎ **Remember**
that using cross-references can help you find additional information on your topic.

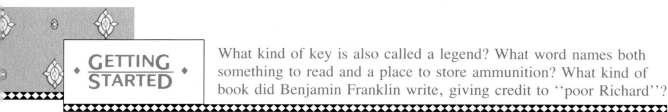

♦ GETTING ♦
STARTED

What kind of key is also called a legend? What word names both
something to read and a place to store ammunition? What kind of
book did Benjamin Franklin write, giving credit to "poor Richard"?

STUDY SKILLS ♦
Using Other Reference Materials

The encyclopedia is a good place to begin research. Other
books, however, may be more useful in finding certain types of
information. Here are some other common reference materials.

Atlas ⟩ An atlas is a collection of maps. Use it to find information about
places. Some maps show political boundaries. Others show land
features, climate, population, or roads.

Almanac ⟩ An almanac is a book of facts, past and present. Since it is
revised each year, it is useful for recent information. An almanac
includes hundreds of charts, tables, and lists of facts on subjects
like these: population; presidents, governors, and mayors; sports
events; postal ZIP codes; book, movie, and music awards; famous
personalities; states and countries; astronomy. Unlike other
nonfiction books, an almanac has its index in the front.

Periodicals ⟩ Periodicals, such as newspapers and magazines, are published at
frequent intervals. They usually have the most current information.
To find magazine articles on a topic, use the *Readers' Guide to
Periodical Literature.* It is an index of articles from many
magazines. Articles are listed alphabetically by subject and author.

In addition to print materials, most libraries have audiovisual
(A-V) materials for researchers. These include films, filmstrips,
slides, mounted photographs, records, tapes, and videocassettes.
CD/ROM (compact disk/read-only memory) is technology that
stores massive amounts of information for reference on a single
compact computer disk. Ask a librarian about A-V materials.

> **Summary** ♦ **Atlases, almanacs, periodicals,** and the
> *Readers' Guide* are useful research tools.

Guided Practice

Tell what is found in each of the following reference materials.

1. atlas **2.** almanac **3.** *Readers' Guide*

Practice

A. Match each kind of information with the best reference source.

4. list of ZIP codes	**a.** *Readers' Guide*
5. facts about yesterday's events	**b.** magazine
6. story about a popular athlete	**c.** newspaper
7. climate regions of Oregon	**d.** almanac
8. list of articles on auto touring	**e.** atlas

B. Write *atlas, almanac, periodical,* or *Readers' Guide* to tell the reference source best suited to answer each question.

  9. Who was President of the United States in 1909?

10. Which states border the Mississippi River?

11. Which issue of *Art News* covers American women artists?

12. Is rain expected tomorrow?

13. How many people live in Cleveland?

14. How many cars were sold in the United States last year?

15. In what part of Alaska is the Copper River?

16. Who won yesterday's tennis match?

17. When did women athletes first participate in the Olympics?

18. Does Interstate Highway 20 pass through Kansas?

C. Write the topic or topics you might look under in the *Readers' Guide* if you needed to answer each question below.

19. What is the proper clothing for bicycling?

20. Is bicycling a good way to achieve physical fitness?

21. What are the features of the latest bicycles?

22. How did Greg Lemond train for the Tour de France?

Apply ◆ Think and Write

Audiovisual Materials ◆ Write a paragraph explaining what audiovisual materials you might use for a report on jazz musicians.

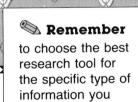

✏️ **Remember**
to choose the best research tool for the specific type of information you need.

STUDY SKILLS: Reference Materials **317**

◆ GETTING ◆
STARTED

A well-known saying is "Too many cooks spoil the broth." Can you think of another way to state this idea, using your own words?

WRITING ◆
Taking Notes and Paraphrasing

Roy needed information on Harriet Morehead Berry, the "mother of good roads in North Carolina." He read this:

> Harriet Morehead Berry (July 22, 1877–March 24, 1940) was born in North Carolina. After college, she taught school for several years. Then she went to work for the North Carolina Geological and Economic Survey. Her work, along with the new popularity of automobiles, made her aware of the need for modern paved roads. Berry became a leading force in the North Carolina Good Roads Association, formed in 1902. She wrote letters, gave speeches, and got public leaders to support her ideas.

Roy wanted to remember the important facts for his report. He took these notes on an index card, according to the hints below.

Harriet Morehead Berry worked for modern roads
— born 7/22/1877, North Carolina
— taught school for a while
— worked for N.C. Geological and Economic Survey
— active in N.C. Good Roads Association
— sought public support for her ideas

Roads and Highways Across America, Hugh Nash, page 38.

Hints for Taking Notes

- ◆ Take notes on lined 3″ × 5″ index cards.
- ◆ Write the main idea at the top of the card.
- ◆ List supporting details below the main idea.
- ◆ Use key words or phrases. Full sentences are not necessary.
- ◆ Do not copy information word for word. Paraphrase, or restate ideas in your own words.
- ◆ Note the title, author, and page numbers of your source.

When you are ready to write your report, you will **summarize** the information you have gathered from various sources. You will select the most important points and state them in your own words.

> **Summary** ♦ Use your own words when taking notes on what you read.

Guided Practice

Restate each sentence in your own words.

1. Roads in swampy areas were often in especially poor condition.
2. Some dirt roads were covered with flat wooden planks.
3. Road planks wore out quickly and had to be replaced.

Practice

A. Rewrite each sentence in your own words.

    4. Berry's work included taking notes and keeping records.
    5. She had to prepare a geology exhibit for the State Fair.
    6. She was consulted by President Wilson during World War I.
    7. Some citizens encouraged Berry to run for governor.

B. Read the paragraph below. Take notes on the paragraph, using your own words. You do not need to use complete sentences.

    Berry knew that the way to get modern roads was for lawmakers to pass a law. In 1920 she worked with politicians on a highway bill, a written idea for a law. The next year the bill passed. It called for the state to spend fifty million dollars to improve its highway system and resulted in nearly 6,000 miles of improved roads.

Apply ♦ Think and Write

Dictionary of Knowledge ♦ Harriet Morehead Berry worked on a bill for new roads in North Carolina. In the entry for **federal laws**, read about how a bill becomes law in the United States. Take notes on the important facts in your own words. Then summarize the article, using your notes.

✎ **Remember**
to use key words and phrases when taking notes.

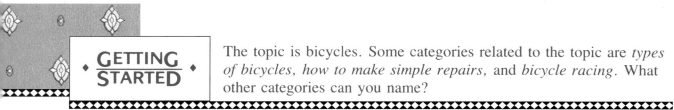

GETTING STARTED

The topic is bicycles. Some categories related to the topic are *types of bicycles, how to make simple repairs,* and *bicycle racing.* What other categories can you name?

WRITING ◆
An Outline

An outline is a written plan. It can help you organize your notes in a logical order before you begin to write a report. Each main idea becomes a main topic of the outline. Main topics are indicated by Roman numerals. Each supporting detail becomes a subtopic. Subtopics are indicated by capital letters. The outline below organizes information about a pioneering mountain climber.

Title ——————————— Fanny Bullock Workman (1859–1925)

Main topic ——— I. Began worldwide bicycle travels in 1895

Subtopics ———
A. Explored North Africa, Europe, Asia
B. Averaged forty to fifty miles per day
C. Endured bad weather, dangers, rough roads

Main topic ——— II. Switched to mountaineering in 1899

Subtopics ———
A. Explored unmapped mountains and glaciers
B. Took photos, kept scientific records, made maps

Main topic ——— III. Made seven expeditions to Asian Himalayas, 1899–1911

Subtopics ———
A. Had no modern equipment or conveniences
B. Set women's world altitude record (21,000 ft.), 1903
C. Reached new record altitude (23,300 ft.), 1906

Guidelines for Writing an Outline

◆ Center the title at the top of the outline.
◆ Place a period after all Roman numerals and letters.
◆ Capitalize the first word of each topic or subtopic.
◆ Indent each subtopic.
◆ Include at least two items at each level of the outline. This means never use a I without a II or an A without a B.

Summary ◆ An **outline** organizes information into main ideas and supporting details.

320   WRITING: Outlines

Guided Practice

Tell the words that complete each sentence about outlines.

1. Main topics are indicated by _____ in an outline.
2. _____ are indicated by capital letters.
3. Be sure to indent each _____ .

Practice

A. 4–11. Rewrite the following outline correctly. Then label the title, the main topics, and the subtopics.

Annie Smith Peck, Mountaineer
1. Early climbs
   a. ascended Mt. Shasta in California
   B. climbed Popocatépetl volcano in Mexico
II. South American climbs
   A. reached summit of Mt. Sorata, Bolivia, in 1904 (21,300 ft.)
   B. tried Mt. Huascarán in Peru three times
   c. set Western Hemisphere record there in 1908 (21,812 ft.)

B. Arrange these main topics and subtopics into an outline titled ''Comparison of Peck and Workman.'' Refer to the information given in the separate outlines about the two women.

12. Annie Smith Peck
13. Both set records
14. Began as bicyclist
15. Climbed in North and South America
16. Climbed a volcano
17. Fanny Bullock Workman
18. Peck and Workman
19. Both climbed in early 1900s
20. Climbed in Asia

C. Use information from the outline on page 320 to write a paragraph about Fanny Bullock Workman. Choose one of the main topics and its subtopics as the basis of your paragraph. You may make up additional information if you wish.

Apply ◆ Think and Write

An Outline ◆ Read a short encyclopedia article on a topic that interests you. Take notes on the article in your own words. Then arrange the main ideas and supporting details in outline form.

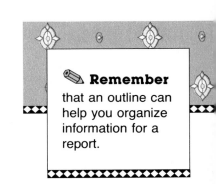

✎ **Remember**
that an outline can help you organize information for a report.

Focus on Fact and Opinion

When you read nonfiction, you often find facts mixed with opinion. How can you tell the difference between them? Sometimes it is difficult. A **fact** is a statement that can be proved true. An **opinion** is a judgment that someone believes to be true. An opinion *may* be true, but it cannot be proved.

> **FACT:** Alice Ramsey was the first woman to drive an automobile across the United States.
>
> **OPINION:** Alice Ramsey was the best woman driver of the century.

As a reader, you must be able to separate fact from opinion. Otherwise, you may take the writer's opinions to be facts. If you do, you may believe more of what the writer says than you should.

As a writer, you have a responsibility to your readers. You need to make clear which statements are facts and which are opinions. You can do this by using certain words and phrases to introduce an opinion.

> I believe (*or* think, feel, imagine, maintain, assume, suppose)
> It seems (*or* appears, is likely that, looks as if)
> In my opinion (*or* view, estimation, judgment)
> Possibly (*or* most likely, probably, chances are)

The Writer's Voice ◆ Many well-known facts (such as "The world is round.") were once opinions. ("Our friend Christopher Columbus maintains that the world is round.") Take a familiar fact from any subject and express it as an opinion.

Working Together

It is important to know how to recognize opinions and how to separate facts from opinions. As your group does activities **A** and **B**, identify facts and opinions.

A. Decide which of the following statements express facts and which express opinions. Record your group's decisions. Then discuss them with the class.

1. In 1909 there were few paved highways in America.
2. Some doctors felt that women became too excited at a car's speed of 15–20 mph and could not sleep.
3. Ramsey's top speed was 42 mph.
4. According to some doctors, riding in a car could produce "automobile face" and sinus problems.
5. Maxwell company officials believed that giving Ramsey a Maxwell for her trip would help to sell Maxwells.

B. With your group, express each statement of fact in activity **A** as an opinion. Then change each statement of opinion into a sentence that seems to make it into a fact.

THESAURUS CORNER • Word Choice

Look up the adverb *well* in the Thesaurus. Write three opinions you have about a favorite entertainer or athlete. In each sentence, use a different synonym listed for *well*. This adverb will indicate your opinion of the person's performance. Be sure that each synonym fits the meaning of the sentence.

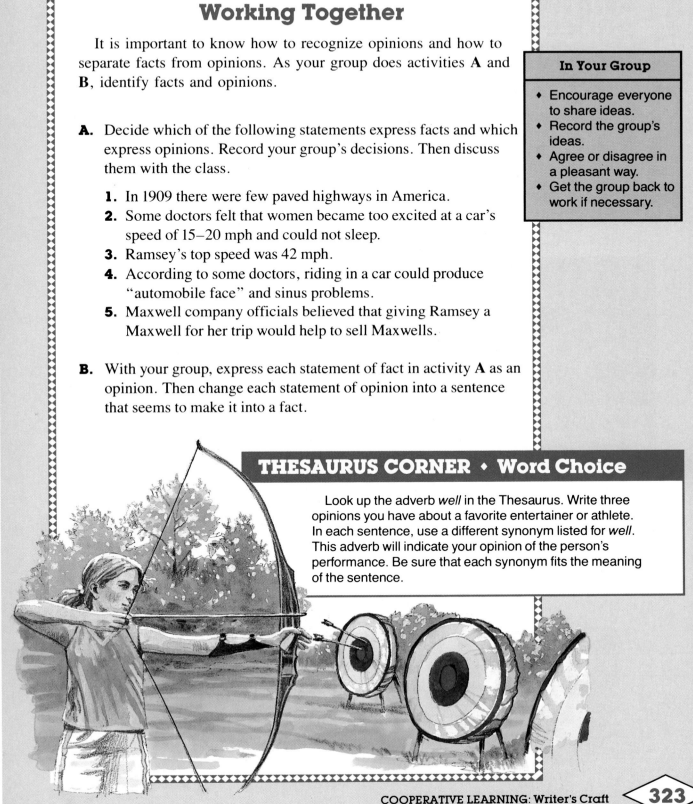

Writing a Research Report

The author of "From Coast to Coast" wove facts about Alice Ramsey into a fascinating true account. To find the facts, she may have interviewed witnesses and consulted old newspaper files, magazines, books, and encyclopedias.

Writers of research reports also gather facts. Like a magazine article, a research report should do more than list facts. It should seize and hold the reader's interest.

Know Your Purpose and Audience

What's MY PURPOSE

In this lesson you will write a research report. Your purpose will be to write about a person who made a contribution to history.

Who's MY AUDIENCE

Your audience will be younger children. Later you can act the part of the person you wrote about or contribute your report to a readers' corner.

1 Prewriting

First you must choose your topic—a person to write about. Then you will need to gather facts about that person.

Choose Your Topic ◆ Start by listing three people who interest you. You might choose a scientist, an artist, or an explorer. Just choose a name that interests you so that you can be sure it will interest your readers.

Think About It

Whom will you list? You might pick someone who is famous now or who was famous in the past. Then check the library to see what information is available about each name on your list. Pick a person about whom you can find information. Then choose one event to write about.

Talk About It

Work with a partner. Scan textbooks and library books for names. You may be able to recognize a name that your partner does not know. Help each other find the most interesting subject for your reports.

Topic Ideas

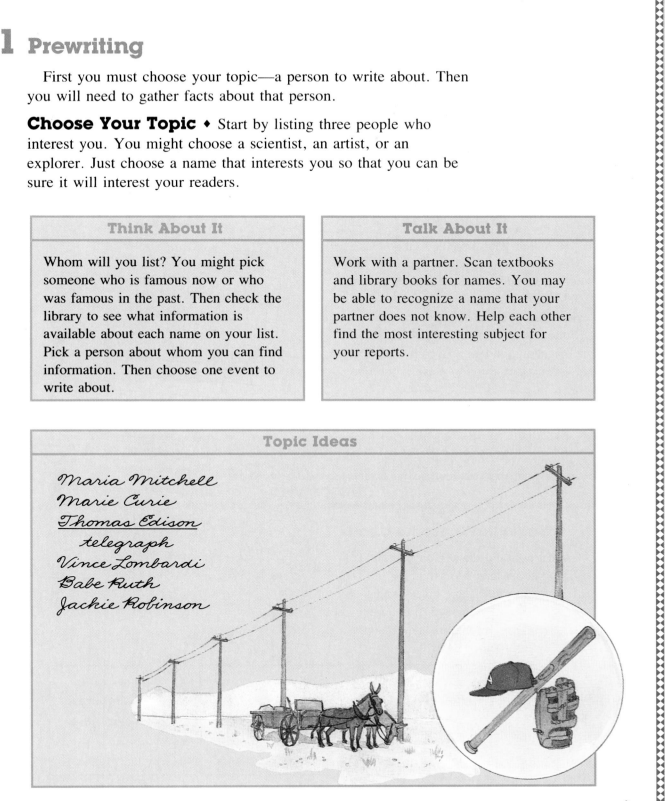

Maria Mitchell
Marie Curie
Thomas Edison
  telegraph
Vince Lombardi
Babe Ruth
Jackie Robinson

Choose Your Strategy ♦ Here are two strategies that can help you find facts for your report. Use the idea you think will be helpful.

PREWRITING IDEAS

CHOICE ONE

Taking Notes

Research your topic and take notes. Make a separate group of note cards for each main idea. The cards should contain supporting ideas. Write your notes in your own words. Make source cards, too. (Follow the examples shown for a book, a magazine, and an encyclopedia.) Then use your note cards to make an outline.

Model

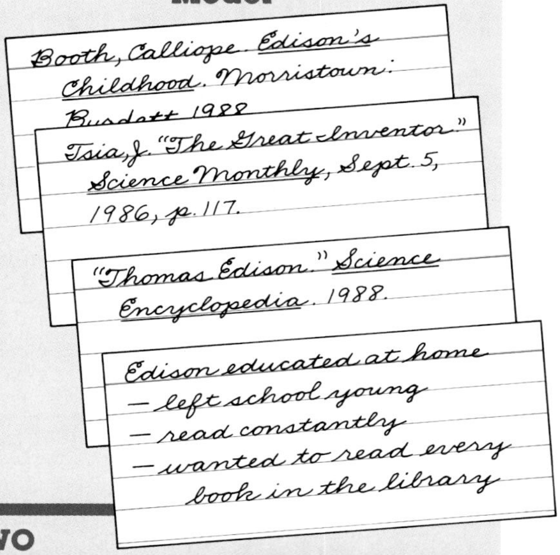

Booth, Calliope. *Edison's Childhood*. Morristown: Burdett 1988

Tsia, J. "The Great Inventor" *Science Monthly*, Sept. 5, 1986, p. 117.

"Thomas Edison." *Science Encyclopedia*. 1988.

Edison educated at home
— left school young
— read constantly
— wanted to read every book in the library

CHOICE TWO

A Goal/Plan/Outcome Chart

What goal did the person you are writing about have? What action did she or he plan to reach that goal? What was the outcome? Making a goal/plan/outcome chart can help you report that person's story in an organized way.

Model

Goal:
Edison wanted more sleep

Plan:
to find a way to send messages automatically

Outcomes:
He invented a signaling device

2 Writing

Have your prewriting notes at hand as you begin writing. You might begin with a statement or a question about your person.

- ◆ Even as a child _____ was interested in _____.
- ◆ Did you know that the inventor of _____ was _____?

As you write, remember that you are writing for younger children. Follow the organization of your note cards, your outline, or your goal/plan/outcome chart. Don't worry about perfection; you can fix things later. Just try to put down all the main facts about this person's contribution to history. Conclude by telling your opinion of the person.

Sample First Draft ◆

Even as a child, Thomas Edison showed signs of being a great inventer. He invented the phonograph, reliable electric lighting, and dozens of other things. He left school at a young age, but he studied hard at home.

At the age of twelve, Edison took a job selling newspapers on a train he admired the telegraphers, who sent messages by wire from one Station to another. He soon became a good telegrapher himself. At night Edison had to send messages every hour, so he couldn't get no sleep. He invented a device to send the signals automaticly. Thomas Edison had used his intelligence to invent a solution to a problem. He did this for the rest of his life. In a way, Edison was a magican. He could turn ideas into realities.

3 Revising

Revise your report to make your meaning clearer and your writing more interesting. The strategy below may help.

REVISING IDEA

FIRST Read to Yourself

Remember your original purpose. Did you write a research report? Did you explain one person's contribution to history? Consider your audience. Will a younger child understand why this person is important?

Focus: Have you included facts? Have you stated your opinion? Put a caret (^) where you want to add information.

THEN Share with a Partner

Remind your partner that your audience will be younger children. Read your report aloud. Ask your partner for helpful comments. The guidelines below may help you both.

The Writer

Guidelines: Ask your partner for specific ideas, but you be the final judge.

Sample questions:
- Will a younger child understand my report?
- **Focus question:** Have I given enough facts to support my opinion?

The Writer's Partner

Guidelines: Be as tactful as you can, but also be honest.

Sample responses:
- I really liked the part where you told about _____.
- What facts support your opinion that _____?

Revising Model ♦ A draft that is being revised often looks messy. The marks show changes the writer wants to make.

The writer thought that this information belonged in the concluding paragraph.

The writer's partner suggested adding a supporting fact.

Proficient is more exact than the overused word *good*.

While reading aloud, the writer heard this double negative.

> Even as a child, Thomas Edison showed signs of being a great inventer. ~~He invented the phonograph, reliable electric lighting, and dozens of other things.~~ He left school at a young age, but he studied hard at home. *He read constantly, once saying he wanted to read every book in the public library.*
> At the age of twelve, Edison took a job selling newspapers on a train he admired the telegraphers, who sent messages by wire from one Station to another. He soon became a ~~good~~ *proficient* telegrapher himself. At night Edison had to send messages every hour, so he couldn't get ~~no~~ *any* sleep. He invented a device to send the signals automaticly. Thomas Edison had used his intelligence to invent a solution to a problem. He did this for the rest of his life. In a way, Edison was a magican. He could turn ideas into realities.

Read the research report above. Read it the way the writer thinks it *should* be. Then revise your own report.

Grammar Check ♦ Double negatives are confusing. Look twice at any sentence that contains a negative.

Word Choice ♦ Do you want to replace inexact or overused words like *good*? A thesaurus can help improve your word choice.

4 Proofreading

A neat copy with all errors corrected is a courtesy to your readers.

Proofreading Model ✦ Here is the draft report about Thomas Edison. Proofreading changes have been added in red.

Even as a child, Thomas Edison showed signs of being a great ~~inventer~~ *inventor.* He invented the phonograph, reliable electric lighting, and dozens of other things. He left school at a young age, but he studied hard at home. *He read constantly, once saying he wanted to read every book in the public library.*

At the age of twelve, Edison took a job selling newspapers on a train. ^he admired the telegraphers, who sent messages by wire from one ~~S~~tation to another. He soon became a ~~good~~ *proficient* telegrapher himself. At night Edison had to send messages every hour, so he couldn't get ~~no~~ *any* sleep. He invented a device to send the signals ~~automaticly~~ *automatically.* Thomas Edison had used his intelligence to invent a solution to a problem. He did this for the rest of his life. In a way, Edison was a ~~magican~~ *magician.* He could turn ideas into realities.

PROOFREADING IDEA

Spelling Check

Here is a trick for focusing on word spellings instead of word meanings. First check all words beginning with vowels. Then check all words beginning with consonants. Use a dictionary if you are unsure about any spellings.

Now proofread your research report and write a title for it. Then make a neat copy.

5 Publishing

Attach a bibliography to your report, listing your sources of information. Alphabetize by author's last name. If no author is named, alphabetize by title.

Bibliography
1. Booth, Calliope. Edison's Childhood. Morristown: Burdett, 1988.
2. "Thomas Edison," Science Encyclopedia. 1988.
3. Tsia, J. "The Great Inventor." Science Monthly, Sept. 5, 1986, p. 117.

A Great Inventor

Even as a child, Thomas Edison showed signs of being a great inventor. He left school at a young age, but he studied hard at home. He read constantly, once saying he wanted to read every book in the public library.

At the age of twelve, Edison took a job selling newspapers on a train. He admired the telegraphers, who sent messages by wire from one station to another. He soon became a proficient telegrapher himself. At night Edison had to send messages every hour, so he couldn't get any sleep. He invented a device to send the signals automatically.

Thomas Edison had used his intelligence to invent a solution to a problem. He did this for the rest of his life. He invented the phonograph, reliable electric lighting, and dozens of other things. In a way, Edison was a magician. He could turn ideas into realities.

PUBLISHING IDEAS

Share Aloud

Visit a younger class. Read your report aloud or wear a costume and act the part. Speak in the first person. For example, you might say, "I'm Thomas Edison. When I was a boy, I wanted to read every book in the library!" Ask your listeners to tell what they learned.

Share in Writing

Assemble your reports in a place where they can be shared. Next to them place construction paper, markers, scissors, and tape. After you read a report, make a bookmark on which you write the most fascinating fact you learned. Attach it to the report or give it to the author.

CURRICULUM
◆CONNECTION◆

Writing Across the Curriculum

Social Studies

In this unit you wrote a research paper about someone who contributed to history. You may have used a goal/plan/outcome chart to show how that person strove to reach a goal. This is a strategy that can help you understand many people in history.

Writing to Learn

Think and Analyze ◆ The picture below is of an early settlement in Quebec, Canada. There was no electricity or running water. There were no shops for many miles. What were the goals of the settlers? Wealth? Happiness? Survival? For one goal you think they had, make a goal/plan/outcome chart. Fill in actions you think they took toward their goal and the likely outcome.

Goal-Plan-Outcome Chart

☐ ▶ ☐ ▶ ☐

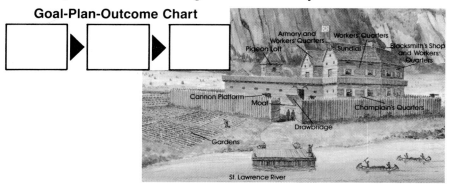

Write ◆ Imagine you are a member of the Quebec settlement. Write a letter to a friend, telling about your life in the settlement.

Writing in Your Journal

In the Writer's Warm-up you wrote about a "pioneering" woman. During the unit you read about other determined, confident women. Are there pioneering women today? In your journal, list women you consider to be modern-day pioneers.

BOOKS TO ENJOY

Read More About It

I Will Be a Doctor! The Story of America's First Woman Physician *by Dorothy Clarke Wilson* In the face of overwhelming prejudice, Elizabeth Blackwell managed to graduate from medical school, practice medicine, and open her own hospital. This biography traces her achievements.

A Woman Against Slavery: The Story of Harriet Beecher Stowe *by John A. Scott* In addition to being an abolitionist and an author, Harriet Beecher Stowe was a pioneer in the movement for women's rights.

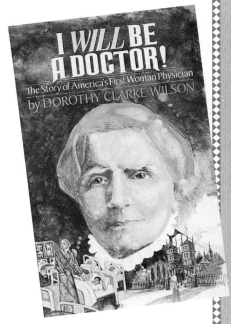

Book Report Idea Talking Book

By becoming a "talking book," you can find new readers for a book you have enjoyed.

Become Your Book ♦ Make and wear a paper T-shirt that shows your title and author. When it is your turn to report, introduce yourself by giving your title, and then ask for questions from the group. Classmates may ask questions such as "What is your setting?" "Will you describe your main characters?" "What problems do the characters face?" "Why should I read you?" Answer the questions in a way that creates interest in the book's contents.

UNIT REVIEW

Unit 6

Adverbs and Adjectives
pages 290–297

A. Write each of the following sentences. Underline each adverb.

1. The old miner slowly climbed the steep trail.
2. He stopped suddenly at a huge tree.
3. There he removed his canteen and drank deeply.
4. His burro lazily drifted toward his side.
5. It brayed loudly until the miner finally gave it some water.
6. Soon the burro had satisfied its thirst.
7. The old man gently scratched the burro behind the ears.
8. It nodded its head contentedly and happily nuzzled its master.
9. After a few minutes man and animal were on the trail again.
10. Both of them climbed energetically to the top of the mountain.

B. Write the word each underlined adverb describes. Then write whether the word is a *verb,* an *adjective,* or an *adverb.*

11. Pedro is an <u>unbelievably</u> fast runner.
12. He <u>usually</u> wins all of his races.
13. His speed is <u>truly</u> remarkable.
14. He competed <u>yesterday</u>.
15. The other athletes raced <u>very</u> quickly.
16. Pedro was <u>even</u> quicker.
17. As before, he won the race <u>easily.</u>
18. When he received the gold medal, he appeared <u>quite</u> happy.
19. The crowd applauded <u>heartily.</u>
20. Pedro <u>casually</u> waved his hand to acknowledge the applause.

C. Write the comparative and superlative forms of each adverb.

21. warmly
22. late
23. seriously
24. powerfully
25. gracefully
26. slowly
27. rapidly
28. stubbornly
29. loudly
30. high
31. well
32. early
33. politely
34. badly
35. quickly
36. fast
37. smoothly
38. casually
39. gently
40. low

D. Write the word in parentheses ( ) that correctly completes each sentence. Avoid double negatives.

41. Charlene doesn't eat (any, no) dessert.
42. Can't (someone, no one) repair this broken chair?
43. Please don't sing (any, no) more.
44. We won't get (nowhere, anywhere) until we make a plan.
45. This violin doesn't have (any, no) strings.
46. Won't (anybody, nobody) give me directions to Broad Avenue?
47. Weren't there (any, no) peanuts left?
48. Don't you (ever, never) rest?

E. Write the word that correctly completes each sentence.

49. The traffic moved (slow, slowly).
50. An old car wheezed (noisy, noisily).
51. Its driver was (impatient, impatiently).
52. He held the wheel (tight, tightly).
53. His mood seemed (bad, badly).
54. A little girl waiting to cross the street smiled (cheerful, cheerfully) at him.
55. He changed (remarkable, remarkably).
56. His face brightened (visible, visibly).
57. He began to grin (happy, happily).
58. The slow traffic no longer felt (unbearable, unbearably).

Synonyms and Antonyms
pages 298–299

F. Write each sentence, replacing the underlined word with a synonym from the list below.

gallant	communication
promptly	insurmountable

59. The dashing hero saved the heroine from the trap.
60. Please do your chores instantly.
61. The odds against his success seemed hopeless.
62. The message was delivered to her.

G. For each of the following words, write the correct antonym.

63. scatterbrained: rapid, reliable, tardy
64. protest: law, scholar, approval
65. precede: run, follow, avoid
66. shy: timid, outgoing, scholarly

Choosing a Topic   *pages 312–313*

H. Write the narrowest topic in each group.

67. Museum of Modern Art, museums, art museums
68. reference books, books, encyclopedias
69. explorers, notable persons, Osa Johnson
70. books, *Little Women*, novels
71. atomic physics, science, physics

Reference Materials   *pages 314–317*

I. For each question, write the key word and the volume number in which you would find it. Use the encyclopedia on page 314.

72. What was Mark Twain's first book?
73. When did the great fire in Chicago occur?
74. What are the common types of kites?
75. Where can gorillas be found?
76. What have scientists learned about neutrinos?

J. Write whether you would choose an *atlas, almanac, periodical,* or *The Readers' Guide* to answer each question.

77. What countries adjoin the United States?
78. Who is the governor of Vermont?
79. What is the population of Sweden?
80. Which book of poetry won the Pulitzer Prize last year?
81. Which issue of *Time* has an article on laser research?

CUMULATIVE REVIEW

Unit 1: Sentences *pages 8–13*

A. Write each complete subject.
Underline each simple subject.

1. Don likes to watch television.
2. His mother worries about him.
3. Some shows can be very interesting.
4. A recent program about Arctic explorers was quite rewarding.
5. Many television comedies are silly.
6. Those evening hours can be spent in other ways.
7. Good books stand on library shelves, waiting to be read.
8. A novel about pioneers in early Kansas was fascinating.
9. My aunt works at our local library.
10. Her advice about interesting and exciting books is invaluable.

B. Write each complete predicate.
Underline each simple predicate.

11. Rita Torres is practicing gymnastics.
12. The team competes at local athletic events.
13. Rita can do a one-handed handstand.
14. She has acquired skill and poise through her training.
15. The other members of the team admire her spirit.
16. They have cheered her on to several gold medals.
17. She will compete at the state level.

18. Rita has overcome a serious handicap on her road to success.
19. She was born blind.
20. Her parents have given Rita the gifts of courage, patience, and hope.

Units 2 and 4: Nouns and Pronouns
page 62–65, 180–189

C. Write the nouns in each of the these sentences. Then write whether each noun names a person, place, thing, or idea.

21. My grandmother was the first schoolteacher in East Frankville.
22. Her school consisted of a single room.
23. Books were scarce at that time.
24. Two students shared a single desk.
25. One farmer didn't want his son to get an education.
26. Learning was a foolish pursuit, in his opinion.
27. My ancestor convinced this stubborn man of his error.
28. His boy grew up to become governor of our state.
29. This statesman wrote a book about his life.
30. His autobiography gives my grandmother much credit for his success.

D. Write whether each noun is common or proper.

31. festival	38. Easter
32. Tuesday	39. bale
33. Karen	40. cousin
34. Ms. Brooks	41. restaurant
35. city	42. Australia
36. carton	43. squirrel
37. Dr. López	44. Rocky Mountains

E. Write the correct word in parentheses ( ).

45. (You're, Your) a very interesting person.
46. (My, Mine) is the coat on the left.
47. (Their, They're) going to a game.
48. Jimmy Wu and (he, him) are members of the club.
49. Help Jill and (I, me) with the boxes.
50. The yellow sports car is (our, ours).
51. Tara told (we, us) about it.
52. Have you seen (my, mine) pet pony?
53. The best-groomed animal at the dog show was (their, theirs).
54. Sandy and (I, me) have lead roles.

Unit 3: Verbs   *pages 120–121, 126–131*

F. Write each of the following sentences. Underline the helping verbs once and the main verbs twice.

55. Janice has mastered many magic tricks.
56. She can take a coin from your ear.
57. She will perform her magic act soon.
58. Tom is learning magic also.
59. He might assist Janice with her act.
60. He does not know all her tricks yet.
61. Tom should practice more often.
62. He may do two or three simple tricks.

G. Write the principal parts of each verb. Use the helping verb *has* with each past participle.

63. stop   **67.** do   **71.** drink
64. write   **68.** lag   **72.** blow
65. fly   **69.** swim
66. choose   **70.** mop

Adjectives and Adverbs
pages 238–249, 290–297

H. Write these sentences. Underline the demonstrative adjective once. Underline the predicate adjective twice.

73. This mystery story is very exciting.
74. That heroine appears very bright.
75. The trap door is important to this plot.
76. Mr. Crow, that sly lawyer, looks evil.
77. As things turn out, these appearances are highly deceptive.
78. He just seems evil in order to fool those real villains.

I. Write the comparative and superlative forms of each adjective.

79. good   **82.** bad   **85.** mighty
80. happy   **83.** large   **86.** beautiful
81. emotional **84.** sad

J. Write the word each underlined adverb describes. Then write whether the word is a *verb*, an *adjective*, or an *adverb*.

87. The tightrope walker was <u>rather</u> quickly crossing the rope.
88. <u>Very</u> unexpectedly the rope snapped.
89. She landed <u>gracefully</u> in the net.
90. Such mishaps are <u>quite</u> common.
91. Our performers are <u>truly</u> expert.
92. They react <u>almost</u> instinctively.

K. Write the comparative and superlative forms of each adverb.

93. badly   **97.** unbelievably
94. early   **98.** quickly
95. high   **99.** unwillingly
96. seriously **100.** fast

LANGUAGE PUZZLERS

Unit 6 Challenge

Tom Swifties

Tom Swifties are puns that are based on adverbs.
Using different adverbs, write some Tom Swifties like
the following:

1. "I'd rather have a hot dog than a hamburger," said
   Tom frankly.
2. "My flashlight battery is almost
   dead," said Tom dimly.
3. "I like my shirts well starched,"
   said Tom stiffly.
4. "I have an appointment with
   Dr. Lee," said Tom patiently.
5. "May I have the toast without
   butter?" asked Tom dryly.

Crossword Adverbs

Draw the crossword graph on a sheet of paper. Then fill
in the words. (Hint: Each answer can be used as an adverb.)

Across
1. the day after today
3. the opposite of *down*
4. not well
6. every day
9. quite
10. also

Down
1. really
2. quickly
5. opposite of *there*
7. neither early nor on time
8. at this time

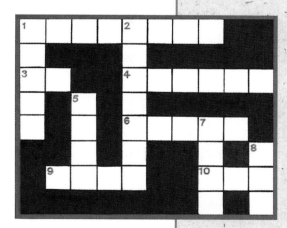

338 Language Puzzlers

Unit 6 Extra Practice

1 Writing with Adverbs   *p. 290*

A. Write each sentence. Underline each adverb.

1. Birds sing sweetly in the trees.
2. Tomorrow spring begins.
3. Flowers will bloom everywhere.
4. I can hardly wait!
5. Soon warm days will arrive.
6. Spring is a very beautiful season.
7. I'll plant my vegetable garden there.
8. Our spring cleaning is already finished.
9. I have almost forgotten winter!
10. The snows have melted now.
11. Streams quickly carry the water to the sea.
12. The alfalfa in the fields is growing rapidly.
13. Soon the apple trees in the orchard will blossom.
14. Baby ducks are swimming quietly in the pond.
15. Lambs run playfully in the meadow.
16. Yesterday a new colt was born.
17. Some friends have started a baseball game nearby.
18. We always play baseball in the spring.

B. Write the adverb in each sentence. Then write *how*, *when*, *where*, or *to what extent* to show which question the adverb answers.

EXAMPLE: We thoroughly enjoyed the game.
 ANSWER: thoroughly, to what extent

19. Today we will shear the sheep.
20. The fence in the pasture should be repaired immediately.
21. The chicken coop really needs paint.
22. Those sacks of seed go there.
23. The ditch is completely clogged with leaves.
24. The tractor is running poorly.
25. Soon we'll fertilize the fruit trees.
26. We'll be working constantly until summer!

Extra Practice   **339**

C. Write each sentence. Underline each adverb.

27. Jim Thorpe was an unbelievably fine athlete.
28. He won many events easily in the 1912 Olympics.
29. Jim Thorpe excelled in very many sports.
30. He was a truly excellent football player.
31. This famous Native American played baseball quite well.
32. He ran track-and-field events extremely quickly.
33. Thorpe was almost always a winner.
34. Jim Thorpe was an exceptionally athletic youngster.
35. He could run really fast.
36. Jim entered the Carlisle Indian School in Pennsylvania very soon after his nineteenth birthday.
37. Almost immediately he joined their football team.
38. Thorpe consistently led Carlisle to victories in football.
39. This small school often beat the best teams.
40. Jim played a truly important role in the 1912 Olympics.
41. He won the pentathlon contest effortlessly.
42. He did not stop there.
43. He won still more events in the decathlon.

D. Write the word that each underlined adverb describes. Then write whether the word is a verb, an adjective, or an adverb.

44. Jim Thorpe didn't keep his Olympic awards too long.
45. It was learned that he had briefly played baseball for money before the Olympics.
46. An extremely sad Jim Thorpe had to return his cherished Olympic medals.
47. Later he played professional football remarkably well.
48. He easily won election to both the college and professional football halls of fame.
49. The Associated Press enthusiastically voted him the best athlete of the first half of the century.
50. His love of sports never ended.
51. His lost awards remained a very bitter memory, however.
52. Thorpe's family worked hard to have his awards returned.
53. In 1982 the family's efforts were finally successful.
54. Officials of the Olympics not only restored his medals.
55. They also restored his place in the record books.

2 Adverbs That Compare

A. Write the comparative and the superlative forms of each adverb.

1. badly
2. gently
3. hungrily
4. high
5. long
6. bravely
7. willingly
8. hard
9. well
10. hopefully
11. sharply
12. loud

B. Write each sentence. Use the correct form of the adverb in parentheses ( ).

13. This morning we got up (early) than usual to jog.
14. Elena ran the (gracefully) of all the joggers.
15. We jogged (quickly) today than yesterday.
16. Tomorrow we may run even (fast).
17. You use oxygen (rapidly) when running than when walking.
18. Therefore, you must breathe (deep) than usual.
19. Carmen seems to breathe the (deep) of everyone.
20. She also runs the (fast) of all.
21. I always manage to run the (slow).
22. You should stretch your leg muscles (thoroughly) than that before running.
23. Beginners should run (slow) than experienced runners.
24. Joggers who practice hard run the (well).
25. You ran (well) this time than last time!
26. I run (comfortably) on grass than on roads.

C. Complete each sentence with the correct form of the adverb in parentheses ( ).

27. Some birds imitate sounds (skillfully) than others.
28. Jays mimic sounds (well) than crows do.
29. Mockingbirds imitate sounds the (convincingly) of all.
30. They copy other birds' calls (closely) than human experts can.
31. They can imitate the sound of machinery even (well) than bird calls.
32. Birds also learn to imitate human speech (easily) than other creatures.
33. Mynah birds learn (quickly) than crows do.
34. The gray parrot of Africa talks the (well) of all birds.

Extra Practice

3 Avoiding Double Negatives *p. 294*

A. Write each sentence. Use the word in parentheses ( ) that makes the sentence negative.

1. What two things can you (ever, never) eat for breakfast?
2. You (can, can't) eat lunch or dinner for breakfast.
3. Why has (nobody, somebody) heard the joke about the bed?
4. (Anyone, No one) has made it up yet!
5. What is of (no, any) use until it is broken? (An egg)
6. (Anybody, Nobody) knows the answers to all these riddles.
7. What falls often but (does, doesn't) ever get hurt? (Snow)
8. What room can (anyone, no one) enter? (A mushroom)
9. What table has (no, any) legs?
10. A multiplication table has (some, none).
11. What wears a cap but (has, hasn't) any head? (A bottle)
12. Why does an elephant (ever, never) forget?
13. It has (anything, nothing) to remember.
14. Why is there (no, any) sport noisier than tennis?
15. (Nobody, Anybody) can play it without raising a racket.

B. Write the word in parentheses ( ) that correctly completes each sentence. Avoid double negatives.

16. Some people cannot (ever, never) remember a joke.
17. What cannot (ever, never) go down a chimney up?
18. An open umbrella won't (ever, never) fit inside a chimney.
19. Why can't (no one, anyone) have a nose twelve inches long?
20. Then it wouldn't be (no, a) nose, but a foot!
21. What has a mouth but doesn't (ever, never) eat? (A river)
22. To what question can't (no one, anyone) answer yes?
23. You can't (never, ever) answer the question ''Are you asleep?'' with a yes.
24. Why can't (no one, someone) with an empty stomach eat two peanuts?
25. After the first, the person's stomach isn't empty (no, any) more.
26. Why are some people like fences? They run around a lot but don't get (nowhere, anywhere).
27. I don't usually tell (no, any) jokes.
28. I can't (never, ever) remember the punch lines!

4 Using Adjectives and Adverbs   *p. 296*

A. Write the word in parentheses ( ) that correctly completes each sentence.

  1. I want a new bicycle (bad, badly).
  2. I don't feel (safe, safely) on my old one.
  3. Unfortunately, bicycle accidents occur (regular, regularly).
  4. Make sure your bicycle is running (smooth, smoothly).
  5. Check it (thorough, thoroughly) before a long trip.
  6. Jeremy rides his bicycle very (careful, carefully).
  7. Bikers should follow traffic laws (careful, carefully).
  8. Don't ride too (rapid, rapidly) on busy streets.
  9. Walk your bike (slow, slowly) through intersections.
 10. Don't move (abrupt, abruptly) from lane to lane.
 11. That worn tire looks (dangerous, dangerously) to me.
 12. Bicycle lights let people see bikers (easy, easily).
 13. Watch for cars that pull out (sudden, suddenly).
 14. Ride (cautious, cautiously) on wet leaves.
 15. Carry tools so you can fix your bicycle (quick, quickly).
 16. Does that wheel feel (loose, loosely) to you?
 17. Check your route (regular, regularly) for loose stones.
 18. Brake (cautious, cautiously) at curves and corners.

B. Write each sentence. Use the word *good* or *well* in place of the blank. Then write whether the word is an adjective or an adverb.

EXAMPLE: It is not _____ to overload a bicycle.
ANSWER: It is not good to overload a bicycle. (adjective)

 19. Don't ride a bicycle if you are not feeling _____ .
 20. It is _____ to give pedestrians the right of way.
 21. Make sure your tires are in _____ condition.
 22. Also make sure that your brakes are working _____ .
 23. A horn or bell is a _____ safety device.
 24. Reflectors work _____ to make you more visible at night.
 25. It is also a _____ idea to wear light-colored clothing.
 26. You can have a _____ time riding a bicycle.
 27. Bicycle riding is _____ exercise.
 28. Exercise can help you stay _____ .

UNIT SEVEN

USING LANGUAGE TO
IMAGINE

Writing
IN YOUR JOURNAL

WRITER'S WARM-UP ◆ What do you know about folklore? You probably know more than you think. For example, holidays usually include some folklore. Choose a holiday you celebrate and write in your journal about its folklore. Describe the legends, the songs, and the customs that are part of the holiday.

Pick an object in the classroom. See if others can guess it by asking questions about its location. For example, *Is it on the wall? Is it near the door? Is it beside the bookcase?*

1 Writing with Prepositions

In the sentence below, the underlined word is a **preposition**.

■ **Folklore has developed throughout history.**

The preposition *throughout* relates the noun *history* to the word *developed*. The noun or pronoun that follows a preposition is the **object of the preposition.** In the sentence, *history* is the object of the preposition *throughout*.

A preposition, its object, and any words that describe the object make up a **prepositional phrase.** In the sentence below, the prepositional phrases are shaded in blue.

■ **Many types of folklore exist in all societies.**

Forty common prepositions are shown below.

about	before	during	off	to
above	behind	for	on	toward
across	below	from	out	under
after	beneath	in	outside	until
against	beside	inside	over	up
along	beyond	into	past	upon
around	by	near	through	with
at	down	of	throughout	without

Summary ◆ A **preposition** relates a noun or pronoun to another word in the sentence. You can use prepositional phrases to make your sentences more specific.

Guided Practice

Name the prepositional phrase in each sentence.

1. Folklore explains the beliefs of a people.
2. Only meaningful folklore is repeated over the years.
3. The rest passes from use and is forgotten.

Practice

A. These sentences tell about different kinds of folklore. Write the prepositional phrase in each sentence.

    4. The myths and tales in books are often folklore.

    5. Proverbs and riddles are told by friends.

    6. Folklore on the playground includes jump rope songs.

    7. Dances and many games also fit into the category.

    8. Can you name some legends about your community?

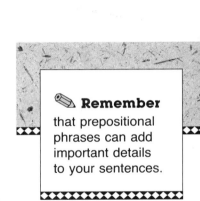

B. Write the prepositional phrase in each sentence. Underline the preposition once and the object of the preposition twice.

    9. People, or "folk," from a common background have the same folklore.

  10. People of the same region often share folklore.

  11. Workers in the same occupations share stories, too.

  12. Across each ethnic group, there is a common folklore.

  13. Do students at your school have their own folklore?

  14. When people move, they take their folklore with them.

  15. True folklore will exist throughout the world.

  16. After many retellings a story or tale changes.

  17. Folklore is not authentic without some variations.

  18. Scholars once collected hundreds of different "Cinderella" versions.

C. Write your own version of the opening of "Cinderella." Add a prepositional phrase to each sentence.

  19. Cinderella lived long ago _____ .

  20. Cinderella had to do all the work _____ .

  21. Her stepmother and stepsisters complained _____ .

  22. One day, Cinderella heard some exciting news _____ .

  23. A great ball would take place _____ .

Apply ◆ Think and Write

From Your Writing ◆ Add clarity and details to the writing you did for the Writer's Warm-up. Change some of your sentences by adding prepositional phrases. Compare and discuss with a partner the two versions of your writing.

> ✎ **Remember**
> that prepositional phrases can add important details to your sentences.

Proverbs are part of our folklore. See how many proverbs you can think of that contain prepositional phrases.

EXAMPLES: *Birds of a feather flock together.*
A bird in the hand is worth two in the bush.

2 Prepositional Phrases as Adjectives

Some prepositional phrases are like adjectives. They describe nouns or pronouns. Prepositional phrases that describe nouns or pronouns and tell *how many*, *what kind*, or *which one* are adjective phrases.

The same word can be described by an adjective or by an adjective phrase.

Adjective	Adjective Phrase
Japanese folklore	folklore of Japan
a storytelling nation	a nation of storytellers

Adjective phrases can describe nouns and pronouns in different parts of a sentence. In sentence **1** below, the adjective phrase describes the subject. In sentence **2** it describes the predicate nominative. In sentence **3** it describes the direct object.

1. The country <u>of Japan</u> has many different folktales.
2. Traditionally, Japan was a land <u>with many isolated villages</u>.
3. Each village developed legends <u>about important events</u>.

> **Summary** ◆ A prepositional phrase that describes a noun or pronoun is an **adjective phrase**. You can use adjective phrases to make your descriptions more interesting.

Guided Practice

Name the adjective phrase in each sentence.

1. Folklore is an important key to a people's culture.
2. Japanese folktales present harmony with nature as a major theme.
3. Stories about rivers are popular.

Practice

A. Write each sentence. Underline the adjective phrase.

4. Legends are partially true stories about real events.
5. The legends of each Japanese village united the community.
6. These legends gave people a connection with the past.
7. The Japanese enjoyed tales about their ancestors.
8. Folktales stressed good relationships with family members.
9. Animals changing their shape is a common theme in Japanese folklore.
10. Animals in human form might harm or help people.
11. Monsters in Japanese folklore were not always bad.
12. Some monsters taught people the skills of swordplay.

B. Write each adjective phrase and the noun it describes.

13. Folklore often taught the qualities of Japanese virtue.
14. Kindness toward others was stressed.
15. Stories about warriors emphasized honor and strength.
16. Hardworking peasants received the reward of happiness.
17. The greedy and lazy suffered losses of their crops.
18. People with modesty gained respect.

C. Use your imagination. Write adjective phrases to complete this Japanese legend. You may use phrases that begin with *of*, *with*, *for*, and *without*.

Long ago, the wife (**19.** _____) was washing sweet potatoes in a stream. A poor stranger (**20.** _____) came by and asked for a potato to eat. ''I have nothing (**21.** _____),'' said the woman. A note (**22.** _____) was in her voice. As the man hobbled off, the stream dried up. From that time on, the people (**23.** _____) suffered hardships.

Apply ◆ Think and Write

Test Construction ◆ Make a complete-the-phrase test for a classmate. Write eight items. Trade papers and have a partner add prepositional phrases that are adjective phrases.

EXAMPLES: folktales <u>of Japan</u>   stories <u>about village life</u>

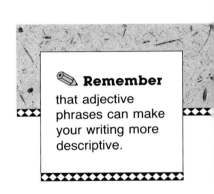

✏️ **Remember**
that adjective phrases can make your writing more descriptive.

Say a sentence containing an adverb. Then challenge someone to replace the adverb with a prepositional phrase that has about the same meaning. For example: *I'll be there immediately*. *I'll be there in a second*.

3 Prepositional Phrases as Adverbs

Adverbs describe verbs, adjectives, and other adverbs. Some prepositional phrases describe these same parts of speech. Prepositional phrases that work like adverbs are called adverb phrases.

> Japanese village life began <u>during the second century</u> B.C.
> No writing system was available <u>at that time.</u>
> The Japanese borrowed Chinese writing late <u>in the 400s.</u>

The underlined words in the sentences above are adverb phrases. In sentence **1**, the phrase describes the verb *began*. In sentence **2**, it describes the adjective *available*. In sentence **3**, it describes the adverb *late*. Like adverbs, adverb phrases answer the questions *How? When? Where?* and *To what extent?*

Some words, such as *around, out, up, near,* and *by,* can be either prepositions or adverbs.

> China is quite <u>near</u>. (adverb)
> China is <u>near</u> Japan. (preposition)

If you aren't sure whether a word is a preposition or an adverb, look at how it is used. A preposition begins a phrase and always has an object. An adverb is used alone. It has no object.

> **Summary** ◆ A prepositional phrase that describes a verb, an adjective, or an adverb is an **adverb phrase.**

Guided Practice

Name the adverb phrase in each sentence.

1. The Chinese writing system spread throughout Japan.
2. Few people could read or write before the 1700s.
3. Oral storytelling was important everywhere in the country.

Practice

A. Write each sentence. Underline the adverb phrase.

    4. Japan was a feudal land, not a democracy, until the 1800s.
    5. The land was ruled by powerful lords.
    6. Each lord reigned over a large territory.
    7. These lords were loyal to a *shogun*.
    8. The shoguns were very powerful during that time.
    9. Warriors called *samurai* worked for each lord.
   10. The samurai lived with the peasants.
   11. The samurai treated peasants with cruelty.
   12. Peasants had no rights under this system.
   13. Education and travel were not available to peasants.

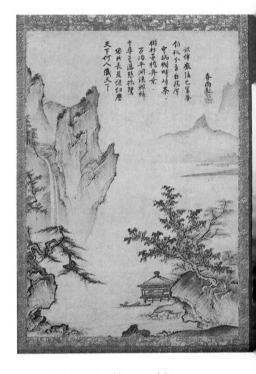

B. Write each adverb phrase and the word it describes.

   14. Peasants lived in unpainted wooden huts.
   15. There were thatched roofs on these simple huts.
   16. Paper walls separated rooms from each other.
   17. Peasants worked late in the day cultivating rice crops.
   18. Vegetable gardens grew near most huts.
   19. People wore loose robes, or *kimonos*, at this time.
   20. Many Japanese wove their own cotton cloth on home looms.
   21. Skillful weavers sold finer fabrics to wealthy lords.
   22. Talented painters told legends with painted scrolls.
   23. These scrolls were beautiful in their design.

The Metropolitan Museum of Art, Purchase. Bequest of Stephen Whitney Phoenix, by exchange, 1985. (1985.7)

C. Imagine that you lived in Japan long ago. Complete each sentence with an adverb phrase.

   24. I awake early ＿＿ .   **27.** My hut is chilly ＿＿ .
   25. I work ＿＿ .   **28.** A garden grows ＿＿ .
   26. I feel peaceful ＿＿ .

Apply ♦ Think and Write

A Poem Pattern ♦ Write a Prepositional Phrase Poem. Try using a poem pattern. Look at the example, then write your own.

Morning bird sings
outside the hut,
in the rice fields,
above the mountains.

✎ **Remember** to use adverb phrases to add variety to your writing.

Say sentences containing prepositional phrases. In how many different ways can the words be arranged and still make sense? For example: *The peasant lived in a hut. In a hut the peasant lived. In a hut lived the peasant.*

4 Using Prepositional Phrases

People sometimes confuse the prepositions *between* and *among*. Use *between* when you refer to two persons or things. Use *among* when you refer to three or more persons or things.

> **The poor peasant's hut was between two tall mountains.**
> **He barely had enough food to divide among his many children.**

When you use a pronoun as the object of a preposition, always use an object pronoun. The object pronouns are *me*, *you*, *her*, *him*, *it*, *us*, and *them*. Be especially careful when the object of the preposition is made up of a noun and a pronoun.

> **"Things are difficult for my family and me," thought the man.**
> **"Perhaps my rich brother will give food to us."**

A prepositional phrase can be part of a sentence with **inverted word order**. In a sentence with inverted word order, the complete predicate comes before the complete subject. Do not confuse the object of the preposition in such a sentence with the sentence subject. Notice the position of the prepositional phrases below.

Normal Word Order: The rich brother lived in a mansion.
Inverted Word Order: In a mansion lived the rich brother.

> **Summary** ♦ Use prepositional phrases carefully. Using prepositional phrases in different positions in sentences can add interest to your writing.

Guided Practice

Name the word that correctly completes each sentence.

1. There were few similarities (between, among) the two brothers.
2. The rich man was (between, among) the greediest men on earth.
3. "I won't give anything to his wife and (he, him)," the greedy brother decided.

Practice

A. Write the words that correctly complete the sentences.

Empty-handed, the disappointed peasant walked home (**4.** among, between) the trees. He worried about his hungry children. What would he say to his wife and (**5.** they, them)? On the way home he met two old men sitting (**6.** between, among) two tall stones. "Have you any food for my friend and (**7.** I, me)?" asked one of the men.

The peasant handed over a tiny rice cake that his wife had given to (**8.** he, him). The two men devoured it (**9.** among, between) themselves. Then, from (**10.** among, between) the many folds of his kimono, one old man produced a stone mortar, or vessel. "This magic mortar will repay you for your generosity."

At home the peasant placed the mortar (**11.** among, between) his wife and (**12.** he, him). "Magic mortar, grind rice for our children and (**13.** we, us)," he pleaded.

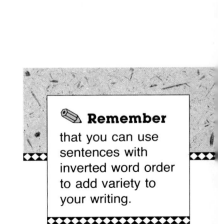

B. Write each sentence with inverted word order in regular word order. Write each regular sentence in inverted order.

14. Out of the mortar streamed a supply of fine rice.
15. From the special utensil also sprang meat, cloth, and money.
16. News of the peasant's good luck came to the greedy brother.
17. The brother's anger and jealousy grew beyond reason.
18. This greedy man stole into his brother's house.
19. With the mortar fled the greedy man.
20. This thief escaped in a boat.
21. For diamonds hoped the greedy brother.
22. From the mortar poured an unending flow of salt.
23. Into the sea disappeared the salt-filled boat and the man.

Apply ◆ Think and Write

Folktale Response ◆ What might a reader learn from this Japanese folktale? Explain your responses. Check to make sure you have used prepositional phrases correctly.

✎ **Remember**
that you can use sentences with inverted word order to add variety to your writing.

Think of pairs of words that are used together and combined with *and*, *or*, or *but*.

EXAMPLES: *cheese and crackers; true or false; slow but steady.*

5 Writing with Conjunctions

The words *and*, *but*, and *or* are conjunctions. In sentences, these conjunctions join nouns, pronouns, verbs, adjectives, or adverbs.

Examples of Conjunctions	
noun + noun	Japanese life and culture are fascinating.
pronoun + pronoun	You or I may visit Japan someday.
verb + verb	The Japanese people appreciate and respect many old traditions.
adjective + adjective	Yet European or American influences are also seen in Japanese life.
adverb + adverb	Creatively but carefully, Japan has blended the old and the new.

Conjunctions can also join groups of words. In your writing you can use conjunctions to combine the ideas in short sentences.

> **Japan borrows Western customs. Japan keeps its best traditions.**
> **Japan borrows Western customs but keeps its best traditions.**

Summary ◆ A **conjunction** joins words or groups of words.

Guided Practice

Name the conjunction in each sentence.

1. The Japanese wear suits and shoes in the workplace.
2. The traditional *kimono* is worn at home or for special events.
3. Traditional shoes include wooden *geta* and *zori* sandals.
4. Both types of footwear are worn outdoors but removed indoors.
5. Many Japanese people wear styles by European and American designers.

Practice

A. Write each sentence. Underline the conjunction.

6. The Japanese borrowed but changed the Chinese language.
7. Students have to write and pronounce 1,850 characters.
8. Each character is a symbol for a sound or a word.
9. Learning to read and write Japanese may take many years.
10. Most students in Japan learn Japanese and English.
11. Houses are one-story or two-story wooden structures.
12. Architecture and landscape are meant to blend.
13. Graceful tile roofs and walled gardens are common.
14. Inside, the Japanese sit on low cushions or *tatami* mats.
15. A room may be used for living by day but for sleeping at night.

B. Write the conjunction in each sentence. Then write *nouns*, *verbs*, *adjectives*, or *adverbs* to show what kind of words are joined.

16. Japanese music may sound different or unfamiliar to Westerners.
17. It features stringed instruments and flutes.
18. Slowly but surely, Western music has become popular.
19. The Japanese produce and attend much traditional drama.
20. The serious *No* plays have themes from history or legend.
21. *Kabuki* plays are colorful and dramatic performances.
22. New drama from Japan or other countries is also presented.

C. Combine each pair of sentences, using a conjunction.

23. The Japanese watch baseball on TV. They also watch sumo wrestling.
24. Many Japanese enjoy golf. Many enjoy judo.
25. Japanese culture is unique. It is also varied.

Apply ♦ Think and Write

Cultural Effects ♦ In what ways has Japan influenced our culture? Write sentences about the effects Japanese traditions, art, and products have had on the West.

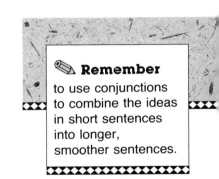

✏ **Remember**
to use conjunctions to combine the ideas in short sentences into longer, smoother sentences.

Make a list of emotions—excitement, disappointment, fear, and so on. Then think of a word to express each emotion, such as—
Hooray! Phooey! Eek!

6 Parts of Speech Summary

The chart below shows the seven parts of speech you have learned. It also shows the eighth part—the **interjection**.

Part of Speech	Definition and Examples
noun	A noun names a person, place, thing, or idea. <u>girl</u> <u>Japan</u> <u>folklore</u> <u>generosity</u>
verb	A verb expresses action or being. <u>walk</u> <u>helps</u> <u>ran</u> <u>is</u> <u>seem</u>
pronoun	A pronoun takes the place of a noun or nouns. <u>she</u> <u>him</u> <u>mine</u> <u>your</u> <u>them</u>
adjective	An adjective describes a noun or pronoun. <u>serious</u> <u>Japanese</u> <u>twenty</u> <u>this</u>
adverb	An adverb describes a verb, an adjective, or another adverb. <u>gladly</u> <u>soon</u> <u>here</u>
preposition	A preposition relates a noun or pronoun to another word in the sentence. <u>at</u> <u>of</u> <u>in</u>
conjunction	A conjunction joins words or groups of words. <u>and</u> <u>or</u> <u>but</u>
interjection	An interjection expresses feeling or emotion. Use an exclamation mark after an interjection. <u>Oh!</u> <u>Wow!</u>

Summary ♦ There are eight parts of speech. A **part of speech** tells how a word is used in a sentence.

Guided Practice

Name the interjection in each sentence.

1. Oh! This garden is perfect.
2. My! It has a peaceful mood.
3. Hush! The wind whispers.
4. Goodness! That's pretty.

Practice

A. Write each interjection below.

 5. Wow! The Japanese have hundreds of different festivals.
 6. Hooray! On Children's Day in May, toys are everywhere.
 7. Gee! Japan's New Year's Day festival begins January 1, too.
 8. Hey! Their celebrations last for three days or more.
 9. Yum! Along with parades and games, there are many feasts.

B. Two words are underlined in each sentence about silk-making. Write the part of speech of each underlined word.

 10. Japanese <u>fabrics</u> have long been admired <u>around</u> the world.
 11. Silk was <u>traditionally</u> worn by the <u>wealthy</u> Japanese.
 12. <u>Wow!</u> Silkworms produce silk; <u>they</u> make cocoons from it.
 13. Workers carefully unwound the <u>cocoons</u> into <u>long</u> strands.
 14. The strands were twisted <u>or</u> spun <u>into</u> strong thread.
 15. Dyes from plants <u>and</u> minerals <u>provided</u> rich colors.
 16. The dyed thread was woven into <u>cloth</u> in <u>simple</u> hand looms.
 17. The woven cloth <u>reflected</u> the skills of <u>its</u> weaver.
 18. Complicated designs <u>and</u> silver and gold threads made some fabrics <u>extremely</u> beautiful.
 19. Both weaving and silk-making <u>are</u> <u>Chinese</u> in origin.

C. Read this traditional Japanese poem. Complete the sentences about the poem, using the parts of speech indicated.

> A solitary frog drenched in rain
> Rides on a lotus leaf,
> Unsteadily.   —Chiyo

Somehow a frog (**20.** verb) the poet's imagination. To Westerners, the (**21.** noun) may seem (**22.** adverb) insignificant. But in Japanese arts, anything having to do with nature (**23.** conjunction) the seasons is (**24.** adjective).

Apply • Think and Write

Dictionary of Knowledge • Read about the Japanese form of poetry called *haiku*. Then write an original example of haiku. How many of the eight parts of speech did you use?

✎ **Remember**
to use the parts of speech correctly to make your meaning clear.

♦ GETTING ♦
STARTED

Can you "translate" these sentences? *A huge bore had tiny mights awl over it's pause and flees awl over it's hare. The pore bore was quite soar.*

VOCABULARY ♦
Homophones and Homographs

Homophones are words that sound alike but have different meanings and spellings. The words *aisle*, *isle*, and *I'll* are homophones.

Some pronouns and contractions are often confused in writing. Do the homophones below cause you trouble?

Pronoun	Contraction
its—belonging to it your—belonging to you their—belonging to them	it's—it is, it has you're—you are they're—they are

Homographs are words that are spelled alike but have different meanings and sometimes different pronunciations. For example, the word *band* meaning "musical group" and *band* meaning "something that encircles or ties together" are homographs. The word *bow* that rhymes with "cow" and the word *bow* that rhymes with "toe" are homographs that have different pronunciations.

Building Your Vocabulary

Spell the contraction that could be used in place of each pair of underlined words. Then name the pronoun that is a homophone of the contraction. Use the pronoun to complete the sentence.

1. It is almost time for the team to play _____ third game.
2. They are looking for _____ first win.
3. "You are going to win _____ game," Tad's mother declared.

Create sentences for the homographs below.

These rhyme with toe: 1. bow   2. row   3. sow
These rhyme with cow: 4. bow   5. row   6. sow

Practice

A. Use each pair of homophones below in a sentence of your own.

    EXAMPLE: haul, hall
    ANSWER: Please help me <u>haul</u> the table down the <u>hall</u>.

    1. feat, feet   **3.** night, knight   **5.** grown, groan
    2. piece, peace   **4.** course, coarse   **6.** tied, tide

B. Use sets of homographs to complete the sentences.

    7. ____ the ____ of paper under the door. (Clue: When you ? you sometimes fall.)

    8. He ____ early in the morning and picked a ____ from the garden. (Clue: ? is also a reddish color.)

    9. Sam likes to ____ up the plane and let it go into the ____ . (Clue: You also ? up a clock.)

    10. It is ____ to the time that these stores ____ . (Clue: One of these words rhymes with the answer to **8**.)

    11. The ____ ____ off the branch as the cat climbed up the tree. (Clue: The ? is a symbol of peace.)

C. Rewrite this nonsense paragraph, using the correct form of each homophone.

    Sum people will dew anything to make a prophet. Won person eye no cells handmaid close. Another sows bridle gowns. Won man makes golf teas. His sun is a cellar of foul. As four myself, eye just heard cattle and raze sheep.

LANGUAGE CORNER ◆ Palindromes

Palindromes are words or sentences that are spelled the same forward or backward.

    kayak level radar

    "Madam I'm Adam."

Figure out what is special about this capitalized palindrome: **NOON**.

How to Combine Sentences

You have been learning how adjectives, adverbs, and prepositional phrases work in sentences. Now you will learn how to take these elements from separate sentences and combine them to form more efficient sentences. For example, consider the sentences below.

1. The Grimm brothers collected folktales.
2. The folktales were German.

Both sentences give information about folktales. Sentence **2** simply adds the information that the folktales were German. These two sentences can be combined because they describe the same thing. The adjective *German* from sentence **2** can be added to sentence **1** to form one strong sentence.

3. The Grimm brothers collected German folktales.

Other parts of sentences can be combined in the same way. Notice how the prepositional phrase *through the ages* was used to form the sentence in example **5**.

4. Many customs and traditions are passed down orally. This happens through the ages.
5. Many customs and traditions are passed down orally through the ages.

The Grammar Game ◆ Now try it yourself! Combine each pair of sentences below, using the underlined words to combine them.

◆ Jody went to the library to get books about folktales.
  She went <u>yesterday</u>.
◆ Did Jody give the books to Eliot?
  Did she give him the books <u>about the folktales</u>?

Working Together

Notice how combining sentences makes your writing more efficient and interesting as your group works on activities **A** and **B**.

In Your Group

- Contribute your ideas.
- Invite others to talk.
- Agree or disagree in a pleasant way.
- Help the group stay on the job.

A. Combine each pair of sentences below. Use the underlined adjectives, adverbs, or prepositional phrases to combine them. Can you identify the underlined sentence parts in your new sentences?

1. Jody learned that folklore often changes. It changes <u>over long periods of time</u>.
2. Fables are a familiar kind of folklore. Fables are <u>about animals with human qualities</u>.
3. Many cultures have superstitions. <u>Some</u> superstitions are <u>curious</u>.
4. Jody studied the topic and delivered a speech. The topic was studied <u>thoroughly</u> and the speech was delivered <u>today</u>.

B. Find pairs of sentences to combine in the paragraph below. Then write your group's new version of the paragraph.

Folklore reflects a culture's attitudes and ideals. The culture's attitudes and ideals are unique. Folklore has made a major contribution. It has contributed to the world of the arts. Many writers are inspired by folklore. This happens often. For example, some of Shakespeare's plays are based on folktales. These are some of his greatest plays, including *King Lear*.

WRITERS' CORNER ◆ Positioning Phrases

Make sure your prepositional phrases are correctly placed. Sometimes an incorrectly placed phrase can completely change the meaning of your sentence.

EXAMPLE: **Many students from our school heard the expert speak.**
CHANGE: **Many students heard the expert from our school speak.**

Read what you wrote for the Writer's Warm-up. Look carefully at the prepositional phrases you used. Are they correctly placed?

THE EAST RIVER (1901)
painting by Maurice Prendergast
Collection, The Museum of Modern Art, New York.
Gift of Abby Aldrich Rockefeller.

USING LANGUAGE
TO
IMAGINE

PART TWO

Literature *The Crane Wife* translated by Katherine Paterson
A Reason for Writing Imagining

CREATIVE
Writing

FINE ARTS ◆ The painting at the left takes us to the East River in New York City many years ago. Put yourself in the picture. Some of these children are probably singing a song. Write the words to the song the children are singing. You may make up a new song or write new lines to an old song.

CREATIVE THINKING ◆
A Strategy for Imagining

A THOUGHT BALLOON

A great deal of imagination goes into the creation of a folktale. A writer must imagine how each character would think and feel. The character's point of view determines how that character will act. After this lesson you will read "The Crane Wife" by Sumiko Yagawa. Later you will use your imagination to write a story of your own.

In "The Crane Wife," a young Japanese peasant named Yohei finds a wounded crane. Here are some lines from the story. When Sumiko Yagawa wrote them, she imagined Yohei's feelings.

> Now Yohei could see that the bird was in great pain, for an arrow had pierced its wing. He went to where the crane lay, drew out the arrow, and very carefully tended its wound.

How might the author have decided how Yohei would feel when he found the wounded crane? How do you imagine the crane felt?

Learning the Strategy

How can you figure out someone else's point of view? Understanding your own feelings can help. Imagine that you are at a pool waiting in line for the diving board. A friend is ahead of you. How do you think that person feels when about to dive off the board? How will you feel when you dive? Your feelings about diving would depend on whether you have dived before. You could probably guess your friend's point of view about diving if you knew whether he or she had dived before. Now suppose you receive a letter from your cousin saying his family is moving. Put yourself in his place. What would be your point of view about moving? What do you think his point of view would be?

Making a thought balloon is a strategy that can help you imagine another person's point of view. Here is a thought balloon for your cousin who has to move. What ideas might you change or add in this thought balloon?

I'm excited about living in a new place. I wonder if I'll like my new school. I hope my new classmates will like me. I'm going to miss my old friends.

cousin

Using the Strategy

A. Suppose someone brought a lost dog to class. How do you think your teacher would feel about it? Make a thought balloon to show what you imagine your teacher's point of view would be. Then ask your teacher to give his or her actual point of view about a situation like this.

B. In "The Crane Wife," Yohei helps a wounded crane. Think about how the crane might have felt toward Yohei. Make a thought balloon. Show what the crane's thoughts might be. As you read "The Crane Wife," see if the author had the same idea you had about the crane.

Applying the Strategy

♦ How did drawing and writing a thought balloon help you imagine your teacher's thoughts about the lost dog?

♦ Why is it important to understand others' viewpoints?

LITERATURE

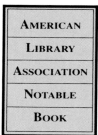

The Crane Wife

Retold by SUMIKO YAGAWA   Translated by KATHERINE PATERSON

Illustrated by SUEKICHI AKABA

This story of a poor farmer who rescues a wounded crane from death is perhaps Japan's best-loved folktale. Japanese children grow up hearing this tale. As adults they continue to enjoy it, since it has been made into plays, movies, and even an opera.

In a faraway mountain village, where the snow falls deep and white, there once lived all alone a poor young peasant named Yohei. One day, at the beginning of winter, Yohei went out into the snow to run an errand, and, as he hurried home, suddenly *basabasa* he heard a rustling sound. It was a crane, dragging its wing, as it swooped down and landed on the path. Now Yohei could see that the bird was in great pain, for an arrow had pierced its wing. He went to where the crane lay, drew out the arrow, and very carefully tended its wound.

LITERATURE: Folktale

Late that night there came a tapping *hotohoto* on the door of Yohei's hut. It seemed very peculiar for someone to be calling at that time of night. When he slid open the door to look out, there before him stood a beautiful young woman.

"I beg you, sir," she said in a voice both delicate and refined, "please allow me to become your wife."

Yohei could hardly believe his ears. The more closely he looked, the more noble and lovely the woman appeared. Gently he took her hand and brought her inside.

"Yohei has got some fine wife at his house," the villagers gossiped among themselves.

And it was true. The young woman was modest and kind, and she served Yohei faithfully. He could no longer recognize the cold, cold dreary hut where he had lived all alone, his house had become so bright and warm. The simple Yohei was happier than he could have ever dreamed.

In reality, however, with two mouths to feed instead of one, poor Yohei became poorer than he was before. And, since it was winter and there was no work to be found, he was very quickly coming to the bottom of what he had stored away.

At this point the young woman had a suggestion. "The other women of the village have looms upon which to weave cloth," she said. "If you would be so kind as to allow it, I should like to try my hand at weaving too."

In the back room of the hut, the young woman set up a loom and closed it off with sliding paper doors. Then she said to Yohei, "Please, I beg you, I beg you never look in upon me while I am weaving."

Tonkara tonkara. For three days and three nights the sound of the loom continued. Without stopping either to eat or drink, the young woman went on weaving and weaving. Finally, on the fourth day, she came out. To Yohei she seemed strangely thin and completely exhausted as, without a word, she held out to him a bolt of material.

And such exquisite cloth it was! Even Yohei, who had absolutely no knowledge of woven goods, could only stare in astonishment at the elegant, silken fabric.

Yohei took the cloth and set out for town. There he was able to sell it for such a high price that for a while the two of them had enough money to live quite comfortably and pleasantly.

The winter, however, stretched on and on until, finally, there was very little money left. Yohei hesitated to say anything, so he kept quiet, but at last the young woman spoke up. "I shall weave on the loom one more time. But, please, let this be the last." And, once more, having been warned not to look in on the woman as she wove, the simple Yohei settled down to wait outside just as she asked.

This time the weaving took four days and four nights. A second time the young woman appeared carrying a bolt of cloth, but now she seemed thinner and more pathetic than before. The fabric, moreover, was lighter and even more beautiful. It seemed almost to glow with a light all its own.

Yohei sold the material for an even higher price than the first time. "My," he marveled, "what a good wife I have!" The money bag he carried was heavy, but Yohei's heart was light, and he fairly skipped as he hurried home.

Now the man next door had noticed that Yohei seemed to be living far more grandly than he had in the old days, and he was most curious. Pretending to be very casual about it all, he made his way through the snow and began to chat. Yohei, being a simple and innocent fellow, told the neighbor how his wife's woven goods had brought a wonderful price.

The man became more curious than ever. "Tell me," he said, "just what kind of thread does your wife use? My woman's cotton cloth never fetched a price like that. If your wife's stuff is as marvelous as you say, you ought to take it to the capital, to the home of some noble. You could probably sell it for ten times—for a hundred times more. Say, how about it? Why don't you let me do it for you? We'd split the profits right down the middle. Just think of it! We could live out the rest of our lives doing nothing but sitting back and fanning ourselves."

Before Yohei's very eyes, gold coins great and small began to dazzle and dance. If only he could get his wife to relent, if only he could persuade her to weave again, they could seize such a fortune as had never been known before.

When Yohei presented her with this idea, the young woman seemed quite perplexed. "Why in the world," she asked, "would anyone need so much money as that?"

"Don't you see?" he answered. "With money like that a man's problems would all disappear. He could buy anything he liked. He could even start his own business."

"Isn't it plenty to be able to live together, just the two of us?"

When she spoke this way, Yohei could say no more. However, from that time on, whether asleep or awake, all he could do was think about money. It was so painful for the young woman to see Yohei in this state that her eyes filled with tears as she watched him, until finally, unable to bear it another day, she bowed to his will.

"Very well then," she said. "I will weave one more time. But truly, after this, I must never weave again." And once more she warned the now-joyful Yohei, saying, "For the sake of heaven, remember. Do not look in on me."

Yohei rubbed his hands together in his eagerness and sat down to wait.

Tonkara tonkara. The sound of the loom continued on and on into the fifth day. The work in the back room seemed to be taking longer than ever.

Yohei, no longer the simple fellow that he had once been, began to wonder about certain peculiar things. Why did the young woman appear to grow thinner every time she wove? What was going on in there behind those paper doors? How could she weave such beautiful cloth when she never seemed to buy any thread?

The longer he had to wait, the more he yearned to peep into the room until, at last, he put his hand upon the door.

"Ah!" came a voice from within. At the same time Yohei cried out in horror and fell back from the doorway.

What Yohei saw was not human. It was a crane, smeared with blood, for with its beak it had plucked out its own feathers to place them in the loom.

At the sight Yohei collapsed into a deep faint.

When he came to himself, he found, lying near his hand, a bolt of fabric, pure and radiantly white, through

which was woven a thread of bright crimson. It shone with a light this world has never known.

From somewhere Yohei heard the whisper of a delicate, familiar voice. "I had hoped," the voice said sorrowfully, "that you would be able to honor my entreaty. But because you looked upon me in my suffering, I can no longer tarry in the human world. I am the crane that you saved on the snowy path. I fell in love with your gentle, simple heart, and, trusting it alone, I came to live by your side. I pray that your life will be long and that you will always be happy."

"Wai-t!" Yohei stumbled in his haste to get outside.

It was nearly spring, and, over the crest of the distant mountains, he could barely discern the tiny form of a single crane, flying farther and farther away.

Library Link ♦ *Another collection of tales from Japan that you may enjoy is* The Magic Listening Cap: More Folk Tales from Japan *by Yoshiko Uchida.*

 Reader's Response

"The Crane Wife" is a beloved folktale of the Japanese people. Why do you think this story is so popular?

The Crane Wife

 ## Responding to Literature

1. Sometimes a folktale reveals the culture of its people. What does this beautiful story tell you about those who tell it to their children and grandchildren?

2. Perform a Read-Around of ''The Crane Wife.'' Designate a starting reader. In turn, different people in the class will read one paragraph each. When it is your turn to read, remember to speak clearly and use your voice well.

3. With a small group, write another ending for ''The Crane Wife.'' Compare your ending with this author's ending. Tell which one you prefer and why.

 ## Writing to Learn

Think and Imagine ◆ Imagine Yohei's distress when he discovered his wife's secret. Sketch a picture of Yohei and add a thought balloon above his head. Add words to the balloon to tell what Yohei might have thought at that moment.

Thought Balloon

Write ◆ Write a journal entry from Yohei's point of view at the moment he discovered that his wife was leaving. Imagine what he thought. Put his thoughts into words.

Be a critic! What television program that you watched recently did not live up to your expectations? Why were you disappointed?

SPEAKING and LISTENING ◆
Critical Listening

Do you enjoy listening as someone tells or reads a story to you? There are times when your main reason for listening is just that—listening for enjoyment. However, even when you are listening for enjoyment you evaluate, or make judgments about, what you hear. Listening to make a judgment about what you hear is critical listening.

You have already read one version of "The Crane Wife." Now you will read aloud and listen to parts of another version of the same folktale. As you listen, think about which one you like better. You and your classmates will probably not all agree on which is the "better" version, just as movie critics and book reviewers do not always agree. That does not matter. The important thing is to have reasons for your judgments. The critical listening guidelines below will help you do this. Guidelines for reading aloud are also given.

Reading Aloud	1. Slow down! Most people read aloud too fast. 2. Practice until you can read aloud with ease. 3. Read with expression. Change your tone of voice to fit the characters and the action.
Being a Critical Listener	1. Compare: How is the selection like or different from others of its kind? If comparing two versions, think about what is the same. What is different? 2. Judge: Does the selection capture and hold your interest? Can you picture the details? Is the language of the story appealing? Do you think the author achieved his or her purpose? What is your overall opinion of the selection?

Summary ◆ **Critical listening** is listening closely to make a judgment about what you hear.

Guided Practice

Here are the openings from two versions of the Japanese folktale about the crane wife. Listen as they are read aloud. Then tell which you prefer. Give reasons for your choice.

In a faraway mountain village, where the snow falls deep and white, there once lived all alone a poor young peasant named Yohei.

Once upon a time there was an old man who lived in the country all alone with his old wife. They had no children.

Practice

A. The passages below are from two versions of the same folktale. Listen as they are read aloud. Then write which you prefer, and why. Use the guidelines in this lesson as you give your reasons.

1. One day I was in the swamp when I saw a Canada goose in the water near me. Geese need open space; they should never be in the swamp. The bird had been shot, and its wing was broken. It could scarcely move. I picked it up, carried it home, and nursed it back to health. In a few weeks it flew away.

2. One day, at the beginning of winter, Yohei went out into the snow to run an errand, and, as he hurried home, suddenly *basabasa* he heard a rustling sound. It was a crane, dragging its wing, as it swooped down and landed on the path. Now Yohei could see that the bird was in great pain, for an arrow had pierced its wing. He went to where the crane lay, drew out the arrow, and very carefully tended its wound.

B. Choose the passage you liked most from "The Crane Wife" on pages 366–372. Read the passage aloud to a partner, and tell why you chose it. Does your partner agree with your choice?

Apply ◆ Think and Write

Evaluating a "Read-Aloud" ◆ Write a paragraph telling what kind of story you think makes a good "read-aloud." Does it need conversation? Action? Description?

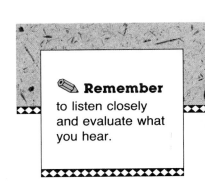

✎ Remember
to listen closely and evaluate what you hear.

If you could put yourself into a story, which story would it be? What character would you most enjoy meeting? What place would you want to see?

WRITING ◆
Character and Setting

Do people fascinate you? Do you notice their clothes, their gestures, their facial expressions? Do you pay attention to what they say and how they say it? Are you curious about what they do and why they do it?

Are you intrigued by places? Do you notice details of a location? Can you picture a place you have been? Can you remember its sounds, its smells, and how you felt when you were there? If you enjoy observing people and places, you already have material to create two essential parts of a story: characters and setting.

Characters	The people (or animals) in a story *Sherlock Holmes; Scarlett O'Hara; the black stallion*
Setting	Where and when the story takes place *A mysterious castle in England, centuries ago*

Experienced writers tell about their characters through the characters' actions and words. They let the characters speak for themselves. Characters often tell readers about a story's setting as well. Authors also weave descriptions of characters and setting through their stories. In these ways, writers create characters that are convincing and settings that readers can easily picture.

> **Summary** ◆ Two basic elements of a story are its **characters** and its **setting**.

Guided Practice

Tell whether each of these describes a character or setting.

1. The modest young woman worked diligently.
2. Behind the house, the hillside sloped down to a swift stream.
3. A pale beam of moonlight fell softly on the floor of the simple hut where the woman sat.
4. The man's heart filled with sadness as he watched the crane fly gracefully toward the distant mountains.

Practice

A. Read these sentences from ''The Crane Wife.'' Write *character* or *setting* to show what each one illustrates.

5. He could no longer recognize the cold, cold dreary hut where he had lived all alone, his house had become so bright and warm.

6. In the back room of the hut, the young woman set up a loom and closed it off with sliding paper doors.

7. ''Why in the world,'' she asked, ''would anyone need so much money as that?''

8. ''I fell in love with your gentle, simple heart, and, trusting it alone, I came to live by your side.''

B. Think of a favorite story that you have read recently. Write answers to these questions about the story.

9. What is the name of the story, and who is the main character?

10. What is the character like? Describe the character's physical appearance. Describe something the character did, and tell why he or she did it.

11. What is the setting of the story?

Apply ◆ Think and Write

Imagining a Setting ◆ The same folktale often exists in different versions in different countries. The various versions may have different settings. Write a description of a setting for a modern version of ''The Crane Wife'' or for another folktale.

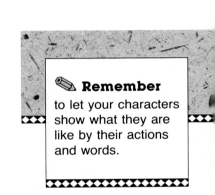

✎ **Remember**
to let your characters show what they are like by their actions and words.

Imagine a different ending for "The Crane Wife." Begin at the point where Yohei is about to open the door of the room where his wife is weaving. What happens next in your version?

WRITING ◆
Story Plot

You have studied two basic elements of a story—character and setting. The third element is **plot**. Notice what part each plays.

> **Characters**   Who is in the story?
> **Setting**   Where and when does the story take place?
> **Plot**   What happens?

Plot is the story's action, or the sequence of events that takes place. Writers often use the incidents in the plot to create suspense, to make readers want to find out what happens next. Basic to every plot is conflict. There must be a clash, a problem, a struggle, or there is no story. A conflict is two suitors and one princess, two armies and one victor, or two dogs and one bone. A conflict is someone trying to get something and being opposed.

The structure of a plot is often explained like this: The *beginning* of the story introduces the characters, setting, and conflict, or problem. The *middle* of the story shows the characters struggling—the clash of opposing forces. Suspense builds to a peak. Then *something happens*! The conflict is resolved. The *end* of the story is a matter of explaining the solution and tying up loose ends.

> **Summary** ◆ The **plot** of a story tells what happens. It introduces a conflict or problem for the characters to resolve.

Guided Practice

Below is a list of characters. For each one, invent a conflict for a story plot. Name a goal for the character. Then tell a possible problem in reaching the goal.

1. Wanda, a girl who is an excellent swimmer
2. Bruce, a dog whose owner has moved away
3. Rinaldo, a teenager who has lost something valuable

Practice

A. Four characters are described briefly below. For each character, invent a conflict for a story plot. Write a goal for the character and a possible problem in reaching the goal. Tell what obstacle the character might face.

    4. Stephanie, an overworked traffic officer
    5. James, a potential basketball star
    6. Troog, a creature from outer space
    7. Champ, a dog lost far from home

B. Answer these questions about a story you have read recently.

    8. What are the most important events that take place in the story?
    9. What conflict, or problem, does the main character face?
   10. How is the conflict resolved?

C. Choose one of the situations you wrote for **Practice A**. Expand it into a plot outline. Include these details.

   11. the characters
   12. the setting
   13. the story's conflict, or problem
   14. how the main character tries to get whatever it is he or she wants
   15. the opposition the main character meets
   16. the point of greatest conflict in the story—the deciding struggle
   17. how the story ends

Apply ◆ Think and Write

Dictionary of Knowledge ◆ Sometimes the conflict in a story involves a struggle with a natural force, such as a violent storm, a serious drought, or a harsh environment. Read about the Gobi Desert in the Dictionary of Knowledge. Then write about the obstacles its severe environment might place in the path of a story character who is trying to cross this desert.

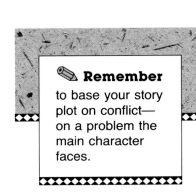

✎ Remember
to base your story plot on conflict— on a problem the main character faces.

Focus on Folktales

Folktales, as their name suggests, are tales that come from the folk, or people. The authors and the origins of folktales are unknown, for the stories are very, very old. Folktales are passed down by storytellers from one generation to the next. No matter what their country of origin, folktales are alike in a number of ways.

Purposes   A folktale entertains listeners or readers with a suspenseful story. It also teaches values such as kindness, honesty, courage, lack of greed. "The Crane Wife," which you read earlier, has these characteristics.

Character, Setting, Plot   The characters and setting of a folktale are introduced early in the story. The plot is important and develops quickly. Characters are all good or evil, wise or foolish. In "The Crane Wife," for example, the wife is beautiful, good, humble, patient, and loving. There is never any confusion about who is the hero or the villain of the story.

Magic   Folktales regularly make use of magic. There may be talking animals, magical objects, wishes supernaturally granted, a long sleep, impossible tasks and trials, or transformation of an animal into a human or vice versa. In "The Crane Wife" the young wife is a crane that fell in love with the peasant Yohei.

The Writer's Voice ◆ Folktales often have things occurring in threes — three wishes, three tasks to perform. Give an example from a familiar folktale of something that occurs in threes.

◆ Name a folktale character who is all good or all evil.

◆ Give an example of a folktale animal that talks or changes into a person.

Working Together

Folktales have a number of elements that you will notice as you read them. Keep these elements in mind as you work with your group on activities **A** and **B**.

A. With your group, invent two characters for a folktale. Then write a brief description of each character. Follow the guidelines below. You may make a drawing of the characters, too, if the group wishes to do so.

   1. Invent one character who will be all good.
   2. Invent an opposing character who will be all evil.
   3. Give each character a name.
   4. Make sure each character has a distinct personality. Tell what he or she looks like, sounds like, and wears.
   5. Invent an expression for each one — something that the character says again and again.

B. Decide on a setting and story problem for the two characters your group invented in activity **A**. Where and when will the story take place? Why and how will the two characters oppose each other? Write down what your group decides. Then choose someone to tell the rest of the class about the story your group has created.

> **In Your Group**
>
> - Contribute ideas to the group.
> - Build on other people's ideas.
> - Help the group reach agreement.
> - Record the group's ideas.

THESAURUS CORNER • Word Choice

Look up the entry for *good* in the Thesaurus. Choose four synonyms that best describe your folktale hero who is good. Use a different synonym for *good* in each sentence and underline it. Then go back and underline and label each preposition and each conjunction in the sentences you have written.

WRITING PROCESS

IMAGING

Writing
a Folktale

A folktale is a fantasy tale that often teaches a lesson about human nature. In ''The Crane Wife,'' the characters you met were Yohei and his lovely, mysterious wife. You found out how they survived the winter without much money. You also learned something about the importance of keeping a promise.

Know Your Purpose and Audience

In this lesson you will write a folktale. Your purpose will be to tell a story about a character with a problem to solve.

Your audience will be your classmates. Later you and your classmates can dramatize your folktales or make a book.

What's MY PURPOSE

Who's MY AUDIENCE

1 Prewriting

Before you write your folktale, choose a topic. Your topic will include a character, a setting, and a plot idea. Then you will use some prewriting strategies to develop ideas for your story.

Choose Your Topic ◆ You need to pick a character, a setting, and a plot for your story. You might use a chart such as the one below in Topic Ideas. Make sure you choose the story ideas that you like the best.

Think About It

Could you create a modern version of an old folktale? Perhaps you would rather create an original folktale. It might help to read some traditional folktales to get ideas for your story. Take care to create a story you like.

Talk About It

On the chalkboard make a large chart of characters, settings, and plots. Add as many as you can. Then discuss how mixing and matching story parts can give you ideas for original stories.

Topic Ideas

Main Character

Cinderella
17-year-old girl
Brown hair,
    brown eyes
Gentle, kind,
patient

Plot

Mean
stepsisters
try to keep
her from
attending a
special dance

Setting

A Friday
    in spring
A big old
    mansion

Choose Your Strategy ◆ Here are two strategies for developing story ideas. Read both. Use what you find helpful.

PREWRITING IDEAS

CHOICE ONE

Asking Questions

One way to gather plot ideas for your story is to ask and answer questions. Work with a partner to develop questions about your story. Discuss possible answers. Write your answers after the questions.

Model

What is my main character's problem?
Wants to go to the dance
What happens at the beginning?
Mean stepsisters give her chores
What happens next?
Does chores, has only rags to wear
How does the character solve the problem?
Gets animals to help her

CHOICE TWO

A Thought Balloon

In a story you want to do more than just tell plot events. You want to tell how your character feels or what kind of person your character is. Put yourself in your character's place. As the plot unfolds, how does he or she feel? Make a thought balloon for your main character. You might also make thought balloons for other characters.

Model

Why are my stepsisters so mean? I'm determined to be happy anyway!

Cinderella

2 Writing

Before you begin to write, practice telling your folktale to a partner. This may help you to find and fix plot problems or to fill in details you haven't thought about.

Now begin to write your folktale. Introduce your character and his or her problem at the beginning of the story. As you write, include descriptive details to help readers picture the setting. Show how your characters feel. Remember that a folktale usually tells something about human nature.

The main thing is just to keep writing until the character has solved the problem. Then your story is finished.

Sample First Draft ◆

Cinderella's horrible stepsisters laughed as they tried on their dresses. The dresses were for the spring dance. "Too bad you can't go," they jeered at Cinderella

By that evening Cinderella had washed, dusted, polished, and vacumed every inch of the creaky old mansion. Cinderella longed to go to the dance, but she had to clean the entire mansion. "Besides," she said aloud, "I have only these old jeans to wear. I don't own a pretty dress." She looked out the open window of her dingy attic room. Tears gathered in her eyes as she watched her sisters zoom away in their shiny Sports Car. Just then a bluebird flew into the room. A yellow butterfly followed. Cinderella heard a soft, feathery voice say, "don't worry, Cindi. We're going to help you get to the dance."

3 Revising

Now that you have written the first draft of your folktale, you may want to improve it. This idea may help you.

REVISING IDEA

FIRST   Read to Yourself

As you read, review your purpose. Did you write a story about a character with a problem to solve? Consider your audience. Will your classmates understand and enjoy the story?

Focus: Does your story have the elements of a folktale? Is it a fantasy? Does it reveal something about human nature? Place a caret (^) where you want to add a detail.

THEN   Share with a Partner

Ask a partner to read your folktale aloud to you. Then ask for your partner's ideas. These guidelines may help you both.

The Writer

Guidelines: As your partner reads, listen as if you were another person hearing it for the first time. Note the parts you would like to improve.

Sample questions:
- What part did you like best?
- **Focus question:** Does my story sound like a folktale? Does it have the elements of a folktale?

The Writer's Partner

Guidelines: Read the story to the writer with expression. Give helpful suggestions.

Sample responses:
- The part I liked best was _____.
- You could make it more like a folktale by _____.

Revising Model ♦ This beginning of a folktale is being revised. The marks show the writer's changes.

The writer combined sentences with a prepositional phrase.

The character's problem was moved closer to the beginning.

Gazed is a more precise word than *looked*.

The writer's partner suggested adding this fantasy element.

Cinderella's horrible stepsisters laughed as they tried on their dresses. ~~The dresses were~~ for the spring dance. "Too bad you can't go," they jeered at Cinderella

By that evening Cinderella had washed, dusted, polished, and vacumed every inch of the creaky old mansion. ~~Cinderella longed to go to the dance, but she had to clean the entire mansion.~~ "Besides," she said aloud, "I have only these old jeans to wear. I don't own a ~~pretty dress.~~" She ~~looked~~ *gazed* out the open window of her dingy attic room. Tears gathered in her eyes as she watched her sisters zoom away in their shiny Sports Car. Just then a bluebird flew into the room. A yellow butterfly followed. Cinderella heard a soft, feathery voice say, "don't worry, Cindi. We're going to help you get to the dance." *It was the bluebird who had spoken.*

Read the above folktale beginning the way the writer has decided it *should* be. Then revise your own folktale.

Grammar Check ♦ Combining sentences can make writing less choppy.

Word Choice ♦ Do you want a more precise word for an overused word like *look*? A thesaurus can help you.

4 Proofreading

Proofread your folktale for mistakes. Making sure that your writing is correct shows consideration for your readers.

Proofreading Model ♦ Here is the folktale draft. Notice how red proofreading marks have now been added.

Proofreading Marks

capital letter =

small letter /

indent paragraph ¶

check spelling ⬭

Cinderella's horrible stepsisters laughed as they tried on their dresses. ~~The dresses were~~ for the spring dance. "Too bad you can't go," they jeered at Cinderella.
¶By that evening Cinderella had washed, dusted, polished, and (vacumed) *vacuumed* every inch of the creaky old mansion. ⟨Cinderella longed to go to the dance, but she had to clean the entire mansion. "Besides," she said aloud, "I have only these old jeans to wear. I don't own a pretty dress."⟩ She ~~looked~~ *gazed* out the open window of her dingy attic room. Tears gathered in her eyes as she watched her sisters zoom away in their shiny S̶ports C̶ar.¶ Just then a bluebird flew into the room. A yellow butterfly followed. Cinderella heard a soft, feathery voice say, "d̲on't worry, Cindi. We're going to help you get to the dance." *It was the bluebird who had spoken.*

Proofreading Checklist

- ☐ Did I spell words correctly?
- ☐ Did I indent paragraphs?
- ☐ Did I use capital letters correctly?
- ☐ Did I use correct marks at the end of sentences?
- ☐ Did I type neatly or use my best handwriting?

PROOFREADING IDEA

Spelling Check

To be sure you find all spelling errors, try checking every other word. On your second reading, check the other words. This way you will focus on word spellings rather than meanings.

Now proofread your folktale. Add a title for it, and then make a neat copy.

5 Publishing

Now it's time to share your folktale with others. Try one of these ideas.

A Modern Cinderella

Cinderella's horrible stepsisters laughed as they tried on their dresses for the spring dance. "Too bad you can't go," they jeered at Cinderella.

Cinderella longed to go to the dance, but she had to clean the entire mansion. "Besides," she said aloud, "I have only these old jeans to wear. I don't own a pretty dress."

By that evening Cinderella had washed, dusted, polished, and vacuumed every inch of the creaky old mansion. She gazed out the open window of her dingy attic room. Tears gathered in her eyes as she watched her sisters zoom away in their shiny sports car.

Just then a bluebird flew into the room. A yellow butterfly followed. Cinderella heard a soft, feathery voice say, "Don't worry, Cindi. We're going to help you get to the dance." It was the bluebird who had spoken.

PUBLISHING IDEAS

Share Aloud	Share in Writing
Read your folktales to a small group of classmates. Then ask your group to help you dramatize your tale for the class.	Make a book of folktales for the class library. Assemble all the folktales. Decorate the book's cover with illustrations, and include a blank page after each story for remarks.

CURRICULUM ·CONNECTION·

Writing Across the Curriculum   Science

In this unit you read a folktale and then wrote one. In planning your story you reviewed the importance of point of view, and you may have made a thought balloon. Putting yourself in another person's place can help you with your science studies, too.

Writing to Learn

Think and Imagine ◆ Skim your science textbook and choose a person who made an important discovery. Imagine you are that person. Why do you feel your work and your discovery were important? Make a thought balloon for the person you chose.

Thought Balloon

Write ◆ Use your thought balloon to write a paragraph from the point of view of the person you chose. Describe your discovery and tell why you feel it was important.

Writing in Your Journal

In the Writer's Warm-up you wrote about folklore. In this unit you learned many facts about Japan, its people, and their beliefs. In your journal, record the things that you learned about Japanese folklore.

BOOKS TO ENJOY

Read More About It

The Dancing Kettle and Other Japanese Folktales *retold by Yoshiko Uchida*
These fourteen folktales present many of the themes that are common in Japan's folklore.

Of Nightingales That Weep
by Katherine Paterson
This colorful and romantic story depicts life in feudal Japan. Takiko, the daughter of a samurai warrior, personally experiences both the luxury of court life and the poverty of the peasant villages.

The Girl Who Cried Flowers and Other Tales
by Jane Yolen
Jane Yolen wrote these beautiful stories in the best folklore tradition. They are new stories, but they are written with the threads of the past woven throughout.

Book Report Idea   Character Interview

Have you ever wished you could meet a character in a story or a book? An imaginary interview is one way you can. It is also a good way to share a character or book with your classmates.

Write a Script ♦ Write your interview in the form of a script. Your questions and the character's answers should include information about the book. Write the answers that your character would give.

Interviewer: Sam, in *My Side of the Mountain*, you spent the winter inside a tree on a mountain. What did you miss most about home during that time?

Sam Gribley: I was really too busy surviving and enjoying the wild to miss very much. I did miss my family, though, which surprised me.

UNIT REVIEW

Unit 7

Prepositions   *pages 346–353*

A. Write each prepositional phrase. Underline the preposition once and the object of the preposition twice.

1. We went to the theater.
2. Perry sent this for your birthday.
3. Father took the pizza from the oven.
4. The parachutist landed in the pond.
5. My dog walked behind me.
6. The science museum is near my house.
7. The group of fans cheered the team.
8. The raccoon leaned against the fence.
9. The store across the street just opened.
10. Beneath the great oak tree were several tiny acorns.
11. Inside the room was a table of oak.
12. We took a shortcut through the park.
13. Tiny silver fish swam rapidly below the surface.
14. The woman from my mother's class is visiting us.
15. We strolled along the beach.

B. Write each prepositional phrase. Write *adjective* if it describes a noun. Write *adverb* if it describes a verb, an adjective, or an adverb.

16. My aunt just traveled for six months.
17. She is one of our great travelers.
18. Her stories about her travels are fascinating.
19. She flew over the Himalayas.
20. Her tour group visited Tibet, among other places.
21. A Tibetan lama chanted a blessing for her.
22. I can show you a photograph of her.
23. She is smiling at the lama.
24. A small Tibetan boy with a scroll is holding her hand.
25. He is grinning at her.
26. A woman stands in a corner.
27. She is leaning against a pillar.
28. A white shawl is draped over her.
29. My aunt told me the woman with the shawl is the boy's mother.
30. The lama is the older brother of the boy.

C. Write the word in parentheses ( ) that correctly completes each sentence.

31. Share the fruit (among, between) the three of you.
32. Ms. Lange gave the books to Jean and (I, me).
33. This poem is for (she, her).
34. A little girl stood (among, between) the two men.
35. Emilio solved the problem for (we, us).
36. We shall have to walk around (they, them).
37. (Among, Between) Charles, Lin, and Pedro we would have a hard time choosing the friendliest person.
38. Did you make the bed for (she, her)?

Conjunctions *pages 354–355*

D. Write each sentence. Underline the conjunction.

39. The lesson went slowly but surely.
40. Bart and I look forward to spring.
41. They missed the warning sign or ignored it.
42. Italy and France are noted for their fine chefs.
43. The work crew scraped off the old paint and put on a new coat.
44. This novel is complicated but good.
45. Will you write or type your report?
46. The trail up the mountain is long and winding.

Interjections *pages 356–357*

E. Write each sentence. Punctuate the interjection correctly.

47. Ugh This room is a complete mess.
48. Wow That monster movie was scary.
49. Ouch I hit my knee on the table.
50. Hooray Our team won the game.
51. Aha I've found you at last.
52. Whew That test was tough.
53. Oh There's a hole in my sock.
54. Eek A black bat just brushed me.

Homophones and Homographs *pages 358–359*

F. Write the correct word in parentheses ( ) to complete each sentence.

55. (Its, It's) a beautiful evening.
56. The cobbler (died, dyed) the boots.
57. The boat swayed as the (tied, tide) came in.
58. Let me give you a clean (peace, piece) of paper.
59. (Their, They're) rehearsing for a rock concert.
60. Is the dog's (tale, tail) wagging or just the opposite?
61. The cat licked (its, it's) fur.
62. The juggler performed a challenging (feat, feet).
63. Tell me when (your, you're) ready to leave.
64. The war was over and (peace, piece) (rained, reigned) throughout the land.
65. She told us a (tale, tail) of (nightly, knightly) deeds of long ago.
66. Of (coarse, course) you may go to the movie.

Character, Setting, and Plot *pages 376–379*

G. Tell whether each of the following is an example of character, setting, or plot.

67. Except for the hooting of an owl, the night was still.
68. The old man whistled to himself to keep up his courage.
69. Ahead of him stood the old dark house, its spires outlined in the moonlight.
70. He paused, his hands trembling, his heart shaking within him.
71. "Be courageous!" he kept telling himself, but even so he could not bring himself to enter.
72. He had promised his friend he would never go there alone.
73. He had argued with his friend about going there in the first place.

LANGUAGE PUZZLERS

Pict-O-Grams

Figure out each of the following sentences. (Hint: Each contains a prepositional phrase.)

1. FRIEND There R ~~secrets~~ FRIEND
2. TOTHECIRCUSISWN

3.

4.

There's 0 new

5. Climb

Hide some other prepositional phrases the way the ones above were hidden.

Preposition Tic-Tac-Toe

Play Preposition Tic-Tac-Toe with a classmate. Score a point for each preposition that can be made in one move.

Play until no more words can be made. You may write the words across, diagonally, and from bottom to top as well as from top to bottom.

EXAMPLE:

Player A
(two points:
for, of)

```
  f | o | r
 ---+---+---
    |   |
 ---+---+---
    |   |
```

Player B
(two points:
of, off)

```
  f | o | r
 ---+---+---
    | f |
 ---+---+---
    | f |
```

Player A
(three points:
off once, *of* twice)

```
  f | o | r
 ---+---+---
    | f |
 ---+---+---
  o | f | f
```

Player B
(two points:
to twice)

```
  f | o | r
 ---+---+---
  t | f |
 ---+---+---
  o | f | f
```

Player A
(four points:
for once, *of* three times)

```
  f | o | r
 ---+---+---
  t | f | o
 ---+---+---
  o | f | f
```

Totals: Player A has nine points. Player B has four points.

Unit 7 Extra Practice

1 Writing with Prepositions

p. 346

A. Write the prepositional phrase in each sentence.

1. Europe is a continent of large peninsulas.
2. Greece is located on the Balkan Peninsula.
3. Italy is a boot-shaped peninsula in the Mediterranean Sea.
4. Spain covers a large part of the Iberian Peninsula.
5. Norway shares a peninsula with Sweden.

B. Write each sentence. Underline each prepositional phrase.

6. Southern Europe's peninsulas are crossed by mountains.
7. The Pyrenees run along the Iberian Peninsula's base.
8. The Balkan Mountains cover much of the Balkan Peninsula.
9. The Alps stand at Italy's northern border.
10. The Alps rise more than 13,000 feet above sea level.
11. High in the Alps four important rivers begin.
12. The Rhine River empties into the North Sea.
13. The Danube River empties into the Black Sea.
14. The Rhone flows south through France.
15. The Po River flows east across northern Italy.

C. Write the prepositional phrase in each sentence. Underline the preposition once and the object of the preposition twice.

EXAMPLE: Forests once covered most of this continent.
 ANSWER: of this continent

16. Europeans have changed their land greatly over the years.
17. They have drained swamps and cleared forests for farms.
18. Rich farmland can be found throughout Europe.
19. Much coal and iron ore lie beneath European soil.
20. Oil deposits can be found under the choppy North Sea.
21. Europeans have built great cities with their resources.
22. Ships travel across many nations, using canals and rivers.
23. Fine roads and tunnels carry people past high mountains.
24. Large industries contribute to the European lifestyle.
25. Europe's universities are admired around the entire world.

Extra Practice **395**

2 Prepositional Phrases as Adjectives

p. 348

A. Write each sentence. Underline each adjective phrase.

1. The Sahara is the largest desert in the world.
2. This African desert is the size of the United States.
3. The other two thirds of the continent is a high plateau.
4. Much land on this plateau is savanna, or grassland.
5. Mountains with high peaks are also found there.
6. Mount Kilimanjaro is higher than any mountain in Europe.
7. Africa also has large forests with rainy climates.
8. The longest river in the world is Africa's Nile River.
9. The length of this river is more than 4,000 miles.
10. The Congo and the Niger are rivers with many waterfalls.

B. Write the adjective phrase in each sentence. Then write the noun the phrase describes.

11. Much soil in Africa is not rich.
12. The savannas, however, produce good harvests of grain.
13. Farmers on the savannas raise cattle and sheep.
14. Africans have cleared much land in the rain forests.
15. Forests throughout Africa produce coconuts and cacao.
16. Cacao is the main ingredient of chocolate.
17. Rubber for tires is another forest crop.
18. Africa also produces a large amount of coffee.
19. Sisal, a plant with strong fibers, grows well.
20. Sisal is used to make rope of all kinds.

3 Prepositional Phrases as Adverbs

p. 350

A. Write the adverb phrase in each sentence.

1. Mr. Kelso planned his trip for weeks.
2. He would travel around Asia.
3. Asia's northernmost parts lie in the frozen Arctic.
4. Southern Asia ends near the equator.
5. Mr. Kelso flew to China first.
6. He toured Peking, China's capital, with great interest.

B. Write each sentence. Underline each adverb phrase.

7. Mr. Kelso reached the Himalayas by July.
8. These mountains lie in central Asia.
9. Mount Everest, the world's highest mountain, is in the Himalayas.
10. Mr. Kelso toured India for several weeks.
11. He traveled down the Ganges River.
12. Many people live and farm along this river.
13. The Ganges flows into the Bay of Bengal.

C. Write the adverb phrase in each sentence. Then write the word the phrase describes.

14. Mr. Kelso also visited Indonesia on his trip.
15. The Indonesian islands lie near Malaysia.
16. They stretch along the equator.
17. Finally, he flew over Iran and Iraq.
18. Even those countries are within Asia's boundaries.
19. Mr. Kelso is eager for his next trip.

4 Using Prepositional Phrases   *p. 352*

A. Write the word that correctly completes each sentence.

1. There are many similarities (among, between) Australia, the United States, and Canada.
2. Mother went to Canberra with Father and (I, me).
3. Canberra is (among, between) Sydney and Melbourne.
4. The city will be interesting for you and (he, him).
5. The land (among, between) the Pacific Ocean and the Great Dividing Mountains gets the most rain in Australia.

B. Write each sentence with inverted word order in regular word order. Write each regular sentence in inverted order.

6. From the Latin word for "southern" comes the name *Australia*.
7. In Australia work many iron, bauxite, and nickel miners.
8. The Great Barrier Reef lies off the northeastern coast.
9. Kangaroos and bandicoots wander across the interior.
10. In rural areas live most of the Aborigines.

C. Write the word in ( ) that correctly completes each sentence.

11. "Much of Australia was claimed by England in 1770," Mother explained to Father and (I, me).
12. "James Cook explored it," I said to Father and (she, her).
13. "The New South Wales region was named by (he, him)."
14. Father pointed out to (we, us) that the first Australian settlement was a prison colony.
15. England had sent (among, between) 160,000 and 170,000 convicts to the country by 1868.
16. There are many farms (among, between) Australia's coast and inland deserts.
17. Today Australia is (among, between) the world's four greatest producers of wheat and beef.
18. (Among, Between) all wool producers, it is ranked first.
19. Differences (among, between) city life and country life in Australia are relatively few.
20. Over half of the country's population is divided (among, between) the six state capitals.

5 Writing with Conjunctions   *p. 354*

A. Write the conjunction in each sentence.

1. Many states celebrate Arbor Day in March or April.
2. Planting a tree is hard but satisfying work.
3. Arbor Day began and grew popular in Nebraska.
4. The once treeless but fertile prairies in Nebraska were called The Great American Desert.
5. J. Sterling Morton spoke and wrote about the need for trees on the prairies of Nebraska.
6. He wanted every Nebraskan, young or old, to plant trees.
7. Eventually Nebraska's lawmakers introduced and passed a law making April 10, 1872, the first Arbor Day.
8. *Arbor* is a Latin word meaning "tree" or "shrub."
9. Prizes were given to persons and groups for planting trees.
10. A million or more trees were planted that first Arbor Day.
11. By 1888, Nebraskans had planted 350 million trees and shrubs.
12. Other states and countries followed Nebraska's lead.

B. Write the conjunction in each sentence. Then write *nouns*, *pronouns*, *verbs*, *adjectives*, or *adverbs* to show what kind of words are joined.

13. More and more people now recognize the value of trees.
14. They appreciate and encourage planting trees.
15. Connecticut celebrates Arbor Day in spring and fall.
16. Some trees should be planted or transplanted only in fall.
17. This tree is small but healthy.
18. Birds live happily and well in trees.
19. Trees are important for them and us.
20. Trees provide people with food and lumber.

6 Parts of Speech Summary   *p. 356*

A. Write each interjection below.

1. Oh! Look at these pictures of imaginary animals!
2. Hooray! Here is a picture of a griffin.
3. Aha! It's half lion, half eagle, and very beautiful!
4. Eek! What's coming out of that fire?
5. Wow! It is a phoenix, of course.

B. Two words are underlined in each sentence. Write the part of speech of each underlined word.

EXAMPLE: The phoenix rises from its own ashes.
ANSWER: verb, noun

6. The awful Hydra had at least 100 heads.
7. Many heroes tried to kill the Hydra.
8. They attempted to cut off its heads.
9. However, two new heads quickly replaced each lost head.
10. The Leucrocotta was an imaginary animal from India.
11. It had the tail and chest of a lion.
12. People thought it could imitate the human voice.
13. I'm really glad there aren't any around now!
14. The unicorn is my favorite imaginary animal.
15. It looks much like a white pony.
16. However, it has a magical horn on its head.
17. People hunted the unicorn for its magical horn.

UNIT EIGHT

USING LANGUAGE
TO

CLASSIFY

═══════════ **PART ONE** ═══════════

Unit Theme   *Wildlife Conservation*

Language Awareness   Sentences

═══════════ **PART TWO** ═══════════

Literature   *Project Panda Watch* by Miriam Schlein

A Reason for Writing   Classifying

Writing
IN YOUR JOURNAL

WRITER'S WARM-UP ◆ What do you know about efforts to preserve wildlife? Perhaps you have read about why certain species have become extinct. You may have seen TV shows about special efforts to save endangered animals. Write in your journal about what can be done in your community to preserve wildlife.

GETTING
STARTED

Think of pairs of nouns or verbs that are used together—*food and drink, friend or foe, live and learn, wait and watch.* Say one of the words and ask a partner to guess the other.

1 Compound Subjects and Predicates

The simple subject is the main word in the complete subject of a sentence. The simple predicate is the main word or words in the complete predicate. In the sentence below, the simple subject is shown in blue and the simple predicate in green.

■ The black-and-white **panda** **looks** like a cuddly bear.

Some sentences have more than one simple subject. Two or more simple subjects with the same verb are called a compound subject. A conjunction such as *and* or *or* usually joins the simple subjects. Other sentences have more than one simple predicate. Two or more verbs that have the same subject are called a compound predicate. A compound predicate is also called a compound verb.

Pandas and **bears** have thick coats. (compound subject)
Pandas **climb, move,** and **sit** like bears. (compound predicate)

You can often combine short sentences with repeated ideas into one sentence with a compound subject or a compound verb.

Bears are like pandas. Raccoons are like pandas.
Bears and raccoons are like pandas.

> **Summary** ◆ A **compound subject** is two or more simple subjects that have the same verb. A **compound predicate** is two or more verbs that have the same subject.

Guided Practice

Name the compound subject or predicate in each sentence.

1. China and Tibet are the native habitats of giant pandas.
2. Bamboo and other plants make up the panda's diet.
3. The Chinese people admire and protect these rare animals.

Practice

A. Write the compound subject or predicate in each sentence.

4. The 300-pound giant panda sits and walks like a bear.
5. The red panda looks and moves like a raccoon.
6. Its small body and ringed tail are raccoonlike.
7. Red pandas and their giant cousins have a false thumb.
8. Pandas grab and hold objects with this extra wrist bone.
9. The morning and the evening are the panda's active periods.
10. Myths, tales, and legends mention the ''white bears.''
11. Westerners discovered and named the giant panda in 1879.
12. Explorers and hunters sought pandas for museum collections.
13. However, thick forests and high mountains provided protection.

B. Write and label each compound subject and compound predicate. If a sentence has no compounds, write *no compound*.

14. Fewer than one thousand pandas still live in China.
15. Scientists travel to China and study the panda.
16. The few pandas in Western zoos often aged and died without offspring.
17. In 1972 the United States and China developed better relations.
18. Hsing-Hsing and Ling-Ling were China's gift to the Americans.

C. Add a noun or verb to complete the compound subject or predicate of each sentence. Write the sentence.

19. In 1936 European and American hunters ____ and shipped the first live pandas.
20. Europeans and ____ fell in love with the gentle beasts.
21. The pandas' beauty and ____ captured people's hearts.
22. At zoos, millions watched and ____ the pandas.
23. Zoologists could now ____ and examine live pandas.

Apply ◆ Think and Write

From Your Writing ◆ Look back at what you wrote for the Writer's Warm-up. Did you use any compound subjects or predicates? Could your writing be improved by combining the subjects or predicates of some of your sentences?

✎ **Remember**
that compound subjects and verbs help to condense your writing and avoid repetition.

• GETTING •
STARTED

Play "Animal Charades." Make up two brief sentences about animals. Act out the sentences and have others make guesses. Write the correct answers on the board as a single sentence.
Birds fly. Apes eat fruit. = Birds fly, and apes eat fruit.

2 Compound Sentences

So far you have studied simple sentences. A simple sentence expresses one complete thought and has a subject and a predicate.

■ The world's wild land is disappearing rapidly.

A compound sentence consists of two or more simple sentences. In the following compound sentences, pairs of simple sentences are joined by the conjunctions *and*, *or*, and *but*. Notice that a comma is placed before the conjunction.

> Open land disappears, and wild animals lose their habitats.
> Some species have become extinct, but zoos have saved others.
> Zoos breed their own animals, or they buy animals.

Instead of a comma and a conjunction, a semicolon (;) is sometimes used to join two simple sentences.

■ Zoos display animals; zoologists study them.

Do not confuse a compound sentence with a simple sentence that has a compound subject or a compound predicate.

Compound Sentence: Zoos keep animals, and they care for them.
Compound Predicate: Zoologists study and describe animals.

> **Summary** ◆ A **compound sentence** consists of two or more simple sentences.

Guided Practice

Tell whether each sentence is simple or compound.

1. Zoos entertain visitors, but they also educate them.
2. In zoos people learn about the needs of wildlife.
3. The Chinese created a zoo three thousand years ago; they called it the Garden of Intelligence.

Practice

A. Write *simple* or *compound* for each sentence.

4. Animal parks were first called zoological gardens, but later the name was shortened to *zoo*.
5. Zoology is the science of animals; it is a branch of biology.
6. Zoos collect facts about animals and share them with others.
7. The London Zoo has the world's largest zoological library, and it publishes *The Zoological Record* for scientists.
8. A good zoo need not be big, but its animals must be healthy.
9. Sluggish, caged animals were once common; this is changing.
10. Good diets and imaginative display areas keep animals alert.
11. Healthy animals will breed, and offspring will survive.
12. Zoos today produce more and more of their own animals.
13. Extra animals go to other zoos, or they return to the wild.

B. Write *compound sentence*, *compound subject*, or *compound predicate* for each sentence.

14. Some animals are put on islands, and they are isolated.
15. These displays and shows please visitors.
16. Zookeepers are well trained, but they need to use care.
17. Children and adults enjoy the zoo.
18. They take the rides and see the whole zoo from above.

C. Write each pair of sentences as a compound sentence. Use a comma and a conjunction to combine each pair.

19. The Bronx Zoo is in New York City. You would never know it.
20. Here you can find deserts and jungles. You might prefer to see the pampas and the caves.
21. A herd of bison roams its prairie. Wolves howl in the woods.
22. Thunderstorms occur regularly. Only the reptiles get wet.

Apply ◆ Think and Write

Creative Writing ◆ Imagine you are in charge of mammals at a zoo. What might your daily tasks be? Write a paragraph that tells about a zookeeper's day. Try to use some compound sentences.

✎ **Remember**
that you can combine simple sentences with related ideas into compound sentences.

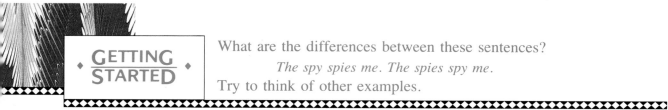

What are the differences between these sentences?
The spy spies me. The spies spy me.
Try to think of other examples.

3 Making Subjects and Verbs Agree

Like nouns and pronouns, verbs have singular and plural forms. The singular form must be used with a singular subject, and the plural form with a plural subject. When the correct verb form is used in a sentence, the subject and verb are said to agree.

Subject-Verb Agreement

1. Singular nouns and the pronouns *he*, *she*, and *it* use a present-tense verb ending in *-s* or *-es*.

The panda lives in China. It searches for bamboo all day.

---

2. Plural nouns and the pronouns *I*, *you*, *we*, and *they* use a present-tense verb not ending in *-s* or *-es*.

Many rare animals live in the Far East. We study them.

The verb *be* has special forms you must learn.

Subject	Forms of *Be*	Examples
1. The pronoun *I*	uses *am* or *was*	I am a zoologist.
2. Singular nouns and *she, he,* and *it*	use *is* or *was*	She is a zoologist.
3. Plural nouns and *we, you,* and *they*	use *are* or *were*	They were zoologists.

Summary ◆ A verb must agree with its subject.

Guided Practice

Tell which verb in parentheses ( ) agrees with the sentence subject.

1. Wild tigers (is, are) endangered animals.
2. The big striped cats (prowls, prowl) Indian forests.
3. In cold Siberia a tiger (grows, grow) a shaggy winter coat.

Practice

A. Write the form of the verb in parentheses ( ) that correctly completes each sentence.

4. A yak (is, are) a wild ox of Asia.
5. It (inhabit, inhabits) the high plateaus of Tibet.
6. These wild beasts (is, are) agile on rocks and ice.
7. The smallest ape, the gibbon, (weighs, weigh) fifteen pounds.
8. Tailless gibbons (ranges, range) over Southeast Asia.
9. Another Asian ape, the orangutan, (is, are) much rarer.
10. Powerful but peaceful, it (live, lives) in Sumatra and Borneo.
11. Many orangutans (reaches, reach) a height of five feet.
12. Tiny musk deer (roams, roam) in some Asian forests.
13. They (stands, stand) less than two feet high.

B. Write a present-tense verb to complete each sentence.

14. Many animals _____ fascinating stories.
15. When frightened, one kind of deer _____ a barking sound.
16. The Himalayan black bear _____ throughout Central Asia.
17. These fierce creatures often _____ cattle, horses, and people.
18. Komodo dragons _____ members of an ancient lizard family.
19. These lizards _____ in caves on Indonesian islands.
20. A large Komodo dragon _____ a length of over ten feet.
21. Do you _____ about Przewalski's horse?
22. Only about thirty of these Asian horses _____ in the wild.
23. They _____ truly wild horses, not descendants of runaways.

C. Use each word below as the subject of a sentence. Use a form of *be* as the verb in each sentence.

24. peacocks   **25.** you   **26.** people   **27.** we   **28.** panda

Apply ◆ Think and Write

Sentence Marathon ◆ Use these words to write as many sentences as possible in ten minutes.

I	they	he	we	you	she
am	is	are	was	were	study
zoologists	a scientist	wildlife	habitats	unique	animals

◆ GETTING STARTED ◆

Play "Coming to an Agreement." Take turns putting nouns together to form compound subjects. One person says two nouns. The next person finishes the sentence "agreeably."

EXAMPLE: *Two eaglets and a condor circle above us.*

4 Using Verbs with Compound Subjects

A compound subject is two or more simple subjects that have the same verb. When the parts of a compound subject are joined by *and*, the verb is always plural.

> People and their activities <u>endanger</u> wildlife.
> Agriculture, industry, and construction <u>limit</u> the available space.

When *or*, *either/or*, or *neither/nor* join the parts of a compound subject, the verb is sometimes singular and sometimes plural. Use a singular verb when both parts of the subject are singular. Use a plural verb when both parts are plural.

> Soil conservation or forest management <u>protects</u> some animals.
> Wildlife refuges or national parks <u>protect</u> animals, too.

When one part of a compound subject is singular and one part is plural, the verb agrees with the nearer subject.

> The federal government or the states <u>provide</u> protected areas.
> Neither laws nor conservation <u>brings</u> back extinct animals.

Summary ◆ Compound subjects joined by *and* use the plural form of the verb. Compound subjects joined by *or*, *either/or*, or *neither/nor* sometimes use the singular form of the verb and sometimes the plural.

Guided Practice

Name the verb that correctly completes each sentence.

1. A plant or animal species (becomes, become) extinct every day.
2. Neither nature nor science (protects, protect) them now.
3. In many cases their beauty and value (was, were) great.
4. Further study or thoughtful measures (is, are) needed.

Practice

A. Write the verb that correctly completes each sentence.

The place and the time (**5.** is, are) the Midwest in 1840. A passenger pigeon flock or horde (**6.** fly, flies) past. For a while neither sun nor clouds (**7.** is, are) visible. Acorns and beechnuts (**8.** makes, make) up the birds' diet. Meanwhile, farmers and loggers gradually (**9.** clears, clear) the hardwood forests. The birds' nesting areas and food supply (**10.** disappear, disappears). This bird and its young (**11.** turns, turn) to eating grain. They are killed as pests. The pigeons' bright feathers and tasty meat (**12.** attracts, attract) hunters, too. The number of pigeons dwindles. However, neither individuals nor the government (**13.** acts, act) to protect them. In the end neither the game preserves nor the zoo (**14.** is, are) able to save the few remaining birds. In 1914 the last passenger pigeon died.

B. Write a present-tense verb to complete each sentence.

The bald eagle and the California condor (**15.** _____) similar problems. Pesticides or other poisons (**16.** _____) the birds' ability to lay healthy eggs. Expanding urban areas or new industry (**17.** _____) the available territory for the birds. Fortunately, private organizations and government agencies (**18.** _____) to save these endangered species. High fines or a jail term (**19.** _____) anyone who harms these birds. At present, Alaska and other states (**20.** _____) bald-eagle eggs to special eagle-breeding labs. Studies and experience (**21.** _____) that eagles bred in labs survive in their new habitats. More bird sanctuaries or a condor-breeding program (**22.** _____) necessary to preserve the California condor.

Apply ◆ Think and Write

Dictionary of Knowledge ◆ Read about the dodo in the Dictionary of Knowledge. Write a paragraph that describes the animal and tells about the causes of its extinction. Use some compound subjects. Check your verbs to make sure they agree with the subjects.

✎ **Remember**
to make sure that verbs agree with compound subjects.

Play "One Word at a Time." One person says the first word of a sentence. Others in turn add a word to build a sentence. The one who adds the word that makes the sentence complete may suggest a word to begin a new sentence.

GETTING STARTED

5 Avoiding Sentence Errors

Remember that a sentence has a subject and a predicate and expresses a complete thought. A group of words that does not express a complete thought is called a sentence fragment. You can correct a fragment by adding words to make it a complete thought.

Fragment: Can help us appreciate animals.
Complete Sentence: Naturalists can help us appreciate animals.

A run-on sentence strings sentences together incorrectly. The following are run-on sentences.

> John James Audubon was a naturalist he painted American birds.
> John James Audubon was a naturalist, he painted American birds.

You can correct a run-on sentence by separating each thought into a sentence of its own. You can also use a comma and a conjunction between the thoughts. A third way you can correct a run-on sentence is to use a compound subject or predicate.

> Audubon was a naturalist. He painted American birds.
> Audubon was a naturalist, and he painted American birds.
> Audubon was a naturalist and painted American birds.

> **Summary** ◆ A **sentence fragment** is a group of words that does not express a complete thought. A **run-on sentence** is two or more sentences not separated by correct punctuation or connecting words. Avoid these errors in your writing.

Guided Practice

Tell whether each group of words is a sentence or a fragment. Add words to each fragment to make a complete sentence.

1. Painted birds in their natural surroundings.
2. Audubon's *Birds of America* was a very important work.
3. These colorful, realistic, and popular paintings.
4. An appreciation of our natural heritage.

Practice

A. Write *sentence* or *fragment* for each group of words. Add words to each fragment to make a sentence. Write the sentence.

5. Some people study animal life.
6. Named plants and animals.
7. Scientists all over the world.
8. Identified hundreds of kinds of animals.
9. This was an important discovery.
10. Not found outside China.
11. Lived in parks and zoos.
12. Still survive today.
13. They came from China.
14. In other parts of the world.
15. We still identify rare animals today.

B. Correct these run-on sentences. Rewrite each run-on sentence as two separate sentences, as a compound sentence, or as a sentence with a compound predicate.

16. Rachel Carson was a biologist she wrote about nature.
17. Carson's popular books described the ocean they also warned people about pesticides.
18. Pesticides kill harmful pests birds and fish also die.
19. Imagine a spring without birds Carson's *Silent Spring* tells of such a sad season.
20. Her arguments were effective, pesticide use was restricted.
21. Jane Goodall is an English zoologist she worked in Africa.
22. Goodall had daily contact with chimps she won their trust.
23. Her careful observations led to many discoveries scientists have had to change their beliefs about apes.
24. Chimpanzees hunt pigs for food they use tools.
25. The social order in a chimpanzee group is fascinating, they groom and care for each other daily.

Apply ◆ Think and Write

Classifying Sentences ◆ Write three complete sentences and three sentence fragments. Read them aloud. Have your listeners identify the fragments and tell how they can be corrected.

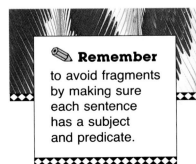

✎ **Remember**
to avoid fragments by making sure each sentence has a subject and predicate.

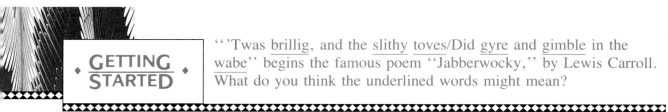

GETTING STARTED

"'Twas brillig, and the slithy toves/Did gyre and gimble in the wabe" begins the famous poem "Jabberwocky," by Lewis Carroll. What do you think the underlined words might mean?

VOCABULARY ◆
Context Clues

When you read, you often come across unfamiliar words. Sometimes the **context**, or the words that surround an unknown word, will give you clues to a word's meaning. Such clues are called **context clues**. The chart below gives examples of different kinds of context clues.

Kinds of Clues	Examples
A *definition* of the new word	The natives told them to be careful of the cassowary. *The cassowary is an Australian bird with powerful legs and sharp claws.*
Further information about the new word's meaning	The mayfly's life span is ephemeral. *It often lives only a few hours or days.*
A *synonym*, or a word with a similar meaning	The chameleon uses its tongue to ensnare, or *trap*, insects.
An *antonym*, or a word with an opposite meaning	The lion is kindred, not *unrelated*, to the jaguar.

Building Your Vocabulary

Tell whether each example gives a definition, further information, a synonym, or an antonym as a context clue for the underlined word.

1. Most cats are carnivores, or meat eaters.
2. Herbivores are animals that eat plants.
3. Humans domesticated, or tamed, many animals for food and as beasts of burden.
4. Goats and sheep were first raised for their palatable, not untasty, meat.
5. Their wool is used to make apparel that is worn by people all over the world.

Practice

A. Write *definition, further information, synonym,* or *antonym* to name the context clue given for each underlined word.

1. Several people from our class made an <u>excursion</u> to a farm the other day; it was a pleasant trip.
2. The farmer was in the fields with a <u>reaper</u>, cutting wheat.
3. The wheat was then run through a <u>thresher</u>, to separate the grain from the straw.
4. The farmer was <u>renowned</u>, or known by many, as a storyteller.
5. His stories were <u>engrossing</u>, not at all boring.
6. He told us about an <u>itinerant</u>, or wandering, cow.
7. The cow was a famous <u>soprano</u>, a high-voiced singer.
8. She sang <u>arias</u>, beautiful melodies, to the farmers she met.
9. Her songs told of <u>verdant</u> pastures of luscious green grass.
10. We found his story <u>implausible</u>—that is, most unlikely!

B. Use the context to determine the meaning of each underlined word. Write the meanings.

11. Many farmers leave half of their land <u>fallow</u>, and they plant the other half.
12. The unplanted fields can regain important <u>nutrients</u>, such as nitrogen and moisture, which help plants to grow.
13. Farmers must <u>replenish</u> the soil every other year, by adding back essential nutrients.
14. Some pastures must be set aside as <u>forage</u>, which livestock can graze upon.
15. <u>Husbandry</u> is a very important industry. It produces the plants and animals that we use for food.

LANGUAGE CORNER • Ancient Roots

A pedometer is a device to measure how far one has walked. *Pedometer* comes from the Latin root *pes-,* meaning "foot," and the Greek root *metron,* meaning "measure."

Can you think of other words that end in *-meter*? What do they mean?

How to Combine Sentences

You can combine two simple sentences that have ideas that go together into one compound sentence. Combining sentences can add variety to your writing and show relationships between ideas.

> **1.** The word *aardvark* means "earth pig."
> **2.** The word *aardwolf* means "earth wolf."

Both sentences give information about the meaning of words. Both sentences are equally important. They can be combined into one compound sentence by adding a comma and the word *and*.

> **3.** The word *aardvark* means "earth pig," and the word *aardwolf* means "earth wolf."

Sometimes two sentences have related but contrasting ideas. The contrasting sentence can be combined with the first sentence by adding a comma and the word *but*, as is shown in example **5** below.

> **4.** The aardvark has a piglike snout. It does not resemble a pig in any other way.
> **5.** The aardvark has a piglike snout, but it does not resemble a pig in any other way.

Two sentences can also be related by offering possible choices. Such sentences can be combined with a comma and the word *or*.

> **6.** Is this a picture of an aardwolf? Is it a spotted hyena?
> **7.** Is this a picture of an aardwolf, or is it a spotted hyena?

The Grammar Game ◆ Create examples! Write pairs of sentences that can be combined with a comma and the words *and, but,* or *or.* Exchange papers and combine each other's sentences.

Working Together

Work with your group to combine the sentences in activities **A** and **B**. Notice that combined sentences add variety to your writing.

A. Combine each pair of sentences below, adding a comma and the word *and*, *but*, or *or*. The group must agree on the choices.

1. Aardvarks and aardwolves are rare animals. They are both native to Africa.
2. Does an aardvark eat meat? Is it a vegetarian?
3. One might think that an aardvark is a pig. It is actually a member of the anteater family.
4. An aardvark hunts at night. Ants and termites are its favorite prey.
5. Aardvarks are not fierce animals. They will attack if necessary.

B. Find sentences to combine in the paragraph below. Remember to think about how ideas in the sentences could go together. Then write the new paragraph.

   Is the aardwolf a typical hyena? Is it different from other hyenas? The aardwolf is different in a few ways. Most hyenas have powerful jaws and strong teeth. The aardwolf's teeth are small and weak. Other hyenas have four toes on each foot. The aardwolf has five toes on its front feet and four on its hind feet.

WRITERS' CORNER • Stringy Sentences

Be careful not to string together too many sentences with conjunctions. Stringy sentences can be hard to read and understand.

The word *aard* is Dutch, and it means "earth," and aardvarks and aardwolves both live in the ground, and both animals eat insects, but neither animal is found in the United States.

Can you improve this sentence by forming several shorter ones? Read what you wrote for the Writer's Warm-up. Did you use any stringy sentences? If you did, can you improve them, too?

SURPRISE!
painting by Henri Rousseau
Reproduced by courtesy of the Trustees,
The National Gallery, London.

UNIT EIGHT

USING LANGUAGE
TO
CLASSIFY

=== **PART TWO** ===

Literature *Project Panda Watch* by Miriam Schlein
A Reason for Writing Classifying

CREATIVE
Writing

FINE ARTS ◆ The painting at the left is called "Surprise!"
Is the tiger surprised, or is the tiger about to surprise
something else? Write a story called "Surprise." Tell what
the surprise is and who is surprised.

CRITICAL THINKING ◆
A Strategy for Classifying

A VENN DIAGRAM

Classifying is sorting things into groups, putting together things that belong together. One way to classify is to compare and contrast, or explain how things are alike and different.

After this lesson you will read part of *Project Panda Watch*. In it the author compares and contrasts pandas with other animals. Later you will write to compare and contrast.

In this part of *Project Panda Watch*, we learn how scientists compared and contrasted the giant panda and the red panda.

> Certainly Père David's animal [the giant panda] and the red panda did not *look* alike. One was large and bearlike, the other small and raccoonlike. But they did have other important things in common. Their skulls were both short-muzzled and similar in shape. . . . They both ate bamboo.

How were the giant panda and the red panda alike? How were they different? Would you guess that the giant panda and red panda belong to the same family of animals? Why or why not?

Learning the Strategy

Considering likenesses and differences is often important. For example, do you know the brother or sister of a friend? What could be wrong with assuming that the brother or sister is just like your friend? Suppose you have been winning short sprints for your track team. Now you want to enter some longer races. Would your experience in sprinting help you or hinder you? Why? Suppose you attended a live concert of your favorite musical group. You are telling a friend about it. How was the concert like and different from the two of you listening to tapes together?

A Venn diagram can help you sort out likenesses and differences. Draw two overlapping circles. Write the differences between two items on the outsides. Write the likenesses in the center. The example below is about a live concert and a tape recording. What ideas would you add?

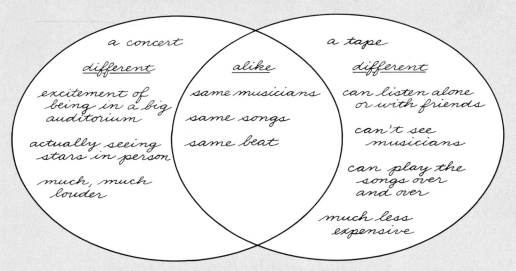

a concert

different

excitement of being in a big auditorium

actually seeing stars in person

much, much louder

alike

same musicians

same songs

same beat

a tape

different

can listen alone or with friends

can't see musicians

can play the songs over and over

much less expensive

 Using the Strategy

A. Do you remember first grade? What were you like then? What are you like now? What has changed? What is still the same? Make a Venn diagram to show likenesses and differences between you in first grade and you today.

B. Giant pandas are those lovable black and white animals from China sometimes seen in zoos. Some scientists believe pandas are related to bears. Others think they are not. Use what you already know about pandas and bears to compare them in a Venn diagram. Then read *Project Panda Watch* to find out more about the scientific puzzle of classifying pandas.

 Applying the Strategy

♦ Besides a Venn diagram, what other ways could you use to sort out and write down likenesses and differences?

♦ Describe one time in the past week when you noticed how two things were alike or different, and why you noticed.

YOU BE THE SCIENTIST

from **PROJECT PANDA WATCH**

by MIRIAM SCHLEIN

illustrated by Robert Shetterly

High in the Himalayas of China lives a gentle animal species called the giant panda. The pandas live in forests, where bamboo is their main source of food. For a long time, when bamboo was plentiful, pandas thrived in China. Then bamboo became scarce, and many pandas died. Without enough bamboo to eat, the giant pandas are threatened with extinction. Only about 1,000 pandas are still alive.

Worldwide concern for the pandas' problem led China and the World Wildlife Fund to start a program called Project Panda Watch. In 1980, Chinese scientists invited George Schaller, an animal expert from the Bronx Zoo in New York, to join the first scientific team ever to study pandas in the wild. Such studies are needed, for little is known about these unusual animals. More than a hundred years after the pandas' discovery by Père David, scientists are working to protect them and help them survive.

The Panda was not always known by the name "panda."

The Chinese had always thought it was a kind of bear. Sometimes they called it the clawed bear or the bamboo bear. Other names for it were the harlequin bear, the speckled bear, and the cat-bear. Most often, it was called "bei-shung"—the white bear.

Is the panda a kind of bear?

In size and shape, it looks a lot like a bear. It climbs trees like a bear. And it moves and sits in a bearlike way. There is another way it resembles a bear. Its young are unusually small at birth as compared to the size of an adult. A mother grizzly bear may weigh 500 pounds (226 kilograms). Her newborn cub weighs about a pound (less than half a kilogram).

When Père David discovered the panda in 1879, he also thought it was some kind of bear. Since the person who discovers a new species has the honor of naming it, Père David gave it the name of *Ursus melanoleucus.* This means, in Latin, "black and white bear."

Excited by his discovery, he sent a specimen of the animal—a skin and skeleton—to his friend, Professor Alphonse Milne-Edwards, in Paris. There, at the natural history museum, the new specimen was eagerly examined. Soon they saw things that made them disagree with Père David. They did not think the animal was a bear.

When scientists try to decide which animals are in the same "family" and are most closely related to each other, they don't just go by what the animal looks like, or by its behavior. There are other things they consider more basic. A similarity in the bone structure is considered important, especially foot and leg bones. Teeth and skull are also important. (Thus, for example, the hippo is considered more closely related to the giraffe than it is to the rhino, even though a hippo and rhino *look* more alike.)

Examining the remains of the panda, this is what Milne-Edwards and the others saw:

The skull did not resemble that of a bear. It was different in shape; shorter in the muzzle, and also heavier and more solid than a bear skull.

The jaws and teeth were not like those of a bear, either. Nor were the feet and legs. The skeleton in general was not really bearlike.

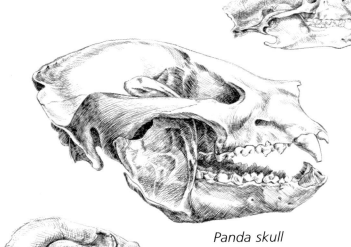

Bear skull

Panda skull

Red panda skull

Then, examining the foot and leg bones more carefully, they saw the most telling feature of all—the extension of the wristbone, creating the unusual sixth claw, or "panda's thumb."

No bear has anything like that. But they knew another animal that did; it was called the red panda. It was a small animal with reddish fur, a bushy, ringed tail and a foxlike white face. It was in the raccoon family. Its scientific name was *Ailurus fulgens,* meaning "fire-colored cat."

Certainly Père David's animal and the red panda did not *look* alike. One was large and bearlike, the other small and raccoonlike. But they did have other important things in common. Their skulls were both short-muzzled and similar in shape. Their jaws and teeth were also quite similar. They were alike in another curious way: they both ate bamboo. (Panda is a Nepalese word meaning "bamboo-eater.")

As the scientists examined Père David's new specimen, they became more and more convinced that these two animals were closely related. If so, since the red panda was in the raccoon family, they felt the newly discovered animal must also be in the raccoon family. It was not a bear at all!

This meant it could not keep the name *Ursus* (bear) given to it by Père David. Its name was changed to *Ailuropoda melanoleucus*—meaning "black and white catfoot."

As time went on, the larger panda was known as the Great Panda, and the small, fire-colored one called the Lesser Panda. We now call the large one the Giant Panda.

But the change in name did not settle the argument. Through the years, many scientists have felt that Père David *was* right, and that the giant panda does belong in the bear family. In their view, the fact that both kinds of pandas have the "panda's thumb" doesn't prove the giant panda is in the raccoon family, or even that the two animals are closely related. They feel that the red panda and the giant panda may simply have developed this unusual feature independently.

They feel the similarity in the two animals' teeth doesn't prove a close relationship, either. It is possible, they say, that both animals developed the same type of teeth because they both eat the same diet—bamboo.

They feel the two pandas are not in the same family, but belong in two different families: the giant panda in the bear family, and the lesser panda in the raccoon family.

New lab techniques developed in recent years have provided evidence for both sides of the panda argument. Blood can now be analyzed. The blood of the giant panda has been found to be more like bear blood than red panda blood.

That doesn't prove anything, say the people who believe the giant panda is a member of the raccoon family, because they have another new fact on *their* side. The giant panda has the same number of chromosomes as the raccoon (42). Different kinds of bears have been shown to have either 56 or 74 chromosomes.

Chromosomes are that part of the cell that carry the genes, which determine an animal's qualities. So this would seem to be an important point. We also know the stomach, liver and intestines of the giant panda are more like that of a raccoon than that of a bear.

So, although the giant panda was discovered more than 100 years ago, the argument about it is still going on:

Is the giant a super-huge raccoon-type animal? Or is it a rather unusual bear-type animal?

George Schaller and many Chinese scientists do not agree with either side. They have a different point of view altogether. A giant panda is not a raccoon, they say. And it is not a bear. They feel the panda is a sufficiently different kind of animal to be in a family of its own. "A panda is a panda," says George Schaller.

The red panda is in the raccoon family.

What do *you* think? *You* be the scientist.
Think of all the important points. List
them. Maybe it would help you to do some
extra reading about bears and about raccoons.
You may also want to read a little about
animal classification. (This is our system of
placing animals in different "families" and
other groupings.) Then try to come to your
own conclusion.

Do you think the panda belongs in the
bear family, or in the raccoon family? Or do
you think the giant panda is an animal special
enough to be in a family of its own?

Library Link ♦ *To learn more about the panda, read Miriam
Schlein's* Project Panda Watch. *You may enjoy other scientific
books by her, too.*

 Reader's Response

Would you like to read scientific studies of other animals? Explain.

PROJECT
PANDA WATCH

 Responding to Literature

1. If you had a panda, what would you name it? Where would you keep it? What would you feed it?

2. The panda is a rare and precious animal. Design a sweatshirt with a panda message. Compose a slogan encouraging preservation and care for this popular animal.

3. Père David discovered the panda in 1879. Make up a new animal as your ''discovery.'' Draw a picture of your animal and write its name on the drawing. Tell classmates where you discovered your animal. Tell about its habits. Finally, tell what animal family it belongs to and why.

 Writing to Learn

Think and Decide ♦ Use the Venn diagram below to help you organize information on the likenesses and differences between the panda and the raccoon.

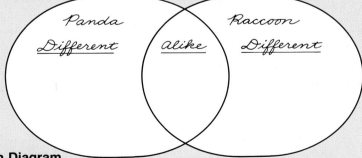

Venn Diagram

Write ♦ Is the panda a separate species? Can raccoons claim the panda as a cousin? Put your ideas in writing and support your conviction with evidence.

Should there be commercials on television? Think about that question. Would you be <u>for</u> or <u>against</u> commercials? Take turns answering the question.

SPEAKING and LISTENING ♦
Group Discussions

Mr. García's class is studying the local bird population. They want to find out which varieties of birds inhabit their area and how numerous each kind is. One species has created problems in the community. In your class do you sometimes talk about problems in your community? Do you talk about the community's good news?

Holding a group discussion is an excellent way to share ideas and information and to solve problems. A discussion is more than just talking. It is talking together with a *purpose* in mind. Here are guidelines that will help you achieve your purpose when you hold a group discussion.

	Discussion Guidelines
Speaking	1. Know the purpose of the discussion. Know what needs to be decided or accomplished. 2. Help the group stick to the purpose of the discussion without getting sidetracked. 3. If your discussion involves facts, get the facts beforehand. Be prepared by having all the information you need. 4. Contribute to the discussion, but do not talk too much. 5. Use your voice, gestures, and facial expressions to communicate enthusiasm and feeling.
Being an Active Listener	1. Listen carefully to the comments of others. 2. Do not interrupt a speaker. 3. If you disagree with what is said, do not make faces or shake your head. Instead, politely explain why you disagree.

Summary ♦ A **group discussion** provides an opportunity to exchange ideas, information, and opinions. The purpose of a discussion is often to explore ways of solving a problem.

Guided Practice

Tell whether each of these statements agrees with the discussion guidelines. Explain why or why not.

1. **BRAD:** Let's put a bird-feeding station at the lake. Then we can study the birds more easily.
2. **VERA:** That's a ridiculous idea! Who wants to feed those birds?
3. **ROB:** I think Brad's idea makes a lot of sense. We have to come up with a way to get a count of the birds.
4. **JOHN:** Say, speaking of birds, did you ever see that scary Hitchcock movie about birds?
5. **ANITA:** Let's stick to the topic, John. If we make a feeder, we can make a graph to record what kinds of birds and how many of each kind visit it.

Practice

A. Decide if each example below agrees with the discussion guidelines. Write *agrees* or *disagrees* for each example. Then write a sentence to explain your answer.

6. I only like to talk about giant condors. I mention them every chance I get.
7. Nancy's point about sharing responsibility for solving problems in wildlife conservation makes sense to me.
8. I would never agree with your opinion, Ana. Why should I back down? You'd better agree with me.
9. After listening to Tanya, I thought about this issue in a new way, but I disagree with her on one point. . . .
10. Your idea was terrible. Why did you say that?

B. Have a group discussion with four or five of your classmates about a topic that interests you. Follow the guidelines in this lesson. Participate as both a speaker and a listener.

Apply ◆ Think and Write

Discussion Topics ◆ Think of a problem or topic for your class to discuss. Write it down. Then write several sentences stating what you would say about the topic.

✎ **Remember**
that active speakers and listeners get the most from a discussion.

WRITING ◆
A Paragraph That Compares

How is a panda like a bear? How is a panda like a raccoon? Those are the kinds of comparisons that scientists and science writers are concerned with. They look for similarities, or likenesses, as they decide how to classify scientific information. Because comparisons form the basis for classifying information, they are a tool used often by all writers.

Comparisons can enrich and clarify all the writing that you do. Study the example paragraph below. Its detail sentences are from *Project Panda Watch*.

Topic Sentence

Details That Give Likenesses

> A panda is like a bear in several important ways. In size and shape, it looks a lot like a bear. It climbs trees like a bear, and it moves and sits in a bearlike way. There is another way it resembles a bear. Its young are unusually small at birth as compared to the size of an adult. A mother grizzly bear may weigh 500 pounds (226 kilograms). Her newborn cub weighs about a pound (less than half a kilogram).

Summary   A **paragraph of comparison** tells how things are alike. It often begins with a topic sentence.

1 Prewriting

First select a topic—two things you will compare. Then gather ideas about your topic.

Choose Your Topic ♦ Start by choosing a general category that interests you, such as sports, animals, weather, airplanes, or games. Then find two specific items that fit in that category. Choose the pair that you like best.

Think About It	Talk About It
List several pairs in your category. You might compare two kinds of airplanes, like gliders and jets. Look for a pair people think of as different but that have interesting likenesses you can point out.	You can try out possible categories and pairs by reading your lists to classmates. Which items seem to catch their interest? Which ones make them stop to think? Which ones cause them to ask a question? Choose the topic that causes interest.

Topic Ideas

Weather
1. *snow and rain*
2. *different clouds*
3. *hurricanes and tornadoes*
4. *old and new weather warnings*
5. *sleet and hail*
6. *sun and haze*
7. *fog and smog*

Choose Your Strategy ♦ The two strategies below can help you gather supporting details for your comparison article. Read both. Then use the idea you think will work best for you.

PREWRITING IDEAS

CHOICE ONE

A Venn Diagram

Find out facts about your two items. Then use a Venn diagram to group likenesses and separate them from differences. Draw two overlapping circles. Write the differences on the outsides. Write the likenesses in the center. You will base your comparison article on the likenesses.

Model

tornadoes *different* last a few hours start on land narrow path

alike they travel seasonal, spinning violent, damaging

hurricanes *different* can last days tropical seas miles wide

CHOICE TWO

A Fact Chart

Find out facts about your two items. On a fact chart, list facts in several categories. When the chart is complete, analyze it for likenesses. Circle facts that are the same or similar for both items. Those facts will be the basis of your comparison article.

Model

	Hurricanes	Tornadoes
Size	up to 500 miles	100–200 yards
Speed	over 75 mph	very strong
Path	travel many miles	travel far
Place	start in tropics	start on land
Shape	round, spinning	spinning

2 Writing

Now begin to write your comparison article. You might begin with a question or a statement like one of these.

- How is a _____ like a _____?
- A _____ and a _____ share many surprising likenesses.

Now write about the likenesses that appear in the center of your Venn diagram or that are circled on your fact chart. Here is a plan for organizing your article. Write as many paragraphs as you like between the introduction and the conclusion.

Sample First Draft ◆

How are a hurricane and a tornado alike?
They share a number of charatistics.
Tornadoes form over land each spring.
Hurricanes start in summer in hot areas of
the Atlantic ocean. Both tornadoes and
hurricanes are seasonal storms.
      Each storm is round and hollow with high
winds at the outside. The center, called the
Eye, is clear and calm.
      Both hurricanes and tornadoes have
strong winds. Hurricane winds can reach up
to one hundred fifty miles per hour. Tornado
winds can reach six hundred.
Both storms travel. A hurricane can travel
thousands of miles, a tornado up to one
hundred. A hurricane can be five hundred
miles wide, but a tornado is much smaller.
      The most important way hurricanes and
tornadoes are alike is that they can kill. Take
both kinds of storms seriously!

Introduction   Name the two items.   Say they are alike.
Paragraph 2   Tell likenesses in   one category.
Paragraph 3   Tell likenesses in   another category.
Conclusion   Sum up how th_   items are alik_

3 Revising

Does your comparison article say what you wanted it to say?
This idea may help you revise to clarify meaning.

REVISING IDEA

FIRST   Read to Yourself

As you read, review your purpose. Did
you write an article that compares two
things? Consider your audience. Will
your classmates understand and enjoy
your article? Circle any confusing words
or phrases you may want to change.

Focus: Have you clearly described the likenesses of two items? Have
you omitted details about their differences?

THEN   Share with a Partner

Ask a partner to be your first
audience. These guidelines may help
you work together on your comparison
article.

The Writer

Guidelines: Ask your partner to
read your article silently and to
respond.

Sample questions
- Are there any details that don't
  belong?
- **Focus question:** Can you think
  of other ways these items are
  alike?

The Writer's Partner

Guidelines: Read carefully. Make
comments that are honest but
polite.

Sample responses:
- You might take out this detail
  about differences.
- Another way they are alike
  is _____.

WRITING PROCESS: Article That Compares

Revising Model ◆ This comparison article is being revised.

Revising Marks

cross out   ——

add   ∧

move   ⟋

How are a hurricane and a tornado alike? They share a number of charatistics.

~~Tornadoes form over land each spring.~~ ~~Hurricanes~~ start in summer in hot areas of the Atlantic ocean. Both tornadoes and hurricanes are seasonal storms.

tropical

Each storm is ~~round and hollow~~ with high winds at the outside. The center, called the Eye, is clear and calm.

shaped like a donut

Both hurricanes and tornadoes have strong winds. Hurricane winds can reach up to one hundred fifty miles per hour. Tornado winds can reach six hundred. Both storms travel. A hurricane can travel thousands of miles, a tornado up to one hundred. ~~A hurricane can be five hundred miles wide, but a tornado is much smaller.~~

and

The most important way hurricanes and tornadoes are alike is that they can kill. Take both kinds of storms seriously!

Tropical is a more precise word than *hot*.

The writer's partner suggested moving the topic sentence up.

The writer decided this comparison made the meaning clearer.

The writer combined sentences to form a compound sentence.

Details about differences do not belong in a comparison.

Read the article with the writer's changes. Then revise your own comparison article.

Grammar Check ◆ Sometimes you can combine choppy sentences to form compound sentences.

Word Choice ◆ A thesaurus can help you find precise words.

Revising Checklist

☐ **Purpose:** Did I write an article that compares two things?

☐ **Audience:** Will my classmates understand and enjoy my article?

☐ **Focus:** Did I clea[...] describe likenes[...] Did I omit det[...] about differe[...]

4 Proofreading

Check your comparison article for surface errors. Neat, correct writing is easier to read and understand.

Proofreading Model ♦ Here is the article about hurricanes and tornadoes. Proofreading changes have been added in red.

How are a hurricane and a tornado alike? They share a number of ~~charatistics~~ *characteristics*.

¶ Tornadoes form over land each spring. Hurricanes start in summer in hot areas of the Atlantic ocean. Both tornadoes and hurricanes are seasonal storms.

Each storm is ~~round and hollow~~ *shaped like a donut* with high winds at the outside. The center, called the eye, is clear and calm.

Both hurricanes and tornadoes have strong winds. Hurricane winds can reach up to one hundred fifty miles per hour. *and* Tornado winds can reach six hundred.

¶ Both storms travel. A hurricane can travel thousands of miles, a tornado up to one hundred. ~~A hurricane can be five hundred miles wide, but a tornado is much smaller.~~

The most important way hurricanes and tornadoes are alike is that they can kill. Take both kinds of storms seriously!

Proofreading Checklist

- ☐ Did I spell words correctly?
- ☐ Did I indent paragraphs?
- ☐ Did I use capital letters correctly?
- ☐ Did I use correct marks at the end of sentences?
- ☐ Did I use my best handwriting?

PROOFREADING IDEA

Handwriting Check

Make sure that your letters are clearly formed. For example, check to see that your *a*'s do not look like *o*'s. Check that your *n*'s do not look like *m*'s. Poorly formed letters can make your writing difficult to read.

Now proofread your comparison article and make a neat copy.

5 Publishing

Here are two ways to share your article with classmates.

How are a hurricane and a tornado alike? They share a number of characteristics.

Both tornadoes and hurricanes are seasonal storms. Tornadoes form over land each spring. Hurricanes start in summer in tropical areas of the Atlantic Ocean.

Each storm is shaped like a donut with high winds at the outside. The center, called the eye, is clear and calm.

Both hurricanes and tornadoes have strong winds. Hurricane winds can reach up to one hundred fifty miles per hour, and tornado winds can reach six hundred miles per hour.

Both storms travel. A hurricane can travel thousands of miles, a tornado up to a hundred miles.

The most important way hurricanes and tornadoes are alike is that they can kill. Take both kinds of storms seriously!

PUBLISHING IDEAS

Share Aloud	Share in Writing
Have a "team read-around." Form a small group and read your comparison articles aloud. Ask your listeners to name one more likeness between your two items. If they can, they score a point!	With your classmates, make a class magazine of articles. Include a cover, a table of contents, an index, and illustrations. Share the magazine with another class at your grade level. Include a few blank pages for readers' comments.

CURRICULUM
◆CONNECTION◆

Writing Across the Curriculum

Mathematics

In this unit you wrote an article comparing two things—that is, you told how two different things are alike. Comparing is also an important skill in mathematics, as is contrasting—telling how things are different.

Writing to Learn

Think and Compare ◆ Imagine that your class earns money to buy food for wild birds. You want to spend the money as wisely as possible. Look at the picture below. Make a Venn diagram to compare and contrast the two brands of birdseed.

Venn Diagram

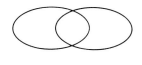

Write ◆ Explain which brand you would choose and why. Explain any mathematical computations you made that helped you choose.

Writing in Your Journal

In the Writer's Warm-up you wrote about conservation. Now look back through the unit to review what you learned about wildlife. For example, what did you learn about extinct birds? In your journal, record the most interesting thing you learned in this unit and tell why you find it interesting.

BOOKS TO ENJOY

Read More About it

Zoos of the World *by Robert Halmi*

Keeping animals comfortable, happy, and healthy should be the goal of every zoo. This book highlights some creative ways in which zookeepers achieve that goal. The author also stresses the important educational and scientific roles of zoos in today's world.

Misty of Chincoteague
by Marguerite Henry

As part of a conservation effort, some of the wild ponies of Chincoteague Island are rounded up each spring and moved. This classic tale is about the adventures of the two children who adopt one of the ponies.

Some Lose Their Way *by Frederick J. Lipp*

Vanessa and David, two young naturalists, study the effects of pollution on birds in their riverside community. Their work leads to a deeper awareness of both their environment and their emotions.

Book Report Idea Acrostic Report

An acrostic is a composition or arrangement of words or sentences in which the first letter in each line taken in order spells a word or name. Try making an acrostic book report that spells out the title of a book you've read and enjoyed recently.

> H obbits are small, good-natured creatures with furry feet.
> O f course, the story has excitement and humor, too.
> B ilbo Baggins finds a magic ring that makes him invisible.
> B e prepared for a real adventure.
>
> I n the end you will want to visit Middle-earth.
> T ry *The Hobbit* for one of the best fantasies ever!

Sentences *pages 402–411*

A. Write the compound subject or the compound predicate in each of the following sentences.

1. Ms. Emerson and our class went to see the giant pandas at the zoo.
2. The mother panda held the baby in her arms and cuddled it.
3. The father sat to one side and watched.
4. Chen and Carmen presented a report on pandas to the class.
5. Both the black-and-white species and the reddish-brown species are called pandas.
6. The two kinds of pandas belong to different animal families and are of different sizes.
7. The giant panda has a white body with black legs and is considered a bear.
8. The red panda is much smaller and belongs to the raccoon family.
9. The red panda weighs six to twelve pounds and is about two feet long.
10. The giant panda feeds mostly on bamboo shoots but also eats other plants and fish.
11. The giant panda and the red panda live in the bamboo forests of Asia.

B. Write *simple* or *compound* for each sentence.

12. Annie, Perry, and their father went fishing.
13. Their father rented a rowboat, and they all got in.
14. They rowed away from the shore and dropped their fishing lines.
15. Annie caught four trout, but Perry didn't have any luck.
16. Their father took the trout and put them in a basket.
17. After a while they rowed back to the shore and put the basket of fish in their car.
18. At home Annie put the fish in the refrigerator, and all three scrubbed their hands clean.
19. Later their mother scaled the fish.
20. Their father breaded and fried them.

C. Write the verb that correctly completes each sentence.

21. This pear (is, are) rotten.
22. Jane Stern or her daughter (has, have) the tickets for the play.
23. A goat and a sheep (grazes, graze) in the meadow.
24. Many fruits (provides, provide) vitamins.
25. Neither Joan nor the Rafferty twins (knows, know) the answer.
26. Lucy Stone (was, were) a great leader of women.
27. The cat and her kittens (romps, romp) in the yard.
28. Every afternoon, Pancho, Frank, and I (walks, walk) home together.

D. Add words to each fragment to make a sentence. Rewrite each run-on sentence as a compound sentence.

29. My father raises cattle my uncle raises pigs.
30. Running down the street.
31. The kitten with the black paws.
32. The squirrel ran up a tree the dog barked at it from below.
33. While going to the supermarket.
34. Celia isn't coming to the party my brother is.
35. Backing the car into the garage.
36. The man wearing the sweatshirt and dirty tennis shoes.
37. The work crew loaded the truck they drove it to the warehouse.
38. Peggy likes potato salad I hate it.
39. The largest balloon in the world.
40. There is a bat in the living room we can't get rid of it.

Context Clues   *pages 412–413*

E. Write *definition, further information, synonym,* or *antonym* to tell which kind of context clue is given for each underlined word.

41. Susan B. Anthony, a <u>feminist</u>, was a staunch defender of women's rights.
42. Mr. Okuma is an <u>ichthyologist</u>, a scientist who studies fish.
43. Mary Turner is a <u>proficient</u>, or skillful, carpenter.
44. The dogs ate <u>voraciously</u>, not moderately.
45. Abraham Lincoln was renowned for his <u>probity</u>, his honesty.

46. Timmie is so <u>loquacious</u> that other people can't get a word in edgewise.
47. Aunt Mae has had a <u>beneficent</u>, not an evil, influence on you.
48. A seaside walk is <u>restorative</u>, in that it refreshes mind and body.
49. Did you get sufficient <u>compensation</u>, or monetary reward, for your work?
50. Ms. Lopez can be called a <u>populist</u>, a believer in the rights of the common people.
51. The heavy meal gave us such a feeling of <u>lassitude</u> that we found it hard to go on with our work.
52. The painting Maria found was <u>authentic</u>, not fake.

Compare and Contrast   *pages 428–431*

F. Compare the items in each pair. List at least two ways in which they are similar to each other.

53. dogs and wolves
54. a scientist and a teacher
55. ice cream and cake
56. an explorer and an astronaut
57. pigs and cattle
58. two of your friends

G. Contrast each pair of items below. List at least two ways in which each is different from the other.

59. cats and rabbits
60. chickens and ducks
61. strawberry pie and beef stew
62. a writer and an actor
63. spring and fall
64. dawn and dusk

CUMULATIVE REVIEW

Units 1 and 8: Sentences *pages 4–15, 402–411*

A. Write the sentences, using capital letters and correct end punctuation. After each sentence write *declarative, interrogative, imperative,* or *exclamatory.*

1. what a clever person you are
2. we all like your jokes
3. did you think of that witty line all by yourself
4. tell me that funny story again
5. are you thinking of becoming a professional comedian
6. perhaps Ms. Hawkins can give you some good tips
7. how funny she is
8. talk to her
9. she has appeared on many television comedy shows
10. you need help in polishing your performance

B. Write the subject of each of the following sentences.

11. Come with me to the ball park.
12. Will Stan attend the game?
13. Joe Wheeler hit a home run.
14. Hand me that bag of popcorn.
15. Did Annie see that double play?
16. We are going to Theo's house after the game.
17. Meet me there at six.
18. Is Carlos going with you?

C. Write the compound subject or predicate in each sentence.

19. Sue and Annie are studying photography.
20. They take pictures and develop the film themselves.
21. Sue's black-and-white photographs and Annie's color slides are excellent.
22. Sue has participated in exhibits and has won several awards.
23. Annie is not as serious about photography and simply enjoys snapping pictures.
24. She takes her camera along on trips and photographs the scenery.
25. Hills and lakes are among her favorite subjects.
26. Sue plans on a professional career and works hard at her art.
27. Her family and her friends admire her work.

D. Write the verb that correctly completes each sentence.

28. The Changs (owns, own) a variety of pets.
29. One of their cats (has, have) a black body and white paws.
30. Two cats and a dog (sleeps, sleep) in the kitchen.
31. Several of the pets (lives, live) in the cellar.
32. The rabbit and the guinea pig (is, are) the best of friends.
33. Neither Mrs. Chang nor her husband (minds, mind) the expense.
34. All of the family members (loves, love) animals.

Unit 2: Nouns   *pages 62–65, 68–71*

E. Write each noun below. Then write whether it is a common noun or a proper noun.

35. Amelia Earhart was among our greatest aviators.
36. This pilot was the first woman to fly across the Atlantic Ocean.
37. Earhart received the Distinguished Flying Cross.
38. This American was born in Kansas.
39. After she dropped out of college, she worked in California, earning money for flying lessons.
40. She flew from Newfoundland to Ireland.
41. Her biggest hope was to fly around the world.
42. The plane she flew disappeared over the Pacific Ocean.
43. No trace of her was ever found.
44. Many people remember Amelia Earhart and her achievements.

F. Write the plural form of each noun.

45. ranch	49. king	53. deer
46. lion	50. goose	54. potato
47. mouse	51. wife	
48. child	52. hobby	

G. Write the possessive form of each noun. Then write whether each noun is singular or plural.

55. nets	59. torpedo	63. board
56. Charles	60. robin	64. sisters
57. elks	61. colony	
58. pictures	62. women	

Unit 3: Verbs   *pages 120–125*

H. Write each sentence. Underline the helping verbs once and the main verbs twice.

65. Teresa Pérez will enter medical school next year.
66. She has won a three-year scholarship.
67. Teresa might specialize in pediatrics.
68. She will decide in a year or so.
69. Her college teachers have praised her work.
70. She is considered an outstanding student.
71. Her relatives have taken great pride in her achievements.
72. They are telling everyone about her scholarship.

I. Write the direct object in each of the following sentences.

73. The seal balanced the ball on its nose.
74. I carried the newspaper under one arm.
75. Sam is reading a book about Japan.
76. The hungry squirrel climbed the oak tree.
77. Jan wrote a letter to her cousin.
78. At the county fair Harry won a stuffed doll.
79. The little old man shook his finger in the waiter's face.
80. Martha threw the ball to me.

J. Write the past and the future tense of each verb. Use *will* with the future tense.

81. stop	83. measure
82. drag	84. taste

Unit 4: Pronouns *pages 180–189, 208–209*

K. Write each sentence. Use the correct pronoun or contraction in parentheses ( ).

85. (Our, Ours) class is holding a hobby show.
86. The hand puppets and the miniature playhouse are (her, hers).
87. (My, Mine) stamp album contains several rare and valuable stamps.
88. Sam showed us (her, hers) table.
89. (Its, It's) a fine skill.
90. (Your, You're) collection of ceramic eggs is exquisite.
91. The Ramos sisters exhibited (their, they're) collection of Mexican pottery.
92. (Their, They're) very proud of its beauty and variety.

L. Write each sentence. Use the correct pronoun in parentheses.

93. The relay runners were (they, them).
94. The winner of the gold medal for the long jump was (she, her).
95. The runner-up was (he, him).
96. The judge of the events was (I, me).

M. Write each sentence. Add commas where needed.

97. Yes my sister wrote this book.
98. You can find her name in the biographical dictionary under Cohen Susan.
99. Did you enjoy reading it Sandy?
100. I think Patricia that my sister is a fine writer.

101. Oh were you surprised by the ending?
102. Did you Domingo expect a different ending?
103. Well I'm glad that you were not disappointed.
104. Sandy would you pass the book along to Tom?
105. Yes I'm sure he will enjoy it as much as you did.
106. Be patient Lonato and Sandy will give you the book.

Unit 5: Adjectives *pages 242–245*

N. Write each sentence. Underline the predicate adjective.

107. After weeks of training, Mike was confident.
108. He felt sure about his skill in archery.
109. His grip on the bow was firm.
110. The target appeared distant.
111. The arrow was swift in its flight.
112. The crowd seemed enthusiastic at Mike's perfect shot.
113. The first-prize gold medal looked beautiful.
114. Mike was proud of his victory.

O. Write each sentence. Underline each demonstrative adjective.

115. Do you see that jet plane?
116. It always takes off at this time.
117. Those people are waiting to travel to Washington.
118. First-class passengers sit in these seats up front.

Unit 6: Adverbs *pages 290–297*

P. Write the word each underlined adverb describes. Then write whether the word is a verb, an adjective, or an adverb.

119. Our trip to Hong Kong and Kowloon was <u>extremely</u> exciting.

120. The people were <u>really</u> friendly.

121. Pedicabs and other vehicles moved <u>slowly</u> down the streets.

122. Our taxicab reached the hotel <u>rather</u> quickly.

123. We <u>truly</u> enjoyed a boat tour of Hong Kong and Kowloon.

124. A trip to a local museum was <u>quite</u> fascinating.

125. By the end of two weeks, though, we could <u>hardly</u> wait to return to our home.

Q. Write the word in parentheses ( ) that correctly completes each sentence.

126. The play was drawing (swift, swiftly) to a close.

127. The hero and heroine were (happy, happily) and smiling.

128. Behind them the frustrated villain glared (angry, angrily).

129. He shook his fist and strode (brisk, briskly) off the stage.

130. The heroine appeared (radiant, radiantly).

131. The hero clasped her (tight, tightly) in his arms.

132. The audience applauded (enthusiastic, enthusiastically).

133. The performers thought the applause was (delightful, delightfully).

Unit 7: Prepositions and Conjunctions *pages 346–355*

R. Write each prepositional phrase. Underline the preposition once and the object of the preposition twice.

134. The dog with the crooked tail howled mournfully.

135. Cara had accidentally stepped on its foot.

136. It looked at her accusingly.

137. She patted it on its head.

S. Write each prepositional phrase. Write *adjective* if it describes a noun. Write *adverb* if it describes a verb, an adjective, or an adverb.

138. The fans cheered the rock group on the stage.

139. The players left during the intermission.

140. The audience rose from their seats.

141. A girl in the lobby was selling souvenir programs.

142. The concert resumed after twenty minutes.

143. The electric guitarist strummed on her instrument.

T. Write each sentence. Underline each conjunction.

144. Mr. Johnson and Mrs. Johnson like to square dance.

145. Their dancing is untrained but fun.

146. They go to dances on Friday night or Saturday night.

147. They dance and socialize with the other dancers.

LANGUAGE PUZZLERS

Unit 8 Challenge

Fragmented Clues

Play this game of trivia by adding words to make each fragment a sentence. Each pair of fragments is about one person, group, or thing.

1. A crown with spikes like sun rays.
   Stands on Liberty Island.
2. Bigger and stronger than anyone else.
   And his blue ox, Babe.
3. A sailing ship called the *Mayflower*.
   Stepped on Plymouth Rock.
4. Was built by Alexander Eiffel.
   In Paris.
5. As high as a three-story building.
   Stretches 1,500 miles across China.

Sentence Palindromes

A palindrome sentence is one that reads the same backward as forward. In some palindromes, whole words reverse.

> **You saw Ted, and Ted saw you.**
> **Live to try, or try to live.**

In other palindromes the spelling of each word, except the conjunction, reverses.

> **Bob saw Dad, and Dad was Bob.**
> **Peels I won, but now I sleep.**

Try writing some palindromes. (Hint: Each must be a compound sentence.)

Unit 8 Extra Practice

1 Compound Subjects and Predicates

p. 402

A. Write the compound subject or predicate in each sentence.

1. A strong wind suddenly arose and blew through town.
2. A storm or tornado was on the way!
3. Thunder rumbled, roared, and echoed through the valley.
4. Dust and leaves sailed overhead.
5. The wind rose and blew harder.
6. Heavy raindrops fell and splashed on the sidewalk.
7. Men, women, and children scurried for shelter.
8. Jan and her mother closed their doors and windows.
9. The clouds opened and released the rain.
10. The gutters and roads filled with water.
11. Paper, wood, and other rubbish floated by.
12. Cars moved slowly or stalled in flooded areas.
13. Emergency workers gathered and helped motorists.
14. Lightning bolts struck and split many trees.
15. Broken trunks and branches fell onto nearby cars.
16. Many orchards and fields were damaged by the winds.
17. Flooded basements and broken windows were common.
18. At last the clouds passed and revealed the sun again.

B. Write each sentence. Underline each compound subject once and each compound predicate twice. If a sentence has no compounds, write *no compound*.

19. This book explains the formation of clouds.
20. Moist air rises from the ground and becomes cooler.
21. The cooler air cannot hold all its water vapor.
22. The vapor condenses and forms clouds.
23. Water droplets in a cloud may form larger droplets.
24. Rain, sleet, or snow falls to the earth.
25. Animals and plants use this water.
26. The water flows into streams and refills lakes.
27. *Cumulus* and *cirrus* are the names of two kinds of clouds.
28. Nimbus clouds are dark rain clouds.

2 Compound Sentences

p. 404

A. Write *simple* or *compound* for each sentence.

1. Anna Jarvis organized the first Mother's Day celebrations.
2. She campaigned for a nationwide Mother's Day in 1907, and the idea became popular.
3. West Virginia celebrated the first Mother's Day in 1910.
4. President Woodrow Wilson made Mother's Day a national observance in 1914.
5. He signed a bill, and Mother's Day became official.
6. Children gave flowers on this day, or they made gifts.
7. Father's Day began in 1910, but it did not become official until 1972.
8. The ancient Romans honored mother goddesses in spring.
9. On Parentalia the Romans remembered dead relatives.
10. The English once honored mothers on Mothering Sunday, but the holiday died out in the 1800s.
11. Children baked cakes, or they did household chores.
12. Mother's Day was a big success in the United States, and other nations soon imitated it.
13. Sonora Dodd of Spokane, Washington, liked Mother's Day, but she wanted a Father's Day, too.
14. Spokane celebrated the first Father's Day in 1910.
15. Mother's Day is the second Sunday in May.
16. Father's Day falls on the third Sunday in June.
17. You can give your father a gift, or you can just thank him.

B. Write *compound sentence*, *compound subject*, or *compound predicate* for each sentence.

18. Mom slept late on Mother's Day and had breakfast in bed.
19. Aaron cleaned the house, and I bought red carnations.
20. Dad made dinner, but he burned it badly.
21. So we went out to dinner and had a great Mother's Day.
22. Aaron and I bought Dad a shirt for Father's Day.
23. Mom picked red roses, and Dad sneezed a lot.
24. Dad got a polka dot tie, but he returned it.
25. Mom, Aaron, and I took Dad on a picnic.
26. Dad swam and played tennis with Mom.
27. Then it started to rain, and we all went home.

3 Making Subjects and Verbs Agree

p. 406

A. This story about Sandra Day O'Connor is written in the present tense. Write the form of the verb in parentheses ( ) that correctly completes each sentence.

1. Sandra Day (grows, grow) up in Arizona in the 1930s.
2. She (works, work) on her parents' ranch.
3. Sandra (finishes, finish) college and law school in only five years.
4. No law firms (gives, give) her a job, though.
5. They (refuses, refuse) to hire women lawyers.
6. Sandra (marries, marry) John O'Connor and raises a family.
7. Later she (decides, decide) to enter politics.
8. The voters (elects, elect) her state senator in Arizona.
9. The people (learns, learn) what a good worker she is.
10. Next the governor (makes, make) her a judge.
11. As a judge she (is, are) always fair.
12. In 1981, President Reagan (chooses, choose) Sandra Day O'Connor for the Supreme Court.
13. The Supreme Court (is, are) the highest court in the land.
14. Sandra Day O'Connor (feels, feel) proud to be the first woman Supreme Court judge.
15. Her court decisions (affects, affect) the nation's future.

B. Write the correct form of the verb in parentheses to complete each sentence.

16. Oceans (covers, cover) more area than all of the land on earth.
17. The largest ocean (is, are) the Pacific.
18. It (cover, covers) more area than all of the land on earth.
19. The Atlantic Ocean (is, are) only half the size of the Pacific.
20. The Atlantic (provide, provides) many more trade routes.
21. Swift streams (flows, flow) through all oceans.
22. Some currents (carries, carry) warm water from the Tropics.
23. Others (brings, bring) cold water from the Poles.
24. Currents (is, are) major influences on the climate of land.

4 Using Verbs with Compound Subjects

p. 408

A. Write the verb that correctly completes each sentence.

1. Honey and fruit (contain, contains) sugar.
2. Cheese and eggs (is, are) rich in protein.
3. Fish or meat also (provide, provides) protein.
4. Bacon, butter, and margarine (provides, provide) fat.
5. Either milk or milk products (supplies, supply) calcium.
6. Neither chocolate nor butter (contains, contain) much iron.
7. Seafoods or iodized salt (is, are) a good source of iodine.
8. Sugar and starches (is, are) carbohydrates.
9. Starches and sugar (is, are) prime sources of energy.
10. Neither body growth nor body repair (takes, take) place without proteins.
11. Fish or meats (provides, provide) complete proteins.
12. Neither beans nor cereal (gives, give) complete proteins.
13. Calcium, phosphorus, and iron (is, are) minerals.
14. Green vegetables or meat (furnishes, furnish) iron.
15. Anemia and other diseases (comes, come) from lack of it.
16. Neither blood nor muscles (stays, stay) healthy without adequate phosphorus.
17. Strong teeth and bone (requires, require) calcium.
18. Cheese or fish (is, are) a good source of phosphorus.

B. Write each sentence. Use the correct present tense form of the verb in parentheses ( ). Then write whether the verb is singular or plural.

19. Poor vision or rough skin (result) from lack of vitamin A.
20. Carrots or butter (provide) this vitamin.
21. Thiamine and niacin (belong) to the vitamin B group.
22. Neither good physical health nor good mental health (seem) possible without them.
23. Meat or beans (provide) most B vitamins.
24. Some vegetables and citrus fruit (furnish) vitamin C.
25. Unhealthy gums or scurvy (result) from no vitamin C.
26. Egg yolks and fortified milk (furnish) us with vitamin D.
27. Strong bones and teeth (need) vitamin D.

5 Avoiding Sentence Errors   p. 410

A. Write *sentence* or *fragment* for each group of words. Add words to each fragment to make a sentence. Then write the sentences.

1. Waved in the breeze.
2. Lisa marched in step.
3. Soldiers in fine uniforms.
4. At the war memorial.

5. The mayor was there.
6. Her shiny trumpet.
7. With their heads high.
8. A fine Memorial Day.

B. Correct these run-on sentences. Rewrite each run-on sentence as two separate sentences, as a compound sentence, or as a sentence with a compound predicate.

EXAMPLE: Most states observe Memorial Day on the last Monday in May, many cities have parades.

ANSWER: Most states observe Memorial Day on the last Monday in May. Many cities have parades.

9. The holiday began in 1866 the people of Waterloo, New York, first observed it.
10. People decorated the graves of soldiers with flowers they placed flags on graves.
11. The nation honored its heroes it recalled their bravery.
12. Now we celebrate Memorial Day we remember our freedoms.
13. Flag Day is another patriotic holiday, it is June 14.
14. Congress authorized the first American flag in 1777 the first Flag Day was in 1877.
15. People display the flag they think about its importance.
16. Schools hold Flag Day programs students learn about the flag.
17. The stripes on the American flag stand for the original thirteen colonies there is a star for each state.

C. Rewrite each run-on sentence as two separate sentences, as a compound sentence, or as a sentence with a compound predicate. Use a semicolon where appropriate.

18. The camp list came last week it surprised us.
19. I am only going for two weeks we need a lot of things.
20. Mom has ordered name tags I will help her sew them on.
21. I signed up for advanced swimming it includes diving, too.

Acknowledgments continued from page ii.

by Marguerite Henry. Reprinted with permission. **Dictionary** 469: Painting by Rudolf Freund, courtesy of The Carnegie Museum of Natural History. 470: Dwight Carter. 471: *l.* Art Resource; *r.* American Museum of Natural History. 473: Private collection. 474: Courtesy of the Shelburne Museum, Shelburne, Vermont. 475: Brown Brothers. 476: © 1990 Olivier Rebbot/Woodfin Camp & Associates. 477: Brown Brothers. 478: Anthony Miles/Bruce Coleman. Every effort has been made to locate the original sources. If any errors have occurred, the publisher can be notified and corrections will be made.

Permissions: We wish to thank the following authors, publishers, agents, corporations, and individuals for their permission to reprint copyrighted materials. Page 24: "This Is About the Old, Old, Tree." From *My Side of the Mountain* by Jean George. Copyright © 1959 by Jean George, renewed 1987 by Jean George. Reprinted by permission of the publisher, E.P. Dutton, a division of NAL Penguin, Inc. Page 80: Excerpt from *Puppeteer* by Kathryn Lasky. Reprinted by permission of Macmillan Publishing Co. and Sheldon Fogelman, New York, NY. Text Copyright © 1985 by Kathryn Lasky. All rights reserved. Page 142: "How Frog Feels About It" by Lilian Moore. Copyright © 1990 by Lilian Moore. All rights reserved. Reprinted by permission of Marian Reiner for the author. First published in *Cricket* magazine. Page 143: "I am the prairie..." from *Cornhuskers* by Carl Sandburg. Copyright 1918 by Holt, Rinehart & Winston, Inc. Renewed 1946 by Carl Sandburg. Reprinted by permission of Harcourt Brace Jovanovich, Inc. From "Mushrooms" Copyright © 1960 by Sylvia Plath. Reprinted from *The Colossus and Other Poems* by Sylvia Plath, by permission of the publisher, Alfred A. Knopf. "Trees: The Seeds" From *Monkey Puzzle and Other Poems* by Myra Cohn Livingston. Copyright © 1984 by Myra Cohn Livingston. Reprinted by permission of Marian Reiner for the author. Page 144: "My Song is a Piece of Jade" from *Poems of Ancient Mexico in English and Spanish*. Adapted by Toni de Gerez. English translation copyright © 1984 by Organizacion Editorial Novaro, S.A. Copyright 1981 by Organizacion Editorial Novaro, S.A. Reprinted by permission of Little, Brown & Co. Page 148: "Living Tenderly" from *Poems to Solve* by May Swenson. © 1963 by May Swenson. Reprinted by permission of the author. Page 149: "Hot volcanoes..." From *Earth Songs* by Myra Cohn Livingston, Poet, and Leonard Everett Fisher, Painter. Text Copyright © 1986 by Myra Cohn Livingston. Reprinted by permission of Marian Reiner for the author. "Under a Telephone Pole" from *Chicago Poems* by Carl Sandburg. Copyright 1916 by Holt, Rinehart & Winston, Inc. Renewed 1944 by Carl Sand-

burg. Reprinted by permission of Harcourt Brace Jovanovich, Inc. Page 150: Excerpted from "Leaning on a Limerick" in *It Doesn't Always Have to Rhyme* by Eve Merriam. Copyright © 1964 by Eve Merriam. All rights reserved. Reprinted by permission of Marian Reiner for the author. Page 151: "A Crusty Mechanic" From *A Person From Britain Whose Head Was the Shape of a Mitten* by N.M. Bodecker. Reprinted with permission of Margaret K. McElderry Books, an imprint of Macmillan Publishing Co. Copyright © 1980 by N.M. Bodecker. "Racing" from *Limericks for Children*. Used by permission of the author Isaac Asimov. Page 152: "River's Song" from *The Golden Hive* Poems and Pictures by Harry Behn. Copyright © 1957, 1962, 1966 by Harry Behn. All rights reserved. Reprinted by permission of Marian Reiner. "The Wind" by James Reeves From *The Wandering Moon and Other Poems*. Reprinted by permission of Laura Cecil on behalf of The Estate of James Reeves. Page 256: Excerpt from *The House of Dies Drear* by Virginia Hamilton. Copyright © 1968 by Virginia Hamilton. Reprinted with permission of Macmillan Publishing Co. and McIntosh & Otis, Inc. Page 264: From *The Mystery of Drear House* by Virginia Hamilton. Copyright © 1987 by Virginia Hamilton. Reprinted by permission of Greenwillow Books (a division of William Morrow & Co., Inc.). Page 266: From *The Mystery of Drear House* by Virginia Hamilton. Copyright © 1987 by Virginia Hamilton. Reprinted by permission of Greenwillow Books (a division of William Morrow & Co., Inc.). Page 306: "From Coast to Coast" by Louise Boyd James. From *Cobblestone's* July 1987 issue The Automobile in History. © 1987 Cobblestone Publishing, Inc., Peterborough, NH 03458. Reprinted by permission of the publisher. Page 357: "A solitary frog drenched in rain..." haiku by Chiyo from *Zen and Japanese Culture* by D.T. Suzuki, © 1959. Bollingen Series LXIV Princeton University Press. Reprinted courtesy of Princeton University Press. Page 366: *The Crane Wife* retold by Sumiko Yagawa © 1979. English translation © 1981 by Katherine Paterson. Illustrations © 1979 by Suekichi Akaba. Used by permission of William Morrow & Co. Page 375: Excerpt from *Dawn* by Molly Bang. Text copyright © 1983 by Molly Bang. Reprinted by permission of Morrow Junior Books (a division of William Morrow & Co., Inc.). Excerpt from "The Fairy Crane" from *Japanese Children's Stories* edited by Florence Sakade. © 1959 Charles E. Tuttle Company. Used by permission of the publisher. Page 420: Excerpt from *Project Panda Watch* by Miriam Schlein. Copyright © 1984 Miriam Schlein. Reprinted with the permission of Atheneum Publishers, an imprint of Macmillan Publishing Co. Pictures copyright © 1984 by Robert Shetterly. Page 477: "Splinter" from *Good Morning, America* by Carl Sandburg. Copyright 1928, 1956 by Carl Sandburg. Reprinted by permission of Harcourt Brace Jovanovich, Inc.

WRITER'S · REFERENCE · BOOK

Study Skills Lessons

Study Habits

1. **Listen in class.** Make sure that you understand exactly what your teacher wants you to do for homework. Write each homework assignment in a notebook.
2. **Have your homework materials ready.** You will need such items as textbooks, pens, erasers, rulers, and your notebook.
3. **Study in the same place every day.** You should try to find a quiet and comfortable place where people will not interrupt you. There should be good lighting, a comfortable chair, and a desk or table. Do not have the TV or radio on while studying. The fewer distractions you have, the better you will study.
4. **Plan your study time.** Develop a daily study schedule. First decide on the best time of the day for studying. Then plan exactly when you will study each of your subjects. It is a good idea to work on your hardest subject first, before you become tired. Include time for chores, or household tasks, and recreation. Write your study schedule, using the one shown below as a guide. Keep your schedule where you do your work, and stick to it.
5. **Set a goal each time you study.** If, for example, you were going to have a social studies test, your goal would be to review and understand the material that would be tested. Keep that goal in mind when you study. If you do, you will concentrate better.

Study Schedule

3:30 to 4:00 P.M. — chores
4:00 to 5:00 P.M. — sports, piano practice
5:00 to 5:30 P.M. — study social studies
5:30 to 6:00 P.M. — study English
6:00 to 7:00 P.M. — dinner and free time
7:00 to 7:30 P.M. — study math
7:30 to 8:00 P.M. — study science
8:00 to 9:30 P.M. — hobbies, reading, TV

Practice

Write a study schedule for yourself. Allow time for each subject you will have to study. Also allow time for chores, dinner, and recreation.

Test-taking Tips

1. **Be prepared.** Have several sharp pencils and an eraser.

2. **Read or listen to the directions carefully.** Be sure you know what you are to do and where and how you are to mark your answers.

3. **Answer the easy questions first.** Quickly read all the questions on the page. Then go back to the beginning and answer the questions you are sure you know. Put a light check next to the questions whose answers you are not sure of or don't know.

4. **Next try to answer the questions you are not sure you know.** If you have a choice of answers, read all the choices. Eliminate the answers you know are wrong. Try to narrow your selection to two answers. Then mark the answer you think is right.

5. **Answer the hardest questions last.** If you can't answer a question at all, don't waste time worrying about it. Skip the question and go on to the next.

6. **Think carefully before answering analogy questions.** An analogy compares two things and shows how they are related. To correctly complete an analogy question, you must figure out the relationship between the first two items. Then complete the analogy so that the second pair has the same relationship.

   EXAMPLE: Circle the correct answer.
   leaf : tree : : hair : _____
   a. twig (b.) head   c. bird   d. curly

7. **Plan your time.** Don't spend too much time on just one question or you may not have time to finish the rest. Check your watch or a clock from time to time as you take the test. Save some time to check your answers.

8. **Check your answers when you have finished.** Make sure you have marked your answers correctly. Unless you're sure you made a mistake, you should not change an answer.

Parts of a Book

The main part of a book is called the body. However, books have other special parts that contain useful information. Study the descriptions of these parts below. Notice that some are in the front of a book and others are in the back.

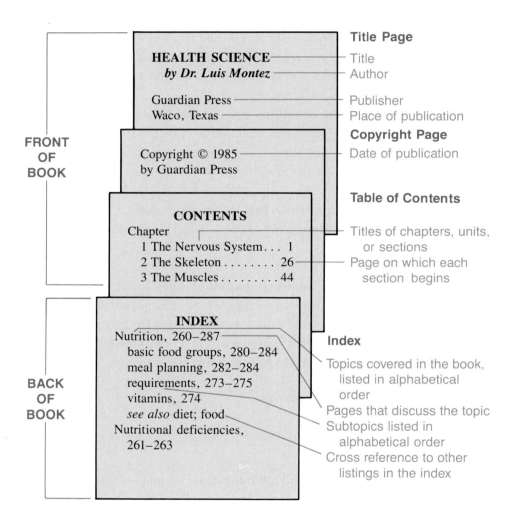

The title page, copyright page, and table of contents are in the front of a book. The index is in the back. Also in the back is the glossary which is described on the next page.

GLOSSARY OF TERMS

Glossary

absorbed Action in which light waves are trapped by matter. *pp. 161, 183*

acid A compound that contains hydrogen and that has a sour taste. *p. 124*

adaptation (ad′əp tā′shən) Any structure or response that helps an organism to survive *p. 35*

adolescence (ad′ə les′′ns) Stage of human life that follows childhood and that involves rapid growth and change. *p. 375*

BACK
OF
BOOK

Special terms used in the book, listed in alphabetical order

Meaning of the word as used in the book

Page where the word is introduced or defined

Pronunciation of difficult words

Practice

A. Write the part of a book in which you would look to answer each of these questions.

   1. when the book was published
   2. on what page Chapter 10 begins
   3. whether the book has any information on the heart
   4. the author of the book
   5. the pages in the book that give information about vitamins
   6. What company published the book?
   7. Does the book have a chapter on nutrition?
   8. Does the book tell who discovered how to prevent people from getting smallpox?
   9. How up-to-date is the information in this book?
   10. Which pages tell about the basic food groups?

B. Use the examples on page 460 to answer these questions.

   11. On what page does the chapter "The Skeleton" begin?
   12. Who wrote *Health Science*?
   13. When was *Health Science* published?
   14. On which pages would you find information on meal planning?
   15. Under what other words in the index can you look to find information on nutrition?

Using the Library

The library is a storehouse of knowledge. No matter what topic you choose, you can learn more about it in the library. First, however, you need to know how to use the library.

Library books are divided into two main categories — fiction and nonfiction. Works of fiction, such as novels and short stories, are arranged alphabetically by the authors' last names. Nonfiction books give facts and are usually arranged numerically under the **Dewey Decimal System**. This system assigns a call number to each nonfiction book according to its subject. History books, for example, have numbers between 900 and 999.

There are two ways you can look for books in a library. Some libraries have card catalogs, which list every book in the library by title, author, and subject on alphabetically arranged cards. Notice the information given on each kind of card.

Many libraries also have computer listings. These contain the same information as card catalogs, but the information is stored in a computer. Most computers have easy-to-follow instructions; if you don't know how to use the computer, ask a librarian.

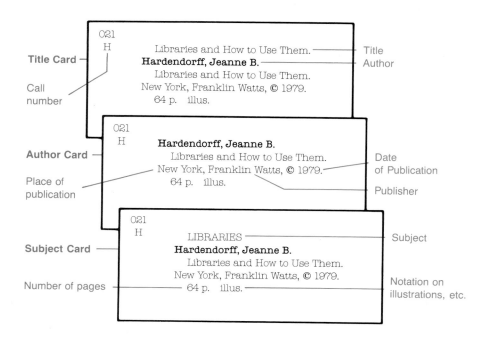

Practice

A. Write the word or words you would look up in the card catalog or computer listing to find the following items.

    1. a book by Virginia Hamilton

    2. the title of a book about figure skating

    3. the call number of the book *The Reasons for Seasons*

    4. the title of a book by Eleanor Estes

    5. the call numbers of books about solar power

B. Write *title, author,* or *subject* to tell what kind of catalog card you would use to answer these questions.

    6. What books by Scott O'Dell are in the library?

    7. How many pages long is the book *Frozen Fire*?

    8. Does the library have any books about opera?

    9. Did the author of *Dragonwings* also write *The Summer of the Swan*?

    10. What books for young readers has Ray Bradbury written?

C. Read the set of computer instructions below.

> To search by author, type **a =** followed by the author's name, last name first. Do not use a comma.
>
> To search by title, type **t =** followed by the title. Do not type *A, An,* or *The* if it is the first word of the title.
>
> To search by subject, type **s =** followed by the subject.

Write what you would type to find the items listed.

    11. the works of Mark Twain

    12. *Ten Thousand Ways to Get Rich Quick*

    13. the *Iliad*

    14. a book about whales

    15. a book of poetry by T.S. Eliot

Using a Dictionary

Of all reference books, the dictionary is probably the one people use most often. A dictionary contains thousands of words in alphabetical order. Each word that is defined is called an **entry word**. If you know the shortcuts to finding words in a dictionary, you can quickly locate the words you need to find.

Front: a, b, c, d, e, f, g
Middle: h, i, j, k, l, m, n, o, p
Back: q, r, s, t, u, v, w, x, y, z

The first shortcut: Think of the dictionary as divided into three parts: the front, *a–g*; the middle, *h–p*; and the back, *q–z*.

When you look up a word, decide in which part of the dictionary it is listed. Then open to that part, trying to open to the first letter of the word you want.

The second shortcut: Use the guide words at the top of a dictionary page. The **guide words** show the first and last entry words on the page. If your word falls alphabetically between the guide words, or if it is a guide word, it will appear on that page. If your word does not fall between the guide words, decide if it comes before or after that page.

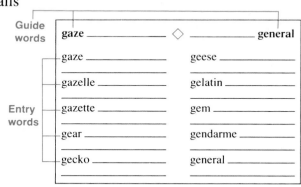

Practice

A. Write each word. Then write *front, middle,* or *back* to show in which part of a dictionary it would be found.

1. frontier
2. usher
3. predict
4. shadow
5. medical
6. talent
7. hacienda
8. eagle
9. quizzical

B. Follow the directions below. Write the words in alphabetical order. Remember, words are put in alphabetical order by the first letter that is different.

   EXAMPLES: <u>b</u>ook, <u>s</u>and   c<u>a</u>pe, c<u>e</u>nt   sh<u>i</u>p, sh<u>o</u>re   bla<u>m</u>e, bla<u>s</u>t

   10. Write four words that name seasons of the year.
   11. Write five words that name pieces of furniture.
   12. Write five words that name things found in a gymnasium.
   13. Write the first names of five classmates.

C. Guide words for imaginary dictionary pages 436–439 are shown at the right. Write entry words **14–22.** Then write the page number for each entry word.

needy 436 **nerve**		**nervous** 437 **neutral**
neutron 438 **newt**		**next** 439 **nimble**

   14. nickel   **17.** newcomer   **20.** nestle
   15. neighbor   **18.** nerve   **21.** neutral
   16. neglect   **19.** niece   **22.** nephew

D. Think of the words *equip* and *error* as guide words. Write *on*, *before*, or *after* to show where each word below would be found.

   23. erupt   **24.** err   **25.** equator   **26.** erase

E. Write each word below. For each word, write an appropriate pair of guide words.

   EXAMPLE: major   **ANSWER:** major; machine, meanwhile

   27. practical   **31.** notch   **35.** morning
   28. saunter   **32.** remedy   **36.** humor
   29. walrus   **33.** exploit **37.** gopher
   30. afternoon   **34.** quiver   **38.** delight

F. Write five words from the Dictionary of Knowledge, which begins on page 468. Scramble the alphabetical order and exchange papers with a classmate. See who can most quickly alphabetize the words and write the Dictionary page number for each word.

What is a *rutabaga*? Does the word spelled *harlequin* mean "a clown"? How is *flange* pronounced? You can find the answers to these questions in the Dictionary of Knowledge, which starts on page 468. Study the sample entry below. It is from the Dictionary of Knowledge.

```
                              Part
              Pronunciation   of speech
                                                           Verb forms
Entry word ——  es•cape   (e skāp')   v. escaped, escaping.
               1. to get free; to break loose. 2. to keep safe from; to
               avoid. Manuela fell on the ice but escaped from being
Definitions —  hurt. 3. to leak out; to flow away. Air was escaping
               from the tire. —n. 1. the act of escaping. Make your
               escape through a window. 2. any way of putting
               problems out of the mind. A long nap is my escape.  —— Example sentence
Etymology ——  [from Latin ex–out of + cappa cloak]
Synonym ————  — Syn. flee. — escaper n. — escapable adj.  —— Derived forms
```

Entry word   This shows how to spell the word. The dots between syllables show how to divide it at the end of a line of writing.

Pronunciation   This tells how to say the word. It is given in symbols that stand for certain sounds. For example, the symbol ā stands for the long a sound heard in *arrange*. The Pronunciation Key on page 468 tells the sound for each symbol.

Part of speech   This label is abbreviated, such as *v.* for *verb*.

Verb forms or plural forms   These are shown when the spelling of the base word changes.

Definitions   The different meanings of the word are numbered.

Example sentence   This helps to make the meaning clear.

Etymology   This is a word history, and it appears in brackets.

Synonym   This is a word that has a similar meaning to the entry word. Its label is abbreviated *Syn.* Antonyms, labeled *Ant.*, are given for some entry words.

Derived forms   These are related forms of the word that are made by adding a suffix to the base word.

Practice

G. Write the answer to each question. Use the dictionary entry on page 466.

    39. How many syllables does the entry word contain?

    40. In the pronunciation, which syllable has an accent mark, showing that it is a stressed syllable?

    41. How many meanings are given for *escape* as a verb?

    42. How many meanings are given for *escape* as a noun?

    43. How many example sentences are included in the entry?

H. Use the dictionary entries below for questions **44–47.**

glad•i•a•tor   (glad′ē āt′ ər) *n.* **1.** a person who fought another person or animal for the entertainment of an audience in ancient Rome. **2.** a person who takes part in any kind of struggle.

glance   (glans) *v.* **glanced, glancing. 1.** to take a quick look. **2.** to strike at a slant and go off at an angle. **3.** to flash or gleam. *Sunlight glanced off the water.*

gland   (gland) *n.* any special organ or tissue in the body that makes chemical substances such as insulin.

    44. What part of speech is *gland*?

    45. What is the number of the meaning that *glance* has in this sentence? *Hail began to glance off the window.*

    46. Which meaning of *gladiator* describes a football player?

    47. Which entry word names a part of the body?

I. Use the Dictionary of Knowledge to answer the questions below.

    48. Which word is spelled incorrectly, and how should it be spelled: *ambassador, improvise, pendent, turtledove*?

    49. Which word names a kind of roof: *opaque, dormer, mansard*?

    50. Is a person in a *coltish* mood feeling tired and run-down?

J. Use the Dictionary of Knowledge to write a word quiz for your classmates. Write three questions like those in **Practice I.** You might exchange papers with a partner and see who can answer the questions in the shortest time.

Dictionary of Knowledge

This Dictionary of Knowledge has two kinds of entries, **word entries** and **encyclopedic entries**. Many of the word entries in this dictionary are taken from the literature pieces found throughout this book. You might use these entries to help you understand the meanings of words. You will use the encyclopedic entries in two "Apply" sections in each unit.

Word Entries ✦ These entries are just like the ones found in the ordinary dictionaries you are familiar with. Each entry includes such elements as pronunciation respellings, definitions, and example sentences.

Encyclopedic Entries ✦ These entries resemble encyclopedia articles. Each entry provides interesting information about a particular topic or person.

Abbreviations Used in this Dictionary			
adj.	adjective	pl.	plural
adv.	adverb	prep.	preposition
Ant.	Antonym	pron.	pronoun
conj.	conjunction	Syn.	Synonym
n.	noun	v.	verb

Full pronunciation key* The pronunciation of each word is shown just after the word, in this way: **abbreviate** (ə brē′ vē āt).

The letters and signs used are pronounced as in the words below.

The mark ′ is placed after a syllable with a primary or heavy accent as in the example above.

The mark ′ after a syllable shows a secondary or lighter accent, as in **abbreviation** (ə brē′vē ā′shən).

SYMBOL	KEY WORDS	SYMBOL	KEY WORDS	SYMBOL	KEY WORDS	SYMBOL	KEY WORDS
a	ask, fat	oo	look, pull	b	bed, dub	v	vat, have
ā	ape, date	ōō	ooze, tool	d	did, had	w	will, always
ä	car, father	yoo	unite, cure	f	fall, off	y	yet, yard
		yōō	cute, few	g	get, dog	z	zebra, haze
e	elf, ten	ou	out, crowd	h	he, ahead		
er	berry, care			j	joy, jump	ch	chin, arch
ē	even, meet	u	up, cut	k	kill, bake	ng	ring, singer
		ɬr	fur, fern	l	let, ball	sh	she, dash
i	is, hit			m	met, trim	th	thin, truth
ir	mirror, here	ə	a in ago	n	not, ton	th	then, father
ī	ice, fire		e in agent	p	put, tap	zh	s in pleasure
			e in father	r	red, dear		
o	lot, pond		i in unity	s	sell, pass	′	as in (ā′b'l)
ō	open, go		o in collect	t	top, hat		
ô	law, horn		u in focus				
oi	oil, point						

*Pronunciation key adapted from *Webster's New World Dictionary; Basic School Edition*, Copyright © 1983 by Simon & Schuster, Inc. Reprinted by permission.

⸻ **A** ⸻

Al•a•mo   (al′ə mō)

The Alamo is a group of mission buildings, including a church, a monastery, and several outbuildings, surrounded by a fortification wall in San Antonio, Texas. On February 23, 1836, the Mexican general Santa Anna and an army of four thousand soldiers attacked the Alamo. The Alamo was the stronghold of the Texans, who were at war with Mexico. Inside the mission, 187 defenders, including frontier heroes Davy Crockett and James Bowie, held off attacks by Mexican soldiers over several days. In the end, however, all the Alamo's defenders were killed. Their actions inspired others, like Sam Houston, who made famous the cry "Remember the Alamo!" A few weeks later the Mexican army was defeated. Texas had won its independence and had become a free nation. It remained independent of both Mexico and the United States for ten years.

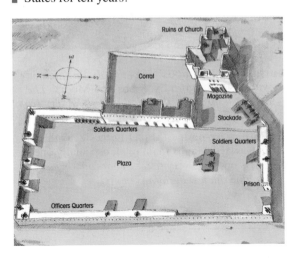

a•loft   (ə lôft′) *adv.* **1.** high up; far above the ground. *The ape swung aloft into the upper branches of the tree.* **2.** in the air; flying. **3.** high above the deck of a ship; near the top of the mast. [from Old Norse *ā* on + *lopt*, loft, upperroom, air, sky.]

am•bas•sa•dor   (am bas′ə dər) *n.* **1.** an official of highest rank sent by a country to represent it in another country. *Clare Booth Luce was the United States ambassador to Italy.* **2.** any person sent as a representative or messenger. *Andrew Young served as the U.S. ambassador to the United Nations.*

ar•chae•op•ter•yx   (är′ kē op′ tər iks)

Archaeopteryx is the scientific name of an extinct animal believed to have been one of the first feathered birds. Scientists think this primitive bird lived about 140 million years ago. The archaeopteryx was about the size of a pigeon and had small wings with claws at the tips, a long bony lizardlike tail, and a beak with teeth. The skeleton of an archaeopteryx, which is more like a reptile's than a bird's, was found preserved between layers of limestone in Bavaria in 1861. Although it clearly had feathers, the archaeopteryx probably could not fly. It could only glide over short distances. Scientists know of a similar bird living today, the hoatzin of the swamplands in Guyana and Venezuela.

The hoatzin has the same unusual claws at its wingtips and can only glide from tree to tree.

The word *archaeopteryx* comes from Greek words *archaeo*, meaning "ancient" or "primitive," and *pteryx*, meaning "wing."

Painting by Rudolf Freund. Courtesy of The Carnegie Museum of Natural History.

a fat	er care	ī bite, fire	oi oil	u up	th thin	ə = a *in* ago
ā ape	ē even	o lot	oo look	ur fur	th then	e *in* agent
ä car, father	i hit	ō go	o͞o tool	ch chin	zh leisure	i *in* unity
e ten	ir here	ô law, horn	ou out	sh she	n̂g ring	o *in* collect
						u *in* focus

ar•tist•ry (är′tis trē) *n.* artistic work or skill. *She uses artistry to create an illusion before our eyes.* [from Latin *ars* art] — *Syn.* **skill**.

B
---

barb•wire (bärb′ wīr′) *n.* wire with sharp points all along it; barbed wire. It is used for fences or barriers. *The barbwire fence kept the animals from straying.* [from Latin *barba* beard]

bo•tan•i•cal (bə tan′i k′l) *adj.* having to do with botany. *Plants are raised in a botanical garden so that they can be studied and exhibited.* Also written *botanic*. [from Greek *botanē* a plant + *al* of]

Brooks, Gwen•do•lyn (brŏŏks′, gwen′d′l ən) 1917–

Gwendolyn Brooks is a black American poet and writer. Brooks was born in Topeka, Kansas, but grew up and went to schools in Chicago's poorer neighborhoods. In her poems and stories, Brooks has in a way never left those places, which she describes as both tough and challenging to the spirit.

In poems like "Vern," from *Bronzeville Boys and Girls,* Gwendolyn Brooks speaks about a rainy walk across a vacant lot with a puppy. A puppy makes a good companion when one has been scolded and feels unloved, she says. The puppy's "wiggly warmness" is comforting. Another poem, "The Bean Eaters," is sadder. Here we meet an old couple who are poor. They go through repeated motions of daily life, remembering good times and bad times while they eat their beans. They live a very simple life. "Narcissa" paints a sparkling picture of a girl who, perhaps like a young Gwendolyn herself, does not play ball or jacks. Narcissa sits and imagines all the wonderful people and things she might be. She revels in imagining.

Bronzeville was Gwendolyn Brooks's name for the inner city. She published her first book, *A Street in Bronzeville,* when she was twenty-eight. Reviewers compared her with writer Edgar Lee Masters. His book *Spoon River Anthology* made use of the voices of ordinary people as it revealed their dreams and their feelings in defeat. Brooks is known less as a writer of social protest than as a knowing or kind observer of strong characters and vivid city places. She has said that people with

"gumption" interest her more than do people who compromise or give up on their dreams for various reasons.

This poet knew she had a special talent early in life. At thirteen her poems were being published by a children's magazine. At sixteen they were published in a newspaper. She won the Pulitzer Prize for poetry for *Annie Allen* in 1950.

bur•noose (bər nŏŏs′ or bur′ nŏŏs) *n.* a cloak with a hood, worn by Arabs and Moors. *The burnoose protects the head and shoulders from the sun.*

by•path *or* **by-path** (bī′path) *n.* a side path; a path away from the main road, especially one that is not used very much. *That road is just a bypath with few buildings on it.*

C
---

ca•reen (kə rēn′) *v.* **1.** to lean or tip to one side, as a sailing ship under a strong wind. **2.** to lean or roll from side to side while moving fast. *The car careened down the bumpy hill.* [from Latin *carina* keel of a ship] — *Syn.* **lean**.

colt•ish (kōl′ tish) *adj.* of or like a colt; especially frisky and frolicsome. *She raced down the hill with coltish leaps and bounds.*–**coltishly** *adv.*

Cru•soe, Rob•in•son (krŏŏ′ sō, rob′ in sən)

Robinson Crusoe is the character invented by Daniel Defoe (1660–1731) in his novel by the same name, published in 1719 in England. Crusoe tells his own story. He describes his running away to sea, his period of slavery among pirates, his shipwreck, and his life on a deserted island off South America. On that island, Crusoe learns to build a civilization on his own.

When Crusoe was first shipwrecked, he returned to the ship on a raft and took certain things from it. He took sailcloth, tools, some lumber, ammunition, and so on. With these he began to make a home. He created a tent from the sailcloth. He used the lumber to brace the walls of a cave and he made a table and a chair. Crusoe grew corn, barley, and rice, which he ground into meal for bread. He even found and tamed some wild goats. In this way he lived for twenty-four years before he saved the life of Friday, who became his friend.

The details of Crusoe's story came from a true account of a shipwreck victim named Alexander Selkirk. Daniel Defoe had read the account, and he used many of the events in the novel *Robinson Crusoe*. Defoe influenced popular writers of his day with his use of realistic detail.

cyl•in•der (sil′ən dər) *n.* **1.** a round figure with two flat ends that are parallel circles. **2.** anything shaped like this, as the chamber in which a piston of an engine moves up and down. *The engine in that car has a cracked cylinder.* [from Greek *kylindros* to roll]

——————————— **D** ———————————

dis•cern (di sʉrn′ or di zʉrn′) *v.* to see or make out clearly; to recognize. *I cannot discern what reason she had for leaving.* [from Latin *dis* apart + *cernere* to separate] — *Syn.* **perceive**.

do•do (dō′dō)

A dodo is a now-extinct flightless bird related to species of pigeons. The dodo was about the size of a male turkey, with a large hooked bill, short thick yellow legs, and gray-and-white feathers. It had small wings and could not fly.

When European explorers discovered the island of Mauritius in the Indian Ocean in the early 1500s, they found the dodo was living in huge numbers in forests there. However, the dodo had never learned to run away from humans. It was easily hunted and killed by settlers and passing sailors. Its nests and breeding grounds were destroyed by livestock such as pigs, which often escaped from the settlements. As the years passed, the dodo failed to adapt to these conditions. By 1700 it had vanished as a species.

From *New Dictionary of Natural History*, 1785 American Museum of Natural History, New York

a fat	**er** care	**ī** bite, fire	**oi** oil	**u** up	**th** thin	ə = a *in* ago
ā ape	**ē** even	**o** lot	**o͝o** look	**ʉr** fur	**_th_** then	e *in* agent
ä car, father	**i** hit	**ō** go	**o͞o** tool	**ch** chin	**zh** leisure	i *in* unity
e ten	**ir** here	**ô** law, horn	**ou** out	**sh** she	**n̄g** ring	o *in* collect
						u *in* focus

dōr•mer (dôr′mər) *n.* **1.** a part that is built out from a sloping roof, containing an upright window. **2.** such a window: *also* **dormer window**. *The dormer let more light into the rooms on the third floor.*

down•y (doun′ē) *adj.* — **downier, downiest** of or like down, or covered with down; soft and fuzzy. *He touched the downy feathers of the duckling's back.* — *Syn.* **silky**. — *Ant.* **rough**.

——————————— E ———————————

eaves (ēvz) *n. pl.* the edge or edges of a roof hanging over the side of a building. *The gutters come at the outer edge of the eaves.* [from Old English *efes* edge, border, eaves]

ed•i•ble (ed′ ə b'l) *adj.* fit to be eaten. *Are these berries edible?* [from Latin *edere* to eat]

en•treat•y (in trēt′ē) *n., pl.* **entreaties**. a pleading or begging; strong request. *The request for emergency aid was an entreaty.*

es•cape (e skāp′) *v.* **escaped, escaping. 1.** to get free; to break loose. **2.** to keep safe from; to avoid. *Manuela fell on the ice but escaped from being hurt.* **3.** to leak out; to flow away. *Air was escaping from the tire.* — *n.* **1.** the act of escaping. *Make your escape through a window.* **2.** any way of putting problems out of the mind. *A long nap is my escape.* [from Latin *ex* — out of + *cappa* cloak] — *Syn.* **flee**. — **escaper** *n.* — **escapable** *adj.*

ex•qui•site (eks′kwi zit or ik skwiz′it) *adj.* **1.** done with great care and skill. *These animal carvings are exquisite.* **2.** very beautiful. *The exquisite silk made an elegant scarf.* **3.** of the best quality; excellent. *The orchestra gave an exquisite performance.* **4.** very great or sharp. [from Latin *ex-* out + *quaerere* to ask] —**exquisitely** *adv.*

——————————— F ———————————

fac•sim•i•le (fak sim′ə lē) *n.* something made to look just like another thing; exact copy. *You may send a label or a facsimile of it.* [from Latin *facere* do and *simile* similar]

fam•i•ly (fam′ə lē) *n., pl.* **families. 1.** a group made up of two parents and all of their children. **2.** the children alone. **3.** a group of people who are related by marriage or a common ancestor; relatives; a clan. **4.** a large group of related plants or animals. *The robin is a member of the thrush family.* **5.** a group of related things.

fed•er•al law (fed′ər əl lô)

A federal law is a law that comes from the federal, or national, government in Washington, D.C. A federal law begins as a bill, a proposal for a new law often written and always introduced by members of the Senate and/or the House of Representatives. These two houses of Congress decide on exact meanings of the new law and how it will be applied, based on their debates and on comments from voters. Each house in turn considers each bill. Then the bill moves to the other house for consideration and debate. If both houses of Congress pass the bill by majority vote, it is sent to the President for signing into law. If the President vetoes the bill, or declines to sign it, Congress can still pass it by a two-thirds majority vote. The vote is called a vote to override the veto. If the bill does not receive a majority vote, it dies and no new federal law is created. Private citizens can share in this process by writing to their representatives about certain bills. Lobbyists also discuss new bills with members of Congress. Lobbyists speak for groups that would like to see particular laws passed.

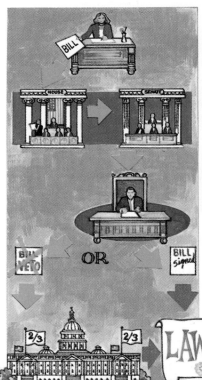

flange   (flanj) *n.* a flat edge that stands out from the rim of a wheel or pipe to hold it in place, give it strength, guide it. *The wheels of railroad cars have large flanges.* [from Old French *flanche* side] — *Syn.* **shield, spine**.

────────────── G ──────────────

glitz   (glits) *n.* gaudy or glittery showiness or attractiveness. *The sequined outfits were more than dressy; they were full of glitz for show.*

Go·bi Des·ert   (gō′ bē dez′ ərt)

The Gobi Desert is one of the largest deserts in the world. It lies between northern China and Mongolia, in the heart of Asia. About half the size of India, the Gobi Desert receives only eight to ten inches of rain per year, and average temperatures run between −40°F. in winter months and 90°F. in summer. It is an area with very cold winters and short, hot summers. Sandstorms and windstorms are common, and most of the soil has been removed by strong winds. Plant growth is sparse in the desert's interior, but its borders of grasslands vary from year to year, due to different amounts of rain. Humans have lived there for thousands of years as nomads, or wanderers, who raise sheep and cattle. Today their communities are more permanent than in previous centuries. Droughts and sandstorms, however, still make the Gobi Desert one of the harshest places to live on the earth.

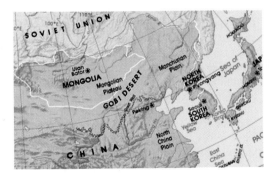

────────────── H ──────────────

hai·ku   (hī′kōō)

Haiku is a form of Japanese poetry. The word means "beginning phrase" and suggests that haiku began as the first or opening images of longer poetic works. Modern haiku poets try to create vivid word-pictures for readers. Each haiku has a very special form. A haiku has three lines and a total of seventeen syllables. The first and third lines each have five syllables. The second line has seven syllables. A haiku should contain a word about nature or a season and should concern one subject. The challenge of haiku lies in using the form while keeping a sense of freedom as well as fresh words and images. A good haiku has some insight or makes a personal comment. Following the form alone does not make a good haiku. Here is an example of a haiku.

> Natural magic;
> Snowflakes become butterflies,
> Brown grows into green.
> — *Peter R. Berkeley*

Butterflies and Spring Grasses, Japanese watercolor on silk Private Collection

har·le·quin   (här′lə kwin) *n.* a clown; a buffoon. *The bear's movements reminded us of the harlequin, the big lumbering overstuffed clown.* —*adj.* **1.** comic, ludicrous. **2.** of many colors; colorful.

a fat	er care	ī bite, fire	oi oil	u up	th thin	ə = a *in* ago
ā ape	ē even	o lot	oo look	ur fur	*th* then	e *in* agent
ä car, father	i hit	ō go	ōō tool	ch chin	zh leisure	i *in* unity
e ten	ir here	ô law, horn	ou out	sh she	ṅg ring	o *in* collect
						u *in* focus

————— I —————

im•merse (i mʉrs′) *v.* **immersed, immersing. 1.** to plunge or dip into a liquid. *The molten steel was immersed in the water to cool.* **2.** to get or be deeply in; to absorb. [from Latin *in* in + *mergere* to dip, plunge into] — *Syn.* **plunge.** — *Ant.* **draw out.**

im•prov•i•sa•tion (im prov′ə zā′shən) *n.* **1.** the act of improvising. **2.** something improvised. *The first time those musicians played together they created a wonderful improvisation.*

im•pro•vise (im′prə vīz) *v.* **improvised, improvising. 1.** to compose and perform at the same time, without preparation. *Some singers improvise verses as they sing.* **2.** to make quickly with whatever is at hand. *We improvised a bed by putting some chairs together.* [from Latin *in* not + *providere* to anticipate or to see ahead of time]

in•her•it (in her′it) *v.* **1.** to get from someone when that person dies; receive as an heir. *Marie inherited her aunt's fortune.* **2.** to have or get certain characteristics because one's parents or ancestors had them. *Ed inherited his father's good looks.* [from Latin *in-* in + *heres* heir]

Ir•ving, Wash•ing•ton (ʉr′vin͠g, wôsh′ in͠g tən *or* wosh′in͠g tən) 1783–1859

Washington Irving is considered America's first writer. He was the author of classics such as "Rip Van Winkle" and "The Legend of Sleepy Hollow." Irving, who was born in New York, developed interests in history and culture in his youth. He began his career with essays and humorous critical pieces on local personalities in New York politics and social life.

Knickerbocker's History of New York (1809) established Irving as a writer, and he began to travel in Europe and America. He had also gained income from the family business, but when the business failed, he increased his writing to support himself. Irving lived in Spain for two years and while there wrote a biography of Columbus. However, his reputation today stands on what he did with various European legends, such as "The Headless Horseman." Irving took certain German tales and retold them in an American setting. This made him one of the first artists to link the Old and the New World.

The story "Rip Van Winkle" first appeared in 1819. The idea for Irving's most popular story came from a folktale. Rip and his dog wander in the Catskill Mountains before the Revolutionary War takes place. He joins a group of little men who play a vigorous game of ninepins. The noise of the rolling balls echoes like thunder in the mountains. Rip is tired from his vigorous playing and falls into a deep sleep. When he wakes up, twenty years have passed. His little world has greatly changed, but so has the country he knew. Now George Washington is President. The author uses this story to contrast the old society with the new.

Rip Van Winkle Asleep, Albertus del Orient Brower, 1879 Courtesy of the Shelburne Museum, Shelburne, Vermont

————— L —————

La Salle, Ro•bert (lə sal′, rō ber′) 1643–1687

Robert Cavelier Sieur de La Salle was a French explorer born in Rouen, France. He studied at first to become a Jesuit priest, but by age twenty-three, in 1666, he was in the New World, exploring French-Canadian territories around Montreal and Lake Ontario. In 1673 he returned to France and received exclusive trading and land rights from King Louis XIV. Soon he returned to North America and, in the early 1680s, explored the Mississippi River valley, which he named *Louisiana*, after his king. La Salle was the first Frenchman to reach the mouth of the river. He returned once more to Europe to arrange for a settlement. Coming back from France, he tried to find the mouth of the Mississippi again, but his ship was driven west to the coast of Texas by a gale. After great difficulties with his followers, La Salle died without having colonized the area.

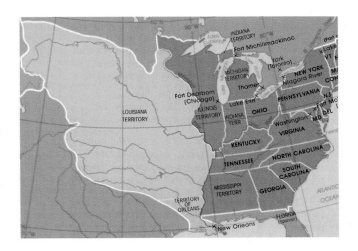

several eastern universities. She became known first as a newspaper columnist and then as an editor of *Vogue* and *Vanity Fair* magazines. Luce also wrote plays, and several of them were produced on Broadway from 1936 on, beginning with *The Women*. During World War II she was a war correspondent and reported directly from battlefronts in the Far East. After the war she ran for public office and became a United States Representative from Connecticut. It was at this time that she married Henry Luce, founder of *Time* magazine. In the 1950s she served as United States ambassador to Italy.

launch¹ (lônch) *v.* **1.** to throw, hurl, or send off into space. *NASA launched the shuttle.* **2.** to cause to slide into the water; set afloat. **3.** to start or begin. *n.* the act of launching a ship, spacecraft, and so on.

launch² (lônch) *n.* an open, or partly enclosed, motorboat.

len•til (lent′′l) *n.* **1.** a plant of the legume family, with small, nearly flat seeds that grow in pods and are used as food. *The lentils are boiled with rice and then steamed with raisins or boiled in a hearty soup.* **2.** the seed itself.

lo•cust (lō′kəst) *n.* **1.** a large insect like a grasshopper, that often travels in great swarms and destroys crops. *The locust swarmed over the fields devouring and destroying the growth.* **2.** a tree with a number of leaflets growing from each stem and clusters of sweet-smelling, white flowers; also, its yellowish, hard wood. *We could smell the sweet flowers on the locust in bloom.* [from Latin *locusta* locust]

Luce, Clare Boothe (lōōs′, kler′ bōōth′) 1903–1987

Clare Boothe Luce became an important figure in journalism and politics in the 1930s. She was born in New York and graduated from

lush (lush) *adj.* growing thick and healthy, or covered with thick, healthy growth. *The plant growth in the rain forest is green and lush.* —*Syn.* **dense.**—**lushy** *adv.*—**lushness** *n.*

--- **M** ---

man•sard (man′särd) *n.* a roof having four sides with two slopes on each side: *also called* mansard roof. *A roof that is mansard often has windows in it.* [from French, after *Mansard*, a French architect]

a fat	er care	ī bite, fire	oi oil	u up	th thin	ə = a *in* ago
ā ape	ē even	o lot	oo look	ʉr fur	th then	e *in* agent
ä car, father	i hit	ō go	ōo tool	ch chin	zh leisure	i *in* unity
e ten	ir here	ô law, horn	ou out	sh she	ŋ ring	o *in* collect
						u *in* focus

mul•lein (mul′in) *n.* a tall plant with spikes of yellow, lavender, or white flowers. *The stems of the mullein were covered with small flowers.* [from Latin *mollis* soft]

⸻○⸻

o•paque (ō pāk′) *adj.* **1.** that cannot be seen through; not letting light through; not transparent. *We could not see through the opaque glass windows.* **2.** not shiny; dull. *The desk had an opaque surface.* **3.** hard to understand. [from Latin *opacus* shade] —*Syn.* **murky.**—*Ant.* **clear.**

⸻P⸻

Peace Corps (pēs′ kôr)

   The Peace Corps was created by Congress in 1961 in an executive order of President John F. Kennedy. Through this organization, American volunteers of all ages are trained and sent to developing countries, called *host countries*, where they help people to learn new skills in agriculture, medicine, and other areas. Any person over eighteen may join the Peace Corps, and the usual assignment overseas lasts for two years. If you have a skill in some technical area, you can probably apply it in Peace Corps work. If not, the Corps will train you according to the kinds of skills needed at your country of destination. For example, you may learn to grow

peanuts and then be sent to teach others how to do it in a country such as Botswana in Africa. Some people find this such rewarding work that it becomes their lifelong career. More than 80,000 Americans have served. For further information, write Peace Corps, 806 Connecticut Avenue N.W., Washington, D.C. 20526.

pend•ant (pen′ dənt) *n.* an ornament that hangs down, as a locket or earring. *Around her neck she wore a long necklace with a pendant.* [from Latin *pendere* to hang]

per•co•late (pʉr′ kə lāt) *v.* **percolated, percolating. 1.** to prepare or be prepared in a percolator, as coffee. **2.** to pass slowly through something that has many tiny holes; filter. *Water gradually percolates through porous limestone.* [from Latin *per* — through + *colare* to strain] — *Syn.* **filter.** — **percolater**, *n.*

per•pet•u•al (pər pech′ ōō wəl) *adj.* **1.** lasting forever or for a long time. **2.** continuing; constant. *The sound of the engine was a perpetual hum.* [from Latin *per* — through + *petere* to strive] — *adv.* **perpetually.**

Pi•noc•chi•o (pi nō′ kē ō)

   Pinocchio is the main character in Carlo Collodi's story *The Adventures of Pinocchio* (1883). In the story a kindly old woodcarver named Gepetto shapes a magical piece of wood into a puppet. The puppet, Pinocchio, then comes to life and goes through various adventures as he grows up. When Pinocchio

lies, his nose grows longer. When he tells the truth, it returns to normal. At one point in the story, when Pinocchio tries to find his way home to Gepetto, he is swallowed by a whale. At last, by learning to be truthful, Pinocchio becomes a real human boy instead of a puppet. Walt Disney made an animated movie of the story in 1940, adding the famous character Jiminy Cricket, who acts as Pinocchio's conscience and guide.

Pinocchio is Carlo Collodi's most famous story. The book first appeared in 1883. Soon it was the most popular of children's stories. It has been translated over and again into many languages. Of course, since Collodi was an Italian journalist, the story was originally written in Italian.

pleu•ri•sy (plŏŏr′ə sē) *n.* a condition in which the membrane lining the chest and covering the lungs is inflamed. It makes breathing painful.

⎯⎯⎯⎯⎯⎯⎯ **R** ⎯⎯⎯⎯⎯⎯⎯

root•let (rōōt′lit) *n.* a little root. *Rootlets began to form on the stem in the water.*

ru•ta•ba•ga (rōōt′ə bāg′ə *or* rōōt′ə bā′gə) *n.* a turnip with a large, yellow root. *I think rutabagas taste delicious when they are cooked.*

⎯⎯⎯⎯⎯⎯⎯ **S** ⎯⎯⎯⎯⎯⎯⎯

Sand•burg, Carl (sand′bərg,′ kärl′) 1878–1967
Carl Sandburg was an American poet, biographer of Abraham Lincoln, and writer in many different forms. The son of poor Swedish immigrants, he grew up in a small town in Illinois called Galesburg. Sandburg fought in the Spanish-American War. Then he put himself through college. After graduation he worked as a newspaper writer. His first book, *In Reckless Ecstacy*, came out in 1904.

Sandburg also traveled widely and is known as the "poet of the prairie West." He wrote about the common people and their relation to the ideals of American democracy. In works

such as *Chicago Poems* and *Cornhuskers*, Sandburg expressed his love of the western landscape, its cities, and his faith in the ordinary citizen. He won a Pulitzer Prize for his six-volume biography of Abraham Lincoln. Some say that his work helped to free American poetry from European influences. Here is one of his poems.

Splinter
The voice of the last cricket
across the first frost
is one kind of good-by.
It is so thin a splinter of singing.

sap•phire (saf′īr) *n.* **1.** a clear, deep-blue, costly jewel. *The stone was a sapphire.* **2.** deep blue color.

a fat	**er** care	**ī** bite, fire	**oi** oil	**u** up	**th** thin	ə = a *in* ago
ā ape	**ē** even	**o** lot	**ŏŏ** look	**ur** fur	**th** then	e *in* agent
ä car, father	**i** hit	**ō** go	**ōō** tool	**ch** chin	**zh** leisure	i *in* unity
e ten	**ir** here	**ô** law, horn	**ou** out	**sh** she	**ŋ** ring	o *in* collect
						u *in* focus

Dictionary of Knowledge

Dictionary of Knowledge

sate (sāt) *v.* **sated, sating. 1.** to satisfy completely. **2.** to supply with so much of something that it becomes unpleasant or disgusting; to glut. *We were sated with all the rich food.*

Sche•he•ra•zade (shə her′ ə zä′ də *or* shə her′ ə zäd′)

Scheherazade is the hero of the main story in the collection of tales known as *Arabian Nights*. These tales come from the Indian, Arabian, and Persian oral tradition.

Scheherazade is married to a harsh king. He marries a bride a day and has her killed the next morning. Scheherazade realizes that she, too, may meet the same fate. However, she has studied poetry and history, and she devises a plan to save her life. She tells a wonderful tale to the king each night, but she keeps the ending secret until the next evening. The king does not have her executed at dawn because he is too curious about how her story will end. Scheherazade continues to tell a new and unfinished story for 1,001 nights, and the king continues to let her live.

One of her stories is about Ali Baba and the forty thieves. Another tells of Aladdin, the lamp, and the genie.

scrab•bly (skrab′lē) *adj.* **scrabblier, scrabbliest. 1.** having a scratching sound. **2.** scrubby or poor. [Colloquial] *That scrabbly tree looked even more bare after the windstorm.*

sen•tin•el (sen′ti n′l) *n.* a person or an animal set to guard a group; a sentry. *Each pair of tall columns were carved sentinels that guarded the door.*

si•nus (sī′nəs) *n.* a hollow place; especially, any of the cavities in the bones of the skull that open into the nose. *He saw the doctor for treatment of sinus.*

skit•ter (skit′ər) *v.* to skip or move quickly, especially on the surface of the water. *The flat rock skittered across the still water.*

spe•cies (spē′shēz) *n., pl.* **species. 1.** a group of plants or animals that are alike in certain ways. *The lion and tiger are two different species of cat.* **2.** a distinct kind or sort. *Her species of bravery is rare.*

spec•i•men (spes′ə mən) *n.* **1.** a part of a whole, or one thing of a group, used as a sample of the rest. *I need a specimen of her handwriting.* **2.** a sample taken for medical analysis.

Stonehenge (stōn′henj)

Stonehenge is today the ruins of an almost four-thousand-year-old stone monument on Salisbury Plain in southern England. Experts on prehistoric cultures still disagree on the exact purpose of Stonehenge's circle of massive stone columns. However, most agree that this was a place of ancient religious importance.

Stonehenge was used to observe the motions of the sun and the moon. Legends say that it was a place of sacrifice and *initiation* (the ritual by which people join a certain organization).

The monument may have been used as an astronomical calendar from which people could tell the day of the year and make predictions about the stars and planets. One of the main pairs of stone columns aligns perfectly with the sun on the longest and shortest days of the year. The oldest parts of Stonehenge date from about 1800 B.C. Evidence shows that people such as the Minoans, from the Mediterranean Sea region, may have been involved with Stonehenge in some way.

swatch   (swoch) *n.* a small piece of cloth or other materials used as a sample. *The salesperson showed us all the color choices in a ring of swatches.* — *Syn.* **sample**.

——————————— **T** ———————————

tar•ry   (tar′ē) *v.* **tarried, tarrying. 1.** to stay for a time. *We tarried in the park till sundown.* **2.** to put off; to delay. *Don't tarry; mail the letter now.* — *Syn.* **delay**.

thresh   (thresh) *v.* **1.** to separate the seed, or grain, from wheat or rye by beating. *The*

machine threshes the grain from the stem. **2.** to move about in a violent or jerky way; to thrash.

tie-rod   (tī′rod) *n.* **1.** a horizontal rod used as a tie. **2.** a rod that connects certain parts in the steering linkage of a motor vehicle. *The tie-rod is a very important connection in the steering mechanism.*

tur•tle•dove   (tur′t′l duv) *n.* a wild dove known for its sad cooing and the love that the mates seem to show for each other. *The two voices sound like turtledoves.*

——————————— **U** ———————————

un•chart•ed   (un chär′tid) *adj.* not marked on a chart or map; not explored or known. *La Salle journeyed through uncharted lands.*

——————————— **W** ———————————

wa•ter ta•ble   (wôt′ər tā′b′l) *n.* the level below which the ground is saturated with water. *The changing level of the saline, or salt, water may affect the water table in this area.*

a fat	er care	ī bite, fire	oi oil	u up	th thin	ə = a *in* ago
ā ape	ē even	o lot	oo look	ur fur	th then	e *in* agent
ä car, father	i hit	ō go	oo tool	ch chin	zh leisure	i *in* unity
e ten	ir here	ô law, horn	ou out	sh she	ṅg ring	o *in* collect
						u *in* focus

Thesaurus

A thesaurus contains lists of synonyms and antonyms. You will use this Thesaurus for the thesaurus lesson in Unit 1 and for the Thesaurus Corner in each Reading–Writing Connection in this book. You can also use the Thesaurus to find synonyms to make your writing more interesting.

Sample Entry

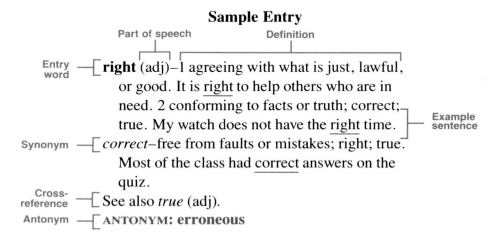

How to Use the Thesaurus Index

To find a word, use the Thesaurus Index on pages 481–484. All entry words, synonyms, and antonyms are listed alphabetically in the Index. Words in dark type are entry words, words in italic type are synonyms, and words in blue type are antonyms. A cross-reference (marked "See also") lists an entry that gives additional synonyms, related words, and antonyms. The page numbers tell you where to find the word you are looking for.

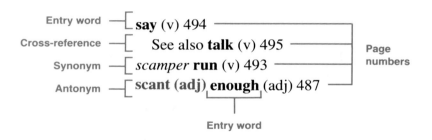

A

afraid (adj)–feeling fear; alarmed; frightened. Were you afraid of the dark when you were small?

anxious–uneasy because of fears or thoughts of what may happen; worried. Daniel was anxious about the first day of school.

fearful–causing fear; terrible; feeling fear; frightened. The fearful person approached the old house with caution.

frightened–afraid; filled with fright. The frightened mouse raced across the ground.

petrified–paralyzed by great fear. The petrified rabbit stayed perfectly still as we ran by.

terrified–suddenly filled with a very great and paralyzing fear. The terrified individual would not move from his chair until all the thunder and lightning had ceased.

ANTONYMS: **bold, brave (adj), courageous, fearless, unafraid, valiant (adj)**

answer (v)–**1** to respond to; to write or speak in response to. Will you please answer these questions right away? **2** to find the solution to. I answered all of the questions on the test correctly.

explain–to tell the meaning of; to make plain or clear; to tell how to. Juan explained how to work out the math problem.

refute–to show an opinion to be incorrect or false; to prove wrong. Can you refute the statement that our school needs a new gymnasium?

reply–to answer by words or action; to respond. I have already replied to the letter that I received yesterday morning.

respond–to reply in words; to answer; to act in answer; to react. I responded to the favorable comment by smiling.

retort–to say in a sharp or quick reply. "I won't go," he retorted.

solve–to find the answer to; to clear up. The detective solved the mystery.

ANTONYMS: **ask, inquire, interrogate, query (v), question (v), quiz (v)**

B

bad (adj)–not good; not as it ought to be; causing harm; troublesome. The bad weather prevented us from going outdoors.

harmful–causing pain, damage, or loss. Because it causes rust, salt can be harmful to automobiles.

mischievous–showing conduct that causes annoyance; naughty. The mischievous children enjoyed playing jokes on one another.

poor–not good in quality; not satisfactory. This jacket is in poor condition.

spoiled–bad or unfit for use; decayed. I hope you will not drink the spoiled milk.

toxic–very harmful to health; poisonous. The water in this stream is toxic.

awful [informal]–very bad or otherwise unusual. It is just awful to be ill with the flu.

See also *wrong* (adj).

ANTONYMS: **beneficial, excellent, fine (adj), good (adj), satisfactory, superior**

big (adj)–great in size or amount; large. That hat is much too big for me.

considerable–in large quantity; much; not a little. If you are still hungry, there is a considerable amount of soup left.

enormous–very large; huge; immense; gigantic. David has an enormous appetite for buttered rolls.

gigantic–of, like, or having to do with a giant; enormous; colossal; huge. During the storm gigantic waves crashed against the cliffs.

huge–very large; unusually large in bulk, dimension, or size; extremely large in number or quantity. Many huge elephants were in the circus parade this morning.

large–of more than the usual amount, number, or size; great; big. Please hand me the large cardboard box that is in the garage.

sizable–fairly large. There is a sizable amount of paperwork on your desk.

See also *great* (adj).

ANTONYMS: **diminutive (adj), little (adj), microscopic, miniature (adj), small (adj), tiny**

buy (v)–**1** to gain ownership of something by the payment of money. I bought this suit on sale in the department store.

acquire–to get by one's own actions or efforts. The museum recently acquired a rare piece of sculpture.

get–to obtain possession of. Let's go to the cafeteria and get our lunch.

obtain–to get or attain, usually through planned action. I obtained the tickets to the concert months ago.

procure–to get or obtain; to acquire. The broker procured many shares of stock.

buy *(continued)*

Thesaurus

purchase–to obtain through the payment of money. They purchased a piano for their living room.
ANTONYMS: **auction (v), market (v), sell (v), vend**

C

call (v)–to say, especially in a loud voice; to cry out or shout. When I call your name, please raise your hand.

cry–to call loudly; to shout. Did someone just cry for help?

scream–to make a loud, piercing cry. Some people screamed while riding the roller coaster at the amusement park.

shriek–to make a shrill or high-pitched sound. As the train approached the station, the whistle shrieked.

yell–to cry out with a loud, strong sound. The children in the playground are yelling.

holler [informal]–to shout or cry loudly. I holler for my dog when he runs away from me.

calm (adj)–not stormy or windy; not stirred up; not excited; peaceful. On that pleasant morning the sea was calm.

peaceful–full of peace; calm; quiet. On a peaceful evening I can hear the gentle, rhythmic chirping of crickets.

placid–pleasantly peaceful or calm; quiet. A placid brook meanders among the rolling hills of the farm.

quiet–moving very little; calm; still. The class was quiet while the test was in progress.

serene–calm; peaceful; untroubled. His serene smile showed that he was happy.

still–without noise; quiet; unruffled or undisturbed; free from waves, violent winds, or the like. Prior to the thunderstorm the air was absolutely still.

tranquil–peaceful; calm; quiet; free from agitation or disturbance; placid. I spent a tranquil day in the park sketching some trees.

ANTONYMS: **fierce, raging, rough (adj), stormy, turbulent, wild (adj)**

D

do (v)–to carry through to completion any work or action; to finish; to perform; to carry out; to make. Rena did all of the work efficiently.

accomplish–to succeed in completing; to carry out or perform a plan or undertaking. What did you accomplish today?

complete–to get done; to end; to finish. She completed her paper after doing research.

finish–to bring an action, work, or anything else to an end; to reach the end of; to complete. Janice finished the race ahead of all the other runners.

perform–to do; to go through and finish; to accomplish. My brother performed well in the school play.

produce–to bring into existence by effort or labor; to create; to make from various materials. That factory produces light bulbs.

See also *make* (v).

E

end (n)–**1** the last part; the conclusion. Their house is at the end of the street. **2** The part where a thing begins or when it stops. Hold the two ends of the string with your left hand.

border–the side, boundary, or edge of anything; a line that separates one country, state, or town from another; a frontier. You must show your passport when you cross the border between some countries.

conclusion–the final part; the end; the close. Before I could read the conclusion of this novel, I fell asleep.

edge–the place or line where something ends; the part farthest from the middle; the side. I cautiously looked over the edge of the rim of the Grand Canyon.

finale–the last part of a play or a piece of music. The finale of Tchaikovsky's "1812 Overture," which includes the sounds of bells and cannon, is very exciting.

termination–the act of ending or the fact of being ended; the end. With the termination of the contract with the builder all construction on the skyscraper ceased.

windup [informal]–an end, conclusion, or finish. At the windup of the festivities, everyone cheered.

ANTONYMS: **beginning (n), commencement, start (n)**

enjoy (v)–to use or have with joy; to be happy with. I enjoy bowling very much.

admire–to regard with wonder, approval, and pleasure; to feel satisfaction or delight in. I admire the astronauts for their courage.

appreciate–to think highly of; to recognize the quality or worth of; to value. Do you appreciate the good things that come your way?

love–to take great pleasure in; to like very much. I love to ride my bicycle in the park.

relish–to take delight or pleasure in; to like the taste of. Kevin relished every moment of his first day in New York City.

savor–to enjoy the taste or smell of; to appreciate by taste or smell. I savored every bite of the food in the Japanese restaurant.

adore [informal]–to like very much. Because she adores horses, Pamela works at the stable whenever she can.

ANTONYMS: abhor, despise, detest, dislike (v), hate (v), loathe

enough (adj)–as much as wanted or needed; sufficient. There is enough fried chicken for everyone to enjoy.

abundant–very plentiful; more than enough. An abundant harvest is the goal in every farmer's mind.

ample–large in degree or kind; more than enough; as much as is needed; sufficient. There is an ample supply of pencils.

minimal–least possible; very small. The tropical storm continued to intensify until it attained minimal hurricane winds.

plenty–abundant; plentiful; enough. Four tomatoes will be plenty.

substantial–important; large; ample. The workers received a substantial increase in salary.

sufficient–as much as is needed; enough. Without sufficient rainfall corn withers.

ANTONYMS: inadequate, insufficient, meager, scant (adj), skimpy

explain (v)–to tell how to do; to make plain or clear; to tell the meaning of; to give reasons for. I will explain how to get there.

clarify–to make clearer; to explain. Please clarify what you mean by that statement.

demonstrate–to show clearly; to explain by carrying out experiments or by showing and explaining samples; to show how something is done. My uncle demonstrated how to make a delicious cheese sauce.

describe–to tell in words how a person acts, feels, or looks, or how a thing, a place, or an event looks or happened; to write or tell about. Betty described her new outfit.

illustrate–to explain or make clear by examples, stories, or comparisons. By using a chart, she illustrated the facts she was presenting.

interpret–to explain the meaning of; to bring out the meaning of a dramatic work, music, or other written material. How would you interpret the meaning of that poem?

justify–to give a good reason for; to show to be right or just. Can you justify spending all that money for a pair of gloves?

ANTONYMS: confuse, misinterpret, obscure (v)

F

fine (adj)–**1** of a very high quality; excellent; good. The city art museum contains a fine collection of paintings. **2** very small or thin. That piece of thread is so fine that it is nearly invisible. **3** not heavy or coarse; delicate. The fine sand on this beach is extremely smooth to the touch.

commendable–deserving approval or praise; praiseworthy. Everyone who helped make the scenery did a commendable job.

delicate–of fine weave, make, or quality; easily torn; thin. Please handle that delicate crystal vase carefully.

powdery–of powder or dust; in the form of powder; dusty. Is powdery snow best for skiing?

pulverized–having been ground into powder or dust; like powder or dust. Is pulverized limestone good for lawns?

slender–thin and long; not big around; slim. I think that the slender tree is a poplar.

splendid–glorious; brilliant; magnificent, grand. The splendid light in the artist's studio is just right for painting.

See also *good*(adj).

ANTONYMS: coarse, inferior, poor, rough (adj), thick, unfinished

funny (adj)–causing laughter; amusing; comical. My sister likes to make funny faces.

amusing–causing smiles or laughter; entertaining. You must tell that amusing story.

comical–funny; amusing. We enjoyed the comical antics of the clowns.

hilarious–very merry; noisily happy; mirthful. Everyone had a hilarious time at Johnny's birthday party.

humorous–full of humor; having an amusing quality; funny. That book contains many humorous stories.

ludicrous–absurd, or not logical or true, but amusing; causing derisive laughter. The little boy and the Great Dane make a ludicrous pair.

witty–full of wit or the ability to perceive quickly and to express cleverly ideas that are striking,

unusual, and amusing; amusing and clever. One
character in the play continually made <u>witty</u>
remarks.

ANTONYMS: grave (adj), melancholy (adj),
mournful, serious, sober, solemn

G

go (v)–to move along; to proceed; to move away;
to leave. Tomorrow I will <u>go</u> to the shopping
mall with my friends.

exit–to go out; to leave. You should <u>exit</u> quickly
and quietly during a fire drill.

leave–to go away; to depart. Our cousins <u>left</u>
shortly after dinner because they had a long ride
home.

move–to pass from one position or place to another; to change position or place. Please <u>move</u>
that chair closer to the table.

progress–to advance; to move forward; to go
ahead. The long freight train <u>progressed</u> slowly
toward its destination.

travel–to go from one place to another; to journey.
My neighbors <u>travel</u> to distant places whenever
they are on vacation.

withdraw–to go away; to leave. Is it true that the
leading lady <u>withdrew</u> from the play?

ANTONYMS: arrive, come, halt (v), remain, stay
(v), stop (v)

good (adj)–**1** having high quality; superior; excellent. The food at this restaurant certainly is
<u>good</u>. **2** as it ought to be; right; proper; desir-
able. It was <u>good</u> of you to visit your ailing
friend. **3** clever, skillful. Obviously, a <u>good</u> artist painted that picture.

considerate–thoughtful of others and their feelings. It was <u>considerate</u> of you to call me when
I was sick.

honest–not cheating, lying, or stealing; fair and
upright; truthful. An <u>honest</u> person returned the
necklace I had lost in school.

proficient–advanced in any science, art, or subject;
skilled. Many of the students in my class are
<u>proficient</u> in spelling.

skillful–having skill or ability; expert. The <u>skillful</u>
carpenter quickly replaced the broken porch
step.

superior–above the average; excellent; higher in
amount, degree, or quality; better. I find the
hamburgers at this restaurant <u>superior</u> to all others I have tasted.

worthwhile–worth attention, effort, or time; having real merit or value. The trip to the historical
site was a <u>worthwhile</u> one.

See also *fine* (adj).

ANTONYMS: awful (adj), bad (adj), improper,
unskilled, worthless, wrong (adj)

great (adj)–**1** large in amount, size, or number;
more than usual. The <u>great</u> ship moved silently
and majestically into the harbor. **2** important;
famous; high in rank. While on our tour of one
of the motion picture studios in Hollywood, we
saw a <u>great</u> actor.

illustrious–very famous; outstanding; renowned.
The <u>illustrious</u> painter greeted all who came to
see the exhibit of his works.

magnificent–noble; impressive; extraordinarily
fine; superb. The <u>magnificent</u> trees of Sequoia
National Park are incredible to behold.

mammoth–gigantic; huge. A <u>mammoth</u> power
shovel was used to dig the trench.

outstanding–standing out from others; important;
well-known. Jack is an <u>outstanding</u> tennis
player.

tremendous–very great; immense; enormous. That
<u>tremendous</u> bridge is over one hundred years
old.

vast–of great area; of immense extent; tremendous.
The continent of Asia is <u>vast</u>.

See also *big* (adj).

ANTONYMS: inconsequential, inconsiderable, insignificant, small (adj), tiny

grow (v)–to become bigger by taking in food;
to develop toward full age or size; to thrive; to
increase. I have <u>grown</u> very much during the
past year.

develop–to come into activity or being; to grow; to
change in character through successive periods;
to evolve; to become bigger or better. Eli <u>devel-
oped</u> strong leg muscles through bicycle riding.

expand–to increase in size; to make grow larger;
to enlarge. A balloon <u>expands</u> when you blow
into it.

flourish–to develop or grow with vigor; to do well;
to be prosperous; to thrive. The marigolds are
<u>flourishing</u> in the garden.

increase–to become greater; to advance in quality,
power, or success; to become more numerous; to
multiply. I will <u>increase</u> the amount of water in
this lemonade.

mature–to come to full growth; to ripen. Tomatoes
that <u>mature</u> before they are picked taste best.

spread–to cover a large or larger area; to expand; to extend or grow outward from a center or trunk. The ivy is spreading over the entire stone wall.
ANTONYMS: **decline (v), decrease (v), diminish, dwindle, shrink (v), wane**

H

have (v)–**1** to hold in one's possession or in one's keeping; to possess. We have two horses in the barn. **2** to experience. We had a wonderful time during our trip to the zoo.
endure–to put up with; to tolerate; to experience. Miyoko endured a toothache for most of the day.
experience–to feel; to meet with; to live through. You haven't experienced sledding until you have gone down the giant hill near the tennis courts.
own–to have or hold as property; to possess. That family owns two automobiles.
possess–to have knowledge, an attribute, or a skill; to have as property. Do you possess the skills needed to do this job?
retain–to continue to hold or have; to keep. She retains much of what she studies.
undergo–to go through; to experience. Will you undergo the minor surgery tomorrow?
ANTONYMS: **lack (v), need (v), want (v)**

hear (v)–**1** to take in a sound or sounds through the ear; to listen to. I heard my favorite song on the radio this morning. **2** to give a chance to be heard; to give a formal hearing to, as a judge does. The judge will hear the case on Tuesday.
eavesdrop–to listen to talk that one is not supposed to hear; to listen secretly to a private conversation. My sister sometimes eavesdrops on my conversations.
heed–to give careful attention to; to take notice of; to mind. Drivers must heed all traffic signals in order to drive safely.
judge–to hear and decide a case in a court of law. That case will be judged next week.
listen–to try to hear; to attend with the ears in order to hear; to pay attention. Please listen carefully to what I am about to say.
perceive–to be aware of through the senses; to hear. I barely perceive the chirping of birds somewhere in the distance.
try–to investigate in a court of law. The defendant was tried and found innocent.

help (v)–to give or do what is useful or needed;

to relieve someone in trouble or distress; to assist; to aid. Tim helped me change the flat tire.
aid–to give support to; to assist. My friends aided me when I fell off my bicycle.
assist–to help someone either when in need or when doing something; to give aid to. I assisted the teacher by handing out the homework papers.
encourage–to give courage, hope, or confidence to; to urge on; to support. My teammates encourage me before every game.
rescue–to save from capture, danger, or harm; to free. During the snowstorm the stranded motorists were rescued by the state police.
support–to give courage, strength, or confidence to; to keep up; to supply with the necessities of life; to provide for. When I was ill my neighbors supported me by cooking all of my meals.
ANTONYMS: **block (v), discourage, frustrate, hinder, obstruct, oppose**

hot (adj)–having a temperature that is relatively high. This coffee is too hot to drink.
scorching–that burns slightly; burning; withering. The scorching sun made it difficult to stay on the playground for long.
sizzling–very hot; burning up with intense heat. The sizzling steaks looked appetizing while they were cooking on the grill.
steaming–emitting steam or vapor; very hot. I would like another steaming bowl of soup.
sweltering–oppressively hot; unbearably hot. On sweltering summer days I like to go swimming.
torrid–parched with heat; scorching. What animals live in the torrid desert climate?
tropical–like the climate of the tropics; very hot; burning. In this tropical weather I really enjoy something cold to drink.
ANTONYMS: **chilly, cool (adj), freezing, frigid, icy**

I

idea (n)–a notion or picture of anything in the mind; a mental image; any result of mental activity; a thought. I have a great idea for a report topic.
concept–an idea or general notion. The concept of transportation takes form in various conveyances, such as automobiles.
impression–an idea or notion. My first impression is that this subject will be difficult.

idea (*continued*)

Thesaurus

notion–an understanding; an idea; an opinion; a belief. I have a notion to go shopping.

opinion–belief not so strong as knowledge; judgment; what one thinks. Can you support your opinion with facts?

theory–an explanation based on reasoning and observation, especially one that has been confirmed and tested as a general principle explaining many related facts; an explanation based on thought. The research scientist developed a new theory.

thought–what a person thinks; a notion; an idea. Many thoughts about the excellent show we saw continue to occupy my mind.

J

job (n)–a piece of work; anything one has to do; work done for pay; employment. My mother has a job with an advertising firm.

chore–a small task; an odd job; a disagreeable or difficult thing to do. I do not mind doing chores around the house.

occupation–the work that a person does regularly or to earn a living; employment; trade. Have you ever thought about what occupation you might want to pursue?

position–a job; employment. Her position in the company is an important one.

profession–an occupation requiring special education, such as law or medicine; any occupation by which a person earns a living. To become a member of the medical profession, a person must study for many years.

task–work assigned or found to be necessary; a duty; work to be done. The task of scrubbing the floor is not pleasant.

work–effort in making or doing something; something to do; employment; occupation. Some outdoor work, such as the repairing of downed power lines, must be done even in inclement weather.

K

keep (v)–**1** to have for a long time; to continue to hold; to have and not let go of. May I keep any seashells I find while at the beach? **2** to hold back; to prevent. The high fence around the playground keeps children from running into the street.

conserve–to keep from loss or from being used up; to preserve. Please conserve water during the drought.

maintain–to keep up; to keep; to preserve. I will maintain the lawn this year by mowing it frequently.

possess–to own; to have as belonging to one; to maintain or keep. My friend possesses many pieces of antique furniture.

prevent–to stop or keep from. The workers prevented people from walking in the wet cement of the new sidewalk.

restrain–to keep in check; to hold back; to keep within limits. Please restrain your dog from chasing my cat.

store–to stock or supply; to put away for later use. Do squirrels store acorns?

ANTONYMS: **abandon** (v), **discard** (v), **free** (v), **lose**, **release** (v), **relinquish**

know (v)–**1** to have understanding of the facts of. I know many of the poems in that book. **2** to be acquainted with. Do you know our neighbors, the Logans?

comprehend–to understand the nature or meaning of something. Do you comprehend that difficult mathematical concept?

grasp–to lay hold of with the mind; to understand. Donny instantly grasped the meaning of what I was saying about the riddle.

perceive–to be aware of through the senses; to feel, hear, see, smell, or taste; to take in the mind. She perceived that they wanted to have a private conversation.

realize–to be fully aware of; to understand clearly. I realized later that I had left my purse under my seat in class.

recognize–to be aware of someone or something previously known. While out shopping, I recognized one of my teachers.

understand–to grasp the meaning of. I understand a few words in French.

L

like (v)–to be pleased with; to be satisfied with; to find agreeable. I like to be with pleasant companions.

admire–to regard with pleasure, wonder, and approval. I admire the crews of the Space Shuttle.

appreciate–to think highly of; to recognize the quality or worth of; to enjoy. Because he appreciates figure skating, he often attends ice shows and skating exhibitions.

cherish–to hold dear; to treat with tenderness. Many people cherish childhood memories.

enjoy–to have or use with happiness; to take plea-sure in. We enjoyed ourselves when we went roller skating last Friday.

prefer–to like better; to choose above another. Do you prefer chicken soup or vegetable soup?

treasure–to value highly; to cherish. I treasure our friendship because you really care very much about me.

ANTONYMS: abhor, detest, dislike (v), hate (v), loathe

look   (v)–to try to see; to see; to direct a glance at. Please look both ways before crossing that busy street.

examine– to look at carefully and closely. The doc-tor examined Dad's eyes and found that his vi-sion was excellent.

gaze–to look steadily and long. She gazed at a puffy cloud as it moved across the sky.

observe–to see and note; to notice; to examine carefully; to watch; to study. Becky often ob-serves the seagulls as they circle near the sandy beach.

peek–to look slyly and quickly; to peep. If you peek into that room, you will see the sleeping kittens.

stare–to look directly and long with the eyes wide open; to gaze fixedly. John stares into space while he is daydreaming.

watch–to look at; to observe with interest or care. While you were at the airport, did you watch the airplanes take off and land?

See also *see* (v).

ANTONYMS: disregard (v), ignore, miss (v), over-look (v)

loud   (adj)–making a great sound; not soft or quiet; noisy. I could hear loud laughter from our neighbor's party yesterday.

blaring–making a loud, harsh sound. Will you please turn down that blaring music.

deafening–that stuns or deafens with noise. With a deafening roar the huge jet aircraft lifted off the runway.

earsplitting–overpoweringly loud; deafening. The racket made by the machines at the construction site is earsplitting.

noisy–making much noise; full of noise. The noisy children were having fun playing baseball.

thunderous–producing thunder; making or accom-panied by a noise like thunder. After the con-cert, the symphony orchestra received a thunderous ovation.

vociferous–noisy and loud; clamoring; shouting. The vociferous crowd cheered enthusiastically for the team.

ANTONYMS: gentle (adj), low (adj), mellow (adj), quiet (adj), soft (adj), subdued

M

make   (v)–**1** to bring into being; to build, form, put together, or shape. She made a delicious meal from only a few ingredients. **2** to cause to; to force to. The teacher made me write my re-port over again.

build–to make by putting materials together; to construct. In my spare time I build model air-planes.

compel–to urge or drive with force; to force. The fierce thunderstorm compelled the pilot to delay the takeoff.

construct–to put together; to fit together; to frame; to build. We carefully constructed the book-shelves according to the instructions that came in the box.

create–to make something that has not been made before; to bring into being. The artist created a beautiful landscape painting.

manufacture–to make by hand or by machine; to make into something useful. Many companies in this area manufacture electrical appliances.

pressure [informal]–to urge or force by exerting a compelling influence. She was pressured by the approaching deadline to work even faster.

See also *do* (v).

ANTONYMS: demolish, destroy, ruin (v), wreck (v)

N

need   (n)–**1** the lack of a desired or useful thing; a want; a lack. We have a need for volunteers to help in the hospital. **2** something that has to be; a requirement; a necessity. There is a need for quiet in the library.

absence–the state of being without; a lack. Darkness is the absence of light.

deficiency–an absence or lack of something needed; an incompleteness. A balanced diet can help to prevent a vitamin deficiency.

lack–the condition of being without; not having enough; a shortage. Because of a lack of inter-est, a course in our town's adult school was canceled.

need (*continued*)

Thesaurus

necessity–that which cannot be done without; a needed thing. Flour is a necessity for many baked items.

requirement–something needed; a necessity. Writing a book report is a requirement in this class.

shortage–too small an amount; a deficiency; a lack. We are fortunate not to have a shortage of food.

ANTONYMS: **abundance, adequacy, affluence, excess (n), wealth**

new (adj)–now first made, thought out, known, felt, or discovered; never having existed before; now first used; not used up or worn. Your new car is just beautiful.

current–of the present time. What are some of the current trends in fashion?

fledgling–just beginning; new or inexperienced. The fledgling store manager soon became quite good at her work.

fresh–newly made, gathered, or arrived; recent; not known, seen, or used before; new. If the cream is not fresh, I do not want it.

modern–of the present time; of times not long past; not old-fashioned; up-to-date. I do not think the telephone is a modern invention.

novel–of a new nature or kind; not known before; unfamiliar; new. Automobiles were novel to people living in the early twentieth century.

recent–made or done not long ago; not long past; modern. Did you see the recent movie that was on television last night?

ANTONYMS: **ancient (adj), antique (adj), old (adj), outdated, outmoded, stale (adj)**

noise (n)–loud, confused, or irritating sounds. The noise of traffic in the street made sleep impossible.

clamor–a loud noise, especially shouting, that goes on continuously. The clamor of the crowd filled the air.

clatter–a rapid succession of sharp, rattling sounds. An awful clatter was coming from the kitchen.

din–loud noise that goes on without letup. The din from the stadium could be heard blocks away.

hubbub–a general confused noise, as of many voices. The speaker waited for the hubbub to die down.

racket–loud, confused noise; loud talk. The sound of everyone talking made quite a racket.

ruckus [informal]–a noisy uproar. After the game,

the winning team raised a ruckus in the locker room.

See also *sound* (n).

ANTONYMS: **calm (n), quiet (n), silence (n), tranquility**

P

place (n)–the part of space occupied by or intended for a person or thing; a definite position in space; a particular portion of space. The corner of this room is a perfect place for my desk.

district–a part of a larger area; a region; a part of a state or city marked off for a special purpose, such as providing schools or law courts. Everyone living in this district attends Mountain Avenue School.

location–a place or position; a locality. Inspiration Point in Yellowstone National Park is an excellent location for taking breathtaking photographs.

region–a place, space, or area; any large part of the earth's surface. Does the northwestern region of the United States receive much snow?

residence–a home or house; a place where a person lives; an abode. My residence is on the other side of town.

site–the place or area upon which something has been, is being, or will be built, done, or made to happen. The site of the monument is right in front of the municipal building.

territory–a geographical area; land. The ancient Roman Empire included a vast amount of territory.

put (v)–to cause to be in some place or position; to place; to lay. I put my shoes under my bed.

deposit–to put or lay down; to put in a place for safekeeping. Carol deposited her paycheck at the local bank.

place–to set in a specified position; to put in a particular place. I placed the mixing bowl on the table for just a moment.

position–to put in a particular place. I will position the painting on this wall.

rest–to place on or against a support. Please rest those boards against the wall.

set–to put in some place. I will set the tray of sandwiches on this table.

situate–to locate or place. Their cabin is situated among the tall pines near the lake.

Q

quiet (adj)–with little or no noise; making no sound; hushed; silent. The class was quiet during the final exam.

inaudible–not loud enough to be heard; that cannot be heard. Can dogs hear sounds that are inaudible to human beings?

noiseless–making no noise; silent; making very little noise; nearly quiet. The noiseless spider was spinning a web.

reserved–showing or having self-restraint; disposed to say little or keep silent. Being a reserved individual, Brian does not dominate a discussion.

silent–quiet; noiseless; not speaking; saying little or nothing. Cynthia usually keeps silent on matters that do not pertain to her.

soft–not loud; subdued; quiet. When I arrived at the store, there was soft music playing in the background.

unvoiced–not expressed in words; not spoken. Although his opinion was unvoiced, I could tell how he felt by the expression on his face.

ANTONYMS: boisterous, clamorous, loquacious, noisy, verbose

right (adj)–**1** agreeing with what is just, lawful, or good. It is right to help others who are in need. **2** conforming to facts or truth; correct; true. My watch does not have the right time.

accurate–without mistakes or errors; exactly right; precisely correct. Electronic devices used to time running races are accurate to a fraction of a second.

correct–free from faults or mistakes; right; true. Most of the class had correct answers on the quiz.

decent–right and proper. A decent person treats others fairly.

precise–accurate; exact; definite. In order to repair the engine, the mechanic needed to know the precise size of the defective part.

proper–right for the occasion; correct; fitting. What are the proper clothes to wear to a job interview?

true–agreeing with fact; not false. Everything you heard on the radio about the accident was true.

See also *true* (adj).

ANTONYMS: erroneous, improper, unethical, unfair, unsatisfactory, wrong (adj)

R

rest (n)–a state of ease and quiet; repose; sleep; ease after effort or work; freedom from anything that tires, troubles, or pains. Do you mind if I take a brief rest before we continue walking up the path?

leisure–time free from required work, in which a person may rest and do enjoyable things. What kinds of hobbies do you pursue at your leisure?

recess–a time during which work stops. We plan to play basketball during recess.

relaxation–relief from effort or work; amusement; recreation. I get relaxation from sketching in the park.

repose–sleep or rest; ease; quietness. At this late hour most of the birds are at repose.

respite–a time of rest and relief; a lull. During the afternoon we had a brief respite from the difficult work we were doing.

letup [informal]–a pause or stop; a lessening of effort. As closing time approached, there was a letup in the store clerk's busy job.

ANTONYMS: activity, disquiet (n), excitement, restlessness, toil (n), work (n)

run (v)–to go steadily by moving the legs quickly; to go faster than a walk; to go in a hurry; to hasten. Marta ran in order to catch the early bus.

hurry–to move quickly or with more than easy or natural speed. People hurry everywhere during the rush hour.

jog–to run at a leisurely pace. Many people jog every day in order to keep in shape.

race–to run swiftly; to run to see who will win; to engage in a contest of speed. I raced my friend to the end of the block and back.

scamper–to run quickly; to go hastily. The chipmunk scampered across the front lawn.

sprint–to run at full speed, especially over a short distance. The runners sprinted across the finish line.

trot–(for four-legged animals) to go at a moderately fast gait by lifting the right forefoot and the left hind foot at about the same time and then the other two feet in the same way. As the horses trotted around the track, they pulled two-wheeled vehicles called sulkies.

ANTONYMS: crawl (v), creep (v), stroll (v), walk (v)

Thesaurus

s

say (v)–to speak; to put into words. I said that I
    thought the meal was delicious.
affirm–to say firmly; to assert; to declare to be
    true. He affirmed that his decision about leaving
    the club was final.
declare–to announce formally or publicly; to make
    known. Did she declare her candidacy for public
    office?
express–to put into words; to utter; to state. I have
    expressed my feelings on this matter many
    times.
impart–to communicate; to tell; to reveal. He im-
    parted to me a great deal of knowledge about
    gardening.
mention–to speak about; to refer to. Taro men-
    tioned that he had traveled extensively.
respond–to reply in words; to answer. Who will
    respond to that challenging question?
See also *talk* (v).

see (v)–**1** to perceive by use of the eyes. Yester-
    day morning I saw a deer in my backyard. **2** to
    form a mental picture of. I still see last year's
    parade as if it were yesterday.
behold–to look at; to observe. We beheld the color-
    ful sunset from the summit of that mountain.
distinguish–to see clearly. Even though the night
    sky was flooded with stars, Maryann dis-
    tinguished many constellations.
notice–to give attention to; to observe; to perceive.
    I noticed that he has not been in school for a
    couple of days.
view–to look at; to see; to behold; to scan. The
    class viewed a film based upon a book that they
    had read.
visualize–to form a mental picture of. Can an artist
    visualize a painting even before it is begun?
witness–to perceive; to see. I know someone who
    witnessed the Olympic Games in person.
See also *look* (v).
ANTONYMS: disregard (v), ignore, overlook (v)

sleek (adj)–smooth and shiny; soft and glossy.
    My cat's fur is sleek.
glassy–smooth; like glass. The ice-covered pond
    had a glassy appearance.
gleaming–sending forth flashes or beams of light.
    After it was waxed, the car once again had a
    gleaming finish.
glossy–having a shiny surface; smooth and shiny.
    It is difficult to read anything written on that
    glossy sheet of paper.

lustrous–having a bright and shining surface; shin-
    ing; glossy. Regular brushing and proper diet
    keep my dog's coat lustrous.
shiny–reflecting light; bright; shining. The sun-
    light reflected off the shiny surface of the lake.
silky–soft and smooth; of or like silk; glossy. That
    black and white kitten has silky fur.
ANTONYMS: coarse (adj), dull (adj), rough (adj)

small (adj)–**1** not large or great; not large as
    compared with other things of the same kind;
    little in size. That small television set would fit
    almost anywhere in the house. **2** not great in
    amount, degree, strength, or value. Only a small
    number of people attended the outdoor cere-
    mony in the rain.
insignificant–having little influence or importance;
    too small to be important. You added such an
    insignificant amount of spice that I can hardly
    detect its flavor in the stew.
microscopic–too small to be seen without a micro-
    scope; extremely small. Are there microscopic
    specks of dust in the air?
miniature–made or done on a very small scale;
    tiny. Many people collect miniature dollhouses
    and furniture.
minor–less important; smaller. That minor error
    will not affect the completion of the work.
slight–not important; not much; small. My
    Chihuahua is so slight that I can carry him in my
    pocket.
teeny [informal]–tiny, very small. Please put a
    teeny amount of sugar in my tea.
ANTONYMS: big (adj), enormous, great (adj), im-
    mense, large (adj), significant

sound (n)–that which is heard; sensation per-
    ceived in the organs of hearing. That strange
    sound came from the other room.
intonation–the manner of producing musical
    notes, especially with regard to pitch; the man-
    ner of speaking, especially with regard to the
    rise and fall in the pitch of the voice. What into-
    nation would you use in your voice to express
    surprise?
monotone–a manner of singing or speaking with-
    out change of pitch; unvaried sound. The guest
    lecturer spoke with such a monotone that many
    in the audience became drowsy.
noise–loud, confused, or irritating sounds. There
    was so much noise in the park that I could not
    concentrate on my book.

pitch–the degree of highness or lowness of a tone or sound. The notes of a muscial scale vary in pitch.

reverberation–the fact or act of echoing back sound; echo. When the car horn sounded in the tunnel, there was a great reverberation of sound.

tone–any sound considered with reference to its quality, pitch, or strength; in music, a sound of definite pitch and character. That violin certainly has beautiful tone.

See also *noise* (n).

ANTONYMS: **quiet (n), silence (n)**

T

take (v)–**1** to grasp; to lay hold of; to seize; to capture. Please take your little brother's hand when crossing the street. **2** to carry; to convey. Is that the plane that will take us to Chicago?

acquire–to get by one's own actions or efforts; to attain; to gain. The museum acquired a valuable piece of sculpture.

confiscate–to seize for the public treasury; to seize by authority. Does the city government confiscate abandoned buildings?

grasp–to seize and hold fast by closing the fingers around; to grip, clutch, or grab. You must grasp the jar firmly to open it.

procure–to get by effort or care; to secure; to obtain. Some people procure large fortunes through wise investment of their money.

seize–to take hold of suddenly; to grasp; to clutch. A long time ago on the high seas, many ships were overrun by pirates who seized valuable cargo.

transport–to carry from one place to another; to convey. The movers will transport all of our furniture to our new home.

ANTONYMS: **give (v), relinquish, return (v), surrender (v)**

talk (v)–to speak; to use words; to exchange words or engage in conversation. I will talk with him after I finish my work.

chat–to talk in an informal and familiar way. My sister and I chat with one another over the phone.

communicate–to give information or news by speaking or writing. You should communicate your feelings to your parents.

converse–to talk in an informal way; to engage in conversation. While he stood in line at the supermarket, Bill conversed with another shopper.

discuss–to talk over; to consider a topic from various points of view. We discussed poetry in class today.

report–to give an account of something seen, heard, read, or done; to relate or tell. Tomorrow I will report on stamp collecting.

speak–to say words; to converse; to talk. Have you spoken to anyone about the class trip?

See also *say* (v).

think (v)–to have an idea or thought in the mind; to picture in the mind. I think it would be a better idea to paint the apartment blue.

conceive–to form in the mind; to think up; to imagine. The writer conceived an unusual plot for his next mystery novel.

contemplate–to think about for a long time; to study carefully. I often contemplate things while walking in the woods.

deliberate–to think over carefully; to consider. The judges of the talent contest deliberated for some time before choosing a winner.

imagine–to form a picture of in the mind; to have an idea of; to think; to fancy. I imagined that I was living in a far-off country a long time ago.

reason–to think things out; to think logically; to solve new problems. The members of the touring group who were lost reasoned that if they remained in the museum, someone would come back and find them.

suppose–to consider as possible; to consider as possibly true. I suppose that someday everyone will be able to travel to distant places in outer space.

true (adj)–agreeing with fact; not false; genuine; real. That movie is based on a true story that occurred during the nineteenth century.

authentic–coming from the stated source; not copied; genuine; worthy of acceptance or belief; reliable. That is an authentic document from the eighteenth century.

certain–without any doubt; sure. It is certain that birch trees will grow in this part of the country if given the proper conditions.

correct–free from faults or mistakes; right; true. Justin had seventeen correct answers on the test.

factual–concerned with or consisting of facts; of the nature of fact. The factual accounts of the hardships endured by many of the pioneers are fascinating.

true (*continued*)

Thesaurus

historical–of or having to do with history; according to history; known to be true or real. I enjoy reading about <u>historical</u> events because in doing so I learn about people in other times and places.

real–not imagined or made up; existing as a fact; actual; genuine. Is that a <u>real</u> diamond or an imitation?

See also *right* (adj)

ANTONYMS: **artificial, false (adj), fictitious, inaccurate, incorrect, untrue**

U

understand (v)–to grasp the meaning of; to know the meaning or idea of; to know well. Because I <u>understood</u> the material, I easily answered the question.

apprehend–to grasp with the mind; to understand; to be aware of; to perceive. After carefully examining the broken motor, Margaret <u>apprehended</u> why it was not running.

comprehend–to understand the nature or meaning of something. I cannot <u>comprehend</u> what you are saying about the math problem.

fathom–to get to the bottom of; to fully understand. Can you <u>fathom</u> the incredible distances to the stars.

grasp–to lay hold of with the mind; to understand. Blanca immediately <u>grasped</u> the impact that the decision would have.

know–to have understanding of the facts of; to have firmly in the mind or memory. The attorney <u>knew</u> the case quite well.

realize–to be fully aware of; to understand clearly. On my way to the beach I suddenly <u>realized</u> that I had left my sunglasses on a table at home.

ANTONYM: **misunderstand**

use (v)–**1** to put into action or service; to utilize; to practice or employ actively; to exercise, especially customarily or habitually. May I <u>use</u> your pen for just a moment? **2** to consume or take regularly; to expend or spend by using. Did you <u>use</u> all of the fertilizer on the lawn?

deplete–to exhaust or empty by using up strength, resources, vitality, or the like. The once abundant coal deposits in this part of the state have been <u>depleted</u> by many years of mining.

employ–to use; to use the services of. We <u>employed</u> a whole new set of tactics to help us win the game.

exercise–to actively use something to cause improvement or to give practice and training. I <u>exercise</u> every day in order to stay in good condition.

exhaust–to empty completely; to drain; to expend. By the end of our three-week vacation in Europe, we had <u>exhausted</u> our funds.

manipulate–to handle or treat with the hands or by mechanical means, especially in a skillful manner. The operator <u>manipulated</u> the power shovel, making it move as if it were a giant animal.

utilize–to make use of; to put to a practical use. When I see the clutter in this office, I wonder if we are <u>utilizing</u> all of our space properly.

ANTONYMS: **conserve (v), preserve (v), save (v)**

W

well (adv)–in a good, favorable, or satisfactory manner; thoroughly; fully; satisfactorily. I am doing <u>well</u> in most of my subjects.

competently–in an able manner. The new carpenter <u>competently</u> performed every task that had to be done.

proficiently–in an advanced or skillful manner; expertly. Janet speaks <u>proficiently</u> in both French and Spanish.

satisfactorily–in a satisfactory, pleasing, or adequate manner; so as to give satisfaction or contentment. Last year I <u>satisfactorily</u> completed a course in first aid.

skillfully–with skill; expertly. The bus driver <u>skillfully</u> eased the large bus around the hairpin turns.

successfully–in a manner that achieves a favorable result or accomplishes what is intended or desired. My older brother <u>successfully</u> completed high school last year.

fine [informal]–excellently; very well. Lien was ill for a little while, but now she is doing <u>fine</u>.

ANTONYMS: **badly, imperfectly, inadequately, poorly, unacceptably, unsatisfactorily**

win (v)–to gain a victory in a contest; to succeed; to get possession of by work or fortune. If our basketball team <u>wins</u> the tournament tomorrow, we will become the new league champions.

achieve–to carry out successfully; to accomplish. Dana <u>achieved</u> her goal this marking period by getting an A in science.

acquire–to get by one's own actions or efforts; to gain; to attain. Since I saw you last year, have you acquired any more merit badges for your Scout work?

earn–to receive in return for work or service; to come to be worthy of or entitled to. I earned enough money from my paper route to buy the radio I want.

prevail–to win the victory; to gain supremacy through strength or superiority. At the international competition the superior gymnasts prevailed over their less skillful counterparts.

reap–to obtain as the result of action or effort. In victory we reaped the fruit of our long hours of practice.

triumph–to be victorious; to win success. Almost every day we read about courageous people who have triumphed over disease or misfortune.

ANTONYMS: **fail (v), fall (v), flop (v), forfeit (v), lose**

wonderful (adj)–causing wonder, or surprise or astonishment; remarkable; marvelous; surprisingly excellent. We had wonderful weather throughout our two-week vacation.

astonishing–very surprising; amazing. The daring feats of the trapeze artist in the circus were astonishing.

extraordinary–beyond what is ordinary; remarkable or very unusual. Pete did an extraordinary job in restoring that old furniture to its present excellent condition.

marvelous–causing wonder; extraordinary. The twinkling stars are a marvelous sight.

remarkable–worthy of notice; unusual. The person who ran into the burning building to save the little child showed truly remarkable courage.

superb–stately and grand; majestic; magnificent. This is a superb hotel.

terrific [informal]–very great or severe; extraordinary; remarkable; very good. My friends are terrific people to talk with as well as to have fun with.

ANTONYMS: **average (adj), common (adj), mediocre, ordinary (adj), uninteresting, usual (adj)**

work (v)–**1** to labor; to do or make something through effort; to do or make something for pay; to be employed. My cousin works for an electronics company. **2** to act; to operate, especially effectively. Does the new farm tractor work as well as the old one?

function–to work; to act; to be in action; to operate. That machine will function properly after it is lubricated.

labor–to do work, especially hard work; to toil. The farmer labored for many hours in order to harvest the wheat.

operate–to be at work; to run; to function. The commuter trains on this line generally operate on schedule.

perform–to do; to go through and finish; to accomplish. The symphony orchestra performed well yesterday evening in the first concert of the season.

toil–to work hard and long; to labor. The workers toiled for several years until the tunnel was completed.

tick [informal]–to function, go, or work. Somehow this complicated mass of gears and valves ticks.

ANTONYM: **play (v)**

wrong (adj)–**1** not right; bad; unlawful; unjust. It is wrong to tell a lie. **2** not true; not correct; not according to truth or facts; incorrect; inaccurate. The final score of the game as printed in this morning's newspaper is wrong. **3** not proper or right according to a code or standard; unsuitable. Yellow socks are wrong for a blue suit.

illegal–not lawful; forbidden by law; against the law. It is illegal to park a car in front of a fire hydrant.

inaccurate–not without errors or mistakes; not exact. You should not make inaccurate statements in a report.

inappropriate–not right or proper; not suitable; improper. It is inappropriate to wear a tennis outfit to a formal dinner party.

incorrect–not correct; containing mistakes or errors; wrong. Your answers for the last two math problems are incorrect.

unethical–not morally right; not in accordance with professional or formal rules for right conduct or practice. It is unethical for a lawyer to discuss with anyone the confidential aspects of a client's case.

unsuitable–not right or fitting; inappropriate. That person is unsuitable for the position in management because he lacks the necessary education.

See also *bad* (adj).

ANTONYMS: **correct (adj), ethical, proper (adj), right (adj), suitable, true (adj)**

Reports, Letters, Notes

Book Reports

A **book report** tells what a book is about and gives an opinion of the book. Read the book report below. Notice that the first paragraph gives the title and author of the book and gets the reader's interest. The second briefly tells what the book is about. The third gives an opinion of the book.

Island of the Blue Dolphins
by Scott O'Dell

"I remember the day the Aleut ship came to our island." This is the way Scott O'Dell begins Island of the Blue Dolphins. The Aleuts are seal hunters who have forced the island tribe to leave their home. In this book, readers will meet a courageous Native American girl. Karana manages to survive all alone on the island.

Karana is one character I will never forget. She is brave and intelligent. In fact, sometimes she really surprised me. Once Karana dove from a ship into the ocean to try to save her brother. Reading about Karana made me wonder what I would do in such a situation.

The book is worthwhile for many reasons. Most important are the ideas about life, survival, and nature. Although Karana's story is an unusual one, I found it believable, and I could understand her, too.

Guidelines for Writing a Book Report

♦ Give the title and author of the book. Underline the title. Capitalize the first word, the last word, and all important words in the title.

♦ Describe the setting of the story — where and when it takes place.

♦ Briefly describe the major characters.

♦ Tell something about the plot, or what happens in the story, but don't give away the ending!

♦ Give your opinion of the book. Explain why you think the book is or is not interesting and worthwhile.

Friendly Letters

A friendly letter has five parts: the heading, greeting, body, closing, and signature. Study the placement of the five parts of this letter.

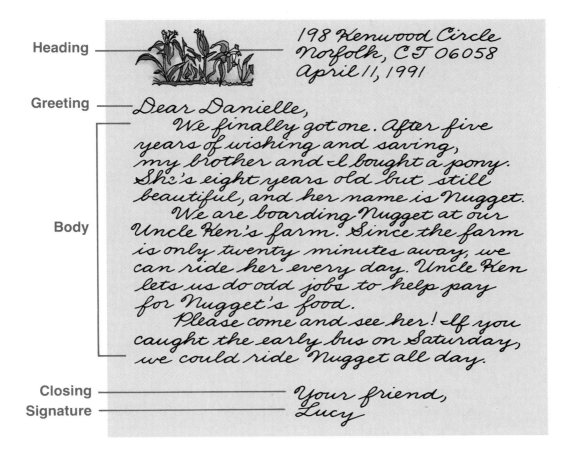

Heading

198 Kenwood Circle
Norfolk, CT 06058
April 11, 1991

Greeting

Dear Danielle,

Body

    We finally got one. After five years of wishing and saving, my brother and I bought a pony. She's eight years old but still beautiful, and her name is Nugget.

    We are boarding Nugget at our Uncle Ken's farm. Since the farm is only twenty minutes away, we can ride her every day. Uncle Ken lets us do odd jobs to help pay for Nugget's food.

    Please come and see her! If you caught the early bus on Saturday, we could ride Nugget all day.

Closing
Signature

Your friend,
Lucy

Follow these rules when writing friendly letters.

- Include your address and the date in the heading. Place a comma between your city and state and between the day and year in the date.
- Capitalize the first word of the greeting. Place a comma after the greeting.
- Place a comma after the closing. Capitalize the first word of the closing.
- Indent each new paragraph.

Social Notes

A **thank-you note** is a short letter of appreciation for a gift or favor. It follows the form of a friendly letter. Like a friendly letter, a thank-you note has five parts: the heading, greeting, body, closing, and signature.

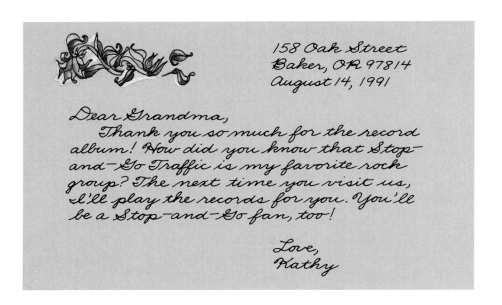

158 Oak Street
Baker, OR 97814
August 14, 1991

Dear Grandma,
    Thank you so much for the record album! How did you know that Stop-and-Go Traffic is my favorite rock group? The next time you visit us, I'll play the records for you. You'll be a Stop-and-Go fan, too!

        Love,
        Kathy

An **invitation** is a note or letter that invites someone to an event. It should name the event, tell where and when it is being held, and tell who sent the invitation.

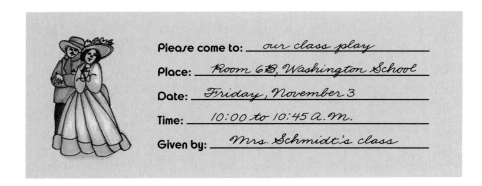

Please come to: _our class play_
Place: _Room 6B, Washington School_
Date: _Friday, November 3_
Time: _10:00 to 10:45 A.M._
Given by: _Mrs. Schmidt's class_

Addressing Envelopes

- When you address an envelope, you write the return address and the receiver's address.

return address
- Write your name and address in the upper left-hand corner. This is the **return address**. It shows where to return the letter if it cannot be delivered.

receiver's address
- In the center of the envelope, write the **receiver's address**. This is the name and address of the person who will receive the letter. For business letters, the receiver's address is an exact copy of the inside address.

state abbreviations
- You may use an abbreviation for the name of a state. See the chart on page 502. It lists the abbreviations approved by the Postal Service.

Return address —— Alice Pavlov
230 Henry Avenue
Carson, CA 90744

Receiver's address ——
Ms. Liz Tanaka
57 Washington Street
Fairfax, VA 22030

State abbreviations ——

Practice

Using a ruler, draw three envelopes like the sample above. Then address each one, using the information given below.

1. *Return address:* Walt Jamison   93 Fox St.   Oxford, NC 27565
   Receiver's address: Mr. Fred Bosch   30 Green Lane   York, PA 17405
2. *Return address:* Leslie Pruce   12 Elm St.   Warwick, NY 10990
   Receiver's address: Mrs. Edna Wright   78 Sunset Dr.   Stanhope, NJ 07874
3. *Return address:* Pedro Sanchez   222 Penn St.   Cody, WY 82414
   Receiver's address: Mr. Justin Mendal   9 Ranch Ave.   El Paso, TX 79910

Abbreviations

Sometimes you do not have to write out a word completely. Instead, you can use an abbreviation. An **abbreviation** is a shortened form of a word. For example, *Sen.* is an abbreviation for *Senator*. Many abbreviations begin with a capital letter and end with a period.

Titles of Persons	Dr.—Doctor Rev.—Reverend Gov.—Governor Mr.—Mister Mrs.—Mistress (a married woman) Ms.—for Miss (an unmarried woman) or Mrs.
Words That Mean Street	St.—Street Rd.—Road Ave.—Avenue Ln.—Lane Dr.—Drive Blvd.—Boulevard Pl.—Place
Days	Sun. Mon. Tues. Wed. Thurs. Fri. Sat.
Months	Jan. Feb. Mar. Apr. Aug. (Other months are Sept. Oct. Nov. Dec. not abbreviated.)
Times	A.M.—*ante meridiem* (Latin for *before noon*) P.M.—*post meridiem* (Latin for *after noon*)

Initials are sometimes used in place of complete names. The name *Sarah Brown Johnson* could be written *S.B. Johnson*. Initials are capitalized and followed by a period.

State Abbreviations   Use these abbreviations of state names when you write addresses. Notice periods are not used.

State	Abbr.	State	Abbr.	State	Abbr.	State	Abbr.
Alabama	AL	Indiana	IN	Nebraska	NE	South Carolina	SC
Alaska	AK	Iowa	IA	Nevada	NV	South Dakota	SD
Arizona	AZ	Kansas	KS	New Hampshire	NH	Tennessee	TN
Arkansas	AR	Kentucky	KY	New Jersey	NJ	Texas	TX
California	CA	Louisiana	LA	New Mexico	NM	Utah	UT
Colorado	CO	Maine	ME	New York	NY	Vermont	VT
Connecticut	CT	Maryland	MD	North Carolina	NC	Virginia	VA
Delaware	DE	Massachusetts	MA	North Dakota	ND	Washington	WA
Florida	FL	Michigan	MI	Ohio	OH	West Virginia	WV
Georgia	GA	Minnesota	MN	Oklahoma	OK	Wisconsin	WI
Hawaii	HI	Mississippi	MS	Oregon	OR	Wyoming	WY
Idaho	ID	Missouri	MO	Pennsylvania	PA	District of	
Illinois	IL	Montana	MT	Rhode Island	RI	Columbia	DC

A Guide to Spelling

Some useful spelling rules are listed below. Learning them will help you to spell words easily. Remember to use these rules when you write.

1. The suffix *-s* can be added to most nouns and verbs. If the word ends in *s, ss, sh, ch, x,* or *zz,* add *-es.*

   Nouns gas   gases   **Verbs**   hiss   hisses
             bush   bushes   match   matches
             fox   foxes   buzz   buzzes

2. If a word ends in a consonant and *y,* change the *y* to *i* when you add a suffix, unless the suffix begins with *i.*

   Nouns cherry   cherries   **Verbs**   study   studies   studied
             baby   babies   try   trying

   Adjectives muddy   muddier   muddiest

3. If a word ends in a vowel and *y,* keep the *y* when you add a suffix.

   Nouns turkey   turkeys   **Verbs**   stay   stayed

4. If a one-syllable word ends in one vowel and one consonant, double the last consonant when you add a suffix that begins with a vowel.

   Nouns swim   swimmer   **Verbs**   stop   stopping

   Adjectives big   bigger   biggest

5. When you choose between *ie* and *ei,* use *ie* except after *c* or for the long *a* sound.
   (Exceptions: *leisure, neither, seize, weird*)

   Nouns field   **Verbs**   shriek
             neighbors   receive

6. If a word ends in a single *f* or *fe*, usually change the *f* to *v* when you add *-s* or *-es*.

NOUNS calf   calves   knife   knives

7. If a word ends in *e*, drop the *e* when you add a suffix that begins with a vowel. Keep the *e* when you add a suffix that begins with a consonant.

VERBS drive   driving   **ADVERBS** sure   surely

8. Add an apostrophe and *s* (**'s**) to a singular noun to show possession, but do not add them to a pronoun. Special pronouns show possession.

doctor   doctor's   Mary   Mary's
his   hers   its   ours   yours   theirs

9. The letter *q* is always followed by the letter *u* in English words. The letter *v* is always followed by another letter; it is never the last letter in a word.

question   give

10. Use an apostrophe (**'**) to show where a letter or letters have been left out in a contraction.

is not   isn't   we are   we're   you will   you'll

Another way to help improve your spelling is to keep a notebook of special words. Collect words you think are interesting or hard to spell. Write them carefully in your spelling notebook. You may wish to add a short meaning next to each word.

Your notebook should have a page for each letter of the alphabet. Keeping these words in alphabetical order will make your personal words easy to find when you need them. If you use a looseleaf binder, you can add pages as your spelling notebook grows.

Words Often Written

The words in the list below came from compositions that were written by students your age. They are the words the students used most often. Are they the words *you* use most often, too?

1.	again	26.	live
2.	always	27.	long
3.	another	28.	made
4.	away	29.	many
5.	been	30.	money
6.	best	31.	mother
7.	better	32.	nice
8.	car	33.	only
9.	decided	34.	person
10.	dog	35.	place
11.	door	36.	right
12.	ever	37.	room
13.	every	38.	should
14.	family	39.	tell
15.	finally	40.	that's
16.	find	41.	these
17.	food	42.	thought
18.	give	43.	three
19.	great	44.	through
20.	green	45.	walked
21.	help	46.	wanted
22.	here	47.	water
23.	last	48.	wish
24.	let	49.	world
25.	life	50.	years

Diagraming Guide

Subjects and Verbs

When you assemble a kite or bicycle, you use a diagram to see how the parts fit together. Similarly, a sentence diagram can help you see how all the words of a sentence fit together.

To begin a sentence diagram, draw a horizontal line. On this line write the subject and the verb of the sentence you wish to diagram. Then draw a vertical line to separate the subject and the verb.

subject	verb

Ann listened.

Ann	listened

Dr. Ramirez was singing.

Dr. Ramirez	was singing

When you diagram an interrogative sentence, write the subject of the sentence before the complete verb.

May we enter?

we	May enter

Did Mrs. Peterson finish?

Mrs. Peterson	Did finish

The subject of an imperative sentence is usually understood to be *you*. In a diagram, write *you* in parentheses in the subject place.

Stop!

(you)	Stop

Do enter.

(you)	Do enter

Notice that a sentence diagram shows the capital letters of a sentence. Punctuation marks, however, are not shown.

> **Summary** ♦ A **diagram** is a line drawing that explains something.

Practice

A. Diagram each of the following sentences.

1. Birds call.
2. Jason is laughing.
3. Did Cara arrive?
4. Leave!
5. Has anyone gone?

6. Gina can dance.
7. She may watch.
8. Do continue.
9. May I speak?
10. Listen.

B. Diagram each sentence.

11. Are you reading?
12. Mrs. Haggerty will sing.
13. Help!
14. Ian was following.
15. Run.

16. Lisa called.
17. Was she working?
18. He has tried.
19. Explain.
20. Will it hurt?

C. Locate the subject and the verb in each sentence. Write the subject and verb on a horizontal line. Then divide them with a vertical line.

> EXAMPLE: In the class the boys were coloring.
> ANSWER: boys | were coloring

21. People seldom walk near the dark castle.
22. A statue of an elf was standing on the lawn.
23. Listen to this tale about a white stag.
24. Always divide carefully.
25. Does this antique globe turn on its axis?
26. During October, the group of actors may travel to Canada and England.
27. The snow on the roads swirled playfully.
28. The children in the movie theater cheered loudly.
29. At the more difficult parts, the teacher paused.
30. Any friend of Hamid's may join, too.

Sentence Parts

Every sentence part can be shown in a sentence diagram. An adjective is written on a slanting line connected to the noun or pronoun it modifies. The articles *a*, *an*, and *the* are also diagramed in this way.

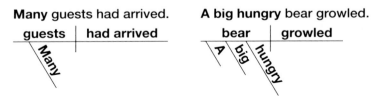

Adverbs are also diagramed on slanting lines. An adverb that modifies a verb appears directly under the verb.

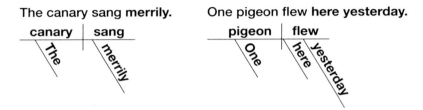

Diagram an adverb that modifies an adjective or another adverb on a slanting line connected to the word modified.

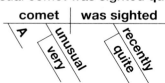

A prepositional phrase is diagramed below the word it modifies. Place the preposition on a slanting line connected to the modified word. Place the object of the preposition on a horizontal line connected to the slanting line.

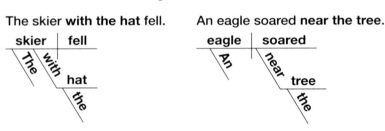

Summary ♦ Adjectives, adverbs, and prepositional phrases are diagramed below the words they modify.

Practice

A. Diagram each sentence. First write the subject and the verb. Then write each adjective and adverb below the word it modifies.

1. The old kettle whistled shrilly.
2. A tall, thin boy was busily sweeping.
3. Did the heavy wrench work well?
4. Speak more clearly.
5. Several rather important books sold quickly.
6. The colorful flag flew proudly.
7. Will the other brother come, too?
8. Three young coyotes stood nearby.
9. The very hungry workers ate quite rapidly.
10. Write soon.

B. Diagram each sentence. Be sure each prepositional phrase is placed below the word it modifies.

11. The tall brown bear lumbered into the forest.
12. We ate on the patio.
13. The girl with the kite was singing.
14. Is the floor of the basement still settling?
15. The young explorers walked quite bravely toward the cave.

C. Diagram each sentence.

16. The happy baby giggled gleefully.
17. Listen very carefully.
18. Several gold coins glistened in the well.

Other Sentence Parts

A direct object receives the action of a verb. (See pages 122–123.) To diagram a direct object, write it on the horizontal line after the verb. Separate it from the verb with a vertical line that does not cut through the horizontal line.

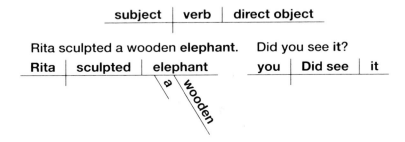

A predicate nominative is a noun or pronoun that renames the subject of the sentence. (See pages 118–119 and 188–189.) In a diagram, place the predicate nominative on the horizontal line after the verb. A line that slants backward separates it from the verb. This slanting line does not cross the horizontal one.

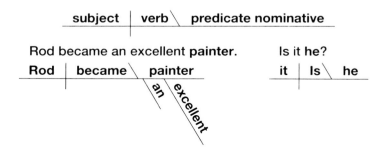

A predicate adjective follows a linking verb and describes the subject. (See pages 242–243.) It also appears after a slanting line in a sentence diagram.

The painting appears so **lifelike!**

| painting | appears \ | lifelike |

The *The* slants below painting; *so* slants below lifelike.

Are they **new?**

| they | Are \ | new |

Summary ◆ Direct objects, predicate nominatives, and predicate adjectives appear after the verb in a sentence diagram.

Practice

A. Diagram each sentence. Be sure your diagrams indicate which words are direct objects.

    1. The teacher left the room.
    2. The tiny kitten grabbed the red ribbon.
    3. Did you understand the question?
    4. Follow the leader.
    5. You may give the correct answer now.
    6. A lost dog followed me yesterday.
    7. Martin cleaned the entire house.
    8. Has anyone seen the new movie?
    9. The young girl chased the pony into the barn.
  10. May I borrow a book about boats?

B. Diagram each sentence. Be sure your diagrams indicate the predicate nominatives and the predicate adjectives.

  11. Ms. Rivera is an excellent leader.
  12. The oral report was quite interesting.
  13. The sweater on the bed looks handmade.
  14. The tall woman with the gray hair is a poet.
  15. Is he a professional actor?

C. Diagram each sentence.

  16. Ed dug the garden.
  17. We were flying the kite yesterday.
  18. Did the child lose a sandal?
  19. Rocky is a gentle horse.
  20. The juicy red strawberries were delicious.

Grammar Handbook

Grammar

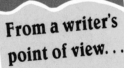

From a writer's point of view...

I create interesting word pictures for my readers by using colorful adjectives to add exact details.

▶ **adjective**   An adjective describes a noun or pronoun. Adjectives often answer the question *What kind?* or *How many?*

> <u>Twelve</u> *roses* arrived today. (describes noun, tells *how many*)
> *They* are very <u>beautiful</u>. (describes pronoun, tells *what kind*)

proper adjective   A proper adjective is formed from a proper noun.

> <u>Italian</u> **border**   <u>Canadian</u> **railroad**   <u>New York</u> **tour**

♦ The ending of a proper noun is usually changed to make a proper adjective. The endings *-ish*, *-an*, and *-ese* are often used to form proper adjectives. Sometimes a proper adjective has the same form as a proper noun.

predicate adjective   A predicate adjective follows a linking verb and describes the subject of the sentence.

> **The apple was <u>delicious</u>.**

demonstrative adjective   A demonstrative adjective points out the noun it describes.

> <u>This</u> **toast is burnt.**   <u>That</u> **hat is mine.**
> **Try one of <u>these</u> muffins.**   <u>Those</u> **students were late.**

♦ *This* and *these* point out people or things nearby. *That* and *those* point out people or things farther away. Use *this* and *that* with singular nouns. Use *these* and *those* with plural nouns.

♦ Sometimes *this*, *that*, *these*, and *those* are used alone in sentences. Then they are pronouns.

> <u>This</u> **is dated 1874.**   <u>These</u> **were built before 1900.**
> <u>That</u> **is an old canal lock.**   **What were <u>those</u> used for?**

comparison of adjectives   Adjectives have different forms to show comparisons.

♦ Use the comparative form of an adjective to compare two persons, places, or things. The comparative is formed by adding *-er* to the adjective. Use the superlative form of an adjective to compare three or more persons, places, or things. The superlative is formed by adding *-est* to the adjective.

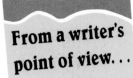

From a writer's point of view...

Adjectives that compare help me describe how things are alike or different.

> **A grapefruit is <u>sweeter</u> than a lemon.**
> **Of a grapefruit, a lemon, and an orange, an orange is the <u>sweetest</u>.**

♦ Use *more* and *most* to form the comparative and superlative of most adjectives with two or more syllables.

> **Roses are <u>more delicate</u> than daisies.**
> **This is my <u>most delicate</u> rose.**

Some adjectives have special comparative and superlative forms:

Adjective	Comparative	Superlative
good	better	best
bad	worse	worst

articles   The words *a*, *an*, and *the* are special adjectives called articles. Use *a* before a word that begins with a consonant sound. Use *an* before a word that begins with a vowel sound.

> **<u>a</u> truck   <u>an</u> automobile   <u>the</u> van**

▶ **adverb**   An adverb describes a verb, an adjective, or another adverb. Adverbs answer the question *How? Where? When?* or *To what extent?*

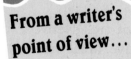

From a writer's point of view...

Adverbs help me add details to my writing—details about actions, times, and places.

> **The baseball team *played* <u>here</u>. (describes verb, tells *where*)**
> **The catcher played <u>rather</u> *well*. (describes adverb, tells *to what extent*)**
> **The game was <u>very</u> *exciting*. (describes adjective, tells *to what extent*)**
> **The fans *cheered* <u>loudly</u>. (describes verb, tells *how*)**

Adverbs often end in *-ly*. Some common adverbs that do not end in *-ly* are shown below.

almost	ever	never	rather	soon
already	here	not	seldom	there
also	just	often	so	too
always	later	quite	somewhat	very

comparison of adverbs   Adverbs have different forms to show comparisons.

◆ Use the comparative form of an adverb to compare two things. One-syllable adverbs usually add *-er* to form the comparative. Use the superlative form of an adverb to compare three or more things. One-syllable adverbs usually add *-est* to form the superlative.

Dan arrived <u>later</u> than I.
The twins arrived the <u>latest</u> of any of us.

◆ Most adverbs that end in *-ly* and adverbs with two or more syllables use *more* to form the comparative and *most* to form the superlative.

The snow melted <u>more rapidly</u> on Monday than on Tuesday.
The snow melted <u>most rapidly</u> of all yesterday.

Some adverbs have special comparative and superlative forms.

Adverb	Comparative	Superlative
well	better	best
badly	worse	worst

double negative   Some negative words, such as *not,* are adverbs. Avoid using two negative words, called a double negative, in the same sentence.

Wrong: Debra <u>don't never</u> eat sugar.
Right: Debra does <u>not</u> ever eat sugar.
Right: Debra <u>doesn't</u> ever eat sugar.

From a writer's point of view. . .

When I proofread my writing, I check to see that I have not used any double negatives.

514   Grammar Handbook

♦ Notice that a double negative can be corrected in different ways. In the second and third sentences above, an affirmative, or "yes" word, has been substituted for one of the negatives. This chart shows the affirmatives for other words.

Negative	Affirmative	Negative	Affirmative
no	any, a, one, some	nothing	anything, something
no one	anyone, someone	nowhere	anywhere, somewhere
none	all, some	nobody	anybody, somebody

♦ See **preposition** if you aren't sure whether a word is an adverb or a preposition.

▶ conjunction   A conjunction joins words or groups of words. The words *and*, *but*, and *or* are conjunctions.

Call a friend <u>or</u> nearby neighbor in an emergency.

<table>
<tr><td colspan="2" align="center">Examples of Conjunctions</td></tr>
<tr><td>noun + noun</td><td>Japanese <u>life</u> <u>and</u> <u>culture</u> are fascinating.</td></tr>
<tr><td>pronoun + pronoun</td><td><u>You</u> <u>or</u> <u>I</u> may visit Japan someday.</td></tr>
<tr><td>verb + verb</td><td>The Japanese people <u>observe</u> <u>and</u> <u>honor</u> many old traditions.</td></tr>
<tr><td>adjective + adjective</td><td>Yet <u>European</u> <u>or</u> <u>American</u> influences are also seen in Japanese life.</td></tr>
<tr><td>adverb + adverb</td><td><u>Creatively</u> <u>but</u> <u>carefully</u>, Japan has blended the old and the new.</td></tr>
</table>

From a writer's point of view...

I use conjunctions to combine the ideas in short sentences into longer, smoother sentences.

▶ direct object   The direct object receives the action of the verb. It is often a noun. It answers the question *whom* or *what*.

Carl raked the <u>leaves</u>.
Susan called <u>him</u> in the afternoon.

▶ interjection   An interjection expresses strong feeling or emotion. Use an exclamation mark (!) after an interjection.

Hooray!   Wow!   Oh!   Gee!

From a writer's point of view...

I use direct objects after action verbs to add information to my sentences.

▶ **noun**   A noun names a person, place, thing, or idea. The chart below shows examples of nouns.

Names of Persons	girl, boy, puppeteer, Shari Lewis
Names of Places	theater, city, Canada
Names of Things	puppet, stage, Bil Baird Marionettes
Names of Ideas	love, enjoyment, peace

<u>Melanie</u> went to the <u>museum</u>.
The <u>show</u> was a huge <u>success</u>.

singular noun   A singular noun names one person, place, thing, or idea.

In 1938, a famous radio <u>star</u> broadcast an amazing <u>story</u> about an <u>attack</u> by aliens.

plural noun   A plural noun names more than one person, place, thing, or idea.

He said that <u>creatures</u> from outer space had landed in the sleepy <u>woods</u> of New Jersey.

common noun   A common noun is the general name of a person, place, or thing.

When they heard about <u>aliens</u> from another <u>planet</u>, <u>people</u> became excited and even frightened.

proper noun   A proper noun names a particular person, place, or thing.

<u>Orson Welles</u> gave an eerie, vivid description of the <u>Martians</u>.

possessive noun   A possessive noun shows ownership.

♦ To form the possessive of a singular noun, add an apostrophe and *s* (**'s**).

The <u>teacher's</u> car stalled.

♦ To form the possessive of a plural noun that ends in *s,* add only an apostrophe (').

The <u>athletes'</u> uniforms are green and gold.

♦ To form the possessive of a plural that does not end in *s,* add an apostrophe and *s* (**'s**).

The storm changed some <u>children's</u> activities.

▶ preposition   A preposition relates a noun or pronoun to another word in the sentence.

We played basketball <u>in</u> the park.

Forty Common Prepositions				
about	before	during	off	to
above	behind	for	on	toward
across	below	from	out	under
after	beneath	in	outside	until
against	beside	inside	over	up
along	beyond	into	past	upon
around	by	near	through	with
at	down	of	throughout	without

object of preposition   The noun or pronoun that follows a preposition is the object of the preposition.

Farmers *in* <u>Idaho</u> grow potatoes.

prepositional phrase   A preposition, its object, and any words that describe the object make up a prepositional phrase.

Their home is located <u>near a slow brook</u>.

♦ A prepositional phrase may act as an adjective or an adverb.

Cheryl admired the *bracelets* <u>with colorful stones</u>. (adjective phrase)
The stones *shone* brightly <u>in the sunshine</u>. (adverb phrase)

adjective phrase   A prepositional phrase that describes a noun or pronoun is an adjective phrase.

> **Luis drank a *glass* <u>of cold water</u>.**

adverb phrase   A prepositional phrase that describes a verb, an adjective, or an adverb is an adverb phrase.

> **I *ate* fried chicken <u>for dinner</u>.**

preposition or adverb?   Some words, such as *around*, *out*, *up*, *near*, and *by*, can be either prepositions or adverbs.

> **China is quite <u>near</u>. (adverb)**
> **China is <u>near</u> Japan. (preposition)**

♦ If you aren't sure whether a word is a preposition or an adverb, look at how it is used. A preposition begins a phrase and always has an object. An adverb is used alone. It has no object.

▶ **pronoun**   A pronoun takes the place of a noun or nouns.

> **The *child* kicked a *ball*.   <u>She</u> kicked <u>it</u>.**

subject pronoun   The subject pronouns are *I*, *you*, *she*, *he*, *it*, *we*, and *they*. Use a subject pronoun as the subject of a sentence and after a linking verb.

> ***Janice* practiced piano for over an hour.**
> **<u>She</u> practiced piano for over an hour.**

> **The owner of the bicycle is *Michael*.**
> **The owner of the bicycle is <u>he</u>.**

object pronoun   The object pronouns are *me*, *you*, *her*, *him*, *it*, *us*, and *them*. Use an object pronoun after an action verb and as the object of a preposition.

> **Bill found an old, straw *basket* in the kitchen closet.**
> **Bill found <u>it</u> in the kitchen closet.**

> **Susan placed apples in the *baskets*.**
> **Susan placed apples in <u>them</u>.**

possessive pronoun   The pronouns *my, your, her, its, our,* and *their* are possessive pronouns. A possessive pronoun shows ownership. Possessive pronouns can replace possessive nouns.

> *Dr. Kern's* office is closed.
> <u>His</u> office is closed.

> Get the keys for *Mom and Dad's* car from *Rita's* jacket.
> Get the key for <u>their</u> car from <u>her</u> jacket.

antecedent   An antecedent is the word or words to which a pronoun refers.

> <u>Elena</u> said *she* would be home later.

▶ sentence   A sentence is a group of words that expresses a complete thought. There are four kinds of sentences.

declarative sentence   A declarative sentence makes a statement. It ends with a period (**.**).

> **Billy Joel is a famous singer, songwriter, and pianist.**

interrogative sentence   An interrogative sentence asks a question. It ends with a question mark (**?**).

> **Did you hear Billy Joel perform on TV last night?**

imperative sentence   An imperative sentence gives a command or makes a request. It ends with a period (**.**).

> **Meet us before the Billy Joel concert at 7 P.M. sharp.**

exclamatory sentence   An exclamatory sentence expresses strong feeling. It ends with an exclamation mark (**!**)

> **I hope Billy Joel performs his hits from *Piano Man*!**

simple sentence   A simple sentence expresses one complete thought and has a subject and a predicate.

> **The world's wild land is disappearing rapidly.**

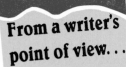

From a writer's point of view...

When I write, I use sentences to express my thoughts clearly. Using different kinds of sentences adds variety to my work.

compound sentence   A compound sentence consists of two or more simple sentences. You can join the simple sentences with a comma and the conjunction *and*, *or*, or *but*. You can also use a semicolon to join two simple sentences.

> **Andrew waited in the rain for an hour, but the bus never arrived.**
> **Andrew waited in the rain for an hour; the bus never arrived.**

sentence error: fragment   A sentence fragment is a group of words that does not express a complete thought. You can correct a fragment by adding words to make it a complete thought.

> **Fragment: Spaghetti with tomato sauce.**
> **Complete Sentence: The chef prepared spaghetti with tomato sauce.**

sentence error: run-on sentence   A run-on sentence is two or more sentences not separated by correct punctuation or connecting words.

> **Nathan delivers newspapers he mows lawns.**

♦ You can correct a run-on sentence by making two simple sentences, by making a compound sentence, or by using a compound subject or predicate.

> **Nathan delivers newspapers. He mows lawns.**
> **Nathan delivers newspapers, and he mows lawns.**
> **Nathan delivers newspapers and mows lawns.**

▶ **subjects and predicates**   The subject and the predicate are the two main parts of a sentence. The subject part always names someone or something. The predicate part always tells what the subject is or does.

complete subject   The complete subject is all the words in the subject part of a sentence. The subject part names someone or something.

> **A herd of deer grazed peacefully near the river.**

From a writer's point of view...

When I proofread my writing, I avoid fragments by checking to see that each sentence has a subject and a predicate.

simple subject   The simple subject is the main word in the complete subject.

A <u>flock</u> of *wild geese* flew over the frozen lake.

compound subject   A compound subject is two or more simple subjects that have the same verb.

<u>Adults</u> and <u>children</u> enjoy the circus.

subject in imperative sentence   *You* (understood) is the subject of an imperative sentence.

<u>(You)</u> Pass me the mustard and the mayonnaise.

complete predicate   The complete predicate is all the words in the predicate part of a sentence. The predicate part tells what the subject is or does.

Africa <u>is home to numerous wild animals.</u>
A colorful tiger <u>roared at the silent sunrise.</u>

simple predicate   The simple predicate, or verb, is the main word or words in the complete predicate.

A gray squirrel <u>darted</u> *up the tree trunk.*

compound predicate   A compound predicate is two or more verbs that have the same subject.

Danielle <u>washed</u> and <u>waxed</u> the family car.

subject-verb agreement   A verb must agree with its subject. That is, a singular verb form must be used with a singular subject and a plural verb form must be used with a plural subject.

♦ Singular nouns and the pronouns *he*, *she*, and *it* use a present-tense verb ending in *-s* or *-es*.

The panda <u>lives</u> in China.
It <u>searches</u> for bamboo all day.

♦ Plural nouns and the pronouns *I*, *you*, *we*, and *they* use a present-tense verb not ending in *-s* or *-es*.

Many rare animals <u>live</u> in the Far East.
We <u>observe</u> them.

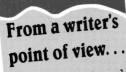

From a writer's point of view...

Using compound subjects and predicates helps me condense my writing and avoid repeating words.

From a writer's point of view...

When I proofread my work, I check to see that each present-tense verb agrees with its subject.

compound subjects   Compound subjects joined by *and* use the plural form of the verb.

> **The tulip and the violet <u>bloom</u> in the spring.**

♦ Compound subjects joined by *or*, *either/or*, or *neither/nor* sometimes use the singular form of the verb and sometimes the plural.

♦ Use the singular verb when both parts of the subject are singular.

> **Usually *Stephen* or *Jill* <u>arrives</u> early.**

♦ Use the plural verb when both parts of the subject are plural.

> **Either *apples* or *peaches* <u>makes</u> great pies.**

♦ When one part of a compound subject is singular and one part is plural, the verb agrees with the nearer subject.

> **Either *butter* or *chocolates* <u>melt</u> quickly.**
> **Neither *lemons* nor a *pickle* <u>tastes</u> sweet.**

▶ **verb**   A verb expresses action or being.

> **An officer <u>directs</u> traffic. (action verb)**
> **The drivers <u>are</u> patient. (state-of-being verb)**

helping verb and main verb   When a verb is more than one word, the most important word is the main verb. Any verb that is not the main verb is a helping verb. A helping verb works with the main verb to express action or being.

> **The world <u>can be seen</u> as one huge ocean.**
> **Here and there the ocean is <u>broken</u> by continents.**
> **Few people <u>are</u> not <u>thrilled</u> by the ocean.**

From a writer's point of view...

When I write, I use verbs that are colorful and precise. This helps my reader picture exactly what is happening.

Some Common Helping Verbs				
am	be	had	did	may
is	being	can	shall	might
are	been	could	should	must
was	has	do	will	
were	have	does	would	

♦ Some verbs in the box, such as *is* and *has*, can stand alone in a sentence. When they stand alone, they are the main verbs.

Waves <u>are</u> rough.   Seas <u>have</u> power.

linking verb   A linking verb connects the subject with a word or words in the predicate.

Katrina <u>is</u> a dancer.   She <u>seems</u> nervous.

Forms of *Be*	Other Linking Verbs
be, am, is, are was, were	appear, become, feel, look, seem, smell, taste

predicate nominative   A predicate nominative is a noun or a pronoun that follows a linking verb and renames the subject.

The *composer* of the song is <u>Marie</u>.
The *composer* of the song is <u>she</u>.

♦ Use a subject pronoun after a linking verb. Pronouns that follow linking verbs are predicate nominatives.

Wrong: The writer of the letter was her.
Right: The writer of the letter was she.

predicate adjective   A predicate adjective follows a linking verb and describes the subject of the sentence.

The *apple* was <u>delicious</u>.

tense   The tense of a verb shows the time of the action.

present tense   A verb in the present tense shows action that happens now.

We <u>sort</u> glass bottles.

past tense   A verb in the past tense shows action that already happened.

Marisa <u>collected</u> newspapers.

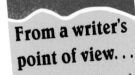

From a writer's point of view...

When I proofread my work, I check that I have used the correct tense to express the time of an idea or event.

future tense   A verb in the future tense shows action that will happen.

   Alberto <u>will save</u> aluminum cans.

principal parts   The principal parts are the basic forms of a verb. They include the present, the past, and the past participle.

Present	Past	Past Participle
arrive	arrived	(has, have, had) arrived

regular verb   A regular verb forms its past and past participle by adding -*ed*.

Present	Past	Past Participle
call	called	(has, have, had) called
splash	splashed	(has, have, had) splashed
worry	worried	(has, have, had) worried
trap	trapped	(has, have, had) trapped

◆ Notice that verbs that end in a consonant and *y*, such as *worry*, change the *y* to *i* and add -*ed* to form the past. One-syllable verbs that end in a vowel and a consonant, such as *trap*, double the final consonant and add -*ed* to form the past.

irregular verb   Irregular verbs do not form the past and the past participle by adding -*ed*.

Present	Past	Past Participle
give	gave	(has, have, had) given

Here are the principal parts of some common irregular verbs.

Present	Past	Past Participle
begin	began	(has, have, had) begun
blow	blew	(has, have, had) blown
do	did	(has, have, had) done
drink	drank	(has, have, had) drunk
eat	ate	(has, have, had) eaten
fly	flew	(has, have, had) flown
give	gave	(has, have, had) given
go	went	(has, have, had) gone
grow	grew	(has, have, had) grown
know	knew	(has, have, had) known
ring	rang	(has, have, had) rung
sing	sang	(has, have, had) sung
swim	swam	(has, have, had) swum
take	took	(has, have, had) taken
throw	threw	(has, have, had) thrown
write	wrote	(has, have, had) written

◆ Some irregular verbs follow a pattern in forming the past and past participle. Others do not.

Some form the past participle by adding -n to the past.

Present	Past	Past Participle
break	broke	(has, have, had) broken
choose	chose	(has, have, had) chosen
freeze	froze	(has, have, had) frozen
speak	spoke	(has, have, had) spoken

Some have the same present and past participle.

Present	Past	Past Participle
become	become	(has, have, had) become
come	came	(has, have, had) come
run	ran	(has, have, had) run

Some have the same past and past participle.

Present	Past	Past Participle
bring	brought	(has, have, had) brought
catch	caught	(has, have, had) caught
say	said	(has, have, had) said
teach	taught	(has, have, had) taught
think	thought	(has, have, had) thought

From a writer's point of view...

When I proofread my writing, I check my use of capital letters.

Capitalization

▶ **sentence**   Begin every sentence with a capital letter.

Soft breezes are delightful in spring.

▶ **proper nouns**   Each important word in a proper noun begins with a capital letter.

♦ Capitalize each word in the name of a person or pet.

the Wildes   John Paul Jones   Minnie the Marvel   Lassie

♦ Capitalize every important word in the names of particular places or things.

Broad Street   New York City   Statue of Liberty

♦ Capitalize names of days, months, holidays, and special days.

January   Friday   Labor Day   Halloween

♦ Capitalize each important word in names of clubs, businesses, and organizations.

**Gardening Club   Hendricks Construction Company
Stamp Collectors of America**

▶ **proper adjectives**   Proper adjectives always begin with a capital letter.

Canadian province   Japanese automobile

▶ **pronoun *I***   The pronoun *I* is always capitalized.

After I finish my homework, I'll play softball.

▶ **abbreviations**   Many abbreviations begin with a capital letter and end with a period.

♦ You may abbreviate titles of persons.

Dr. = Doctor   **Gov. = Governor**   **Mr. = Mister**

♦ You may abbreviate words that mean street.

St. = Street   **Rd. = Road**   **Blvd. = Boulevard**

♦ You may abbreviate names of days and months of the year.

Sun. = Sunday   **Jan. = January**

♦ You may abbreviate words that stand for different times of the day.

A.M. = *ante meridiem* (**Latin for** *before noon*)
P.M. = *post meridiem* (**Latin for** *after noon*)

state abbreviations   You may use the United States Postal Service two-letter abbreviations of state names when you write an address. They have capital letters and no periods.

Alabama	**AL**	Maine	**ME**	Oregon	**OR**
Alaska	**AK**	Maryland	**MD**	Pennsylvania	**PA**
Arizona	**AZ**	Massachusetts	**MA**	Rhode Island	**RI**
Arkansas	**AR**	Michigan	**MI**	South Carolina	**SC**
California	**CA**	Minnesota	**MN**	South Dakota	**SD**
Colorado	**CO**	Mississippi	**MS**	Tennessee	**TN**
Connecticut	**CT**	Missouri	**MO**	Texas	**TX**
Delaware	**DE**	Montana	**MT**	Utah	**UT**
Florida	**FL**	Nebraska	**NE**	Vermont	**VT**
Georgia	**GA**	Nevada	**NV**	Virginia	**VA**
Hawaii	**HI**	New Hampshire	**NH**	Washington	**WA**
Idaho	**ID**	New Jersey	**NJ**	West Virginia	**WV**
Illinois	**IL**	New Mexico	**NM**	Wisconsin	**WI**
Indiana	**IN**	New York	**NY**	Wyoming	**WY**
Iowa	**IA**	North Carolina	**NC**	* * *	
Kansas	**KS**	North Dakota	**ND**	District of	
Kentucky	**KY**	Ohio	**OH**	Columbia	**DC**
Louisiana	**LA**	Oklahoma	**OK**		

▶ **initials** An initial is capitalized and followed by a period.

> **M.L. Starr   Jeff A. Turnbull**

▶ **titles of books, stories, poems, or reports** Capitalize the first word, the last word, and all of the important words in the title of a book, story, poem, or report.

> **<u>A Wrinkle in Time</u> (book)**
> **"A Web of Sunny Air" (story)**
> **"The Rains of Spring" (poem)**
> **How to Raise Hamsters (report)**

▶ **quotations** The first word of a quotation begins with a capital letter.

> **"You should fix your bike," said Bill, "before you go to the park."**

▶ **letters** Capitalize the first word (and the proper noun) of the greeting and the first word of the closing of a letter.

> **Greeting: Dear Ms. Martin,**
> **Closing: Sincerely yours,**

Punctuation

▶ **period** Declarative and imperative sentences end with a period.

> **The ocean is sky blue.   The waves roll gently.**
> **Set up the volleyball net.   Hang the net high.**

♦ Many abbreviations begin with a capital letter and end with a period.

> **Rev. = Reverend   Dr. = Drive**
> **Sept. = September   Tues. = Tuesday**
> **A.M. = *ante meridiem* (Latin for *before noon*)**

For more information, see **Capitalization: abbreviations.**

♦ Initials are capitalized and followed by periods.

B.J. Sanchez   **Michael R. Bates**

♦ When a divided quotation is two sentences, use a period after the words that tell who is speaking.

"We're moving next month," said Susan. "I'll miss my friends."

▶ **question mark**   End an interrogative sentence with a question mark (**?**).

What time will the movie begin?

▶ **exclamation mark**   End an exclamatory sentence with an exclamation mark (**!**).

What a gorgeous day it is!

▶ **comma**   A comma (**,**) shows a reader where to pause.

♦ Use a comma to separate words in a series. No comma is needed after the last item.

Daffodils, tulips, and crocuses bloom in the spring.

♦ Use a comma after *yes*, *no*, or *well* at the beginning of a sentence.

Yes, that is my signature.
No, I've never been to Boston.

♦ Use commas to set off the name of a person spoken to.

Ray, is this your pen?
Your question, Teresa, is a good one.

♦ Use a comma to separate a last name from a first name when the last name is written first.

Bingham, Andrea   **Danzig, Louis**

♦ Use a comma to separate the name of a city from a state or a country.

Jean was born in Toledo, Ohio.
Luisa visited Paris, France.

♦ Use a comma to separate the day and the year.

Christopher Columbus sighted land on October 12, 1492.

♦ In both friendly letters and business letters, use a comma after the last word of the closing. In a friendly letter, use a comma after the last word of the greeting.

Closing: Sincerely yours,   **Greeting: Dear Luis,**

♦ Use a comma before the conjunction in a compound sentence.

On Monday it rained, and on Tuesday it snowed.

♦ Use a comma to separate a quotation from the words that tell who is speaking. The comma comes before the quotation mark.

Carla said, "The streets are very icy."

♦ If a divided quotation is one sentence, use commas to separate the quotation from the speaker.

"The new movie in town," said Shelia, "is hilarious!"

▶ **quotation marks**   Use quotation marks (" ") to show the exact words of a speaker.

"I'm trying out for the swimming team," said Joyce.

♦ Use quotation marks before and after the title of a story, poem, article, or report when you write about it.

You will enjoy this story, "The Lion's Whiskers."

▶ **apostrophe**   Use an apostrophe (') to show where a letter or letters have been left out in a contraction (a shortened form of a word).

> **you + have = you've**   **they + are = they're**

♦ Use an apostrophe to form possessive nouns.

> **That <u>child's</u> crayon is broken.**
> **The <u>artist's</u> carving skills are extraordinary.**
> **The <u>children's</u> creative projects are on display.**

▶ **colon**   Use a colon (:) after the greeting in a business letter.

> **Dear Ms. Sharp:**   **Dear Sir or Madam:**

♦ Use a colon between an hour and minutes.

> **6:35 A.M.**   **12:35 P.M.**

▶ **underlining**   Underline the title of a book, magazine, newspaper, or movie.

> **<u>Freedom Train</u> (book)**   **<u>Denver Post</u> (newspaper)**

Writing and Computers

Along with an imagination, the best friend a writer can have is a computer. It's easy and fun to prewrite, write, revise, and proofread a piece of writing on a word processor. Then, when you've made all the changes, it takes only a few minutes to print a final copy.

Catch the Computer Bug

If you've never used a computer, you may feel just the way a lot of people feel. You may feel nervous or even a little scared. Many people think that computers are difficult and complicated. Some even think that computers are smart! But a computer is just a machine. The only trick you need to know is how to tell it what to do. You need to know how to put your writing into it. Then you need to know how to give it commands so that the computer can help you do your revising and proofreading tasks.

Every computer is slightly different. But each comes with a manual, or handbook, that tells you how to give the commands. Use the manual for help. This list of computer terms, and the chart of computer commands that follows it, will help you understand the directions in your manual.

Computer Terms

Address: numbers or words that label a document or file to show where it is located on the computer's permanent storage.

Backup: a copy of a document that is made to protect the original. The backup is often stored on a floppy disk.

Character: a single letter, numeral, or space. The word *dog* has three characters; so does the number *134*.

Command: an order, such as PRINT or SAVE, that the user gives to the computer.

Computer program: a list or system of instructions that tells the computer what to do; software.

Cursor: the blinking line or square on the screen that shows where the next typed character will appear.

Disk: a magnetic object on which information is stored (See *floppy disk* and *hard disk*).

Document: one or more pages of written material, such as a short story, a report, an essay, or a poem.

Edit: to change what you type into the computer; to revise.

Floppy disk: a small plastic disk used to save and store documents. Sometimes this is called a diskette.

Floppy Disk

Font: any one of various styles of letters that a computer is equipped to use in order to print output.

Format: to prepare a blank floppy disk for use (also called *initialize*).

Function: an operation that the computer does on command, such as SAVE, DELETE, or REPLACE.

Function key: a key that is pushed to tell the computer to do a certain function, such as CUT.

Hard copy: text that is printed out from the computer onto paper.

Hard disk: an internal section of the computer where information is kept in permanent storage. This differs from memory, which is temporary storage of information that is being used at the moment.

Hardware: the machine, including the monitor, computer, and keyboard.

Input: information, including text, numbers, and so on, that the user types into the computer.

Keyboard: part of the computer used to input information. Resembles a typewriter keyboard.

Load: to transfer information from an information storage device, such as a disk, into a computer's memory.

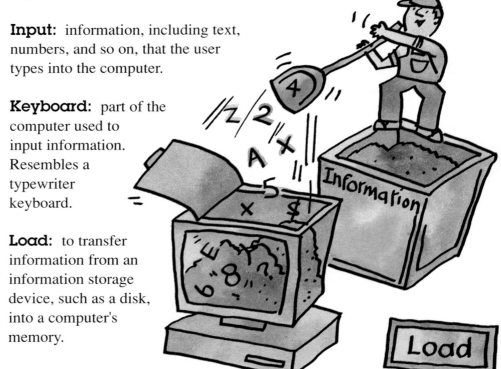

Memory: the part of the computer where programs and text are temporarily stored while they are in active use.

Menu: a list of functions. The user opens the menu, selects a function, and tells the computer to do it.

Modem: the device that allows computers to communicate over telephone lines.

Monitor: the television-like screen on which input and output can be viewed.

Output: text that the computer displays, on the screen or in hard copy.

Printer: the device that prints output in hard copy.

Printout: a copy of your writing made by the printer.

Program: a disk that contains a group of instructions that tells the computer what to do.

Software: programs that run on a computer to allow it to do word processing, math calculations, and so on.

System: the combination of hardware and software that allows the computer to work.

Terminal: includes the keyboard, which loads input into the computer, and the monitor, where output is viewed.

Virus: a set of instructions, hidden in a computer system, that leaves copies of itself in other programs or disks and can erase stored information.

Computer Commands

Cut ▶ Tells the computer to take out, or "cut," a highlighted piece of text.

Delete ▶ Tells the computer to back up one space with the cursor and to remove the character in that space.

Find ▶ Tells the computer to find a certain word within the text.

New ▶ Tells the computer to open a new, blank page so that the user can begin a new document.

Open (or Load) ▶ Tells the computer to open a certain document, identified by its address (or file name).

Paste ▶ Tells the computer to insert a word or group of words in a certain place in the document.

Print ▶ Tells the computer to print out the document in hard copy.

Quit ▶ Tells the computer to close a document.

Return ▶ Tells the computer to move the cursor to the next line of text.

Save ▶ Tells the computer to save a document by putting it into permanent storage.

Shift ▶ Tells the computer to use a capital letter.

Tab ▶ Tells the computer to indent a line of text, as for a paragraph indent.

The Key to Typing

The hardest part of writing on a computer can be learning how to type. The first step is learning which fingers hit which keys. Use the finger diagram below to practice typing "The quick brown fox jumped over the lazy dog." Make sure your fingers are curved and that your hands are parallel to the keyboard. It may be slow going at first, but with practice you'll soon be typing like a pro.

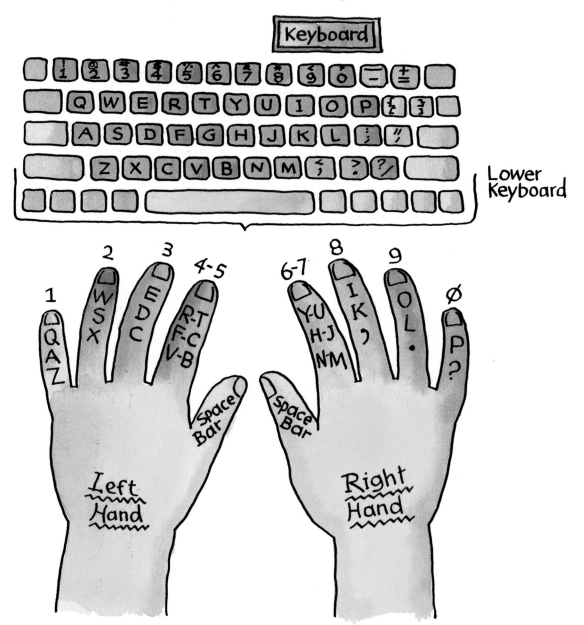

Word Processing

Writing with a computer can make it easier to

- choose topics to write about
- discover your ideas
- organize your ideas
- write your first draft
- revise your writing
- correct your mistakes
- share your writing with others

A word processing program makes the writing process more efficient. The program you use will tell you how to use the computer to enter, save, edit, and print your work. Check your software manual for special features that will help you write. Some programs can catch spelling errors. Others have drawing features (called graphics) that you can use to add pictures or borders to your pages.

Word processing programs cannot do the following things:

- think
- get ideas
- choose the best words
- organize your work
- spell words as you write
- punctuate correctly

You are still in charge of the writing, and you still need to use all of your language skills.

Ready, Set, Write!

Now you are ready to prewrite, write a first draft, revise, and proofread a piece of writing. Follow these steps.

Create a File and First Draft A file is a group of related documents. In a cardboard file folder, you might keep such related papers as prewriting ideas, a first draft, revision, and final copy of a story. A computer can also keep a file for you, but your documents will be stored in computer memory, not on paper. To begin a file:

- ◆ Tell the computer to open a new document.
- ◆ Give the document an address, or name. Some computers ask you to label a document with words; others, with a series of numbers or letters. For example, you might use *SHORTSTOR.DR1*, meaning "short story, draft 1."
- ◆ Now set your margins, font size, and spacing format. (Most papers should be typed double-spaced.)
- ◆ Type a list of ideas, words that describe your topic, or questions about your topic.
- ◆ Type your first draft. Tell the computer to SAVE your work.
- ◆ When your document is complete, follow the directions in your manual for creating a file. Give it an address, or name, such as *SHORTSTOR.FILE*. Put your draft in the file. Take a break! Then begin to revise.

Revise and Proofread Your Draft Now the fun begins! You'll have no more messy papers with arrows, cross-outs, and scribbles in the margins when you revise on a computer. You do the thinking; let the computer do the work! To begin revising:

- ◆ Make a computer document copy of your first draft.
- ◆ Label the new document *short story revision* or *SHORTSTOR.REV.* Save your original draft for reference. Use the new copy for revisions.
- ◆ Move the cursor to a place that needs revision. Give the computer a command. For example, you might tell it to CUT a sentence, move it to another place in your paper, and PASTE the sentence in.
- ◆ Check your writing for errors and correct them.

Make a copy of your document. Decide how to share your writing.

Index

Index